CLARENDON LAW SERIES

Edited by

TONY HONORÉ AND JOSEPH RAZ

CLARENDON LAW SERIES

Some Recent Titles in this Series

PRINCIPLES OF CRIMINAL LAW

ANDREW ASHWORTH

CLARENDON PRESS · OXFORD

Oxford University Press, Walton Street, Oxford OX2 6DP

Oxford New York
Athens Auckland Bangkok Bombay
Calcutta Cape Town Dar es Salaam Delhi
Florence Hong Kong Istanbul Karachi
Kuala Lumpur Madras Madrid Melbourne
Mexico City Nairobi Paris Singapore
Taipei Tokyo Toronto
and associated companies in
Berlin Ibadan

Oxford is a trade mark of Oxford University Press

Published in the United States
by Oxford University Press, New York

First published 1991
Paperback reprinted 1994, 1995

British Library Cataloguing in Publication Data
data available
ISBN 0–19–876144–9
ISBN 0–19–876145–7 (pbk)

Library of Congress Cataloging in Publication Data
Ashworth, Andrew.
Principles of criminal law / Andrew Ashworth.
(Clarendon law series)
Includes bibliographical references.
1. Criminal law—Great Britain.
I. Title. II. Series.
KD7869.A84   1991   345.41—dc20   [344.105]   91–11797
ISBN 0–19–876144–9
ISBN 0–19–876145–7 (pbk)

Printed and bound in Great Britain by
Biddles Ltd, Guildford and King's Lynn

PREFACE

THIS book is intended to be introductory, but not in the sense of describing the main rules of the criminal law in a simplified way. Its foremost aim is to raise questions about the doctrine as well as the rules, and to examine some of the principles and policies at work in the shaping of the criminal law by the legislature, the courts, the law-reform bodies, and academic commentators. This process of examination does not start from the assumption that the criminal law is grounded in a stable set of established doctrines. A more realistic view is that the arguments and assumptions which influence the development of the criminal law form a disparate group, sometimes conflicting and sometimes invoked selectively.

One task is to identify the principles and policies which appear to play a major part, sometimes a part not openly avowed in the reasoning of the courts or the commentators. Then questions are raised about each of these doctrines. Are they soundly based, in moral or social terms? How are they related to the proper aims, forms, and limits of the criminal sanction in modern Western societies? Are there other principles and policies which would be more appropriate? For example, many writers on English criminal law, and some judges, assume, often with little discussion, that fairness requires that no one should be convicted of a criminal offence unless he or she intended it and knew of the circumstances, or a least realized the risk of harm resulting. This 'subjective' principle may then be used as a criterion for determining whether certain defences to crime should or should not be admitted: the tendency is to stress logic or consistency, arguing (or assuming) that the culpability requirements should be the same for all forms of offence. The approach here is to raise questions about such sequences of assumptions. Are there not powerful arguments for restrictions based on 'social defence' or 'welfare'? Do such arguments apply more to some crimes than to others? Are there compelling objections to a system of criminal law which imposes duties on citizens in certain circumstances? But then assertions about 'social defence' should not be taken at face value either: it is important to enquire whether certain restrictions really would advance the cause of social defence.

Many of these issues and conflicts are introduced in Chapters 2 and 3, which have no counterparts in standard works on the criminal law. Chapter 2 explores the relative seriousness of offences, raising questions which are important to the proper shape of the criminal law. Chapter 3 introduces some of the principles and policies relevant to the development of the criminal law. Further doctrines are introduced in their context in Chapters 4, 5, and 6, where the basic elements of culpability, excuse, and justification are examined. Three areas of substantive criminal law are selected for discussion in the chapters which follow: Chapter 7 deals with homicide, Chapter 8 with non-fatal physical violations, and Chapter 9 with offences of dishonesty. The book concludes with Chapter 10 on complicity, and Chapter 11 on inchoate offences. A moderate amount of detail on the legal rules is included—not as much as a textbook, but, it is hoped, sufficient to enable the practical interplay of doctrines to be demonstrated and explored on a sound basis.

The legal focus of this book is upon English criminal law. There are references to the American Law Institute's Model Penal Code, but in general the available space has been used to state and to raise questions about English law rather than to attempt a comparative survey. Several references are made to the draft Criminal Code for England and Wales, published by the Law Commission in 1989 (Law Com. No. 177): the Code, if enacted, may be expected to bring advantages by way of greater accessibility, clarity, consistency of terminology, and so forth, but it is vital that both before and after its enactment these formal virtues do not divert discussion from substantive issues of the proper aims, form, and limits of the criminal law. Indeed, there is an increasing danger that the advancing complexity of the criminal law will result in students spending more time on the dissection of statutes and judgments and less time on issues of structure, policy, and principle. These issues can, of course, be analysed in even deeper terms in the context of political philosophy, the philosophy of action, and moral philosophy. However, the focus here is upon what may be termed middle-range principles and policies, which may be used to link the rules of the criminal law to views about its social function, about the relative importance of particular values and harms, about the strength of various excuses and justifications for causing harm, about the proper division of functions between the legislature and the judiciary, about the proper classification of offences, and so on.

In the course of writing this book I have benefited immensely from discussions with colleagues at King's and, formerly, at Oxford. I am particularly grateful to those who have read and commented on previous drafts of one or more chapters—Kenneth Campbell, Jeremy Horder, Simon Johnson, Nicola Lacey, Roger Leng, Krisztina Morvai, Ken Oliphant, Tony Smith, Andrew von Hirsch, and Martin Wasik. My special thanks go to Edward Griew and to Martin Wasik for reading three chapters each, at relatively short notice, in the late stages of writing. At the Oxford University Press, Richard Hart has shown great patience and faith. Nicola Pike improved the text considerably, and it is on her recommendation that I have returned to the gender-specific 'he' in most places. The vast majority of those tried and convicted are male, and so this concession to elegance has a greater air of social reality in this field than in many others.

I hope that statements about the law were accurate on 1 August 1990; a few subsequent developments have been noted in the appropriate places.

A.J.A.

CONTENTS

TABLE OF CASES

1
CRIMINAL JUSTICE AND THE CRIMINAL LAW

The operation of the criminal law requires little explanation in clear cases. Someone who deliberately kills or rapes another is liable to be prosecuted, convicted, and sentenced. Criminal liability is the strongest formal condemnation that society can inflict, and it may also result in a sentence which amounts to a severe deprivation of the ordinary liberties of the offender. Of course, there are other official deprivations of our liberties: taxation is surely one, depriving citizens of a proportion of their income, or adding a compulsory levy to commercial transactions (for example, value added tax). And taxation, no less than the criminal law, may be seen as justified by the mutual obligations necessary for worthwhile community living. But most cases of taxation do not carry any implication of 'ought not to do', whereas criminal liability carries the strong implication of 'ought not to do'. It is the condemnation conveyed by criminal liability which marks out its special social significance, and it is this condemnation (as well as the liability to state punishment) which requires a clear social justification.

The chief concern of the criminal law is seriously antisocial behaviour. But the notion that the criminal law is *only* concerned with serious antisocial acts must be abandoned, however, as one considers the broader canvas of criminal liability. There are many offences for which any element of stigma is diluted almost to vanishing point, as with speeding on the roads, illegal parking, riding a bicycle without lights, or dropping litter. This is not to suggest that all these offences are equally unimportant: it can be argued, by reference to the danger to others, that exceeding the speed limit ought to be regarded in a more serious light than commonly appears to be the case. Yet it remains true that there are many offences for which criminal liability is merely imposed by Parliament as a practical means of controlling an activity, without implying the element of social condemnation which is characteristic of the major or traditional crimes. An alternative might be to create a new regulatory agency and to invoke some kind of civil process, but this is generally regarded as too complex or too expensive, given that the police force (and some existing regulatory agencies) may be adapted to deal with the problem. Thus, the only feature which distinguishes some of these minor offences from civil wrongs like breach of contract and liability in tort is the decision by Parliament that they shall be criminal offences, attended by criminal procedures and triable in criminal courts. Therefore, although some offences in the criminal law are aimed at the highest social wrongs, there is no general dividing line between criminal and non-criminal conduct which corresponds to a distinction between immoral and moral conduct, or between seriously antisocial and other conduct.

The purpose of this introductory chapter is to convey the 'feel' of the criminal law, in outline, so that it may be developed in the succeeding chapters. It begins with a description of the contours of criminal liability, and follows this with a sketch of the reality of the criminal law. After considering the different viewpoints from which the criminal law may be studied, there is a preliminary examination of its aims and functions.

1.1. THE CONTOURS OF CRIMINAL LIABILITY

When we refer to criminal liability, what sort of conduct are we talking about? The answer may differ not only from one country to another, but also from one era to another in the same country. Some acts of homosexuality and of abortion which were criminal in England before 1967 are not criminal now, whereas some forms of insider trading on the stock-market and of the possession of indecent photographs are criminal now, although they were not until a few years ago. There are certain seriously antisocial forms of conduct which are criminal in most jurisdictions, but there is certainly no straightforward moral or social test of whether conduct is criminal. The only reliable test is the formal one: is the conduct prohibited, on pain of conviction and sentence?

The contours of criminal liability may be considered under three headings: the range of offences; the scope of criminal liability; and the conditions of criminal liability. The range of criminal offences in England and Wales is enormous. There are violations of the person, including offences of causing death and wounding, sexual offences, certain public-order offences, offences relating to safety standards at work and in sports stadiums, offences relating to firearms and other weapons, and the serious road-traffic offences. Then there are violations of general public interests, including offences against state security, offences against public morality, crimes of breach of trust, offences against the administration of justice, and various offences connected with public obligations such as the payment of taxes. A third major sphere of liability comprises violations of the environment and the conditions of life, including the various pollution offences, offences connected with health and purity standards, and minor offences of public order and public nuisance. Then there are violations of property interests, from crimes of damage and offences of theft and deception, to offences of harassment of tenants and crimes of entering residential premises. These are four major spheres of criminal liability, about which more will be said in Chapter 2. As in many other legal systems, there is a whole host of miscellaneous criminal prohibitions as well.

When we turn to the scope of criminal liability, we raise the question of the circumstances in which a person who does not cause one of the above harms may, nevertheless, be held criminally liable. In legal terms, the question has two dimensions: inchoate liability and criminal complicity. A crime is described as inchoate when the prohibited harm has not yet occurred. Several of the offences mentioned in the last paragraph are defined in terms of 'doing an act with intent to cause X', and they do not therefore require proof that the prohibited harm actually occurred. More generally, there are the inchoate offences of attempting to commit a crime, conspiring with one or more other people to commit a crime, and inciting another to commit a crime. These offences broaden the scope of criminal liability considerably, by providing for the conviction of persons who merely tried or planned to cause harm. Turning to criminal complicity, this doctrine is designed to ensure the conviction of a person who, without actually committing the full offence himself, plays a significant part in an offence committed by another. Thus a person may be convicted of aiding and abetting another to commit a crime, or counselling or procuring the commission of a crime by another.

The conditions to be fulfilled before an individual is convicted of an offence vary from one crime to another. There are many crimes which require only minimal fault or no personal fault at all: these are usually termed offences of 'strict liability', and some of them are aimed at companies and their officers. Most of the traditional offences, which have been penalized by the common law of England for centuries, are said to require *'mens rea'*. This Latin term indicates, generally, that a person should not be convicted unless it can be proved that he intended to cause the harm, or that he knew that the prohibited situation existed, or that he knowingly risked the occurrence of the harm or the existence of the prohibited situation. The emphasis of these requirements has been upon the defendant's personal awareness of what was being done or omitted, although some judicial decisions have created exceptions to this. Beyond the *mens rea* requirement, which may differ in its precise form from crime to crime, there is a range of possible defences to criminal liability, so that even people who intentionally inflict harms may be acquitted if they acted in self-defence, whilst insane, whilst under duress, and so on.

The contours of the criminal law are thus determined by the interplay between the range of offences, the scope of liability, and the conditions of liability. Inevitably there are times when the discussion focuses on one of the elements only, but the relevance of the other two must be kept in view if the discussion is not to lose perspective.

I.2. THE REALITY OF THE CRIMINAL LAW

It would be foolish to think that the criminal law as stated in the statutes and the textbooks reflects the way in which it is enforced in actual social situations. The key to answering the question of how the criminal law is likely to impinge on a person's activities lies in the discretion of the police and other law-enforcement agents: they are not obliged to go out and look for offenders wherever they suspect that crimes are being committed; they are not obliged to prosecute every person against whom they have sufficient evidence. On the other hand, they cannot prosecute unless the offence charged is actually laid down by statute or at common law. So we must consider the interaction between the law itself and discretion in the criminal process if we are to understand the reality of the criminal law.

Even before the discretion of law-enforcement officers comes into play, there is often a decision to be taken by a member of the public as to whether to report a suspected offence. Research suggests that as many as three out of four offences are not reported to the police, often because they are thought to be too trivial or because it is thought that the police would be unable to do anything constructive.[1] Thus, if an offence is to have any chance of being recorded, either the victim or a witness must take the decision to report the offence to the authorities. About four-fifths of the offences which come to police attention are reported by the public. This means that people's (sometimes stereotyped) views on what forms of behaviour amount to criminal offences, and also on whether the police should be called, exert considerable influence on the law in action. The remaining offences are observed or discovered by the police themselves. There are some crimes, such as drug-dealing and other so-called 'crimes without victims', which are unlikely to be reported and which the police have to go looking for. And there are other crimes, such as obstructing a police officer and some of the public-order offences, which the police may use as a means of controlling situations—charging the offences against people who disobey police instructions about moving on, keeping quiet, etc.

It will thus be seen that most police investigations of offences are 'reactive', that is, reacting to information from the public about possible offences. Only in a minority of cases do the police operate 'proactively'. Other law-enforcement officials may have a larger proactive role. There are various inspectorates which are required to oversee the observance of legal standards in industry and com-merce—the Health and Safety Executive, the Alkali Inspectorate, the Industrial Air Pollution Inspectorate, and so on. Although these inspectorates do react to specific complaints or accidents, much of their work involves visits to premises or building sites to check on the precautions being taken. It is therefore proactive work, and the number of offences which come to the inspectorate's attention is largely a reflection of the number of visits and inspections carried out. At a time when the staffing of the inspectorates is being tightly controlled, the number of offences which can be discovered is clearly limited.

What happens when an offence has been reported to the police? In most cases the offence is recorded and the police may investigate it. A small proportion of incidents reported as crimes are 'no-crimed'—defined as lost property rather than stolen property, for example, and transferred out of the 'crime' category. Of those which are recorded as crimes, the police trace about one-third to an offender or suspected offender. The proportion of offences thus

[1] Home Office Research Study No. 111, *The British Crime Survey* (1989).

'cleared up' is much higher for offences of violence—where the victim often sees and knows the offender—than for the less serious kinds of property offence, where the identity of the offender is not usually known and the offence is not thought to justify a great investment of police time and resources.

When the police find a suspect, they will invariably question this person. The Police and Criminal Evidence Act 1984 requires them to follow certain procedures before and during any interrogation, including notifying the suspect of his right to a lawyer. The tape recording of suspects' statements will soon become a routine feature at police stations, although statements (allegedly) made elsewhere will remain admissible in evidence. None of this detracts from the proposition that many suspects feel under psychological pressure when questioned by the police, but the result of the 1984 Act appears to have been an improvement in the position of the suspect.[2] The courts also seem to have become more willing to use their power to declare confessions and other unfairly obtained evidence inadmissible.[3] These developments may render it somewhat less likely that persons could nowadays be convicted on the basis of false confessions.[4]

When the police have completed their questioning, they may release the suspect if they have insufficient evidence. If they believe they have sufficient evidence, or if the suspect has admitted guilt, there are choices to be made. The police have three alternatives: to prosecute, to administer a formal police caution, or to take no further action. The cautioning rate has increased in recent years: the police have been encouraged to prefer a formal caution to prosecution where the offence is relatively minor, where the offender is old, infirm, or suffering from mental disturbance, and in other situations where there is little blame. But by far the highest cautioning

[2] This is a reference to the increase in the availability of lawyers in police stations, to the increased use of tape recordings, and to the establishment of Codes of Practice. It is not intended as a complacent suggestion that all is well, and does not ignore the many research findings which demonstrate how, in various ways, the police have striven to retain their position of dominance over suspects. See e.g. I. McKenzie, R. Morgan, and R. Reiner, 'Helping the Police with their Inquiries' [1990] Crim. LR. 22; A. Sanders and L. Bridges, 'Access to Lawyers and Police Malpractice' [1990] Crim.LR 494.

[3] Most of the important decisions are discussed by Di Birch, 'The Pace Hots Up: Confessions and Confusions under the 1984 Act' [1989] Crim. LR 95.

[4] Again, this is not intended as a complacent assumption that there are now no such cases: see e.g. JUSTICE, 33rd Annual Report, and P. O'Connor, 'The Court of Appeal: Re-Trials and Tribulations' [1990] Crim. LR 615.

rate is for juvenile offenders. Some two-thirds of offenders under the age of 17 are cautioned, and only one-third are prosecuted; for first offenders, the proportion cautioned is over 90 per cent. The policy here is to delay the entry of juveniles into the formal criminal-justice system, in the belief that a caution is no less likely to be effective in preventing further offences, and that labelling a juvenile as a delinquent can reinforce that young person's tendency to behave like a delinquent. The result of this is that relatively few of the under-17s are prosecuted for offences—usually, only those who are believed to have committed especially serious offences or who are persistent in their law-breaking. Since the peak age for law-breaking activities is around 15, it will be seen that a large part of the criminal law in action is to provide the background for the administration of formal cautions by the police to juveniles.[5]

The use of alternatives to prosecution is also favoured for offences which are 'policed' by the various inspectorates and by such other public authorities as the Inland Revenue, Customs and Excise, and so forth. Many of these agencies adopt the approach that their main aim is to secure compliance with the law. They therefore tend to rely on informal and formal warnings as a means of putting pressure on companies, employers, taxpayers and the like. The criminal law remains behind them, as the source of the pressure towards compliance which they are able to exert, but most of these agencies regard prosecution as a last resort. Thus, for example, the Inland Revenue brings only a few hundred prosecutions each year, relying chiefly on warnings and on their power to enforce penalties through further taxation as ways of dealing with tax-evaders.[6] In these spheres of behaviour, then, the criminal law is very much in the background, and the criminal process is experienced by relatively few of those caught breaking the law.

Where the police are involved, however, prosecution remains the normal response for persons aged 17 and over. Although the proportionate use of police cautions has increased considerably, it amounts to only some 12 per cent of this group. When the police decide to bring a prosecution, they will charge the suspect and then

---

[5] For discussion of this, see Allison Morris and Henri Giller, *Understanding Juvenile Justice* (1987), esp. Ch. 5; Gelsthorpe and Giller, 'More Justice for Juveniles' [1990] Crim. LR 153; Wilkinson and Evans, 'Police Cautioning of Juveniles' [1990] Crim. LR 165.

[6] An approach commended by the Keith Committee on the Enforcement of Revenue Legislation (1983, Cmnd. 8822); for discussion, see Andrew Sanders, 'Class Bias in Prosecutions' (1985) 24 *Howard JCJ* 176.

pass the papers on to the Crown Prosecution Service (CPS). The CPS has the function of reviewing the case-file to determine whether the prosecution should be carried forward or discontinued. One of the aspects to be considered is evidential sufficiency: is there enough evidence on each of the elements required to prove the offence, so that it can be said that there is a realistic prospect of conviction? The second, related, factor is whether a prosecution would be in the public interest. There is a Code for Crown Prosecutors which provides guidance on this and other decisions which prosecutors must take. This guidance is roughly parallel to the police cautioning guide-lines, enjoining the CPS to discontinue cases where the offence is minor and the likely penalty is nominal, and cases where the defendant is old, infirm, mentally disturbed, and so on.[7] It should be noted, however, that the CPS only deals with those cases which the police decide to prosecute, and that, for example, there has been a tendency not to bring prosecutions in cases involving 'domestic' violence (i.e. violence in the home). It now appears that social attitudes and police practices are beginning to change in this respect.[8]

It will be apparent from the preceding paragraphs that the defendants and offences brought to court form a highly selective sample of all detected crimes. It would not be accurate to say that this sample consists of the most serious offences and offenders, because (i) there are crimes for which a person over 17 would be prosecuted whereas a person under 17 would not be; (ii) fairly serious crimes committed in the home have not been prosecuted whereas less serious offences in the street have been; and (iii) some of the crimes of petty theft which are prosecuted are, by almost any measure, less serious than many crimes which the Inland Revenue or other regulatory agencies deal with by warnings, civil penalties, or other alternative methods. What emerges from this is that adults suspected of committing 'traditional' offences outside their own home are much more likely to appear in court than adults known to have committed 'modern' offences such as tax-evasion, pollution, having an unsafe work-place, and so on. Even leaving juveniles aside, then, court proceedings are a poor representation of the reality of crime in our society.

[7] See Andrew Ashworth, 'The "Public Interest" Element in Prosecutions' [1987] Crim. LR 595.
[8] See the review by Lorna J. F. Smith, *Domestic Violence*, Home Office Research Study No. 107 (1989), esp. Chs. 7 and 8.

It will be evident, too, that it is not rules but discretion which characterizes these early stages in the criminal process. Police decision-making is largely discretionary, structured only by the cautioning guide-lines, local arrangements for dealing with juveniles, police force orders, and internal police supervision. If the police decide to prosecute, the CPS can review the decision, alter the charge, or discontinue the prosecution. If the police decide not to prosecute or not even to record an offence, there is little recourse. The same is largely true of the regulatory and other agencies which have the power to prosecute. Moreover, the elements of discretion do not stop with the decision whether or not to prosecute. A question of particular importance for our present purposes is that of determining what offence to prosecute for. In some cases there is little choice, but there are other cases where the prosecutor can choose between a more serious and a less serious offence. If there is a prosecution for the higher offence, it is usually possible for a court to convict of a lesser offence if it does not find the higher offence proved. But this does not mean that prosecutors routinely try for the higher offence. If, for example, the lower offence is triable only summarily (i.e. in a magistrates' court) whereas the higher offence is triable 'either way' (i.e. in a magistrates' court or at the Crown Court), the prosecutor may prefer the lesser charge so as to keep the case in a magistrates' court—for various reasons, one of which may be the belief that a conviction is more likely if the case is tried by magistrates rather than by a jury.[9] There are other cases where the prosecution may be brought for the higher offence, but where the prosecution and defence have reached an agreement to accept a plea of not guilty to the higher offence but guilty to the lesser offence. This may appear advantageous to the prosecutor, in the sense that a conviction is assured and the hazards of a trial (with the possibility that a key witness will not give evidence convincingly) are avoided. It may also appear advantageous to the defendant, since the conviction is for a lesser offence and the sentence may be lower, too. However, it will probably come to the defendant's attention that a guilty plea is seen as a significant mitigating factor in sentencing: this could place considerable pressure on a defendant to plead guilty even where innocence is maintained, if defence lawyers emphasize the strength of the evidence for the prosecution, etc.,

---

[9] For discussion, see Ashworth, at [1987] Crim. LR 601, and David Riley and Julie Vennard, *Triable-Either-Way Cases: Crown Court or Magistrates' Court*, Home Office Research Study No. 98 (1988).

and there are clearly some cases in which innocent persons feel driven to plead guilty.[10]

Not only, then, are the cases prosecuted a selective sample of all crimes committed, but the offences for which convictions are recorded may be thought to underestimate the true seriousness of the crimes brought to court. It may be in the apparent best interests of both prosecution and defence to settle for conviction of a less serious offence. The way in which offences are defined clearly influences these decisions, and so the criminal law may have a greater direct influence at this point than at some earlier stages in the criminal process.

This brief outline has, it is hoped, demonstrated some of the ways in which the criminal law in action differs from the laws as declared in the statutes and in legal decisions. Little has been said about the ways in which defence lawyers may construct their defences around the legal requirements, but that, too, is a factor in the presentation and the outcome of cases. So far as official agencies are concerned, each case brought to court is the product of a system which is heavily reliant on victims and other members of the public for the detection of offenders and the provision of evidence, and which leaves considerable discretion in the hands of the police, other law-enforcement agencies, and the Crown Prosecution Service. The exercise of discretion is probably more significant with the less serious types of offence, but even at the top end of the scale there are decisions to be taken: Should the charge be murder or manslaughter? Is the evidence strong enough to prosecute for rape? If there is evidence of incest, is prosecution the wisest course?

I.3. OUTLINE OF THE AIMS AND FUNCTIONS OF THE CRIMINAL LAW

Perhaps our first question should be whether the criminal law is necessary at all. It has been suggested from time to time that law in general and criminal laws in particular are necessary only in conflict-ridden societies, and that the establishment of a political system based on consensus would remove the sources of crime and, therefore, the phenomenon itself.[11] This view may be attacked for its

---

[10] Cf. John Baldwin and Michael McConville, *Negotiated Justice* (1977), with Riley and Vennard, *Triable-Either-Way Cases*, 20.

[11] Anarchist theorists such as Godwin held a version of this view (see George Woodcock, *Anarchism* (1962)), and according to Marxist theory, the law would

simplistic assessment of the causes of crime, but it is sufficient for present purposes to state that no modern industrially developed country seems able to dispense with criminal law, and, indeed, that occasional instances of the breakdown of policing have led to increases in certain forms of criminal behaviour.[12] It may therefore be observed that the overall or justifying aim of the criminal law is general prevention or general deterrence—to induce people, by the threat and imposition of punishment, not to cause harms of certain kinds. Central to this is the prevention of attacks on the country itself, in terms of offences against state security. There are difficulties with the breadth of this proposition—for many years the English laws on official secrets were unduly broad,[13] and there are also those who maintain that attacks on the 'common morality' of a country may be interpreted as attacks on the country itself[14]—but it is surely correct that a chief aim of the criminal law is to contribute to the preservation of the society itself, and not just to reinforce the central values of that society.

This general aim is not sufficient to justify all the criminal laws of any particular country. In theory, it is often assumed that the criminal law, being society's strongest form of official condemnation and punishment, should be concerned only with the central values and significant harms. We have already noted that this is not the case in practice: the criminal law is sometimes used against relatively minor kinds of harm, often because the police are available as a convenient means of enforcement. Thus, the reach of the criminal sanction is determined by a number of conflicting social, political, and historical factors. This applies chiefly to the *range* of offences, enlarged on occasion in response to a wave of political concern and without overall consideration of the proper limits of the criminal sanction. The *scope* of criminal liability also bears witness to similar conflicts (e.g. over the extent of the offence of conspiracy); the *conditions* of criminal liability barely conceal the conflicts of principle

wither away on the attainment of perfect communism (see Hugh Collins, *Marxism and Law*, (1982)).

[12] Usually cited in this connection are the police strikes in Liverpool in 1919, and in Melbourne in 1918, and the incarceration of the Danish police force by the Nazis in 1944.

[13] The legislation was recently loosened by the Official Secrets Act 1989. For discussion of the earlier law, see Rosamund Thomas, 'The British Official Secrets Acts 1911–1939 and the Ponting Case' [1986] Crim. LR 491.

[14] See the argument of Lord Devlin, *The Enforcement of Morals* (1965), discussed in Ch. 2.

and policy which have shaped them throughout their years of development, with recurrent debate over the merits of fault requirements, necessitating subjective awareness by the defendant, as against the merits of objective standards of liability, based on what the reasonable person would have appreciated in the defendant's position.

If we turn to the values which underlie the criminal law, one is individual liberty—liberty in the negative sense of freedom *from* coercion, deception, fear, and so on, and also liberty in the positive sense of freedom *to* join a public demonstration (within limits), express one's sexuality (within limits), and so on. Even a casual acquaintance with modern systems of criminal law is enough to sustain the point that not only are there conflicts between the two senses of liberty, but there are also other values which are influential here. There are the collective interests, such as national security, preservation of the environment, the safety of public amenities and so forth. These collective interests inevitably conflict with individual interests at various points, and one can discern paternalistic principles at work in penalizing failures to adopt measures for one's own protection in certain circumstances (e.g. when driving a car, riding a motorcycle, etc.). These factors will be explored in Chapter 2. For the present it is enough to make the point that one cannot simply list the values which the criminal law can justifiably be used to protect, as if they are either self-evident or free from conflict and controversy. They are neither.

1.4. THE CRIMINAL LAW AND SENTENCING

A person who has been found guilty of a criminal offence is liable to be sentenced by the court. The range of sentences available to English courts, and the exercise of their discretion in imposing sentences, are subjects which justify a book on their own.[15] Do they have any relevance to a study of the criminal law? Sentencing has several close links with the criminal law. A criminal law without sentencing would merely be a declaratory system pronouncing people guilty without any formal consequences flowing from that guilt. Informal censure or some other social reaction might follow, but this would be unofficial and probably unstructured. The relation of sentencing to the criminal law itself might appropriately be

[15] e.g. Andrew Ashworth, *Sentencing and Penal Policy* (1st edn., 1983; 2nd edn., forthcoming).

described as 'confirmatory', in the sense that sentencing structures tend to operate largely by way of reinforcement of the values implicit in the offences—broadly reflecting the grading of offences, and giving weight to aggravating and mitigating factors which, if not explicit in the law, may be regarded as implicit in the legal culture. This is not to suggest that sentencers never take account of factors unconnected with the criminal law: clearly they do, and sometimes this leads to objectionable discrimination.[16] But the point is that the sentencing structure is dependent upon, and therefore heavily influenced by, the shape of the criminal law. When it is claimed that the aim of sentencing should be 'just deserts', it is sometimes replied that one cannot hope for 'just' deserts in an unjust society:[17] the sentencing system would merely be reinforcing existing social inequalities, and this would be unjust. The point is an important one, but it is an argument against most other aims of sentencing, too. A deterrent theory seeks to reinforce the value structure inherent in the criminal law. A rehabilitative theory would attempt to mould offenders' behaviour towards compliance with the norms of the criminal law. Whatever is 'just' in the sentencing aim of 'just deserts' is not a wider social justice, but the justice of reflecting sound principles of state punishment. What might these be?

As stated above, the justification for the institutions of the criminal law and sentencing lies in general deterrence and public protection. This does not suggest that the criminal law should be regarded as a primary means of protection of interests. In terms of prevention, more can probably be achieved through various techniques of situational crime prevention,[18] social crime prevention, and general social and educational policies.[19] The fundamental argument, already developed above, is that it would be difficult to ensure even a modicum of restraint and co-operation in most societies without a reasonably authoritative and effective system of criminal law and punishment. Where the so-called theories of punishment differ is at the next stage. Deterrent or preventive

[16] e.g. Ian Crow, *Unemployment and Crime* (1989); D. Farrington and A. Morris, 'Sex, Sentencing and Reconvictions' (1983) 23 *BJ Criminology* 229; Dee Cook, *Rich Law, Poor Law* (1989).

[17] A point made in the early days of the 'just deserts' movement by the American Friends Society, *The Struggle for Justice* (1971).

[18] See Ronald V. Clarke, 'Situational Crime Prevention: Its Theoretical Basis and Practical Scope' (1983) 4 *Crime and Justice: An Annual Review* 225.

[19] See generally A. E. Bottoms, 'Crime Prevention in the 1990s', (1990) 1 *Policing* 3; Michael King, *How to Make Social Crime Prevention Work: The French Experience* (1988), and also his 'Social Crime Prevention à la Thatcher', (1989) 28 *Howard JCJ*.

theories require no further justification, arguing that the fundamentally preventive rationale of punishment will also answer the questions: Who should be punished? And how much should they be punished? A retributive or 'desert' theory maintains that punishment is not only necessary for general preventive reasons, but also grounded in a basic relationship of justice. Some try to derive this from a notion of the 'restoration of the social balance' disturbed by the crime,[20] but that is probably more appropriate as a justification for compensation. The basic relationship is that punishment is deserved for an offence, in the same way as a tort or breach of contract is linked with damages.[21] This regards the relationship between crime and punishment as conceptual rather than something requiring further justification: to argue that certain behaviour is rightly criminalized is also to argue that those who behave thus may properly be punished.[22]

For the criminal lawyer, however, some major questions remain to be answered. Should all crimes be punished equally? Are levels of punishment relevant to the lawyer? The relevance of the sentencing stage to the criminal law is manifest. Much of the doctrine of the criminal law concerns—implicitly and even expressly in places—the different levels of seriousness of crimes. Different maximum penalties may be assigned to offences which turn on the distinction between intention and recklessness: is the distinction really that significant? Some excuses for crime are admitted as complete defences or (in murder) as qualified defences, whereas others go only in mitigation of sentence. There are clear implications within the criminal law when it comes to deciding whether to define an offence broadly, with a high maximum penalty, or to divide it into two or more narrowly defined offences, with graded penalties: broadly defined offences place within the more discretionary realms of sentencing some questions which would be matters of law if there were two or more subdivided offences.[23]

Far from punishing all crimes equally, most systems of criminal

---

[20] See J. M. Finnis, *Natural Law and Natural Rights* (1980), 262–6, and the criticism by Nicola Lacey, *State Punishment* (1988), 22–5.

[21] Michael S. Moore, 'The Moral Worth of Retribution', in F. Schoeman (ed.), *Responsibility, Character and the Emotions* (1987).

[22] Nils Jareborg, 'The Coherence of the Penal System', in his *Essays in Criminal Law* (1988).

[23] D. A. Thomas, 'Form and Function in Criminal Law', in P. R. Glazebrook (ed.), *Reshaping the Criminal Law* (1978); Ashworth, *Sentencing and Penal Policy*, 81–91; and the discussion of dishonesty offences in Ch. 9 below.

law have proportionality as their organizing principle, which leads to a grading of offences and punishments. 'Desert' theory draws a distinction between two kinds of proportionality.[24] One is cardinal proportionality: this requires that the overall level of the penalty scale, both maximum punishment and actual sentence ranges, should not be disproportionate to the magnitude of the offending behaviour. Exactly what that level should be in a particular country is a matter for debate, based on criminological research and, inevitably, restricted by social conventions.[25] The second kind of proportionality, more important for our present purposes, is ordinal proportionality. This concerns 'how [much] a crime should be punished compared to similar criminal acts, and compared to other crimes of a more or less serious nature'.[26] The precise meaning of 'seriousness' here will be explored in Chapters 2 and 5, for it seems to indicate assessments of the harm done or risked and of the culpability of the offender. But this concept of proportionality involves preserving a correspondence between the relative seriousness of the crime and the relative severity of the sentence.

Other approaches to punishment do not necessarily neglect proportionality. Bentham's preventive theory of punishment has general deterrence as its main principle for the distribution and amount of punishments:[27] Would punishment of this class of persons deter others from committing crimes? How much punishment is necessary to achieve this deterrent effect? Even so, Bentham expressed his theory as subject to the parameters of proportionality, since he urged that a greater punishment might be ventured against a greater harm.[28] Modern economic theorists, who propose that punishments should be ranged as a kind of scale of costs for law-breaking, do not insist on proportionality but probably believe that their approach would reflect and even establish proportionality, by showing how much of their liberty or money citizens are prepared to forfeit in order to commit various offences.[29]

These introductory remarks on punishment and sentencing have been designed to show that proportionality, much discussed in

---

[24] See Andrew von Hirsch, *Past or Future Crimes* (1985).
[25] Andrew Ashworth, 'Criminal Justice and Deserved Sentences', [1989] Crim. LR 340, at 344–5.
[26] Von Hirsch, *Past or Future Crimes*, 40.
[27] Jeremy Bentham, *Introduction to the Principles of Morals and Legislation* (1789).
[28] Ibid., Ch. XIV, para. 10.
[29] Richard Posner, *Economic Theory of Law* (2nd edn., 1977), Ch. 7.

those contexts, is a key element underlying the structure of the criminal law itself. It is a major function of the criminal law not only to divide the criminal from the non-criminal, but also to grade offences and to label them proportionately. The criminal law also has other functions which are not justifying aims but which are relevant to decision-making. Thus, although it may be said that the criminal law is merely one means of social control (along with moral codes, religion, education,and so forth), it has considerable symbolic importance. In particular, proposed changes in the criminal law may be interpreted as sending messages to citizens (for example, abolition of the mandatory sentence of life imprisonment for murder may be interpreted as assessing murder less seriously as an offence), to an extent which inhibits legislators from pursuing principles and policies amply justified in themselves.

I.5. THE MACHINERY OF ENGLISH CRIMINAL LAW

The criminal courts in England and Wales are the magistrates' courts and the Crown Court. Those offences considered least serious are summary offences, triable only in the magistrates' courts. Those offences considered most serious are triable only on indictment, in the Crown Court. A large number of offences, such as theft and most burglaries, are 'triable either way', in a magistrates' court or the Crown Court. For these offences the defendant can elect to be tried at the Crown Court, where there is a judge and jury. If the defendant does not wish a Crown Court trial, the magistrates may decide (having heard representations from the prosecutor) that the case is so serious that it should be committed to the Crown Court for trial. The evidence suggests that many defendants regard a Crown Court trial as fairer, and believe that magistrates tend to favour the prosecution,[30] but the maximum penalty in a magistrates' court is limited to six months' imprisonment on one conviction (twelve months' on two or more), and this may provide a defendant with an incentive to prefer the magistrates' court.

I.6. THE SOURCES OF ENGLISH CRIMINAL LAW

The main source of English criminal law has been the common law, as developed through decisions of the courts and the works of such

---

[30] See Riley and Vennard, *Triable-Either-Way Cases*.

institutional writers as Coke and Hale in the seventeenth century, Hawkins, Foster, and Blackstone in the eighteenth century, and East and Russell at the beginning of the nineteenth century. Much of English criminal law is now to be found in scattered statutes. There was a major consolidation of criminal legislation in 1861, and the Offences against the Person Act of that year remains the principal statute on that subject. Some offences are still governed by the common law and lack a statutory definition—most notably, murder, manslaughter, and assault. In the last two decades the Law Commission has embarked on a project of codifying English criminal law which thus far has resulted in several law-reform statutes, such as the Criminal Damage Act 1971, the Criminal Law Act 1977, and the Forgery and Counterfeiting Act 1981. The Law Commission invited a team of academic lawyers to prepare a draft Criminal Code which, using a uniform terminology, would bring together the principal crimes and general culpability requirements in one place. A draft was submitted to the Law Commission in 1985.[31] There were then consultations with members of the legal profession, and the Law Commission published its Criminal Code for England and Wales in 1989.[32] The prospects for its enactment are unclear, but there are several references to its provisions below.

In addition to the benefits of greater certainty and consistency of terminology which might result from codification, there is also a constitutional dimension. If criminal law and punishment are society's most powerful form of coercion, is it not proper that decisions on its scope should be taken by the elected Parliament, after published reports and public discussion, rather than by the judges of the past and present?[33] The case is a strong one, especially since many of the older offences require modernization in any case, and since the common-law offences lack authoritative definitions. But there is also the question of interpretation: any laws created by Parliament fall to be interpreted by the courts, and this inevitably shifts some power back to the judiciary.[34] How do the courts approach the task of interpretation? Practice, as will become apparent, is

---

[31] *Codification of the Criminal Law: A Report to the Law Commission*, Law Com. No. 143 (1985).

[32] *A Criminal Code for England and Wales*, Law Com. No. 177 (two vols., 1989); throughout this book the draft Code and its commentary will be referred to merely as Law Com. No. 177.

[33] A. T. H. Smith, 'The Case for a Code' [1986] Crim. LR 285; and the Law Commission, in Law Com. No. 177, i, 2.2.

[34] A. T. H. Smith, 'Judicial Lawmaking in the Criminal Law' (1984) 100 LQR 46.

characterized by variable policies and principles invoked by different courts. How the courts should approach the task is considered further in Chapter 3: the task of interpretation requires both a consciousness of the power which the court is exercising, and the development of principles and policies to ensure that the power is exercised in a socially acceptable manner.

This book is intended as an exploration of principles of the criminal law. It does not purport to be a textbook, and can therefore afford to be selective in the topics covered. It does, however, attempt to give a general picture of the criminal law in action by including some reference to the myriad laws not usually discussed even in works which are regarded as textbooks. The point of these references is to give some indication of the social context in which the criminal law operates: much more coverage could be given to these contextual issues, such as enforcement policy, police powers, the pre-trial construction of cases, and sentencing, but within the confines of this work that has been treated as less important than the consideration of doctrine. This means that our discussion of the criminal law is largely centred on appellate courts, as opposed to concentrating on the law as it is enforced by the police and others. There is an endeavour to recognize the constitutional responsibilities of the courts in developing the law and interpreting legislation. There is also an endeavour to remain alert to the implications for law enforcement of leaving areas of discretion when formulating laws. But the centre-piece is the doctrine of the criminal law, by which is meant the policies and social values which underlie decisions to increase or decrease the *range* of the criminal law, the principles and values which bear upon decisions about the *scope* of criminal liability, and the principles, policies, and values which relate to the *conditions* of criminal liability.

2

HARM- AND OFFENCE-SERIOUSNESS

What harms justify the imposition of the criminal sanction, and why? When a system of law regards certain offences as more serious than others, what are the grounds for this? Is it merely a matter of tradition or social convention? Is it designed to serve the interests of powerful groups in society? Are there any standards by which it is possible to judge these major decisions on the scope and emphasis of the criminal law?

2.1 WHAT KIND OF BEHAVIOUR SHOULD BE REGARDED AS CRIMINAL?

We have seen that the criminal law may be justified as a mechanism for the preservation of social order. As a type of law, its technique is condemnatory and usually involves the infliction of punishment. Since the criminal law is one of society's innermost defences against antisocial behaviour, its central concern is the reinforcement of those values most basic to proper social functioning—chiefly, physical integrity, but also security of property and environmental probity. The core of the answer to our question about what kind of behaviour should be regarded as criminal is therefore: such behaviour as threatens those values which are basic to proper social functioning. But this can only claim to be the core of the answer. Most modern societies use the criminal law to penalize a much wider range of misbehaviour than could be encompassed by the phrase 'basic to proper social functioning'. The reality is that a great deal of the criminal law consists of relatively minor offences designed as a more or less remote threat to those who might jeopardize the smooth running of road traffic, licensing procedures, urban planning, commercial and financial regulations, and so on. In one form or another, such regulations are essential if the functioning of modern society is to make adequate provision for the realization of social and individual goals. But they are far less central to social order than the preservation of physical integrity, for example. In examining the boundaries of the criminal sanction, we must therefore look further. Since the criminal law is a condemnatory mechanism which usually leads to the infliction of punishment, should we not require a certain degree of social or moral 'objectionableness' or disutility before any conduct or omission is made criminal? Can we identify criteria for the lower threshold of the criminal law?

Let us deal first with the so-called 'regulatory' offences, many of which involve failure to comply with requirements to make returns to official agencies such as the Customs and Excise, the Department of Trade, and so on. Here the criminal law is often invoked as a relatively cheap, convenient, and swift means of reinforcing a system of regulation. This kind of justification makes no attempt to assert that the conduct or omission reaches a sufficient level of social harmfulness to warrant the intervention of a criminal court and the imposition of a criminal sanction. Instead, it treats economic considerations and reasons of expediency as outweighing any argument that the criminal law should be reserved for the most antisocial forms of behaviour. Whether or not the criminal law should be used in this way is debatable. It often seems to be assumed that because the criminal courts are already there, it makes practical sense to use them. There has never been a thoroughgoing examination in this country of the strength of the economic and expediency arguments, and whether some form of non-criminal enforcement could be devised to deal effectively with such matters.[1] Those who believe that the criminal law should be reserved for seriously antisocial behaviour would support such an enquiry, and would regret the way in which the criminal law has been annexed simply as a useful apparatus of control which happens to be available to the government.

But there is another question, no less important, raised by these references to 'regulatory' offences. It is easy to slip into assumptions like 'all regulatory offences are minor' and 'all legislation not concerned with traditional crimes such as theft and violence is regulatory', and thus to conclude that the criminal law should really only be concerned with 'real' or 'traditional' crimes and that regula-

---

[1] There are many academic studies of the operation of laws of this kind, some of which are discussed in Ch. 5.3(*a*) in connection with offences of strict liability. For general surveys of the issues, see K. Hawkins and J. Thomas (eds.), *Enforcing Regulation* (1984), and J. Rowan-Robinson and P. Q. Watchman, *Crime and Regulation* (1990).

tory offences are admitted as a concession to expediency. The assumptions are false, and the conclusion therefore flawed. Statutes such as the Control of Pollution Act 1974, the Health and Safety at Work Act 1974, and the Food Act 1990 create offences which may be much more serious in their consequences than a minor theft or criminal damage. The later parts of this chapter will examine the issue of relative seriousness in more detail. For the present it is sufficient to enter a strong caution against accepting a division of crimes into 'real' and 'regulatory' offences as a basis for deciding where the true boundary of the criminal law should lie.

It could be argued that the key to deciding whether or not behaviour should be treated as criminal is whether or not it is wrong. At the top end of the scale, there are few practical problems with this. Most legal systems are remarkably similar in the types of offence which are triable only in the higher-level criminal courts: homicide, rape, robbery, and serious woundings, for example, are almost invariably treated in this way. But as we move away from these offences and come to less serious and more controversial forms of behaviour, the questions spring forward. Does the term 'wrong' indicate social or moral wrongness? If the standard is a social one, it is readily apparent that there are degrees of social harmfulness, but the appropriate standard at which conduct can justifiably be made criminal is much less apparent. The idea is essentially utilitarian in nature, and so the questions to be asked are whether the behaviour creates a significant degree of social disutility, whether it might be prevented equally effectively by means other than the criminal law, and whether the effects of criminalizing that type of behaviour would produce other disadvantageous consequences which might outweigh the benefits of thus extending the criminal law. Take, for example, the recent creation of an offence of 'behaviour likely to cause harassment, alarm or distress' in section 5 of the Public Order Act 1986. The argument in favour of the offence was that it strikes at disorderly or threatening behaviour which might significantly diminish the quality of life for certain people, creating fear, making them anxious about going out, etc. One of the arguments against it was that the offence is so vague and wide-ranging that it may enable the police to use their powers unfairly against young people who are not doing any real harm, thereby creating 'criminals'. More attention will be given to the detailed arguments elsewhere:[2] at this point it is

[2] See below Ch. 8.3(g).

sufficient to state that the issue may be seen as one of utilitarian balancing, and that, in addition to the difficulties of estimating 'utility' and 'disutility' in many cases, it is also unclear how much surplus disutility in behaviour is necessary before it is right to criminalise it.

Is morally wrong behaviour sufficient justification for the creation of a criminal offence? Few legal systems have followed this to the extent, for example, of creating general offences of telling lies or breaking promises, but there have been vigorous debates about the proper ambit of the criminal law in the realms of sexual morality. In the notable exchanges between Lord Devlin and Professor Hart,[3] Devlin's argument was that a society is entitled to use the criminal law against behaviour which might threaten its existence; that there is a common morality which ensures the cohesion of society; that any deviation from this common morality is capable of affecting society injuriously; and that therefore it may be justifiable and necessary to penalize immoral behaviour.[4] In response, Devlin's opponents have broadly followed the approach of John Stuart Mill[5] in proclaiming that the only acceptable reason for criminalizing behaviour is that it causes harm to others, and that supposed 'immorality' is not a sufficient reason.

Lord Devlin's argument seems to rely on an unacceptably loose concept of morality. He assumes that immorality is to be defined and measured according to the strength of feelings of ordinary people. If certain behaviour evokes feelings of intolerance, indignation and disgust among ordinary members of society, that is a sufficient indication that the behaviour threatens the common morality and is therefore a proper object of the criminal law. The difficulty here is that these feelings of ordinary people may not be moral in nature, but the expression of prejudice. If a person's reaction to certain behaviour is to be termed 'moral', it ought to be grounded in reasons as well as in feelings, and those reasons ought to be consistent with other standards used by that individual to judge personal behaviour. A theory about morality and the criminal law must be based on a secure definition of morality, not one which confuses it with mere feelings of distaste and disgust.[6]

[3] The principal essays written by the protagonists are collected in H. L. A. Hart, *Law, Liberty, and Morality* (1963), and P. Devlin, *The Enforcement of Morals* (1965).
[4] See Ch. 1 of his *The Enforcement of Morals*.
[5] John Stuart Mill, *On Liberty* (1859), *passim*.
[6] R. M. Dworkin, *Taking Rights Seriously* (1977), Ch. 10.

Is there, then, such a thing as a common morality? Whose morals are a guide to this? Although Devlin maintained that morals and religion are inextricably joined, he did not argue that the teachings of the Established Church constitute the common morality. In this he is realistic: British society contains adherents of several religions, with diverse views on abortion, the control of prostitution, euthanasia, and so forth, and there is a large proportion of the population who profess no religion (though their moral codes may bear some traces of religious teachings). Devlin proposed that the common morality could be discovered by assembling a group of ordinary citizens, in the form of a jury, and asking them to reach decisions on certain forms of behaviour. However, not only would this method confound prejudices with moral judgments, but it might also fail to elicit agreement on some subjects such as homosexual behaviour and abortion.

Devlin's opponents have tended to be in the individualistic liberal tradition, linking Mill's principle with Kantian ethics. According to this view, the law should respect the autonomy of each individual above all; it should treat persons as individuals and allow each to pursue his or her own conception of the good life subject only to the minimum number of constraints necessary to secure the same freedom to other individuals.[7] The thrust of this approach is to argue for constraints on lawmaking so as to preserve the individual rights of those whose preferences are out of accord with social convention: democratic rule by majority should not be allowed to trample on the rights of individuals. In the present context it is the right of privacy which is central—a right which derives from the value of personal autonomy and which operates to guard individuals from criminalization in those cases where their behaviour does no harm to others. This view has a stronger theoretical basis than Lord Devlin's, since it is distinctly a moral theory.

However, even for the liberal theorist there must be exceptions, so as to ensure the protection of the young and the mentally disordered. The value of autonomy applies primarily to adults, and it is thought that persons below the designated age of majority should not participate in heterosexual or homosexual activities, in drinking alcohol in public houses, in betting and gaming, etc. (In Britain this age varies according to the activity, and questions may be raised about the justifications for this.) This principle of

[7] See D. A. J. Richards, 'Rights, Utility and Crime' (1981) 3 *Crime and Justice* 247.

paternalism towards young people does not imply that all these activities are 'harmful': rather, it implies that they may have potentially far-reaching consequences for the individual concerned, and that only persons who have reached a certain level of maturity should be allowed to take their own decisions about these potential risks. How well this style of reasoning applies to homosexual acts is a matter of dispute: the possible consequences seem to consist of latent psychological harm, and to be debatable. It is not enough, surely, to state that homosexuals generally lead less happy lives than heterosexuals.[8]

Whilst liberals can, without inconsistency, limit the application of Mill's principle to those adults who are not mentally disordered, they encounter greater difficulties when it comes to supporting the criminalization of drugs, the non-wearing of seat-belts and crash-helmets, and other forms of 'paternalism'. Some liberals might have recourse to the idea of 'harm to others' here: they might use Mill's principle to argue that both drug-taking and the failure to wear seat-belts may result in harm to others, in the sense that the individuals involved might become a burden to others, creating avoidable misery and hardship. It is doubtful whether this style of argument succeeds. Once the concept of harm is extended to cover the risk of indirect hardship to others, Mill's principle is blunted and the possibilities for criminalization are enormous. It is more realistic to accept that there is another principle at work here. Thus Hart qualified his adherence to Mill's principle by supporting paternalism,[9] but a more convincing account may be found in Nicola Lacey's principle of welfare.[10] The significance of welfare is that it is not a qualification or exception to the principle of autonomy but a rival—thus recognizing that decisions on the ambit of the criminal law are, and should be, the result of adjusting competing policies and principles rather than assuming that autonomy is properly regarded as the overriding principle. The concept of welfare refers to those values, needs, and interests which a society has decided (through its democratic processes) are fundamental to its successful functioning. The components of welfare may therefore vary from society to society and from time to time, and may bear the marks of

---

[8] *Per* Devlin, *The Enforcement of Morals*, 134.
[9] Hart, *Law, Liberty and Morality*.
[10] N. Lacey, *State Punishment: Political Principles and Community Values* (1988), esp. Chs. 2 and 7.

several different value systems. What distinguishes them is that they are regarded as basic to social co-operation in that society.

Even though it may be said that this pure concept of welfare is far from the reality in many jurisdictions (because they do not have a fully democratic and dynamic political system, but, rather, a limited democracy with undue pressure from a ruling group), there can be little doubt 'welfare' that considerations do influence decisions about the ambit of the criminal law. Thus, one strong element in criminal legislation is the defence of the community against the loss of lives and the incapacitation of its members. The continued physical well-being of citizens is a key element in welfare, and it would be threatened if individuals were allowed to consent to fights or to travel by car without wearing seat-belts. This provides a prima-facie justification for criminalizing the failure to wear a seat-belt and for ruling out consent as a defence to fighting. A subsidiary element in welfare, also relevant here to some degree, is the financial cost to society of individual 'liberties' such as fighting and not wearing a seat-belt, in terms of the health care and absences from work incurred by those who are thus avoidably injured.

As a principle for the ambit of criminal legislation, the concept of welfare has little difficulty in accommodating criminalization in spheres such as espionage, which strikes at state security, and in other public spheres. This does not mean, however, that it supports Lord Devlin's notion of a common morality which is essential to society's existence. We simply do not know that societies tend to disintegrate if the law permits sexual freedom, abortion, euthanasia, etc.[11] It might seem that Devlin's approach would be endorsed if, by democratic processes, the majority in a particular society defined their fundamental values as being opposed to adultery, homosexuality, prostitution, abortion and so forth. This would constitute that society's definition of welfare, but it would not conclude the case in favour of criminalization, since welfare is not being advanced as an overriding principle but as one of the two leading principles (welfare and autonomy). One critical function of the principle of autonomy, as we have seen, is to defend individual liberty against the 'tyranny of the majority', and to assert individual identity and choice within a community setting. Thus the argument against criminalizing homosexual behaviour between consenting adults would be based on autonomy and privacy—the liberty of individuals

[11] See H. L. A. Hart (1967) 35 *U. Chic. LR* 1.

to pursue their sexual preferences so long as this does not inflict direct harm on others. The adjustment between welfare and auto-nomy is a matter for reasoned debate within each society.

An example of the adjustment of conflicting policies and principles is provided by the report of the Wolfenden Committee on Homo-sexual Offences and Prostitution in 1957.[12] The Committee followed Mill's approach in asserting that 'there must remain a realm of private morality and immorality which is, in brief and crude terms, not the law's business', but it maintained also that this principle must interact with the need to protect the vulnerable against exploitation and corruption, and with the policy of protecting the citizen 'from what is offensive and injurious'. The protection of the vulnerable has already been discussed, but what about protecting all citizens (adults and the young) from 'offence'?

This clearly goes beyond protection from harm, and draws a public–private distinction in respect of decency and shock to feelings; what adults do in private is not the law's business, so long as harm is not inflicted, but what they do in the public domain may be the law's business if it is likely to offend the feelings of ordinary members of the public. Thus prostitution ceased to be an offence with the Street Offences Act 1959, which was based on the Wolfenden proposals, but it is an offence for a woman to solicit for prostitution in a street, and (since 1985) for a man to solicit a woman for prostitution from a motor vehicle. These offences are based on rationales of preserving public decency and preventing public nuisance. Similarly, homo-sexual acts between adult men in private are no longer criminal since the Sexual Offences Act 1967, but homosexual acts in public places (e.g. public lavatories) remain criminal—the public-decency rationale—and homosexual acts involving a person under 21 remain criminal on the rationale of protecting the vulnerable. Another example of the public-decency and offensiveness rationale is provided by the Indecent Displays (Control) Act 1981, which criminalizes the display of any indecent matter which is visible from a public place.

Is this public–private distinction securely based? One view would be that if the criminal law really is not concerned with immorality, it should not object to public manifestations of it. The answer to this seems to be that the psychological effects on ordinary citizens of witnessing events or advertisements which they regard as disgusting or immoral may be so great as to qualify as 'harm' in the same way

----

[12] 1957, Cmnd. 257

that the psychological effects of other crimes (e.g. rape, burglary) are taken to aggravate them. It is one thing to indulge in deviant practices in private, but quite another thing to parade them in public. Acceptance of this, however, still leaves the awkward issue of drawing the line between decency and indecency, a line which fluctuates not only with time but also from locality to locality. Moreover, there are some who argue that the mere knowledge that certain sexual practices are going on in private is strongly offensive to them—for example, where a conventional family lives next door to a homosexual couple. The parents might question the feasibility of bringing up a family in decent surroundings and with proper standards if everyone knows what is going on next door. This, however, is to move the argument a stage too far. If the law were to criminalize conduct simply because it distresses others to know that acts which they regard as disgusting or immoral are taking place, even though they do not witness those acts because they are in private, this would drive a coach and horses through any principle of autonomy and individual liberty. It would be tantamount to enforcing one version of morality, and the arguments against that were set out above. Another, more practical, line of reasoning is that public manifestations of any sexual conduct carry a high risk of affecting the young and other vulnerable groups, and therefore transgress the principle of paternalism. But an equally practical response to this argument is that it depends where the allegedly indecent events or displays occur: if young people have no access to the place, does the argument not fail?

2.2. POLICIES OF RESTRAINT

In addition to the interaction between the principles of autonomy and welfare, there are also various policies which might be brought into the debate. Three will be discussed here. The first is that the consequences of criminalizing certain behaviour should not be as bad as, or worse than, the consequences of leaving it outside the ambit of the criminal law. This is a utilitarian policy which is clearly relevant to any practical adoption of the welfare principle. One oft-cited example is the alcohol prohibition in the United States in the 1920s, which produced a growth in organized crime to combat the prohibition. Some maintain that since this has also been an effect of the increasingly harsh legislation against drugs, society would be better protected by decriminalising drugs (thereby removing the basis for much organized crime) and pursuing the problem through social means. Without evaluating the prospects of this approach, the underlying point about the side-effects of criminalization can certainly be supported. Thus, for example, criminalizing abortion may result in resort to 'back street' abortionists and to the deaths of mothers as well as the removal of foetuses. The unwanted consequences of criminalization do not necessarily indicate the wisdom of decriminalization: there may be other means of reducing them. But these considerations are important if the criminal law is not to be self-defeating in social terms.

Another policy which looks to legal consequences is that the criminal law should not be significantly out of touch with the expectations of members of society. There are several versions of this policy. Sometimes it is said that a law which is widely disrespected and often disregarded is a bad law. To the extent that the criminal law relies for its functioning on co-operation from the public, this has a practical foundation. One bad law may also bring the criminal law into disrepute generally, though this would have to be established as a matter of fact or probability. Another version of this policy is that if the criminal law does not penalize behaviour widely thought to be reprehensible, some citizens might resort to their own informal punishments. Where this is a realistic danger, the question is whether to abrogate the law or to persevere with it and try to control the public reaction. It might be thought that this degree of dissonance between law and citizens should not occur in a true democracy. One answer is that there are few perfect democracies. Another is that legislators do use the law to pursue policies of social engineering: the law which introduced the breathalyser test for drunken driving in 1967 is an example of this, as are the Race Relations Acts which introduced offences of incitement to racial hatred. In these instances the legislature has adopted an objective conception of social welfare, going beyond that shared by many citizens.

Thirdly, there is the policy that the criminal law should be kept to a minimum. With over 7,000 offences in English criminal law, it might be thought that this policy counts for nothing. But it does serve to emphasize that the primary function of the criminal law is to declare and protect fundamental social values; that the criminal law is society's most powerful agency against anti-social conduct; that it is liberty-depriving, coercive, and stigmatic in its operation; and that a justification on grounds of social welfare must be carefully constructed so as to show that welfare could not be achieved by non-criminal regulation. It follows that persuasive social arguments are needed to justify criminalization, over and above the arguments for introducing the regulation of a certain activity or civil liability for its effects. In practice, it seems that this policy is not applied conscientiously to every offence, and that the outer boundaries of the criminal law are not systematically reviewed. For example, the law of attempts extends the ambit of every substantive offence, but there is little evidence that its effects on the overall reach of the law have been considered. Some offences are deliberately defined widely so that law-enforcement agencies are able to select those cases most suitable for prosecution.

These approaches to criminalization run counter to the principle of maximum certainty, to be discussed in Chapter 3.3(j) below, and they also transfer considerable power to the police, the Crown Prosecution Service, and other agencies with the power to prosecute. The tendency in a good deal of criminal legislation has not been to strive for maximum certainty by stating the minimum conduct deemed to constitute an offence, but to leave those engaged in law enforcement to draw the line between what is and what is not serious enough for criminal proceedings. In England and Wales attempts have been made to structure this wide discretion: a Home Office circular is directed at the police,[13] and the Crown Prosecution Service is required to publish its Code for Crown Prosecutors annually.[14] These guide-lines are expressed in similar terms, raising the issues in terms of whether it is 'in the public interest' to prosecute a particular person. To a large extent, the criteria deal with issues of culpability, vulnerability, and sympathy—advising against the prosecution of the very old, the infirm, the mentally disturbed, those suffering from serious illness, etc.—and they say little on the present issue of offence-seriousness. The only relevant provision in the Code for Crown Prosecutors is that prosecutions should not generally be brought where the court 'would be likely to impose a purely nominal penalty'. That provision at least directs prosecutors to divert from the courts those cases which may technically fulfil the definition of an offence but which are in reality only minor infringements. There are internal directives to prosecutors about the non-prosecution of certain forms of offences, but these are not open to public scrutiny. At this

---

[13] Home Office Circular No. 59/1990 'The Cautioning of Offenders'.

[14] The duty is laid on the Director of Public Prosecutions by s. 9 of the Prosecution of Offences Act 1985.

level, then, the criteria for offence-seriousness crumble into unreviewable discretion. Moreover, there is no conscientious attempt to ensure that the different agencies empowered to bring prosecutions (including the Inland Revenue, local authorities, and the regulatory agencies) pursue socially coherent policies when it comes to deciding which offences are too minor to justify taking action.

Another relevant question here is the proper relationship between the criminal and the civil law. Someone who is the victim of a tort or breach of contract may usually sue for damages, or for some other remedy, in the civil courts. The defendant's conduct is wrong in these cases, but it may not amount to a crime. It might be said that the law should grade its responses according to the degree of social mischief involved: cases where a civil action alone is available are regarded as less serious than those which are criminal as well. But occasionally one hears the opposite view, that the criminal law should be available in certain types of case, because it is troublesome, impractical, or unduly expensive to pursue a civil remedy when the swifter approach of a criminal prosecution (for which there are also public officials available—the police, the Crown Prosecution Service, trading-standards officers, etc.) is a possibility. This argument has prevailed on some occasions, producing a proliferation of minor and truly regulatory offences. Another point to be made here is that, whilst in some spheres it might be sufficient to leave aggrieved individuals to sue those who caused them harm, this is not sufficient where the harm is to the public and the offence does not have an individual victim. These are the so-called 'victimless' crimes—like drug offences, some drunken driving, etc.—where no individual will take action if the State does not. It might therefore be justifiable to impose criminal liability in order to ensure that a certain form of antisocial activity is controlled, even though its impact on fundamental social values is rather remote. Before this is accepted, however, alternative modes of preventing the behaviour must be explored, and this is certainly not, as it stands, an argument in favour of strict liability. It is simply to make the point that one cannot assume that, if conduct does not constitute a crime, the laws of tort and contract will enable individuals to pursue wrongdoers in the civil courts. If there is no individual victim, that form of argument is inapplicable.

2.3. THE RELEVANCE OF 'SERIOUSNESS'

The practical importance of the enquiry is manifest. As we have seen, the decision to create a criminal offence to cover certain conduct or omissions has obvious consequences for citizens and law-enforcement officers. Where an offence has been created, the maximum penalty assigned to it determines the extent both of the court's powers and of the offender's liability to punishment. The maximum penalties attached to offences may also be taken to convey the relative seriousness of the types of offence: indeed, one of the main functions of criminal law is to express the *degree* of wrongdoing, not simply the fact of wrongdoing. This is integral to determining the proper label for the offence and the appropriate degree of punishment. Moreover, the differing degrees of serious-ness have wider practical consequences—for the legality of arrest without warrant, for the lawfulness of searches, for the decision to prosecute or to caution, for the decision to try the case in the Crown Court or the magistrates' court, for the sentencing powers of the court, for the decision to release a prisoner on parole, and for many other considerations at various stages in the criminal process. We must enquire, therefore, not only whether the behaviour is serious enough to be made into a criminal offence, but also, if it is an offence, how serious it is when compared with other crimes.

It is not difficult to see some toe-holds for the assessment of relative seriousness. There is a widely held view that, in general, offences of violence are more serious than property offences. However, the very breadth of modern systems of criminal law means that this is no more than a toe-hold. It is not difficult to think of circumstances in which an offence against property (say, stealing a million pounds) might be thought more serious than a particular offence of violence (such as one person pushing another whilst queuing). Thus it is necessary to press the enquiry further, examining those values or interests which are protected by the offence, and those elements which distinguish it from other similar offences. This task soon reveals a bewildering number of separate factors; the challenge is to avoid the banal approach of simply listing the different elements, and instead to attempt to identify some para-meters which enable us to make sense of many different offences. When passing sentence, the courts have to range the different crimes along a single scale of relative gravity (represented by imprisonment, fines, and other non-custodial sentences). Is it possible for the criminal lawyer to range the various offences along a single scale of social seriousness?

There are some who would argue that, ácademically interesting though this enquiry might be, it is quite unnecessary in practice, because most people in most countries agree on the relative gravity of harms. Research by the criminologists Sellin and Wolfgang purported to find considerable agreement in ranking criminal offences, whether amongst people from different countries or from different social groups in one country.[15] However, the questions asked in this research were relatively unsophisticated for the purpose of the criminal law,[16] and its findings cannot sustain the argument that it is unnecessary to think further about the grading of crimes as more or less serious. It is certainly true that those American states which have recently introduced sentencing guide-lines for their courts had no great difficulty in ranking the offences,[17] but that should not stifle deeper enquiry. After all, the 1980s saw several distinct shifts in the seriousness with which certain forms of offence were viewed—for example, rape, drunken driving, reckless driving, corruption of public officials and insider dealing on the stock-market are all offences which have come to be viewed as relatively more serious, as people have become more aware of their consequences. The arguments for and against changes of this kind are based, surely, on the elements of the various crimes and on their value or importance when compared with other crimes. It is arguments of this kind that we are assessing and developing here.

Another claim is that there is no point in considering offence-seriousness without examining the social structure as a whole, since the criminal law is a reflection of the interests of the powerful in society. This is especially true with law enforcement, it is argued, where the often public misbehaviour of the disadvantaged members of society is prosecuted with vigour whilst the often private crimes of the powerful go unprosecuted—the shop-lifter and the late-night brawler go to court, whilst the tax-evader and the industrial polluter go to their club. And, the argument continues, this is also the case

[15] See the Introduction to the revised edition of T. Sellin and M. Wolfgang, *The Measurement of Delinquency* (1978).

[16] Of the many writings on this issue, see P. Rossi et al., 'Beyond Crime Seriousness: Fitting the Punishment to the Crime' (1985) *Journal of Quantitative Criminology* 59; and F. T. Cullen *et al.*, 'Consensus in Crime Seriousness: Empirical Reality or Methodological Artefact' (1985) 23 *Criminology* 99.

[17] See e.g. Ch. 5 of A. von Hirsch, K. A. Knapp, and M. Tonry, *The Sentencing Commission and its Guidelines* (1987).

with the criminal law itself, since the law provides serious offences with heavy penalties for street violence and public disorder, whilst providing few offences with relatively low penalties for offences concerned with industrial safety, product safety, and pollution. Yet the social consequences of the latter offences can be damaging on a widespread scale. An attempt to treat these claims seriously is made below, but their limitations are not difficult to find. It is unlikely to be the case that the whole of the criminal law can be explained in terms of conflicts between different social groups, with the powerful imposing their will and their values on the disadvantaged. There may be some shared values in societies, and one should not rule out the possibility of a kind of fundamental 'moral order'—even a pluralist society with opposing interest groups may share some basic tenets of right and wrong in social behaviour.[18]

This is not to suggest, however, that the best way of understanding offence-seriousness is to conduct opinion polls: even if individuals have devoted thought to the matter, their opinions might be founded on imperfect knowledge of the characteristics and consequences of certain forms of law-breaking, and on fears which are objectively irrational. To understand and evaluate offence-seriousness, one must ascertain whether there are any objective standards which can be used as criteria for assessment. One seemingly indisputable standard might be human rights, but that is more helpful in determining the values or interests to be protected rather than in assessing comparative seriousness. What about economic theory—would it be helpful to use economic criteria for the calculation of relative gravity, arguing that the more one is prepared to pay to be free of a certain offence, the more seriously it may be regarded? Would a more realistic, though more abstract, approach be to assess the impact of various crimes upon one's living standards, using that term to encompass all the stages of existence, from deprivation to luxury? Before we examine the possibility of constructing parameters of offence-seriousness, it is essential to survey the field and to take stock of the rich variety of behaviour with which any general principles would have to deal.

---

[18] See Paul Rock, 'The Sociology of Deviancy and Conceptions of Moral Order' (1974) 14 *BJ Criminology* 139.

2.4. VARIETIES OF HARM

(a) Offences Involving Death

Substantial agreement might be obtained to the proposition that death constitutes the most serious harm, and English criminal law has a range of offences relating to death. Since the seriousness of offences is clearly connected to the culpability with which they are committed, the highest of homicide offences is murder—an offence which, it may be hoped,[19] is designed to comprise the most culpable killings. The crime of attempted murder deals with those who try to commit this offence but do not succeed. Beneath murder are ranked several other offences which include death as an element, such as manslaughter (in other legal systems this may be called culpable homicide or second-degree murder), infanticide, and causing death by reckless driving. Most legal systems also contain various offences of endangerment, designed to reduce the danger to life by penalizing conduct which both creates and is known to create a risk of death— offences connected with explosives and firearms, placing a dangerous device on an aircraft or causing damage (usually by fire) which endangers life. Beneath these offences are various provisions dealing with the safety of work-places and sports stadiums, and the carrying of weapons, all concerned to protect both life and limb. These offences are often neglected in an exposition of the criminal law, perhaps because they are not 'traditional' offences. Other types of offence may also be linked to the preservation of human life: the purpose of speed limits is to promote safety, a concept which includes human life, and it has been claimed that one major reason for controlling the importation and supply of hard drugs is the danger that these substances pose to the lives of users.

This general discussion of homicide offences has already shown that there are at least two dimensions of offence-seriousness apart from the intrinsic value of the harm being protected. One is the degree of culpability involved in the offence, and the other is the degree of remoteness from the infliction of the harm. Thus, one may regard causing death by reckless driving as an offence designed to recognize the special value of life, but can the same be said about reckless driving, drunken driving, speeding, and so on, as the offences become more remote from the actual causation or threat of

---

[19] See below, Ch. 7.3 and 7.4.

harm. More will be said about this below, after some other categories of crime have been outlined.

(b) Offences Involving Physical Violation

Beneath homicide come the non-fatal offences of violence. These range from torture and the deliberate and unjustifiable infliction of serious injury, through the less serious crimes of wounding, injury, and bodily harm, down to the basic offence of common assault. The purpose of these offences is to recognize the value of physical integrity and freedom from attack, a value which is indisputably lower than that of death. There is immense variation within these crimes; some of the non-fatal offences will place the victim close to death, and others will be little more than a push or kick; sometimes this group of offences is taken to include sexual offences, sometimes the two are regarded as separate. By no means all sexual offences involve some kind of physical injury (and if they do, they can involve a separate charge of an offence of violence), but they do typically involve an invasion of physical integrity. Both crimes of violence and sexual offences may involve considerable psychological trauma, although this is more commonly discussed in relation to sexual offences. Few legal systems take account of these psychological effects when defining crimes of violence or sexual offences, but that is no reason to ignore them when assessing relative seriousness. The reality of psychological hurt can be more painful, and certainly longer-lasting, than physical hurt. To read victims' accounts of the effects of rape is to realize that it is difficult to separate the relative gravity of serious sexual invasion and of serious wounding.[20] The two types of offence may therefore be placed together provisionally, bearing in mind, however, that sexual offences may also vary from the deeply serious to the relatively minor sexual touching.

(c) Offences against Public Order

What values are public-order offences supposed to uphold? To some extent, crimes such as riot, violent disorder, and affray appear as inchoate offences of violence or even actual offences of violence. If so, it is largely a matter of putting a different label on an offence of violence which occurs during public disorder. It is doubtful whether the creation of public-order offences could be justified on the basis of promoting the peaceful passage of ordinary citizens' daily business,

[20] For a summary of the literature, see J. Temkin, *Rape and the Legal Process* (1987), 1–6.

since many of the incidents could equally be prosecuted as offences or inchoate offences of violence. But they might be justified as recognizing the psychological effects on some citizens of marauding groups of people in public places and the fear which may be instilled by that kind of conduct. Questions will be raised later about the need for broad public-order offences which go beyond the offences against the person and which bestow considerable powers on the police.[21] For the moment, the respects in which public-order offences extend beyond ordinary offences of violence may be regarded as promoting the value of freedom from fear among members of the public, and freedom from abuse and nuisance. Viewed in this light, they would not be placed high on the scale of relative seriousness. However, English law does define some of the offences as covering situations of fairly serious violence or threatened violence, requiring those offences to be placed on a level with non-fatal offences against the person.

(d) Road-Traffic Offences

Some road-traffic offences have already been mentioned. Clearly, one purpose of having such offences is to create an orderly flow of traffic, so that there is a single set of rules to which all road-users conform. Beyond that, the penalties for infringing the rules are designed to criminalize those who deviate from the rules, thereby creating a risk of damage to property or to the individual. The offence of reckless driving marks out the creation of an obvious risk of such harm; the offence of careless driving is applicable to lesser risks of lesser harm; the offence of driving with excess alcohol ('drunken driving') contains no reference to particular consequences, but can be said to constitute the creation of an unacceptable risk to the safety of other road-users. The same comment can be made about the offence of exceeding the speed limit, although here the risk is thought to be more remote (if it is not, then a more serious offence such as reckless or careless driving should be charged). What we see in the road-traffic offences, therefore, is a range of offences differing primarily in the nature and degree of risk to person and property. Generically, they are closer to offences of violence than to property offences; it is relatively rare for a motor vehicle to create a risk to property that could not also be said to constitute a risk of harm to a person. Road-traffic offences are

[21] See below, Ch. 8.3(g) and 8.3(k).

therefore a diluted form of offences of violence, diluted in so far as typically, the risk of injury may be low and the culpability may be relatively low. But of course there will be cases in which the degree of risk and culpability will render a driving offence significantly more serious than an intentional but moderate assault on another person.

(e) Safety Offences

Also designed to penalize those who create risks to the physical safety of citizens, these offences are concerned with safety at work, the safety of consumer products, the safety of sports stadiums, safety in transport systems, and so forth. These are sometimes offences of negligence and sometimes offences of failing to comply with directions from the appropriate regulatory agency. There is a tendency for these offences to be regarded as a lesser species of criminality, as 'not real crime', since on the relatively rare occasions on which prosecutions are brought, the defendants are persons who might be regarded as respectable members of the community. However, one benefit of the present approach of seeking to identify those values which offences aim to protect is to show that safety offences ought to come fairly high on any comparative assessment of the seriousness of crimes. True, the seriousness of these offences might be reduced where the culpability is not high and where the risk created is fairly remote; but there will assuredly be cases where that is not so. Moreover, some of these cases will involve risks to the safety of considerable numbers of people, and that ought to increase their relative seriousness.

Figure 2.1 (overleaf) consists of a somewhat basic diagrammatic representation of the position so far, showing offences involving death, non-fatal offences of violence, sexual offences, public-order offences, safety offences, and road-traffic offences. Seriousness appears to be constructed from four main components—nature of harm, intensity of harm (number of victims, actual or potential), proximity of harm (degree of risk), and culpability of harm-doer.

(f) Offences against the State

Turning to an entirely different group of offences, we come to those crimes surrounding the functioning of the State and its legal system. Treason covers such conduct as levying war against the State or giving aid or comfort to the enemy in times of war: the offence aims to protect the foundations of the State in its existing form, and may

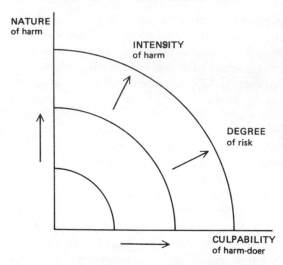

FIG. 2.1. *Measuring the seriousness of offences*

therefore be regarded as basic to the continuance of 'life as we know it'. It does not, however, involve death or even injury to anyone. This makes it difficult to draw a comparison between the various offences concerned with death and physical harm on the one hand, and offences against the State on the other. It can be argued that it is necessary to preserve peace and good order, and that stability of government is a major factor in this; therefore offences which penalize attempts to destabilize a lawful government strike at a fundamental aspect of the legal system. This is an argument which begs various questions about political obligation and the requirements of allegiance to a particular system.[22] If it can be assumed that the system is worthy of allegiance, then it is surely justifiable to penalize those who attempt to destabilize it by illegal means. Once again, however, there are degrees of challenge to the State. Treason is one thing, but contraventions of the Official Secrets Acts in Britain may be something far less, since the Acts have tended to cover both serious breaches of security, involving highly sensitive defence secrets, and relatively minor disclosures of the contents of government documents to which the extensive prohibitions apply.[23] Account must also be taken of the anti-terrorism laws, which

[22] See further, Lacey, *State Punishment* esp. Chs. 4 and 6.
[23] The broader provisions in earlier statutes were significantly curtailed by the Official Secrets Act 1989.

include such offences as belonging to a proscribed organization, arranging meetings of such an organization, wearing the uniform of such an organization, and so on. These offences lie rather remote from a direct challenge to the State—they are preparatory offences, and more serious offences may be charged where the challenge goes further. Also, there are other offences which involve less of a direct challenge to the authority of the State than an attempt to undermine its proper functioning—perverting the course of justice, perjury, bribery of public officials and so forth.

Thus the offences against the State show the same differences of degree as other groups of offences, but the key problem is still how to compare this group with offences of violence. How can the death of one citizen be compared with a threat to the defences of a nation? How can the serious injury of a citizen be compared with an act of assistance to an enemy in time of war, such as the making of propaganda broadcasts? One approach would be to argue that the death of an individual must remain the supreme harm, and any challenge to the State's authority which does not involve any deaths is less serious. The opposite approach would regard the continuation of a national identity as supreme, in comparison with which, any individual's life is necessarily secondary. The latter view goes to great lengths in affirming that the present system is preferable to all others.

(g) Offences against Property

The vast bulk of recorded crimes falls into the category of property offences. Robbery is usually regarded as the most serious of this group. It involves theft and the use or threat of force at the time of the stealing. It is, therefore, a combination of two generically different elements, one against property and one against the person; as such, it straddles the categories of property and violence. If there were no offence of robbery, this kind of situation could be covered adequately by the separate offences of theft, carrying firearms or offensive weapons, and any offence of violence actually committed. The same cannot be said of another serious 'property' offence, namely, causing damage to property with intent to endanger life or knowing that life may be endangered thereby. Clearly, this is a hybrid offence, involving property damage and danger to life, but English law does not contain a separate offence of reckless endangerment which could deal with these cases in the absence of this aggravated crime of criminal damage.

Turning to the general property offences, criminal damage covers offences of damaging or destroying another's property, whilst theft deals with those individuals who dishonestly appropriate property belonging to another with the intention of depriving the other person of it permanently. Thus, both offences tend to protect property interests—both interests of ownership and interests of possession—by penalizing those who destroy or challenge them. A welter of other crimes is concerned with different methods of destroying or challenging property rights: offences of obtaining by deception proscribe a particular method of challenging property rights, as do false accounting, abstracting electricity, making off without paying for goods or services, and so on. The crime of handling stolen goods strikes at those who help to make property crimes economically worth while, by criminalizing those who assist in the realization of the proceeds. We can leave until later the debate about whether handling ought to be regarded as more serious than stealing; our present concern lies not with the relatively small differences between property offences, but with the comparison between this type of offence and other kinds of crime.

Before attempting this comparison, attention should be drawn to three further types of hybrid offence in this category. First, blackmail consists of making an unwarranted demand with menaces: the demand is usually an economic one, which places the offence in the property category, but the method involved may be the threat or use of violence. Some, but not all, of these cases might fall within the definition of offences of violence. Blackmail is therefore an offence which may straddle the property and the violence categories. Second, there is a group of offences whose purpose is to criminalize those who threaten a citizen's home, such as the offences of harassment of a tenant, threatening violence in order to secure entry to premises, and adverse occupation of residential premises. There are varying elements in these crimes—the threat of force and the psychological efforts of harassment, as well as the deprivation of the use of property—and they may therefore be regarded as more serious than simple stealing. The third hybrid offence is burglary, which involves either theft or an intention to steal when trespassing on premises belonging to another. There is no general crime of trespass in English law, although, as we have just seen, there are some crimes protecting the home, but one major element in burglary (not mentioned by the legal definition) is the invasion of privacy and the resulting psychological effect on many victims. It is not merely a question of property loss; indeed, this often seems to be less important both in the short run and in the long run than such psychological effects as feeling that one's possessions have been sullied (sometimes amounting to feeling that one has been intimately assaulted), and being afraid that, once again, someone else may be in one's home.[24] Thus, whereas the law draws no distinction between burglary of a home and burglary of commercial premises, the reality is that the former is felt to be more heinous than the latter because of the generally more serious psychological effects. This may be taken to raise residential burglary out of the 'property' category into some sort of equivalence with the lower levels of sexual offences.

How can one compare the simple, non-hybrid property offences, such as damage, theft, and deception, with other classes of offence, such as violence and road-traffic offences? There is a need for a common denominator among such disparate kinds of offending behaviour, something which will measure their centrality to the conditions of life. There is a powerful intuition that, in general, property offences are less serious than offences of violence. The intuition may be based on the replaceability of much property, on the greater feeling for one's body than for one's possessions, and on the futility of property without the life and health to enjoy it.

(h) Moral and Paternalistic Offences

Legal systems vary in the number of offences which they create and enforce in order to protect citizens from themselves. One major reason for such offences is to protect those who are unable to protect themselves, notably the very young. But the offences invariably cast their net more widely, and there are various offences designed to protect adults from themselves. High among these are the various offences involving the importation, supply, cultivation, and possession of dangerous drugs and narcotics. The addictive and potentially destructive nature of narcotics, coupled perhaps with the social consequences of their wide use (lower economic productivity, inferior family relations, and so on), are taken to justify severe restrictions. There are arguments that the law is framed unnecessarily widely, in that cannabis and soft drugs are included when some allege that their use is no less socially deleterious than the permissible use of tobacco and alcohol, but the most serious cases involve the importation of millions of pounds' worth of hard

---

[24] M. Maguire, 'The Impact of Burglary upon Victims' (1980) 20 *BJ Criminology* 261.

drugs, some of which might well find their way to very young people. This is why some regard these hard-drugs offences as preserving the value of life, and why they would place them alongside life-threatening conduct in terms of seriousness: it is one thing for an adult to be found in possession of a quantity of a controlled drug for personal use; it is quite another thing to import these drugs on a large scale.

Among other offences in this broad category are those of failing to wear a seat-belt in the front seat of a car and failing to wear a crash-helmet when riding a motor cycle, both paternalistic in nature and supported (as we saw in section 2.2 above) on the grounds that the State knows better than individuals when it comes to the risk of death or injury, and that the State may, by this law, reduce its expenditure on medical treatment. Then there are the laws against obscene publications, obscene displays, living on the earnings of prostitution, and other offences against 'public morality'. These are mostly hybrid offences, concerned not only with protecting individuals against themselves but also with protecting vulnerable members of society (the very young) and with controlling the organization of prostitution (even though prostitution itself is not a crime), since it might otherwise involve the exploitation of women and, perhaps, the formation of organizations which might commit other crimes.

The variation of offences within this category is great. If the argument relating hard drugs to deaths is sustained, then there is a strong case for regarding such offences as equivalent in seriousness to other offences of endangerment. Otherwise, these offences against public morality seem more concerned with the protection of the vulnerable and with the quality of the living environment of others, two justifications which indicate substantially different rankings on any scale of comparative seriousness.

(i) Offences Concerned with the Environment

Obviously falling within this category are the various pollution offences, particularly those relating to rivers and to the sea. The tendency has been to place these offences relatively low on the scale in terms of maximum penalties, and it is a sphere in which supposed justifications such as the conduct of a business employing many people have been assumed to reduce the seriousness of the damage to the animals, fish, and birds which either do or would inhabit these waterways, and of the general damage to public amenity. However, there is now greater consciousness of the lasting effects of pollution on food and health, and a higher respect for the value of pleasant, pollution-free living conditions. Counter-arguments based on increased costs for industrial enterprises tend to receive less weight.

Also in this group of offences are some of the public-order offences, such as those concerned with using abusive or insulting words or behaviour or disorderly behaviour likely to cause harassment, alarm, or distress, those concerned with soliciting for prostitution, offences of obstruction, and so forth. No tangible harm is required for these offences: their essence lies in their capability of causing a public nuisance, and therefore of significantly reducing the quality of life for ordinary citizens. The same might be said of some of the morality offences considered previously: adults who see or hear obscene matters may be temporarily shocked, and the publication of such matters may be regarded as lowering the quality of life significantly. These considerations seem to suggest that, in general, this category may be thought to be the least serious of the nine considered. This does not mean that every property crime (even stealing goods worth £1) is rightly assessed as more serious than every crime against the environment (such as releasing a large quantity of poisonous effluent into a hitherto clean river where people fish and swim, and from which water is drawn for purification). Indeed, pollution crimes ought to be regarded as more serious than many property crimes because of the potentially large-scale consequences of a single offence. But the remaining offences in this category, consisting mainly of public nuisance, should be treated as minor.

2.5. THE SEARCH FOR PRINCIPLES

Nine different categories of offence have been established above, and even that has been achieved at the cost of considerable simplification. Nevertheless, some of the principal antinomies which make this exercise so difficult have been identified. To assess the relative seriousness of harms on a single scale is not only a matter of identifying the values behind each class of offence and then ranking those values in order of priority. The issues revolve not around this single axis but around several axes, of which the most important are:

high culpability > low culpability;
virtual certainty of harm > remote risk of harm;

actual occurrence of harm > non-occurrence of harm;
widespread effects > effects confined to small area;
significant psychological trauma for victim > no psychological
    trauma for victim;
no social justification for activity involved > some social justifica-
    tion for activity involved.

Only by reference to these other axes can one find a principled
answer to the comparison between, say, a negligent homicide and
an intentional robbery involving only slight injury; or between, say,
reckless driving and intentional pollution of clean waters. Many
other complexities will also be apparent. The seriousness of an
offence may be greatly affected by the position of the offender (for
example, breach of a position of trust in relation to the victim must
aggravate the offence) and of the victim (for example, theft from a
person living on social-security payments must be more serious than
theft of an equivalent amount from a wealthy person or company, at
least if the offenders know of the relative wealth of their victims).
But, beneath all these complexities of detail, are there any general
principles which can serve to point the way to meaningful com-
parisons?

It was argued above that references to human rights, whilst
importing some much-needed objectivity into this sea of plural
values, are unhelpful in determining relative seriousness. Agreements on human rights are designed to guarantee certain basic
rights and liberties, not to rank values in order of priority. On the
other hand, the economic theory of crimes, which assesses their
seriousness according to the price which might be paid in order to be
free of them, is a conscientious attempt to reduce the myriad crimes
to a single scale, but the objectivity of this exercise crumbles when
one considers that the valuations merely reflect the impressions of
the individuals involved, most of whom will have little practical
experience of the various forms of victimization and of the real
'costs' involved. The empirical element in this approach is therefore
inferior to surveys of victims and victims' families; and the 'principle'
which underlies it is simply one of reflecting people's feelings rather
than arguing about desirable priorities. The economic theory may
therefore be little more than a formalized version of an approach
which purported to rank the seriousness of crimes simply according
to public views. As argued above, such opinions may be based on
imperfect knowledge: moreover, even a perfectly designed survey

might offer no explanation of those views, nor any criteria for their appraisal and subsequent change. The proper task is to construct principles for making sense of views which are assumed to be widely held.

One deeper approach is that of Joel Feinberg, who proposes a threefold division of individual interests—welfare interests, security interests, and accumulative interests.[25] His purpose in making this division is rather different from our purpose here, but the methodology is none the less instructive. 'Welfare interests' are those which individuals need to have satisfied in order to have any significant capacity to choose their way of living. They include such basic interests as human life and a modicum of personal property. 'Security interests' are those which may be said to cushion welfare interests, by providing a reasonable measure of security above the bare essentials of life, and which thus enhance an individual's capacity to choose a way of life. The lowest of Feinberg's categories is 'accumulative interests', the consequences of the choices one makes if one's security interests are assured—the acquisition of personal property and the existence of pleasant living conditions.

Feinberg's classification marks an important step in thinking about this difficult area, but it has manifest drawbacks as a model here. Three levels of values/interests would be unlikely to capture the essence of the rich variety of crimes depicted in section 2.4 of this chapter. Feinberg expressly confines his scheme to individual interests, leaving state and collective interests out of account. The classification lays heavy emphasis on the importance of choice in determining relative seriousness, but it is unclear whose choice is the crucial measure. The effect of a given crime may have a far greater impact on the life choices of some victims than of others, and prevailing principles of criminal culpability give considerable attention to the choice and knowledge of the offender. Is it possible to improve upon Feinberg's approach and to meet these criticisms? One proposal, by Andrew von Hirsch and Nils Jareborg,[26] is aimed specifically at assessing offence-seriousness. The first question to be asked, following their approach, is what interests are violated or threatened by the standard case of this crime. Their analysis, which is confined to crimes with individual victims, identifies four generic interests:

---

[25] J. Feinberg, *Harm to Others* (1984).
[26] A. von Hirsch and N. Jareborg, 'Gauging Criminal Harm: a Living Standard Analysis' (1991) 11 *Oxford JLS* (forthcoming).

    (i) physical integrity: health, safety, and the avoidance of physical pain;

    (ii) material support and amenity: includes nutrition, shelter, and other basic amenities, various material comforts, and luxuries as well;

    (iii) freedom from humiliation or degrading treatment;

    (iv) privacy and autonomy.

Their approach would be to ask which of these interests are affected by a standard house burglary, rape or shop theft.

The four types of interest listed are intended to be illustrative and not exhaustive: the authors' method could accommodate more such interests. Once the nature of the violated interests has been determined, the second stage is to apply a scale of seriousness to each one affected. The scale which they put forward has five bands of effect on the 'living standards' of victims:

(1) subsistence: survival with maintenance of elementary human functions—no satisfactions presupposed at this level;

(2) minimum well-being: maintenance of a minimum level of comfort and human dignity;

(3) adequate well-being: maintenance of an 'adequate' level (but no more) of comfort and dignity.

(4) significant enhancement: significant enhancement in quality of life above the merely 'adequate' level;

(5) marginal impact: living standards not significantly affected.

Once again, the differences between the levels are couched in fairly vague terms, such as 'adequate' and 'significant', but that is surely inevitable if one is seeking general principles, and it is also appropriate in view of the cultural relativity of offence-seriousness: what is crucial in a cold country or a poor country might be peripheral in a hot country or an affluent country. The five-band division not only allows more scope than Feinberg's threefold classification, but it also shifts the emphasis away from the effect on the individual victim's capacity of choice to the means and capabilities which ordinarily help one to achieve one's conception of a good life. The key issue becomes the effect of the offence (which violates certain types of individual interest) upon the conditions for enjoying some 'quality of life'. But whose view of these conditions should be treated as determinative? The value-preferences of each individual victim should not usually be allowed to determine offence-seriousness, but where the offender knows of the special situation of the victim, it is right to take this into account. For the general run of cases, however, the criterion should be the typical impact on victims of this kind of offence. This allows monetary value to be a primary determinant of seriousness in property and drug offences, and it also allows the psychological impact of residential burglary to be given some weight in assessing the seriousness of this crime. Should a particular offender be allowed to argue that he or she failed to realize the emotional after-effects of this kind of crime? Surely not: it should be assumed that there is general awareness of the common effects of most types of crime, and the psychological trauma caused by certain kinds of burglary may be regarded as a common effect. The typical impacts of crimes on victims should be incorporated into any assessment of their seriousness, whether the offender was aware or not. One practical consequence of taking this approach is the need for more empirical research into the effects of victimization, followed by publicity to ensure that these effects are widely known in the community.

Assessments of offence-seriousness should therefore be concerned with the standard impact and effects of the type of offence. On this approach, offences involving death would be ranked at the top level, 'subsistence', on the 'living standards' scale proposed by Von Hirsch and Jareborg. Serious offences against the person, such as grievous bodily harm, would be ranked at the first or second level. Rape unaccompanied by serious physical injury might be ranked at the second level, 'minimum well-being', taking account both of the physical threat and of the extreme humiliation and degradation. Offences such as reckless driving, drunken driving, and unsafe working conditions may well be placed at the first or second level, though undoubtedly some of the offences towards the lower end of each scale would rank at the third level or below. This suggests that even the ninefold division of types of crime described in section 2.4 above is not detailed enough for our purposes. However, there is no doubt that the higher offences in each of these categories is properly placed at the second level of seriousness of harm. Property offences, likewise, straddle the third, fourth, and fifth levels, according to the value of what is taken or damaged and the effect it has upon the victim. Most shop thefts will be in the fifth category, whereas some larger offences of theft and deception involving elderly victims would be at the third level or even higher. Thus one strength of the 'living standards' framework is that it enables one to rank offences in a more sophisticated way than the legal categories themselves would allow: an offence falling within the legal category of theft might be ranked at a different level of seriousness, depending on the impact of a standard case of that kind. Moreover, the 'living standards' approach can be adapted to take account of such other variables as high or low culpability, high or low risk of harm, occurrence or non-occurrence of harm, high or low psychological effects, and low or moderate social justification for the offence. It would take a complex mathematical model to show how these could be brought into the calculation, but it is relatively straightforward to take account of one variable, such as the degree of risk inherent in the offence. Figure 2.2 is a two-dimensional grid which, having plotted harm against risk of harm, is able to yield some assessment of the seriousness of an offence.

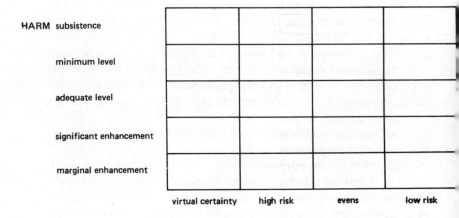

FIG. 2.2. *The von Hirsch–Jareborg scale for ranking harms*

The complexity of judgments of offence-seriousness, however, makes it necessary to search for a model which takes account not merely of two dimensions but of several. That requires a considerable degree of mathematical sophistication, which will not be attempted here, but it is evident that the conscientious judge and legislator already performs this kind of exercise in a rough and ready form. Many assessments of offence-seriousness do attempt to take proper account of various factors which are, in reality, operating on different scales. To take even three major factors—intrinsic gravity of harm, culpability, and degree of risk of harm—and to produce an intelligible joint scale is not easy. If the calculation is not accomplished mathematically, then there is inevitably room for error or for the infiltration of extraneous opinions and factors. What the present enquiry might be able to offer is a framework for identifying the weight that should be given to the various factors, and a clearer basis for social argument.

The drawback of using 'living standards' as this framework is that it is limited to individual interests and harms. It cannot deal with offences against the State, with moral/paternalistic offences, or with environmental interests. Although the notion of 'living standards' is not so obviously tied to liberal individualism as Feinberg's threefold model, it does not incorporate references to the effect of certain types of offence on the social setting or community in which individuals interact. There must surely be a more explicit accommodation of judgments of social welfare within the evaluation of offence-seriousness. Both legal authority and the existence of certain community amenities are important to the realization of individual liberty. Thus, an offence of espionage which involved the betrayal of crucial information about national defence might have little impact on the individual citizen, but it may be directly related to the conditions of security which are necessary if individual citizens are to be able to realize their conceptions of the good life. This is a difficult argument to press to a conclusion, of course, since it depends on the justifications for state authority and on other arguments about political obligation and legitimacy which would stray too far from the purposes of this book.[27] But it is important to remember that the relative seriousness of offences against the State depends ultimately not only on the centrality of that offence's challenge to state authority, but also on the legitimacy of the State itself. Such lofty considerations are likely to be less relevant to an offence such as perjury, which would have an impact on any system of justice. Perjury *can* affect the fate of individuals, but the essence of the offence is the undermining of the system of justice. If perjury were to be placed on the same scale as the offences against individual interests, the most appropriate level would probably be that of an 'adequate' level of well-being—witnesses who lie in court do not generally affect individuals' subsistence or the minimal level of self-respect, and yet it would trivialize perjury to claim that it is merely concerned with enhancements (whether significant or marginal) of individual well-being.

[27] See above, n. 22.

In this chapter we have considered some of the major questions of value which are involved both in the overall structure of the criminal law and in its practice. The structural issues concern the outer limits of the criminal law and the ranking of crimes in terms of maximum penalties. The practical implications concern not only maximum penalties, mode of trial, and so forth, but also the assessment of the seriousness with which any particular manifestation of an offence should be regarded. It was argued that the debate about law and morals might be better viewed in terms of the interaction of a liberal individualistic approach, promoting 'autonomy' and a more social conception of 'welfare'. Thus, contrary to the impression given by some writers who might be termed 'libertarian', the ideal of autonomy should not be treated as a sufficient or as an overriding consideration, but merely as one of the major values relevant to decisions about the ambit of the criminal law.

Whilst the 'law and morals' issues have attracted the greatest discussion, wider and deeper questions about the relative seriousness of offences have received less attention. One reason for this is that they have often been thought of as non-controversial,[28] but that view can hardly be sustained after the significant changes of the 1980s. Why is rape regarded as more serious now than it was ten years ago? Probably because there is a greater awareness of the psychological effects of the offence, and because a higher value is placed on the physical integrity of women than used to be the case. Why are drunken driving and reckless driving regarded as more serious than ten years ago? Because there is greater awareness of the connection between these kinds of behaviour and injuries and loss of life, so that the idea of treating these crimes as simply motoring offences is giving way to the sense that they are inchoate offences against the person. Why is taking a motor vehicle without consent regarded as less serious than ten years ago? Probably because it is accepted nowadays that non-violent, non-sexual, and non-frightening offences should be differentiated more clearly from those more serious forms of antisocial behaviour. Similar analyses could be applied to the rise in relative seriousness of pollution offences and offences relating to the safety of transport systems. A combination of greater awareness of their effects (through research or major events) and a willingness to link offences to such underlying values as personal safety has resulted in this re-evaluation. This

[28] Advisory Council on the Penal System, *Sentences of Imprisonment: A Review of Maximum Penalties* (1978).

shows that arguments can be made about offence-seriousness, and that some parameters can be clearly stated, even though the relative importance of certain values (e.g. a pure and peaceful environment as against some minor properly interests) is difficult to settle. The values of autonomy and welfare interact constantly with a number of other principles and policies, and several different dimensions of harm (e.g. degree of risk, remoteness of harm, non-occurrence of harm) have to be allowed for. The notion of 'living standards' is a helpful tool in analysing the arguments, but it needs to be supplemented by more explicit standards for public harms—such as the principle of welfare. Whilst it is difficult, and probably fruitless, to seek a 'correct' ranking of offences even within a fairly homogeneous society, it is possible to make some progress in the theoretical structure and factual basis of the relevant arguments.

As for the ambit of the criminal law, the interaction between the principles of autonomy and welfare has also been shown to be relevant. Three distinct policies were suggested: (i) that the consequences of criminalization should not be worse than the consequences of not criminalizing the behaviour; (ii) that there should not be great dissonance between the criminal law and public opinion; and (iii) that the criminal law should be kept at a minimum and reserved for significant wrongdoing. This third policy raises the question of the appropriateness of using the criminal law as a simple and swift method of enforcing relatively minor regulations, and hence the importance of regulating prosecution policies.

3

SOME PRINCIPLES AND POLICIES

There is some utility in describing the practical operation of the criminal law as a set of rules laid down by Parliament and applied by the courts, but it is a very limited utility. It certainly conveys an impression of what goes on in magistrates' courts most of the time, and in the Crown Court some of the time. Where there is a guilty plea—over 90 per cent of cases in magistrates' courts and some 50 per cent in the Crown Court—this invariably means that there is no legal argument in court about the scope of the applicable rule. The rule determines the case.

But the limitations to this approach are manifold. Not all the rules have been laid down by Parliament; some have been developed at common law (e.g. many of those relating to murder, manslaughter, and assault), and it remains open to the courts to modify their definitions further. Even where a guilty plea is entered, it might be to a lesser offence than originally charged: thus, it may be the working practices of prosecutors and defence lawyers, as much as the substantive rules of the criminal law which influence the construction of the case, which the court then deals with as a guilty plea. Then there are all the cases in which a not guilty plea is entered and a trial takes place: whilst most of them involve disputes about the facts rather than arguments on the law, there is a significant minority of cases which do involve some point of law. There may be controversy over whether an issue is one of fact or of law,[1] a distinction which has considerable consequences for the allocation of decision to judge or jury, for the need to give reasons (not required of juries), and for the availability of an appeal (restricted on issues of fact). There are also cases in which the interpretation of 'facts' is not such a pure and value-free exercise as is sometimes supposed. For

---

[1] For discussion, see G. Williams, 'Law and Fact' [1976] Crim. LR 472 and 432; and D. W. Elliott, 'Law and Fact in Theft Act Cases' [1976] Crim. LR 707.

example, points of law are not infrequently entangled with issues of fact in prosecutions for the possession of an offensive weapon, since the court may have to determine whether the article is 'made or adapted for use for causing injury'.[2] And although it has been held that the decision whether or not certain conduct was 'dishonest' is not one of law, it is certainly a decision which involves a moral or social evaluation of a person's conduct.[3]

Courts and lawyers have to draw upon sources, ideas, and concepts extrinsic to the rules themselves when applying or interpreting the rules. Linguistic conventions and other maxims for interpreting legal rules may be invoked; there is also a stock of doctrines, principles, and policies which have acquired some legitimacy in the criminal law through being relied upon from time to time; and there are other policies which appear to be influential but which are rarely spelt out by police, prosecutors, or courts. The idea that the criminal law is a set of clearly stated rules which is mechanically applied to citizens must be banished. Rather, the reality consists largely of a structure established by the rules but mediated in practice by the policies, principles, and working philosophies employed by all those involved in the administration of the criminal law, from police through to appeal-court judges. The pre-trial role of police, prosecutors, and others has already been discussed (see Chapter 1.2); the focus here is upon the legislature and the judiciary.

The purpose of this chapter is not to attempt a comprehensive assessment of the principles and policies relevant to legislative and judicial determinations, but to introduce some which may help to explain the structure and operation of the criminal law. It may be seen as a preliminary exploration of the ideology of English criminal law. Section 3.2 will examine some of the values which relate to the boundaries of the criminal sanction, expressed here in terms of principles and policies. This section refers back to Chapter 2, and to the conflicts of value inherent in decisions whether or not to criminalize certain types of behaviour. Section 3.3 moves on to consider various 'fairness' principles, a term usually applied to individual rights but actually involving a constant pull of community-based considerations. The various paragraphs of section 3.3 attempt to

---

[2] See e.g. *Williamson* (1977) 67 Cr. App. R 35, *Simpson* [1983] 1 WLR 1494, and *Houghton v. Chief Constable of Greater Manchester* (1987) 84 Cr. App. R 319.

[3] See *Feely* [1973] QB 530, *Ghosh* [1982] QB 1053, and the discussion below, Ch. 9.2(*e*).

demonstrate the conflicting values and goals which interplay in the development of the criminal law, and to recognize also the constitutional context, in terms of the respective roles of legislature and courts. From time to time particular principles are promoted as if they are fundamental and incontrovertible (e.g. the presumption of innocence in England, the principle of legality in the United States), whereas there are invariably both theoretical and practical arguments the other way. For this reason, the approach throughout sections 3.2 and 3.3 of this chapter is to present the various principles and policies in pairs, examining first (usually) a principle and then (usually) a policy which may derogate from it. The same policy might be regarded as running counter to more than one principle; readers will find, for example, that the broad policy of social defence is mentioned frequently in this connection.

The approach of this chapter is to be 'normatively' exploratory: that is, to raise some of the theoretical and practical problems which might result from relying on each of the principles and policies identified. The source of most of the principles and policies is empirical: most of them have been stated as a reason for, or a rationalization of, some development in the criminal law, whether by Parliament or by the courts, and some attention will therefore be paid to those occasions on which the arguments have been invoked. Our primary purpose, however, is to give a critical airing to a set of propositions which may have considerable influence on the development of English criminal law, but which have rarely been brought together for critical appraisal.[4] A similar approach is pursued in subsequent chapters when dealing with the conditions of criminal liability—the fault requirements—and none of those principles or policies is discussed in this chapter.

3.2. THE OUTER LIMITS OF THE CRIMINAL LAW

The preceding chapter illustrated the difficulties involved in deciding which interests the criminal law should protect, and in ranking harms so as to achieve some kind of proportionality. Clearly, a primary aim of the criminal law is to provide for the conviction of those who cause major harms to other citizens or to the community, but it has already been noted that the criminal law contains a myriad of less serious or more controversial offences. What principles and

[4] But see Glanville Williams, *Criminal Law: The General Part* (2nd ed., 1961), Ch. 12, and Nicola Lacey, *State Punishment* (1988), Ch. 5.

policies are relevant to the decisions to expand or contract the criminal law in these spheres? The enquiry begins by summarizing two policies already discussed in Chapter 2, and then moves on to consider other relevant policies and principles.

(a) The Policy of Minimum Criminalization

This policy, which was discussed in Chapter 2.2, is that the ambit of the criminal law should be kept to a minimum. In its favour are the individualistic notion of maximising liberty and freedom of choice, and the more community-oriented notion that since the criminal law is society's strongest response to wrongdoing, it should not be over-used lest its effect be blunted. These are strong arguments, but many modern systems of criminal law allow this policy to be outweighed by conflicting policies based on cost and convenience: the criminal courts and the police already exist, whereas it may be onerous for an individual citizen to bring a civil action against a malefactor; and a criminal prosecution may be a powerful threat for a regulatory agency to have in reserve, especially if success in such prosecutions is made easier by the availability of a strict liability offence. Commitment to this first policy is therefore not great in England and Wales.

(b) The Policy of Social Defence

Perhaps the strongest arguments against minimum criminalization are thought to derive from the policy of social defence. According to this view, the criminal law may properly be used against any form of activity which threatens good order. When the government feels impelled to take action against some activity which is causing public concern, resort to the criminal law is frequent: it is a sure sign that 'something is being done about' the public concern. In practice, as Chapter 1.4 suggested, it does not follow that the criminal law and sentencing are the most effective means of dealing with such an activity: various social, educational, and other preventive techniques might bear more fruit. There is a danger, moreover, in accepting the use of the concept of 'social defence' without question: it is one thing to defend existing political arrangements and agreed social principles, but it is quite another thing to protect the interests of particular groups within society.

Are extensions of the criminal law invariably examples of political posturing, or are there occasions when it can be justified on grounds of social defence? In England, as in most countries, the criminal law has accumulated a number of anomalies over the years. Rectification of an anomaly (for example, the current English ruling that a husband cannot be convicted of the rape of his wife[5]) may well lead to a new sphere of criminalization; so may the extension of the criminal law to cover a newly arising mischief, such as computer crime.[6] These examples are important, if only so as to counteract the libertarian argument underlying the policy of minimum criminalization. One might well agree that we all prefer our behaviour to be subject to as few constraints as possible, but that preference must be placed in the context of our membership of a community. Certain constraints may be reasonable in the interests of the community at large, even though they restrict particular individuals. These notions are more fully developed by Nicola Lacey in her concept of 'welfare'.[7] This does not mean that there should necessarily be more criminal law rather than less: one can perfectly well argue for the creation of new offences so as to deal proportionately with new or neglected social harms, whilst supporting the policy of minimum criminalization. For one thing, the extension of the criminal law into areas such as computer fraud and, especially, marital rape may be more significant for its declaration of the degree of wrongdoing inherent in the conduct than for its production of more convictions. And, more generally, one aspect of a real policy of minimum criminalization is to urge a reduction in the number of minor offences which have found their way into the statute-book. This requires a systematic re-evaluation of the myriad crimes thus created.

(c) The Principle of Liability for Acts not Omissions

This principle has often been cited, in the courts and elsewhere, as a reason for restricting the ambit of the criminal sanction.[8] In fact, Parliament has greatly increased the number of offences which penalize persons for 'failing to' fulfil certain requirements, usually concerned with motoring, business, and finance. But when a statute or a judicial precedent falls to be interpreted by a court, its extension to cover omissions is often regarded as exceptional and in need of special justification. The main reason is that positive duties to act

[5] See below, Ch. 8.5(b).
[6] See the Computer Misuse Act 1990, and below, Ch. 9.9.
[7] Lacey, State Punishment, 100–5.
[8] See further A. Ashworth, 'The Scope of Criminal Liability for Omissions' (1989) 105 LQR 424.

are regarded as an incursion on individual liberty: negative duties, which require citizens to avoid certain behaviour, leave them free to pursue their own desires in other directions, whereas a positive duty to act prevents them from doing anything else at the time. Familial ties and voluntarily assumed obligations are fair enough as bases for criminal liability, it is argued, but it would be wrong to introduce a general duty to assist strangers or to take steps towards enforcing the law. This viewpoint is grounded in a highly individualistic concept of liberalism, which is considered more fully in Chapter 4.4 below.

(d) The Principle of Social Responsibility

This countervailing principle is grounded in .the proposition that society requires a certain level of co-operation and mutual assistance between citizens. The recognition of social duties is therefore essential if individuals are to realize their full potential, and the imposition of duties backed by the criminal sanction may be justifiable to safeguard important values (such as life and physical integrity), if this can be done without risk or hardship to the duty-bound citizen. According to this view, the value to be promoted and the harm to be avoided are of greater social importance than the act–omission distinction. The principle of social responsibility would therefore support, for example, an offence of failing to render assistance to a citizen in peril, where that assistance can be accomplished without danger to the rescuer. It might also support the imposition of a duty on a man to make proper·enquiry of a woman before having sexual intercourse with her—in effect, insisting on a requirement of reasonableness for mistake in rape cases.[9] Social responsibility may be regarded as a more appropriate principle for a legislature to pursue, after due deliberation on the community's interests, whereas it might be thought that a presumption against applying liability to omissions is consonant with the courts' adherence to the principle of legality. The general arguments on omissions liability are developed more fully in Chapter 4.4(c) below.

(e) The Principle of Social Justification

There may be circumstances in which it is socially justifiable to inflict harm on another person or another person's property. This

---

[9] See below, p. 165 and Ch. 8.5(c).

principle states that, where necessary in the enforcement of the law, the apprehension of a suspected offender, the prevention of crime, or the protection of an individual from attack, it is justifiable to inflict reasonable harm on another. This is to place society's interest in the prevention of crime and the protection of victims above the interests of an attacker or suspected offender. It favours exceptions to the criminalization of harm-doing in defined circumstances, and is developed more fully in Chapter 4.7 below.

(f) The Principle of Proportionate Response

This principle operates so as to place limitations on the degree of harm which may lawfully be inflicted under the principle of social justification. No individual, even an offender, should have his or her interests sacrificed except to the extent that it is both necessary on the grounds of social justification and reasonably proportionate to the harm committed or threatened. A sharper formulation of this principle would be that social justification grants the authority to inflict only the minimum harm necessary—a version of the view that one is only justified in using force if it is a lesser evil than allowing events to take their course.[10] The concept of reasonableness is usually imported here, in deference to the fact that many situations of justifiable force arise suddenly, without warning, and thus give rise to an instinctive rather than a measured response. It must be borne in mind, however, that this is not always the case, and that in some instances there is ample time for reflection (see Chapter 4.7 below). Further, the assumption that the user of force is innocent and the other party is the wrongdoer does not apply to cases of putative justification, discussed in Chapter 6.6.

This brief discussion of six principles and policies, set out as antithetical pairs, has said little about the practical resolution of the apparent conflicts. This is taken further in the appropriate chapters below. The main point has been to demonstrate that there are deep social principles relevant to the determination of the ambit of the criminal sanction, and that sometimes the rhetoric used (e.g. a pressing social need for a new law, or the concept of 'reasonableness' in the sphere of justifiable force) is apt to conceal—and may be designed to conceal—the social and political dimensions of what is being done.

---

[10] Discussed further below, Ch. 4.7 and 4.8.

3.3. 'FAIRNESS' PRINCIPLES

It is here, in the sphere of what may be termed 'fairness principles', that some of the deepest difficulties in the development of the criminal law may be found. Perhaps the essence of these difficulties lies in a conflict between the criminal law as a form of moral/social labelling of wrongdoers, and the criminal process as a coercive mechanism which should only be allowed to impinge on citizens' lives if fair procedures have been satisfied. Although, as we saw in Chapter 2.2, there is controversy about some of the outer limits of criminal law, that leaves a substantial middle ground where there is widespread agreement about the appropriateness of the criminal sanction. Yet, even in that relatively uncontroversial sphere, there is the expectation that the law will be applied so as to respect the rights of individual citizens and to protect them from any abuse of power by state officials. This expectation may be summed up in the phrase 'the rule of law', a phrase with a powerfully righteous, and sometimes abused, appeal, which is invoked here in its minimal sense of 'being governed by rules which are fixed, knowable and certain'.[11] In this sense, the rule of law may seem to express an incontrovertible minimum of political decency—informing citizens clearly before bringing the criminal sanction down on them—but the discussion below will suggest that, with this principle as with any other, there are conflicts to be resolved and possibly trade-offs to be made. Reverence for 'rule of law' values also serves to indicate the constitutional context of the development of the criminal law. Questions about the proper roles of the legislature, the courts, and law-enforcement agents press forward as we consider the various principles and policies below.

(g) The Non-Retroactivity Principle

It is usual to begin a discussion of general principles of the criminal law by stating the maxim *nullum crimen sine lege*, sometimes known as the principle of legality. But the connotations of the principle of legality are so wide-ranging that it is preferable to divide it into three distinct principles—the principle of non-retroactivity, the principle of maximum certainty, and the principle of strict construction of penal statutes.

The essence of the non-retroactivity principle is that a person

---

[11] J. Raz, *The Authority of Law* (1979), 214–15.

should never be convicted or punished except in accordance with a previously declared offence governing the conduct in question. The principle is to be found in the European Convention on Human Rights, article 7: 'No one shall be held guilty of any offence on account of any act or omission which did not constitute a criminal offence under national or international law at the time when it was committed.' This principle, also enunciated in article 1 of the United States Constitution, forbids a legislature to create a criminal offence which applies to behaviour prior to its enactment. How does it apply to the courts? It may seem equally obvious to state that they should not invent crimes and then punish people for conduct which falls within the new definition. But how would the common law have developed if such a power had not been exercised? The courts have developed and extended English criminal law over the years, untrammelled by the non-retroactivity principle. To 'adapt' the law is a great temptation for a court confronted with a defendant whose conduct it regards as plainly wicked but for which existing offences do not provide.

The conflict between the non-retroactivity principle and the functioning of the criminal law as a means of social defence reached its modern apotheosis in *Shaw v. DPP* (1962).[12] The prosecution had indicted Shaw with conspiracy to corrupt public morals, in addition to two charges under the Sexual Offences Act 1956 and the Obscene Publications Act 1959. The House of Lords upheld the validity of the indictment, despite the absence of any clear precedents, on the grounds that conduct intended and calculated to corrupt public morals is indictable at common law. The decision led to an outcry from lawyers and others. One objection to *Shaw* is that it fails to respect citizens as rational, autonomous individuals: a citizen cannot be sure of avoiding the criminal sanction by refraining from prohibited conduct if it is open to the courts to invent new crimes without warning. What happened in *Shaw* was that a majority of the House of Lords felt a strong pull towards criminalization because they were convinced of the immoral and antisocial nature of the conduct—thus regarding their particular conceptions of social defence[13] as more powerful than the liberty of citizens to plan their lives within the law.

But there are two more, interconnected, objections to this decision.

---

[12] [1962] AC 220.

[13] For the controversial nature of their approach to the relationship between law and morality, see Ch. 2.1 above.

First, the new crime was even less defensible, since it concerned a socially controversial realm of conduct (prostitution) rather than behaviour widely accepted as a social evil: if the courts are to legislate, they should confine themselves to clear cases. Second, this realm of conduct had only recently been considered by Parliament, which had introduced limited reforms in the Street Offences Act 1959; thus it could be argued that if Parliament did not then extend the law to penalise conduct such as Shaw's, the courts would be usurping the legislative function if they did so. This constitutional dimension of the decision should not be underestimated. The proper procedure is for a democratically elected legislature to create new offences. What *Shaw* seems to admit is that the police and prosecution may prefer to press a hitherto unknown charge, and the courts may uphold its validity at common law. This accords great power to the executive and the judiciary, and since an offence thus created operates retrospectively on the defendant, it fails to respect the citizen's basic right that the law be knowable in advance. The criminal law embodies the height of social condemnation, and its extent should surely be determined in advance by accountable democratic processes rather than *ex post facto* by judicial pro-nouncement.[14]

The decision in *Shaw* is unrepresentative of judicial decision-making in criminal law. It is now more usual for courts to disclaim a lawmaking power and to leave the creation of new offences to the legislature.[15] But there have been two recent decisions in Scotland which go against the non-retroactivity principle—one criminalizing the sale of glue-sniffing equipment,[16] and the other extending the crime of rape to a husband still cohabiting with his wife.[17] If these cases had been decided in England, the latter decision would be assailable on similar grounds to *Shaw*: Parliament has recently legislated on sexual offences without altering this aspect of the law of rape,[18] and the Criminal Law Revision Committee was divided on this very issue.[19] One might think that the sale of glue-sniffing

---

[14] A. T. H. Smith, 'Judicial Lawmaking in the Criminal Law' (1984) 100 LQR 46.

[15] Cf. *Knuller v. DPP* [1973] AC 435, and *Tan* [1983] QB 1053.

[16] *Khaliq v. HM Advocate* 1983 SCCR 483.

[17] *S v. HM Advocate* 1989 SLT 469; on the questions of principle raised by this and the *Khaliq* decision, see T. H. Jones, 'Common Law and Criminal Law: The Scottish Experience' [1990] Crim. LR 292.

[18] Sexual Offences (Amendment) Act 1976, Sexual Offences Act 1985.

[19] Criminal Law Revision Committee (CLRC), 15th Report, *Sexual Offences* (1984, Cmnd. 9213).

equipment to young people would be widely condemned as anti-social, and thus that the former decision is more defensible. But it is possible that the defendant knew that such sales had not been declared criminal, and believed that it would take an Act of Parliament to render them so. The first belief was correct, and the second was reasonable. Indeed, Parliament did subsequently pass the Intoxicating Substances (Supply) Act 1985. Both the Scottish decisions may therefore be thought objectionable, for the courts were usurping the legislative role which belongs constitutionally to Parliament.[20]

But the reliance argument, grounded in a citizen's right to know in advance what constitutes criminal conduct, is not relevant at all to excusatory defences. Where the defence is in the nature of an excuse (e.g. insanity, intoxication, mistake), this concerns a mental state of the defendant at the time of the conduct which is utterly inconsistent with the kind of reliance presupposed by the idea of fair warning. These excusatory elements in the criminal law constitute rules of adjudication for the courts rather than rules of conduct to guide citizens, in contrast to the definitions of offences and of the justificatory defences (e.g. self-defence, prevention of crime), which can be relied on by citizens in planning their behaviour. It therefore follows that the usual 'reliance' arguments against judicial creativity do not apply in the sphere of excusatory defences.[21] It may be thought, too, that the constitutional arguments are less troublesome when the courts are dealing with excusatory defences: even if it is not proper for the courts to pursue their own conception of social defence, it may be proper for them to give effect to considerations of individual culpability. This assumes that the function of the courts in criminal matters is to adopt only reasons which favour the defendant, and that whenever they rely on any wider 'public interest' reasons they are trespassing upon the role of the legislature. Such a self-denying ordinance in favour of the liberty of defendants has certainly not been characteristic of judicial decision-making in English criminal law, and there are strong arguments that it should not be.[22]

[20] Cf. John C. Jeffries, 'Legality, Vagueness and the Construction of Penal Statutes' (1985) 71 *Virginia LR* 189, with A. T. H. Smith, 'The Interpretation of Penal Statutes' (unpublished).

[21] See Paul H. Robinson, 'Rules of Conduct and Principles of Adjudication' (1990) 57 *U. Chic. LR* 729, and Peter Alldridge 'Rules for Courts and Rules for Citizens' (1990) 10 *OJLS* 487. Cf. Law Com. No. 177, cl. 4(4).

[22] See Andrew Ashworth, 'Interpreting Criminal Statutes: A Crisis of Legality?' (1991) 107 *LQR* (forthcoming).

(h) The 'Thin Ice' Principle

A counterpoint to the non-retroactivity principle is provided by what may be called the 'thin ice' principle, following Lord Morris's observation in *Knuller* v. *DPP* (1983) that 'those who skate on thin ice can hardly expect to find a sign which will denote the precise spot where he [*sic*] will fall in'.[23] Thus the essence of the principle seems to be that citizens who know that their conduct is on the borderline of illegality take the risk that their behaviour will be held to contravene the law. Another popular phrase for this would be 'sailing close to the wind'. On occasions the courts have applied this principle both to the creation of a new offence and to the extension of an existing offence.[24] The arguments in favour of it seem to combine moral/social and political elements. The social element might be that the criminal law ought to penalize conduct which is widely regarded as immoral; the political element might be that since citizens ought to know that the purpose of the criminal law is to penalize antisocial and immoral conduct, they ought also to know that there is a risk of criminal liability being extended to cover activities on the fringe of illegality. There are obvious counter-arguments. The principle appears to assume that 'immorality' is a sufficient reason for criminalizing conduct, whereas that has never been maintained in England (for example, neither adultery nor prostitution is a criminal offence); it also appears to assume a consensus on what is or what is not immoral, whereas this is increasingly less common in a pluralist society (although there might be a consensus against selling glue-sniffing kits to young people). The principle also neglects the possibility that the defendant may have read about the existing law, or even taken legal advice on it, and then proceeded with the activity in the belief that it was not criminal.

Where the 'thin ice' principle is accorded priority over the non-retroactivity principle, the court is both placing strong emphasis on its own conception of social defence and assuming the function of lawmaker. When this amounts to creating a new offence at common law, as in Shaw's case, this is surely an usurpation of the constitutional function of the legislature. To protest that Parliament is too busy and therefore too slow to respond to new social evils is not persuasive,

[23] [1973] AC 435.
[24] For the former, see *Shaw* v. *DPP* [1962] AC 220; for the latter, see *Tan* [1983] QB 1053.

since there have been notable recent examples of swift legislative action.[25] It is surely preferable that lawmaking be publicly debated, non-retroactive, created by a democratically elected body, and publicly announced. But the arguments alter somewhat when the issue is the interpretation of statutes rather than the creation of new common law crimes, as we shall see below.

(i) The Principle of Maximum Certainty

The next principle—maximum certainty in defining offences—is largely a restatement of the so-called 'fair warning' and 'void for vagueness' principles in United States law. All these principles may be seen as constituents of the principle of legality, and there is a close relationship between the principle of maximum certainty and non-retroactivity principle. A vague law may in practice operate retroactively, since no one is quite sure whether given conduct is within or outside the rule. The reason for departing from the American terminology is that the term 'void for vagueness' refers directly to the power of United States courts to declare criminal legislation unconstitutional if it is unduly vague, a power not available in the United Kingdom; and the idea of 'fair warning' directs attention to the defendant's awareness of the existence and extent of the rule. The argument is that respect for the citizen as a rational, autonomous individual and as a person with social and political duties requires that he should have fair warning of the criminal law and no undue difficulty in finding it out. Thus, even within a system which accepts social obligations as part of the criminal law,[26] there is a proper place for a circumscribed defence of ignorance of the law.[27]

There are also two separate political/constitutional aspects to the principle of maximum certainty. The first concerns the preference for a codified criminal law rather than a system based on common law. English criminal law still contains several common-law offences with no authoritative definition and therefore much uncertainty, together with many scattered statutes. One argument for codification of the criminal law is that this would bring together in one place the definitions of the major crimes, thereby enhancing the fair warning

---

[25] e.g. the Intoxicating Substances (Supply) Act 1985 (sale of glue-sniffing kits) and the Sexual Offences Act 1985 ('kerb-crawling'); such reforms are often introduced into Parliament as Private Members' Bills which receive government support.

[26] As in the imposition of criminal liability for omissions: see below, Ch. 4.4(b).

[27] e.g. in Scandinavian legal systems: see below, Ch. 6.7; cf. the discussion below, text at nn. 32 and 33.

to citizens. Moreover, the enactment of a criminal code would make 'a symbolic statement about the respective constitutional roles of Parliament and the courts, in a way that makes it plain that it is the legislative will that should be the predominant one'.[28] Codification of English criminal law might therefore both increase the certainty and fairness of warning for citizens and reduce the creative (and necessarily retroactive) powers of the courts. The second aspect is that, if rules are vaguely drafted, they bestow considerable power on the agencies of law enforcement; the police or other law-enforcement agents might use a widely framed offence to criminalize behaviour not envisaged by the legislature. Thus the offence would take on the definition of the law-enforcement agents instead of one provided by the legislators.

It will be noticed, however, that the principle is stated in a circumscribed form—the principle of *maximum* certainly, not *absolute* certainly—which indicates the compromise already inherent in the principle before it is weighed against other principles and policies. In its pure form, the 'rule of law' insists on complete certainty, but this is not always practical in view of the varying elements which may bear on the characterization of conduct as criminal. It is occasionally prudent for the criminal law to resort to such open-ended terms as 'reasonable' and 'dishonest' rather than to devise an immensely detailed and lengthy definition which might be extremely complicated to apply and which might still fail to cover the ground. The same might also be said of the English offence of unlawful sexual intercourse with a girl under 16: it is widely accepted that no prosecutions should be brought where the girl is 15 and the boy is only slightly older, but proposals to narrow the offence by exempting cases in which the age difference is, say, only two years have been rejected on the grounds of undue technicality, as has the proposal to have a separate, more serious offence which applies where the man occupies some position of authority over the girl.[29] We therefore tolerate an offence which has what the Americans call 'overbreadth', in the belief (discussed critically in Chapter 2.2 above) that prosecutorial discretion is a more reliable means of identifying truly criminal incidents than legal definition.

To claim that such derogations from certainty may be prudent, largely for practical reasons of administering the law, should not be taken to minimize the importance of striving for maximum certainty.

[28] See Smith, 'The Case for a Code', at 289, and Law Com. No. 177, i, 2.2.
[29] CLRC, 15th Report, part V.

As the US Supreme Court put it in *Connally v. General Construction Co.* (1926): 'A statute which either forbids or requires the doing of an act in terms so vague that men of common intelligence must necessarily guess at its meaning and differ as to its application, violates the first essential of due process of law.'[30] The same might be said of common-law crimes such as outraging public decency, public nuisance, and perverting the course of justice, no less than of some English statutes.

(j) The Policy of Social Defence

The policy of social defence runs counter to the principle of maximum certainty. It draws strength from the social function of the criminal law in labelling and punishing antisocial behaviour, and maintains that some vagueness in criminal laws is socially beneficial because it enables the police and the courts to deal flexibly with new variations in misconduct without having to await the lumbering response to the legislature. The policy of social defence thus supports the same concept as the 'thin ice' principle. It also suffers from the same defect, in terms of differing opinions of the social interests to be defended by means of the criminal law, but it is potentially far-reaching. It would support the enactment of laws vague enough to leave room for the police to apply them to new forms of antisocial action: section 5 of the Public Order Act 1986 might be an example here, penalizing any person who 'uses threatening, abusive or insulting words or behaviour, or disorderly behaviour . . . within the hearing or sight of a person likely to be caused harassment, alarm or distress thereby'.[31] To the objection that this delegates far too much *de facto* power over citizens' lives to law-enforcement agents, proponents of social defence would reply that this should be tackled by means of internal guide-lines and police disciplinary procedures rather than by depriving the police and courts of the means of pursuing conduct which arouses social concern.

Similar policy arguments are sometimes used to support the argument that ignorance of the criminal law should be no excuse. Thus English law authorises the conviction of persons who were unaware of the existence of a crime, even in circumstances where it would have been difficult for them to find out that they were committing it.[32] This derogation from the notions of maxi-

[30] (1926) 269 US 385, at 391.
[31] See A. T. H. Smith, *Offences against Public Order* (1988), Ch. 7.
[32] Discussed below, Ch. 6.7.

mum certainty and fair warning is usually justified in terms of consequentialist arguments of social defence, but they are unpersuasive in theory and practice.[33]

The policy of social defence may be used to point out a distinct social dysfunction of the principle of maximum certainty. If members of society can rely upon criminal laws being drafted precisely and upon enforcement agents and the courts keeping within those boundaries, it is open to ingenious citizens to devise ways of circumventing those laws—conforming to the letter of the law, whilst dishonouring its spirit. Where this kind of activity is pursued in a systematic way—with financial backing, for example—it may be regarded as sufficiently antisocial to justify criminalization. It is said that there are those in the financial and business worlds who make their living on these fringes of legality, exploiting the principle of maximum certainty as a shield to protect them from conviction.[34] But how can these people be distinguished from Shaw, Knuller,[35] and others? It is doutbful whether a distinction between sexual and financial morality would be sufficient to justify a difference in approach. There seems to be a direct conflict between the principle of maximum certainty and the policy of social defence, rather than a dissonance which can be accommodated by means of an exception or compromise. Is the idea of 'fair warning' redundant when most citizens do not trouble to ascertain the law, and most of those who do are bent on exploiting its limitations? Probably not: those who honestly try to ascertain the law must be protected,[35a] and surely it is unwise to give the police, the courts, and prosecutors the power to extend the law without imposing any clear limits on this power. The notion of *ex post facto* lawmaking in only acceptable if there is a broad consensus on what kinds of conduct are sufficiently antisocial to justify the criminal sanction. The extent to which such a consensus exists on certain issues is difficult to judge.

(k) The Principle of Strict Construction

Two of the principles which are often brought under the umbrella of the principle of legality have already been discussed (non-retroactivity, maximum certainty); the principle of strict construction is the third. The difference here is that whereas the non-retroactivity

---

[33] See *Cambridgeshire and Isle of Ely CC v. Rust* [1972] 2 QB 426; cf. *Lim Chin Aik v. R* [1963] AC 160.

[34] See Doreen McBarnet, 'The Limits of the Law' (unpublished, 1987).

[35] See above, nn. 12 and 15.

[35a] Would a viable defence of mistake of law be sufficient?

principle applies to the lawmaking activities of Parliament and the courts, this principle relates to the courts' task in interpreting legislation. The formulation of the principle is a matter for debate. In its bald form, it appears to state that any doubt in the meaning of a statutory provision should, by strict construction, be resolved in favour of the defendant. One justification for this might be fair warning: where a person acts on the apparent meaning of a statute but the court gives it a wider meaning, it is unfair to convict that person because that would amount to retroactive lawmaking. Historically speaking, the principle seems to have originated as a means of softening the effect of statutes requiring capital punishment, through the notion of construction *in favorem vitae*. This carries over into the declaration in *Taylor* (1950) that where the Court of Appeal (Criminal Division) is faced with a conflict of precedents, it should adopt the view which favours the defendant.[36] The foundation of this view probably lies in the inequality of power and resources between the individual defendant and the State, a justification also influential in the presumption of innocence.[37]

The status of the principle of strict construction is unclear. References to it have been fitful both in England and the United States, leading to the claim that it is invoked more to justify decisions reached on other grounds than as a significant principle in its own right.[38] There is certainly no difficulty in assembling a list of cases in which it appears to have been ignored.[39] But it may be that it was not properly understood in its more sophisticated form in England, since it is only recently that a sequence of principles to be applied when interpreting criminal statutes has been established. It now appears that, rather than (for example) being bound by any particular dictionary definition of a crucial word in a statute, the courts should construe a legislative provision in accordance with the perceived purpose of that statute.[40] In order to ascertain that purpose, a court may consult a government White Paper or the report of a law-reform committee so as to ascertain the gap in the law which the legislation was intended to remedy, although it is not permitted to use such a report as an authoritative guide to the

---

[36] [1950] 2 KB 368.   [37] See below, Ch. 3.3(*h*).

[38] Jeffries, 'Legality, Vagueness and the Construction of Penal Statutes'.

[39] e.g. *Caldwell* [1982] AC 341, and *Ayres* [1984] AC 447 in the House of Lords, and many Court of Appeal decisions.

[40] *Attorney-General's Reference (No. 1 of 1988)* (1989) 89 Cr. App. R 60, affirming the Court of Appeal's decision at (1989) 88 Cr. App. R 191.

meaning of a particular word[41]—often a distinction which becomes utterly unpractical. If there is still ambiguity after this enquiry, that ambiguity should be resolved in favour of the defendant. This is the more sophisticated version of the principle of strict construction: it should not be represented as a principle to be applied at the first stage of interpreting a statute, but rather as a principle whose power should be exerted after the enquiry into purpose has failed to reveal a clear answer.[42] Those who disagree with the principle have sought to ridicule it by arguing that no system of criminal law can function adequately if absolutely every ambiguity has to be resolved in favour of the defendant.[43] But this line of attack misunderstands the true role of the principle, which has now been reasserted in the courts. Its proper place is in a sequence of points to be considered by a court when construing a statutory offence.[44] It will be an important advance in the development of English criminal law if other courts routinely follow the approach now established by the House of Lords, but it certainly does not answer all the questions about statute interpretation. For example, uncertainty still prevails over the proper approach to interpreting statutory offences which do not include a fault requirement in their definition: the courts are still without a coherent approach to the question of strict liability.[45]

What is the argument in favour of the more sophisticated version of the principle of strict construction? The 'fair warning' argument undoubtedly plays a part, but the primary argument is constitutional. In terms of interpreting statutes, the courts are the constitutionally authoritative agency. Just as the principles of non-retroactivity and maximum certainty ought to be recognized by the legislature, so they should be recognized by the courts when engaging in interpretation. Indeed, the argument is even stronger for the courts, for they are the ultimate agency for determining the practical limits of the law, and yet they are an unelected group. Parliament should retain the main responsibility for the extent of the criminal law, and, indeed, it has the right to determine the courts' approach towards the task of interpretation (for example, by including some

[41] *Black-Clawson International Ltd. v. Papierwerke Waldhof-Aschaffenberg AG* [1975] AC 591.
[42] Lord Reid, in *DPP v. Ottewell* [1970] AC 642, and Smith, 'The Interpretation of Penal Statutes'.
[43] Jeffries, 'Legality, Vagueness and the Construction of Penal Statutes', and Law Com. No. 177, para. 3.17.
[44] See further, Ashworth, 'Interpreting Criminal Statutes'.
[45] See below, Ch. 5.3(a).

canons of interpretation in the Criminal Code[46]). The courts, because of the practical authority of their interpretations, should exercise restraint in their interpretive role, rather than adopting broad constructions of criminal statutes.[47]

Militating against the principle of strict construction is, once again, the policy of social defence. Why should the courts allow those who indulge in obviously antisocial behaviour to escape conviction by reference to a principle which assumes that citizens take care to ascertain the law beforehand (which they usually do not), and which also assumes that the government and Parliament can be left to deal promptly with antisocial behaviour which becomes a problem (which they usually cannot, because of pressures on parliamentary time)? Powerful as these arguments against strict construction may seem, there are objections to each of them. Some citizens do make an effort to ascertain the law, and it is the policy of English law (manifested in the proposition that ignorance of the law is no excuse) to encourage this. It is therefore unfair for the courts to extend the law retroactively by adopting broad constructions of statutes. As for the question of trusting the government to respond to new forms of antisocial behaviour, this has not been put to the test, because the courts have not established a tradition of strict construction. If they had either brought in acquittals or quashed convictions in every case where the application of a statutory provision left some room for doubt, then the government would have been highly likely to set up a regular system for redrafting and amending criminal laws. For instance, in the case of *Charles* (1976)[48] the Court of Appeal favoured the acquittal of a man who, in spite of his bank's prohibition, had deliberately and substantially overdrawn on his bank account, because the court found it difficult to bring the conduct within the definition of the offence charged. Bridge LJ recognized that social defence might be better served by a conviction, but he did not regard it as the court's function to stretch the words of the statute. The House of Lords had no such compunction: it did stretch the statutory wording, and restored the conviction.[49] Had the House of Lords adopted the same approach as the Court of Appeal, then the government and Parliament would have been left to decide on the need for an amendment to the law.

[46] Cf. Law Com. No. 177, para. 3.17, criticized by Ashworth, 'Interpreting Criminal Statutes'.
[47] Smith, 'Judicial Lawmaking'.
[48] (1976) 63 Cr. App. R 252.   [49] [1977] AC 177.

In the meantime, Charles and a few others would have gone free. It is this consequence which the courts, regarding themselves as custodians of the public interest, have sought to avoid by adopting broad interpretations of statutes. Yet Professor A. T. H. Smith has argued convincingly that the decision in *Charles* demonstrates plainly the inadequacy of 'judicial lawmaking' of the kind effected by the House of Lords in its broad interpretation of the Theft Act.[50] There are several avenues to explore before it can be concludeed that social defence supports a conviction in this type of case, as Lord Lane, CJ recognized a few years later,[51] and a court construing a statute is unlikely to receive evidence on these wider social issues and is hardly the most appropriate body to resolve them anyway. On the other hand, the criminal law should not simply be regarded as a body of rules enshrined in legislation, either currently or under the proposed Criminal Code.

The conflict between the principle of strict construction and the policy of social defence should not be resolved simply by maintaining that courts should only adopt reasons which favour the liberty of the defendant. One good argument against that approach is that the idea of 'fair warning' which underlies several of the principles clustered beneath the principle of legality is inapplicable in some situations. It would be preferable from the social point of view if the courts were to adopt an approach to statutory interpretation which restrained them from taking defendants by surprise, by extending the law when they might fairly have relied on its previous limits, and yet which permitted them to advance the purpose of the legislation by taking proper account of relevant principles and policies. These arguments are pursued elsewhere.[52]

(l) The Principle of Fair Labelling

This principle is chiefly applicable to the legislature. Its concern is to see that widely felt distinctions between kinds of offences and degrees of wrongdoing are respected and signalled by the law, that offences should be divided and labelled so as to represent fairly the nature and degree of the law-breaking.[53] One good reason for respecting these distinctions is proportionality: one of the basic

---

[50] See Smith, 'Judicial Lawmaking', 52–4.

[51] *Clarke* (1982) 75 Cr. App. R 119; see below, Ch. 9.7(c).

[52] Ashworth, 'Interpreting Criminal Statutes'.

[53] A. Ashworth, 'The Elasticity of Mens Rea', in C. Tapper (ed.), *Crime, Proof and Punishment* (1981); and Glanville Williams, 'Convictions and Fair Labelling' [1983] CLJ 85.

aims of the criminal law is to ensure a proportionate response to law-breaking, thereby assisting the law's educative or declaratory function in sustaining and reinforcing social standards. This argument is sometimes grounded exclusively in popular opinion: the law must keep in close touch with the sentiments of ordinary people. This point of view is sometimes advocated as the reason for keeping the two offences of murder and manslaughter rather than having a single offence of culpable homicide—people believe that the most heinous killings should be labelled separately.[54] But should the argument be not so much about what it is politically prudent to do but rather about what it is right to do? Fairness demands that offenders be labelled and punished in proportion to their wrongdoing; the label is important both in public terms and in the criminal justice system, for listing previous convictions, prison classification, and so on. Consequentialists might add that any blurring of this labelling might encourage offenders to reason that they might as well be hanged for a sheep as for a lamb, inducing them to commit significantly more harm because it might appear to involve no greater condemnation.[55]

A second justification for the principle of fair labelling does have a more direct connection with common patterns of thought in society. It is that where people generally regard two types of conduct as different, the law should try to reflect that difference. This argument was raised against the possibility of combining the crimes of theft and obtaining by deception into a single offence: people regard stealing and swindling as distinct forms of wrongdoing, and the law should not obscure this.[56] It is worth noting also that both these proposals would have strained the principle of maximum certainty, since one consequence of moving towards broader definitions of offences is that they may give wide discretionary powers to the police in enforcement and to the courts in sentencing. The spirit of the principle can then be honoured only by structuring and controlling the discretionary powers.

However, the principle of fair labelling is no more of an absolute injunction than the principle of maximum certainty. Divisions between offences are not self-evident and immutable. Reforms of the law may properly lead to the eradication of some distinctions,

---

[54] See below, Ch. 7.3.

[55] Bentham was aware of this: see his *Introduction to the Principles of Morals and Legislation* (1789), Ch. XIV, para. 8.

[56] See below, Ch. 9.7.

and there are many possible formats (such as a single offence with two or three alternative penalty structures).[57] Full adoption of this principle would not necessarily lead to a massive code of finely graded and differentiated offences, sometimes derided as 'the law professor's dream'. The strength of the principle is to ensure that arguments of proportionality, fairness to individuals, and the proper confinement of executive and judicial discretion are taken seriously when new offences with broad definitions and high maximum penalties are under consideration. Is it right that English law should have a single offence of theft, with a maximum penalty of ten years' imprisonment?[58] Is it right that sexual assaults should be divided, effectively, into only the two categories of rape (defined narrowly) and indecent assault (with a ten-year maximum)?[59] Questions of this kind have too frequently been resolved (usually in favour of 'social defence' or economy) without reference to the principles or to the values they uphold.

(m) The Policy of Efficient Administration

The pull towards fewer and broader categories of offence with high maximum penalties derives from the desire to secure greater efficiency in the administration of criminal justice. To some extent, the reasons are economic: broader offences, with fewer boundaries between them, can be expected to lead to fewer disputes in court and to more guilty pleas. The expectation is a welcome reduction in public expenditure on the court system. The labels given to offences are regarded as less important than the actual assessment of culpability, and this can be done expeditiously at the sentencing stage. A further efficiency argument stems from the limitations of juries and lay magistrates: the criminal law must be kept as simple as possible so as to avoid confusing lay people and producing erroneous verdicts, and this argues against finely graded offences which necessitate complex instructions on the law. The policy of social defence also weighs in favour of fewer and broader offences, since they increase the discretion of police, prosecutors, and courts, and make it more likely that antisocial behaviour will result in conviction. Lastly, there is a principled argument to be borne in mind here: it is

[57] e.g. Misuse of Drugs Act 1971, and s. 4 of the Criminal Law Act 1967, both discussed by D. A. Thomas, 'Form and Function in Criminal Law', in P. R. Glazebrook (ed.), *Reshaping the Criminal Law* (1978).

[58] Under the Criminal Justice Act 1991, this maximum will be lowered slightly to 7 years, but the offence will remain undivided.

[59] See the discussion below, in Ch. 8.6(c).

contended that some issues are more appropriate for determination at trial (e.g. yes/no issues) whereas others, particularly questions of degree, are more appropriately dealt with at the sentencing stage.[60] This may lead to a move away from fair labelling towards a conception of efficient administration.

One example of the policy of efficient administration gaining priority over the principles of fair labelling and maximum certainty is the common-law offence of conspiracy to defraud, left untouched by the 1977 reforms of conspiracy law and covering a broad expanse of financial dealings, with little indication of its boundaries.[61] Action has been taken to structure the discretion of prosecutors in invoking this charge, but this still leaves the label vague and the sentence at large. Many of the reforms brought about by the Theft Act 1968 and the Criminal Damage Act 1971 favoured the policy of efficient administration, thereby eroding the principle of fair labelling. However, as already noted, some respect was shown for fair labelling by, for example, retaining the separate offences of theft and deception, when it would have been possible to combine the two.[62]

(n) The Presumption of Innocence

The principle that a person should be presumed innocent unless and until proved guilty is a fundamental principle of fairness, although its relation to the law of evidence means that it is not always included in discussions of the criminal law. The justifications for the principle may be found in the social and legal consequences of being convicted of a crime, and in the immense power and resources of the State compared to the position of the defendant. So strong are these justifications that they support not only the presumption of innocence but also the requirement of a high standard of proof before a conviction may be returned: in England the prosecution has the burden of proving guilt 'beyond reasonable doubt'. The opposite rule—a presumption of guilt upon all those prosecuted for an offence—would impose an oppressive burden on individual citizens, and would place immense power in the hands of the state officials who decide on prosecution. It is distaste for such a regime which underpins the declaration of Lord Sankey LC in *Woolmington v.*

---

[60] This is the argument of Thomas, 'Form and Function'.
[61] Conspiracy to defraud is discussed in Ch. 9.8.
[62] Criminal Law Revision Committee, 8th Report, *Theft and Related Offences* (1966), (Cmnd. 2977), para. 38.

DPP (1935)[63] that 'throughout the web of the English criminal law one golden thread is always to be seen—that it is the duty of the prosecution to prove the prisoner's guilt'. The principled basis for this is plain, but does it represent rhetoric or reality so far as English law is concerned?

(o) The Policy of Ease of Proof

The presumption of innocence is much neglected nowadays: many offences are defined in such a way that the prosecution has to prove little before the burden swings to the defence. Hundreds and thousands of offences have been lifted out of the presumption's ambit, either by the plain words of certain statutes or by section 101 of the Magistrates' Courts Act 1980, which places on the defendant the burden of proving any excuse, exemption, proviso, or qualification in the definition of the offence. Neglect of the presumption has not only been a feature of so-called regulatory offences, but it has also been central to legislation with severe maximum penalties, such as the Public Order Act 1986. There is little evidence that Parliament accords significant weight to the presumption of innocence in most of its legislation. The reason for this neglect is prosecutorial con-venience: at a time when law-enforcement agents and prosecutors are hard pressed, it is expedient to require defendants to prove elements in the crime. Sometimes an attempt is made to justify this transfer of burdens by claiming that it is right to expect the defendant to prove elements relating to the defence. The difficulty here is that there is no satisfactory analytical distinction between offence and defence.[64] Legislative draftsmen do not follow a single drafting rule, and it may often be a matter of chance whether a given element is expressed as a defence or is rolled up into the definition of the crime.[65] A more reliable argument is that certain matters are much easier for one party to prove than the other: it is generally far easier for a defendant to prove that he or she had a licence or permit than for the prosecution to prove the absence of one. But even this argument cannot be used to support the almost routine placement of burdens on the defendant by modern legislation, although it may

[63] [1935] AC 462.
[64] See the discussions by Glanville Williams, 'Offences and Defences' (1982) 2 *Legal Studies* 233, Paul Robinson, 'Criminal Law Defenses: A Systematic Analysis' (1982) 82 *Columbia LR* 199, and Kenneth Campbell, 'Offence and Defence', in I. Dennis (ed.), *Criminal Law and Criminal Justice* (1987).
[65] As demonstrated by A. A. S. Zuckerman, 'The Third Exception to the *Woolmington* Rule' (1976) 92 LQR 402.

be influential in judicial decisions about this placement in cases where the statute is silent on the matter.[66] Much recent legislation is clearly influenced by a policy in favour of ease of proof by the prosecution, thereby embracing the policies of social defence and efficient administration to effectuate a significant erosion of the fairness principles.[67]

The purpose of this discussion to has been to identify some of the 'fairness' principles relevant to the general shape and form of the criminal law, to illustrate briefly how they and their conflicting policies have interacted in the development of English criminal law, and to make some suggestions for the resolution of these conflicts. It is quite clear that there has been no systematic legislative or judicial recognition of these principles, but there has been the occasional official reference to most of them. Those principles aimed at fairness to the individual citizen—the non-retroactivity principle, the principle of maximum certainty, the principle of strict construction, the principle of fair labelling, and the presumption of innocence—tend to emphasize the value of predictability in the law and the importance of protecting citizens from state officials with wide powers. Those principles and policies driven by a conception of fairness to the community—the 'thin ice' principle, the policy of social defence, the policy of efficient administration and the policy of ease of proof—seek to ensure that the criminal law is capable of dealing with new manifestations of antisocial behaviour in the swiftest, surest, and least expensive manner. The principles and policies discussed above are not exhaustive—for example, the government's tendency to draft offences in an inchoate rather than a result-oriented mode is another contribution to ease of proof and social defence, and is discussed in its context below[68]—and each of the following chapters identifies various principles and policies bearing upon the specific subject-matter of that chapter. It is hoped that, by considering these broader aspects of criminal jurisprudence, it is possible to develop a more realistic critical framework for the the analysis of legislative and judicial decisions on the criminal law.

---

[66] See the House of Lords decision in *Hunt* [1987] AC 352, discussed by J. C. Smith, 'The Presumption of Innocence' (1987) 38 *NILQ* 223, and by A. A. S. Zuckerman, *The Principles of Criminal Evidence* (1989), Ch. 9.

[67] For some elaboration, see [1987] Crim. LR 153–5.

[68] See below, Ch. 11.9.

In relation to the principles of policies discussed above, it has been suggested that the principles of fairness to the individual should have a general priority on account of the disparity in resources between individual and State, and the degree of social condemnation implicit in criminal conviction. However, individual fairness is not regarded as an absolute here; its inherent conception of fairness is capable of different interpretations and certainly needs careful examination. It should be emphasized that this fairness does not presuppose individuals in isolation but individuals as members of a community. Individuals tend to place a high value on interpersonal contacts, relationships, mutual support, access to facilities, and the fulfilment of obligations. A society which values collective goals and collective goods may therefore provide a wider range of worthwhile opportunities for individual development, and a more acceptable form of liberty.[69] It may be quite justifiable in some circumstances for individual liberty to be overridden by principles and policies of fairness to the community. On the other hand, one should be swift to scrutinize the use of such broad and malleable concepts as 'social defence', and there are constitutional considerations to be taken into account too. In principle, lawmaking should be the province of the legislature, and the courts should confine themselves to the interpretation, individuation and application of laws. Yet, as suggested above, there may be situations in which a court is justified in using a principle or policy in the interpretation of a vague statutory provision. Some conflicts among the various standpoints will be discussed in particular contexts in the remainder of this book.

[69] See J. Raz, *The Morality of Freedom* (1987), esp. 206–7, and Lacey, *State Punishment*, 172–81.

4

CRIMINAL CONDUCT

4.1. THE GENERAL PART OF THE CRIMINAL LAW

This chapter and the following two chapters discuss what is usually known as the general part of the criminal law—that which is common to all, or at least to many, offences. It has been traditional for writers on the criminal law to approach the analysis of offences by means of two concepts with Latin names, '*actus reus*' and '*mens rea*': the *actus reus* consists of the prohibited behaviour or conduct; the *mens rea* is usually described as the mental element—the intention, knowledge, or recklessness of the defendant in relation to the proscribed conduct. This way of dividing up the general elements in crimes is rather 'rough and ready', and is certainly a better servant than master. It has some merits—for example, if the unlawfulness of the conduct is treated as an element of the *actus reus*, then it must be proved that the defendant knew the facts giving rise to the unlawfulness. A defendant who was mistaken about these facts might not, therefore, be culpable.[1] But the traditional framework also has its shortcomings if it purports to cover all the elements of crimes, since many of the accepted 'defences' to crime cannot be explained in terms of lack of *mens rea*—such defences as duress and even intoxication require a more complex account. The terminology is therefore less important than an enquiry into that which it might obscure, i.e. 'what the preconditions to criminal liability really are, and how far they really reflect the principles they are commonly supposed to encapsulate'.[2]

For convenience, our discussion of the general part of the criminal law has been spread over three chapters. Contrary to tradition, it will not be assumed that the general propositions discussed ought to apply to all offences, irrespective of the nature and seriousness of the harm itself. Chapter 5 will deal with what are termed 'positive fault requirements', broadly, those elements which the prosecution

---

[1] See the further discussion of this principle in Ch.5.3(*d*) below.
[2] A. T. H. Smith, 'On Actus Reus and Mens Rea', in P. R. Glazebrook (ed.), *Reshaping the Criminal Law* (1978), 95.

has to establish in order to construct a case for the defence to answer. Chapter 6 will discuss the 'negative fault requirements', broadly, those elements which do not correspond with positive fault requirements and of which the defendant has to provide some evidence in order to raise them as live issues in a case. This division of material is not advanced as an impermeable scheme,[3] but rather as a convenient basis for exploring the foundations and limits of the traditional propositions. At appropriate points in the discussion, questions will be raised about whether the 'logic' of the general part of criminal liability should prevail over the seriousness of the harm or interests involved in the conduct, or over the situation in which the conduct took place.

This chapter deals with aspects of the conduct element in criminal liability. The precise conduct required will vary from crime to crime, but there are some general issues which bear on this element in almost all crimes—such as the need to establish human agency, the requirement of causation, and the question of social and legal justification for harms. The relative seriousness of harms, already discussed in Chapter 2, becomes relevant later in this chapter when discussing justifications for the infliction of harm on others. Before that, we shall examine the basic issues of responsibility in terms of human agency and causation. Among the consequential issues raised are: is a law which has developed for individual actors equipped adequately to deal with corporate harm-doers? How far has the criminal law moved, and how far should it move, from the proposition that only acts and not omissions should attract criminal liability? Is the requirement of causation a meaningful limitation on criminal liability? What limits should be set to the legal justifications for inflicting harm on another person?

4.2. THE PRINCIPLE OF INDIVIDUAL AUTONOMY

At the foundation of criminal liability lies the principle of individual autonomy—that each human being should be treated as responsible for his or her own behaviour. The very idea of a voluntary action cannot be entertained unless this principle is accepted, nor can the various fault requirements. It would be unfair to blame people for actions if they could not control them. The argument against the principle is that all human behaviour is determined by causes, many

---

[3] Cf. P. Robinson and J. Grall, 'Element Analysis in Defining Criminal Liability: The Model Penal Code and Beyond' (1983) 35 *Stanford LR* 681.

of which are known but some of which are unknown. This determinist view does not mean that the criminal law should dispense with all its recognized excuses (e.g. for the insane, those under duress, etc): what it might mean is that any excuses would have to be based on purely utilitarian grounds, and therefore available only when the prospect of liability and punishment could not affect the deliberations of a citizen in that position.[4] As a result, criminal liability would not be dependent on ideas of blame and desert which are normally influential in everyday social practices; much would turn on predictions of what approach, legal or extralegal,[5] would be most effective in preventing or reducing harm-doing.

It has been convincingly argued, however, that there is no real evidence for the truth of determinism, in the strong sense that all our behaviour is fully determined. This does not mean that the opposite proposition is true, that all human actions (or even all actions by those not insane or very young) are completely free. This is not the place to analyse the various possible forms of 'compatibilism' which have enabled writers to accept the fundamental proposition that behaviour is not so determined that blame is generally unfair and inappropriate, and yet to accept that, in certain circumstances, behaviour may be so strongly determined (e.g. by mental disease or by threats of death from another) that the individual should not be blamed.[6] One can adopt the view that most of human life is conducted on the basis of some such form of compatibilism, and that only if there were to be compelling evidence to the contrary should this be abandoned. It is, however, important to note the ambiguity of the principle of individual autonomy in this connection. The principle is usually assumed rather than stated in legal doctrine, and the assumption is sometimes that of complete freedom of the will. If the principle is stated in that extreme form, it will be relatively easy to demonstrate that the criminal law departs from it in several places, by allowing excuses (e.g. duress, necessity) grounded in severe restrictions on freedom of choice. If, however, the principle is expressed in terms of sufficient freedom in most situations, making it fair to use concepts such as 'desert', 'choice', and 'control', that expresses more accurately the position which the

---

[4] See H. L. A. Hart, *Punishment and Responsibility* (1968), Chs. 2 and 6, and M. Moore, *Criminal Law Theory* (1900).

[5] In Bentham's utilitarian theory, punishment was an evil to be avoided, and therefore other methods (e.g. education) were preferable: see J. Bentham, *Introduction to the Principles of Morals and Legislation.*, Ch. XIII.

[6] For a stimulating discussion, see Moore, *Criminal Law Theory*.

criminal law has reached. It also accords with the political under-pinnings of the law, namely, that citizens should be regarded as rational, choosing individuals whose autonomy the law should respect. But it should not blunt enquiries into the various dividing lines between responsibility and non-responsibility. We shall need to keep an open mind about whether a given condition ought to be admitted as an excuse or a defence, and, if so, whether it is defined so as to draw an acceptable line between 'sufficiently free' conduct and 'significantly restricted' behaviour.

4.3. PERSONALITY

(a) Natural and Corporate Personality

If one major plank of the principle of individual autonomy is that it coincides with our perception of ourselves and how we organize our lives, then similar reflection would lead to a recognition of the deep involvement of corporate activities in much modern social life—through companies as employers, as providers of goods and services, as providers of transport and of recreational facilities, and so forth. The criminal law has made increasing inroads into these spheres in recent years: the courts have developed doctrines of vicarious and corporate liability, and the legislature has introduced new offences directed specifically at corporate activities in the financial and commercial spheres (e.g. Financial Services Act 1986, and the Companies Acts 1985–89). But historically, and to a large extent currently, the criminal law is constructed around the notion of individual human beings as the bearers of rights and duties. The idea of companies as separate legal entities from their shareholders and their management was established in the nineteenth century: a limited liability company was even treated as a separate legal entity from the one man who controlled it.[7]

The present theory, then, is that corporate personality attaches to companies just as natural personality attaches to individuals (with certain modifications). But does this theory, which has a firm hold in company law, mean that companies can be convicted of offences? The courts moved slowly in this direction in the mid-nineteenth century. Although still doubtful whether companies could be said to *do* 'acts', the courts overcame any reluctance to hold companies

[7] *Salomon v. Salomon* [1897] AC 22.

liable for *failing* to act[8] and for committing a public nuisance.[9] The driving force behind these innovative decisions, both concerning railway companies in the early days of rail travel, was not legal theory but pragmatism: 'There can be no effective means of deterring from an oppressive exercise of power, for the purpose of gain, except the remedy by an indictment against those who truly commit it, that is, the corporation acting by its majority.'[10] And from there the law developed towards criminal liability for companies, acting through their controlling officers.[11]

(b) Towards Corporate Criminal Liability

This subject has been given a pressing social importance by the series of recent disasters connected with corporate activites and involving considerable loss of life—for example, the Bhopal chemical factory disaster, the Piper Alpha oil rig explosion, and the capsize of the ferry *Herald of Free Enterprise*. There are few who believe that these disasters can be presented as the responsibility of a few individuals. Indeed, enquiries into the disasters have tended to emphasize the role of deficiencies in the systems of management and accountability. Major disasters apart, the newspapers offer evidence of a constant stream of incidents of industrial pollution, unsafe working conditions, impure foods, and unfair business practices which impinge upon, or threaten to impinge upon, the lives of individual citizens.

Growing recognition of the significance of corporate harm-doing has not, however, been accompanied by substantial alteration of the framework of criminal liability. The trend, as we shall see, has been to attempt to fit corporate liability into the existing structure rather than to consider its implications afresh. And, more important in social terms, there has been little change of approach at the level of enforcement. It is one thing to have a set of laws which penalizes corporate wrongdoing as well as individual wrongdoing. It is quite another thing to have a balanced machinery of enforcement which strives to ensure the proportionate treatment of individuals and companies according to the relative seriousness of their offences:

---

[8] *Birmingham and Gloucester Railway Co.* (1842) 3 QB 223.
[9] *Great North of England Railway Co.* (1846) 9 QB 315.
[10] Per Denman CJ at 320.
[11] The landmark case was *Moussell Bros. v. London and North-Western Railway Co.* [1917] 2 KB 836. For discussion of the history, see L. H. Leigh, *The Criminal Liability of Corporations in English Law* (1969), Ch. 2, and G. Williams, *Criminal Law: The General Part* (2nd edn., 1961), Ch. 22.

present arrangements seem to draw a strong line between frequent police action against individuals and the relatively infrequent action of the various inspectorates, government departments, etc. against companies. However, the social calculation cannot be presented simply as an imbalance in treatment between 'crime in the streets' and 'crime in the suites'. We must also take into account the finding of social surveys that street crimes cause real harm and fear to people, not least to those who are already among the most disadvantaged in society,[12] and be prepared to question the appropriateness of criminal prosecutions for dealing with corporate harmdoing. The latter issue can be left until the framework of the common law has been outlined.[13]

One straightforward application of the doctrine that a company is a legal person, separate from the individuals involved in its operations, is that a company can commit many offences of strict liability: it can cause pollution, sell goods, fail to submit annual returns, etc. An offence of strict liability is one which requires no fault for conviction: any person may be found guilty simply through doing or failing to do a certain act.[14] Thus, if a company owns the business or premises concerned, it may be convicted for failing to submit returns to the relevant authorities, failing to control emissions of pollutants, etc. Outside the criminal law there have been further developments, and the law of torts has established a doctrine of vicarious liability of employers for the conduct of their employees.[15] There is no such general doctrine in the criminal law, but two exceptions have gained a foothold. One is the 'delegation principle': where a statute imposes liability on the owner, licensee or keeper of premises or other property, the courts will make that person vicariously liable for the conduct of anyone to whom management of the premises has been delegated.[16] This applies whether the defendant is an individual or a company. Pragmatism would appear to be the underlying reason for this principle: such offences would otherwise be unenforceable, since delegation would remove responsibility from the

[12] T. Jones, D. Maclean, and J. Young, *The Islington Crime Survey*; M. Gottfredson, *Fear of Crime*, Home Office Research Study No. 84 (1985).

[13] See below, section 4.3(*d*).

[14] See above, *Birmingham and Gloucester Railway Co.*, and the discussion of strict liability in Ch. 5.3(*a*).

[15] P. S. Atiyah, *Vicarious Liability in the Law of Torts* (1967).

[16] Cf. *Allen v. Whitehead* [1930] 1 KB 211, with *Vane v. Yiannopoullos* [1965] AC 486; see P. J. Pace, 'Delegation: A Doctrine in Search of a Definition' [1982] Crim. LR 627.

person in effective control. However, this is surely not the only way
of making such offences workable. The second exception revolves
around the interpretation of such key words in statutes as 'sell',
'use', and 'possess'. The clearest example is where a statute prohibits
the selling of goods in certain circumstances. *Coppen v. Moore (No. 2)*
(1898)[17] held the shop owner liable as the person who sold the goods
in law, even though he was away from the shop at the time and an
assistant carried out the transaction—in breach of the instructions
left by the owner. So long as the assistant is acting as an agent rather
than as a private individual, 'vicarious' liability is imposed. Once
again, practicality is said to provide the justification for this approach.

   In addition to these cases in which companies may be held
vicariously liable for the acts and omissions of employees, a direct
form of corporate liability has grown up. For this, it must be
established that a person who 'represents the directing mind and
will of the company' (sometimes termed a 'controlling officer'[18])
committed the act or omission specified in the offence, and had the
required fault element. In *Tesco Supermarkets v. Nattras* (1971),[19] it
was held that the manager of one of the company's supermarkets
was not sufficiently high up in the organization to 'represent the
directing mind and will of the company', with the result that the
company was not liable for giving a wrongful impression of prices.
The decision demonstrates the narrowness of the existing doctrine:
unless the prosecution can identify someone who both holds a
sufficiently influential position to be a 'controlling officer' and who
had the required fault element, corporate criminal liability cannot
be sustained.[20]

(c) Individualism and Corporatism

The history of legal developments in this sphere suggests a somewhat slow progress towards integrating corporations into a legal
framework constructed for individuals, with few gestures towards
the differences between corporations and individual human beings.[21]
There are those who argue that this is only right; social phenomena
can only be interpreted through the actions and motivations of
individuals, and abstractions like corporations constitute barriers to

[17] [1898] 2 QB 306.
[18] As in the draft Criminal Code (Law Com. No. 177), clause 30.
[19] [1972] AC 153.
[20] For further discussion, see Leigh, *The Criminal Liability of Corporations.*
[21] From among the plentiful literature on this, see particularly C. D. Stone, 'The
Place of Enterprise Liability in the Control of Corporate Conduct (1980) 90 *Yale LJ* 1.

proper understanding.[22] Only individuals can *do* things, and so the law is right to concentrate its attentions upon them; indeed, any other view might threaten the principle of individual autonomy.

The weakness of this argument is that individual actions can often be explained fully only by reference to the social and structural contexts in which they were carried out. When a government minister is announcing a new policy, he is speaking not merely as an individual but also as a representative of the government; when a managing director is initiating a commercial strategy, he is acting not merely as an individual but also as an officer of the company. Without reference to the structure and policies of the company and to that person's role within it, there can be no proper explanation of what was said and done. The argument, therefore, is that the behaviour of individuals is often shaped by their relationship to groups and collectivities—'shaped' in a meaningful sense, not 'determined' in the sense that individual autonomy is lost in the process (since individuals normally have some liberty to disengage themselves from the corporation). The thrust is that companies often acquire a momentum and a dynamic of their own which temporarily transcend the actions of their officers. Perhaps the clearest application of this can be found in offences of omission, particularly those involving strict liability. In a case like *Alphacell Ltd. v. Woodward* (1972),[23] where polluting matter escaped from the company's premises into a river, it seems both fairer and more accurate to convict the company rather than to label one individual as the offender: where the law imposes a duty, the company should be organized so as to ensure that the duty is fulfilled.

None of this is meant to suggest that individuals within a corporation should not bear responsibility for their conduct. It may well be right that they should do so. The point is that companies should be held both criminally and civilly liable, since it is they who create the structural context for the individual's conduct *qua* company officer. The corporation appoints the individual and sustains him in his position—the individual is in that place, doing that thing, because of the corporation—it is right that the corporation should at least have concurrent liability with its officer. That, however, is at the level of social theory. Our argument has been founded on the operation of large, profit-making corporations; some details would

---

[22] Cf. S. Lukes, *Individualism* (1973), Ch. 17.
[23] [1972] AC 824; cf. the early decision in *Birmingham and Gloucester Railway Co.*

need adjusting for small, even one-person, companies and also for non-profit organizations. Moreover, the argument leaves open the question whether the criminal law in its traditional form is the most appropriate means of dealing with corporate harm-doing.

(d) A New Form of Corporate Liability?

The theoretical arguments in favour of corporate criminal liability seem strong, but developments at common law have made this possible only to a limited extent, since the 'controlling officer' test in *Tesco Supermarkets v. Nattrass*[24] has a relatively narrow sphere of operation, and expansion of the 'vicarious liability' approach depends on already strained judicial interpretations of statutes. An alternative strategy of placing the emphasis on individual liability would be unlikely to work. Any particular individual might be dispensable within a corporation (e.g. the 'Company Vice-President responsible for going to gaol'), allowing the company continue on its course with minimal disruption; or it might be difficult to identify the individual responsible, not least because companies sometimes have convoluted lines of accountability. A further alternative strategy would be to rely even more on new offences of strict liability to punish corporate harm-doing, but this might not be a sufficient response to some of the disasters mentioned earlier, or to other harm-doing on a broad scale.

Reasoning of this kind has led to Fisse and Braithwaite's entirely new approach to corporate criminal liability, using concepts not applicable to individuals.[25] Their strategy rests on three key elements: 'enforced accountability'; a new concept of corporate fault; and a fresh approach to sanctions. The idea of 'enforced accountability' is that the law should recognize the complexity of lines of accountability in some corporations, and, rather than expending prosecutorial energy and court time trying to disentangle them, should require a company which has caused or threatened a proscribed harm to take its own disciplinary and rectificatory measures. The State should order the company to activate its own private justice system, and a court should then assess the adequacy of the measures taken. As this suggests, the concept of fault would then

---

[24] [1972] AC 153.
[25] B. Fisse and J. Braithwaite, 'The Allocation of Responsibility for Corporate Crime: Individualism, Collectivism and Accountability' (1988) 11 *Sydney LR* 468; see also L. H. Leigh, 'The Criminal Liability of Corporations and other Groups' (1977) 9 *Ottawa LR* 247; and J. Braithwaite, *Corporate Crime in the Pharmaceutical Industry* (1984).

become a *post hoc* phenomenon. Rather than struggling to establish some antecedent fault within the corporation, the prosecution would invite the court to infer fault from the nature and effectiveness of the company's remedial measures after it had been established that it was the author of a harm-causing or harm-threatening act or omission. The court would not find fault if it was persuaded that the company had taken realistic measures to prevent a recurrence, had ensured compensation to any victims, and had taken the event seriously in other respects. This 'reactive corporate fault' is a far cry from the notions of *mens rea* and prior fault which dominate criminal-law doctrine. The third element in the scheme is that the courts should be able to impose new penalties, specially designed for application to companies. Under the present system, a company can hardly be imprisoned, moderate fines can be swallowed up as business overheads, and swingeing fines might have such drastic side-effects on the employment and livelihoods of innocent employees as to render them inappropriate. The proposal is for a range of special penalties, some of which are rehabilitative (putting corporations on probation to supervise their compliance with the law), some of which are deterrent (punitive injunctions to require resources to be devoted to the development of new preventive measures), and others of which have mixed aims (e.g. community service by companies).

Fisse and Braithwaite's proposals for a radically new legal regime for corporate crime are grounded in arguments of prevention. They emphasize the enormity of the harms which corporations both cause and risk causing, and contend that the primary search should be for a regime which ensures maximum prevention. This is inconsistent with an approach to liability and punishment based on 'just deserts': the authors explicitly reject the idea of holding corporations criminally liable according to their culpability in causing the harms, not merely because it is difficult in practice to make such enquiries, but also because they believe that the prevention of future harm is of greater social importance in this sphere than any abstract notion of 'justice' based on past events.[26] 'Desert' theory would, however, make a clearer distinction between preventive measures and conviction and sentence. In principle, punishment for corporations, no less than for individuals, should be proportioned to culpability: if

---

[26] See further J. Braithwaite, 'Challenging Just Deserts: Punishing White Collar Criminals' (1982) 73 *J. Crim. Law & Criminology* 723, and the reply by A. von Hirsch, 'Desert and White Collar Criminality: A Reply to Dr Braithwaite' ibid. 1164.

that proves impossible in practice, for the reasons given by Fisse and Braithwaite, then that is an argument for legal presumptions or other special doctrines, but not for abandoning the distinctive aims of the criminal law and punishment. Broader preventive measures, perhaps through regulatory mechanisms, should be put in hand in order to reduce the risk of further harms from similar sources. The extent to which criminal offences should be appended to such regulatory schemes will be discussed in Chapter 5.3(a), and there is also the wider problem of ensuring parity of enforcement and proportionality in the impact of the criminal law, so that individuals are not pursued for minor offences, whereas companies can commit more serious offences with impunity.

4.4. ACTS, STATES OF AFFAIRS AND OMISSIONS

It is often assumed that the most basic requirement for criminal liability is an act: a person cannot be, and should not be, convicted for doing nothing. One problem with this assumption lies in the definition of an act, since people's bodies may occasionally move independently of their direction (this is the problem of 'involuntary conduct', discussed in section 4.5). Another problem with the general assumption is that it takes no account of the possibility of, and the justifications for, criminal liability based on states of affairs or on omissions. These issues are explored here.

(a) Situational Liability

It is generally thought to be objectionable to convict a person simply because a state of affairs exists and not because that person 'did' anything. The leading case is *Larsonneur* (1933),[27] where D left England because the duration of her permitted stay had come to an end. She went to Ireland, from where she was deported back to this country. On her return, she was convicted of 'being found in the United Kingdom' contrary to the Aliens Order 1920. Her appeal, based on the argument that her return to England was beyond her control, was dismissed by the Court of Criminal Appeal. The case is widely criticized: her return to this country was not her own act; it was as if she had been returned by compulsion. To convict a person simply for 'being found' leaves little room for the normal grounds of exculpation—even if D's return was not voluntary and

[27] (1933) 149 LT 542.

hardly bore the stamp of an individual behaving autonomously.[28] Perhaps, in order to prevent unfairness, the court should have striven to find a defence of compulsion (see below, section 4.5). But what is striking is the wording of the offence, simply 'being found': is this unusual?

In fact, English criminal law has acquired a number of offences which simply penalize a state of affairs and impose what Glazebrook has termed 'situational liability'.[29] In section 4.3(b) we saw how, in certain situations, the courts have imposed 'vicarious liability' on shop owners and employers by construing statutory words so as to achieve this result. In effect, these individuals and companies are being held liable simply for states of affairs—for the fact that an employee sold American ham as Scottish ham, for example, even though the shop owner had specifically warned against this.[30] It is not simply that this may mean conviction without fault; it also means conviction without anything on the part of the shopowner which could be termed an 'act'. How strong is this line of objection? Surely a rational criminal code might well penalize employers whose failure to organize their business or to supervise their staff causes harm, and it might well penalize them for negligence as well as for intentional or reckless failures.[31] It may therefore be quite defensible to impose situational liability if the law were so phrased as to ensure that defendants are in control of their activities and know about their duty to avoid certain situations, and if there were, for example, a requirement of proof of negligence.[32] The objection to the Aliens Order, and to the imposition of 'vicarious liability' by the courts, is that no such principled approach was taken. The same might also be said, although to a lesser degree, about the various possession offences in English criminal law (possessing an offensive weapon, controlled drugs, etc.), where the requirements of knowledge are not entirely sufficient to avoid the conviction of an innocent recipient.[33]

---

[28] Cf. the analysis by D. J. Lanham, 'Larsonneur Revisited' [1976] Crim. LR 276, which suggests that the decision may have been based on prior fault (see below, Ch. 5.2(e)).

[29] P. R. Glazebrook, 'Situational Liability', in Glazebrook (ed.), *Reshaping the Criminal Law*, 108.

[30] As in *Coppen v. Moore*.

[31] See the discussion of strict liability in Ch. 5.3(a) below.

[32] See the discussion of negligence in Ch. 5.3(f) below.

[33] *Warner v. Metropolitan Police Commissioner* [1969] 2 AC 256.

(b) Omissions Liability in English Law

English criminal law has adopted an ambivalent stance towards criminal liability for omissions to act. There has been a steady growth in the number of statutory crimes of omission: many of these are commercial and industrial offences, in the form of 'failing to register . . .' and 'failing to submit' required returns; others penalize omissions in the context of positive activities such as driving a motor vehicle—driving without insurance, without road tax, and without a licence. But the difficulties arise with common-law or statutory crimes whose definitions do not expressly refer to omissions: can they be committed by omission? In order to resolve the matter, courts have tended to discuss whether the language of the definition will allow an extension to cover omissions and, if so, whether the situation is one in which a duty to act should be recognized. The linguistic approach has led to a variety of decisions on different statutes,[34] without much discussion of the general principles underlying omissions liability. The Law Commission's draft Criminal Code signals the continuation of this approach, by redefining the homicide offences in terms of 'causing death' rather than 'killing', and redefining the damage offences in terms of 'causing damage' rather than 'damaging', so as 'to leave fully open to the courts the possibility of so construing the relevant (statutory) provisions as to impose liability for omissions'.[35] A similar ambivalence has been evident in the courts' development of common-law offences. Liability for omissions is not a new phenomenon at common law, but the courts have tended to pursue a restrictive policy in general. There are now authorities for the propositions that parents can be convicted of murder or manslaughter (according to the degree of their culpability) for failing to feed or call medical attention to their young child;[36] that a person who voluntarily undertakes the duty of caring for another and then neglects that duty may be held liable for causing the consequence of that neglect;[37] that the owner of a house or car may be convicted as an accomplice to offences committed on or with the property in the owner's presence if the owner takes no

---

[34] With different interpretations of words such as 'cause': see G. Williams, 'What should the Code do about Omissions?' (1987) 7 LS 92.

[35] Law Com. No. 177, ii, para. 7.13; see generally paras. 7.7–7.13.

[36] Gibbins and Proctor (1918) 13 Cr. App. R 134.

[37] Instan [1893] 1 QB 450; see P. R. Glazebrook, 'Criminal Omissions: the Duty Requirement in Offences against the Person' (1960) 76 LQR 386.

steps to prevent the offences;[38] and that a person who accidentally or mistakenly commits an act which causes harm, and who then becomes aware of the act and its results, becomes liable for the results if he or she fails to do what is reasonable to prevent their occurrence.[39]

These, however, are specific instances which do not indicate any coherent approach to omissions liability. The general ambivalence may be illustrated by comparing two manslaughter cases decided in the 1970s. In *Lowe* (1973)[40] the Court of Appeal quashed the conviction of a father for the manslaughter of his child by failing to summon a doctor, commenting that 'there is a clear distinction between an act of omission and an act of commission likely to cause harm', and continuing:

if I strike a child in a manner likely to cause harm, it is right that if the child dies I may be charged with manslaughter. If, however, I omit to do something with the result that it suffers injury to health which results in its death, we think that a charge of manslaughter should not be an inevitable consequence, even if the omission is deliberate.[41]

This strong view may be contrasted with the finding in *Stone and Dobinson* (1977)[42] that both defendants had assumed a duty to care for the deceased woman—Stone because the deceased was his sister and was occupying a room in his house, and Dobinson because she had by conduct 'undertaken the duty of trying to wash [the deceased], and of taking such food to her as she required'. Since the defendants were found also to have satisfied the culpability requirements for manslaughter,[43] their convictions were upheld by the Court of Appeal.

(c) Omissions, Duties, and Criminal Liability

Clearly there are differences, at the level of analysis, between acts and omissions. Rather than concentrating on those differences[44] however, our discussion will focus on whether a distinction ought to be drawn between acts and omissions in terms of criminal liability.

---

[38] *Du Cros v. Lambourne* [1907] 1 KB 40; *Tuck v. Robson* [1970] 1 WLR 741.
[39] *Miller* [1983] 2 AC 161; draft Criminal Code (Law Com. No. 177), clause 23.
[40] [1973] QB 702.   [41] Ibid. 709, per Phillimore LJ.
[42] [1977] QB 354; see I. Dennis, 'Manslaughter by Omission' [1980] CLP 255.
[43] See below Ch. 7.5(*d*).
[44] For references, see A. Ashworth, 'The Scope of Criminal Liability for Omissions', (1989) 105 LQR 424, at 433–6; cf. A. Leavens, 'A Causation Approach to Omissions' (1988) 76 Cal. LR 549.

One way of answering this question would be to demonstrate that there are points at which the distinction has hardly any true bearing on culpability at all: for example, is it fair to say that a hospital nurse who decides not to replace an empty bag for a drip-feed has made an omission, whereas another nurse who switches off a ventilator has committed an act?[45] Surely an act-omission distinction should not influence the law's response to the two situations.

In approaching the matter from the point of view of broad principle, two possible foundations for the law may be contrasted. One is individualism, which argues that although it is necessary to place citizens under certain duties so that taxes are paid and businesses are properly conducted, the only other positive duties which the criminal law should recognize are duties towards those people with whom the individual has a special relationship, such as children and the parties to any contracts or voluntary undertakings. A law which recognized positive duties to render assistance to any other person in peril, for example, would constitute too great a restriction on the liberty of citizens. A citizen's plans would be liable to be disrupted by chance occurrences, preventing him or her from pursuing personal goals.[46] The 'social responsibility' view is in direct contrast to this, emphasizing the need for individuals to co-operate in the achievement of general social goals. Perhaps the most significant point is that this view challenges the link between individualism and the principle of individual autonomy outlined earlier.[47] It argues that individual autonomy is better realized not in a society which regards the preservation of individuals' maximum liberty as the supreme aim, but in a community which accepts that human interdependence, mutual support, and the fulfilment of interpersonal obligations are necessary for the fullest development of individuals.[48]

It would be tempting to say that the difference between the two views is one of degree, but it does have a much broader significance. In practice, there are few advocates of either extreme position, in relation to the criminal law, and the debate therefore tends to be about the middle ground—notably, whether a system of criminal

---

[45] For references, see Ashworth, 'The Scope of Criminal Liability for Omissions', 437; cf. I. M. Kennedy, *Treat me Right* (1988), 167–74.

[46] For elaboration of the points in this paragraph, see Ashworth, 'The Scope of Criminal Liability for Omissions', esp. 427–33. For criticism, see G. Williams, 'Criminal Omissions', (1991) 107 LQR 86.

[47] See above, section 4.2.

[48] See J. Raz, *The Morality of Freedom* (1987), Chs. 10 and 15; N. Lacey, *State Punishment* (1988), 172–81; and above, p. 77.

law should include an offence of failing to take reasonable steps to assist another citizen in peril. Individualists may rule this out as going too far in restricting the liberty of citizens; the social responsibility view would cite it as a prime example of a positive duty imposed for socially justifiable reasons. One point in favour of this latter view is that it takes full account of the value involved (i.e. the life or safety of the person in peril), whereas the individualist view seems not to place this in the balance with the citizen's liberty to pursue his or her own interests—or at least, to accord it less weight. Is there not a case for arguing that as the values at stake become more central (life and physical safety being uncontroversial examples of this), it is right for the criminal law to adopt the social responsibility approach and to impose positive duties on citizens to do what is reasonable to avert the serious consequences?[48a] This suggests that the legislature should consider the enactment of new offences in England, similar to those in other European countries, imposing a 'duty of easy rescue'.[49] It also suggests that the judiciary, in their interpretive role and in developing the common law,[50] ought to devote more explicit attention to the arguments of principle rather than appearing as slaves to the vagaries of language. The fact that a life could have been saved without danger to the rescuer should matter more than the fact that the law uses the word 'kills' rather than the words 'causes death'.

4.5. INVOLUNTARY CONDUCT

(a) Automatism and Authorship

Automatism is often regarded as an excuse for, rather than as an essential component of, criminal conduct, but its appearance in this chapter reflects its fundamental nature. It is not merely a denial of fault or of responsibility. It is more of a denial of authorship, a claim that the ordinary link between mind and behaviour was absent; the person could not be said to be acting as a moral agent at the time— what occurred was an involuntary set of movements of the body rather than 'acts' of D. The usual examples of this are sleep-

---

[48a] This line of argument is accorded insufficient weight in the critique by Williams, 'Criminal Omission'.

[49] For discussion, see A. Ashworth and E. Steiner, 'Criminal Omissions and Public Duties: The French Experience', (1990) 10 *Legal Studies* 153.

[50] A task which will be left to them under the draft Criminal Code: see above, p. 90.

walking, concussion, being physically overpowered by another person, and being attacked by a swarm of bees whilst driving.

It seems to be accepted that automatism prevents liability for all crimes, including crimes of strict liability. One way of rationalizing this within the traditional framework of *actus reus* and *mens rea* is to maintain that automatism negatives *actus reus*, since it shows that the conduct or omission was not the result of the defendant *acting* but of something *happening to* the defendant. Since all crimes require *actus reus*, even if some of them do not require *mens rea*, it follows that automatism may be a defence to any and every crime. But there is another side to this: since automatism is so powerful a defence—being available to all crimes—the courts have attempted to circumscribe its use, holding that freedom from liability for causing harm should only be available to those who are free from fault. We shall therefore see that automatism itself is defined fairly narrowly, and that the courts have evolved three major doctrines of limitation.

It is common to refer to automatism as a 'defence', even though the defendant has only to adduce some evidence for the burden of negativing involuntariness to fall to the prosecution. Thus, when it is said that 'voluntary action is a fundamental requirement of criminal liability', it should not be overlooked that voluntariness is assumed in all cases and that it is only rarely challenged.

(b) The Essence of Automatism

Examples of forms of involuntariness which might amount to automatism have been given—sleep-walking, concussion, etc. Criminal lawyers used to express the legal position in terms of a requirement of a voluntary act, going on to say that an act is voluntary if it is willed.[51] One criticism of this is that it does not explain how the act of will occurs, and suggests an infinite causal regress;[52] another is that it misrepresents and exaggerates our awareness of the movements involved in our behaviour.[53] These criticisms have led Hart to propose a 'negative' definition, describing involuntary actions as 'movements of the body which occurred though the agent had no reason for moving his body in that way'.[54] This switches attention to rare occasions of involuntariness, for

---

[51] The classic statement is that of J. Austin, *Lectures on Jurisprudence* (5th edn., 1885), 411–24.

[52] A. I. Melden, 'Willing', in A. R. White (ed.), *The Philosophy of Action* (1968), 77.

[53] H. L. A. Hart, *Punishment and Responsibility* (1968), 103.

[54] Ibid. 255–6, reformulating (in response to criticism) the passage appearing at 105.

which two types of situation might be identified—behaviour which was uncontrollable, and behaviour which proceeded from severely impaired consciousness. Uncontrollable behaviour might be illustrated thus: D is physically overpowered by X and is made to stab V: in these circumstances it is fair to say that this was not D's *act* but something which *happened to* D. Other examples might be conduct during an epileptic fit, and reflex actions. Turning to behaviour proceeding from a lack of consciousness, this can be illustrated by things done during a hypoglycaemic episode or whilst sleep-walking. It seems from the decided cases that the courts have not insisted on a total absence of consciousness here: what is required is consciousness which was significantly reduced or impaired.[55] There are several examples of harms inflicted whilst sleep-walking for which a defence of automatism has been upheld.[56] It should be noted that both types of automatism apply equally to offences of omission, excusing those who fail to fulfil a legal duty through physical incapacity arising from inability to control behaviour or through significantly reduced consciousness.[57]

This brings us to a reconsideration of the essence of automatism. Hart's definition depends upon the absence of a reason for the movements of the body, whereas the cases seem to have more to do with an absence of capacity. Glanville Williams, taking this point, argues that movements are involuntary if D is unable to avoid them.[58] Not only does this involve a shift of emphasis to capacity, but it also strikes an unusual note in asking not whether D did control the movements (were they uncontroll*ed*?), but whether D could have controlled them (were they uncontroll*able*?). Williams's approach is preferable here, as the draft Code recognizes; Hart's test dwells on cognition, whereas the essence of automatism is lack of volition. But there is no concealing the questions of judgment it leaves open. The draft Code includes within automatism any movement which '(i) is a reflex, spasm or convulsion; or (ii) occurs while he is in a condition (whether of sleep, unconsciousness, impaired consciousness or otherwise) depriving him of effective control of the act'.[59] The key here is 'effective control', and this, combined

---

[55] e.g. *Charlson* [1955] 1 WLR, 317, *Kemp* [1957] 1 QB 399, and *Quick* [1973] QB 910. [56] e.g. *Boshears, The Times*, 18 Feb. 1961.

[57] See Model Penal Code, art. 2. 01(1), draft Criminal Code (Law Com. No. 177) clause 33(2), and A. Smart, 'Responsibility for Failing to Do the Impossible' (1987) 103 LQR 532.

[58] G. Williams, *Textbook of Criminal Law* (2nd edn., 1983), Ch. 29.

[59] Law Com. No. 177, clause 33(1).

with 'impaired consciousness', shows how difficult it is to eliminate questions of degree even from such a fundamental aspect of criminal liability. The *essence* of automatism may lie in D's inability to control the movement (or non-movement) of his body at the relevant time, but it is thought unduly harsh to phrase the law in terms of the deprivation of all control, and so the phrase 'depriving him of effective control' leaves the courts free to evaluate and judge D's worthiness for a complete acquittal. The advantage of this formula is to allow sensitivity to the special facts of unusual cases; its disadvantage is to allow courts to incorporate extraneous considerations into their judgments.

At common law the courts have narrowed the defence of automatism in at least three major respects, by excluding cases of insanity, intoxication, and prior fault, and it is to these developments that we must now look.

(c) Insane Automatism

Even if D's bodily movements were uncontrollable or proceeded from reduced consciousness, the defence of automatism will not be available if the cause of D's condition was a mental disorder classified as insanity. The courts have developed this policy for reasons of social defence, since it ensures that those who fall within the legal definition of insanity are subject to the special verdict (with its consequence of indefinite detention[60]) rather than being allowed to argue that their condition rendered their acts uncontrollable, and that they should therefore have an unqualified acquittal on the grounds of automatism. Thus, if D bases his defence on automatism but the judge rules that, since the origin of D's condition was a 'disease of the mind', the defence should be treated as one of insanity, D may decide to plead guilty to the charge rather than to persist with an insanity defence.

The social policy behind this judicial approach was at its clearest in Lord Denning's speech in *Bratty v. Attorney-General for Northern Ireland* (1963).[61] D based his defence to a murder charge on psychomotor epilepsy, but the trial judge refused to let automatism stand here, advising that the true nature of the condition was a disease of the mind and that therefore insanity was the only defence. The House of Lords upheld the trial judge's approach, and Lord Denning affirmed that 'it is not every involuntary act which leads to

---

[60] Criminal Procedure (Insanity) Act 1964, s. 5; see below, Ch. 6.2(*b*).
[61] [1963] AC 386.

a complete acquittal'. D's behaviour may have been involuntary, 'but it does not give rise to an unqualified acquittal, for that would mean that he would be let at large to do it again'. The proper verdict is one of insanity, 'which ensures that the person who suffers from the disease is kept secure in a hospital so as not to be a danger to himself or others'. Moreover, Lord Denning was inclined to give 'mental disease' a broad definition for this purpose, so as to include 'any mental disorder which has manifested itself in violence and is prone to recur'. This decision confirmed the dominance of the policy of social defence over considerations of individual responsibility.

Further questions about the dividing line between automatism and insanity were raised in *Quick* (1973),[62] where D's defence against a charge of causing actual bodily harm was that the attack occurred during a hypoglycaemic episode brought on by the use of insulin and his failure to eat an adequate lunch. The Court of Appeal held that a malfunctioning of the mind does not constitute a 'disease of the mind' within the insanity defence if it is 'caused by the application to the body of some external factor such as violence, drugs, including anaesthetics, alcohol, and hypnotic influences'. This 'external factor' doctrine was accepted by the House of Lords in *Sullivan* (1984),[63] where it was also restated that a disease of the mind may be either permanent or transitory. Thus, where D's condition is caused by an external factor, the legal classification is automatism rather than insanity. This leads to the apparently strange result that a hypoglycaemic episode (resulting from the taking of insulin to correct diabetes) falls within automatism, whereas a hyperglycaemic episode (resulting from a high blood-sugar level which has not been corrected) falls within insanity, since it is an internal condition rather than a condition caused by an external factor.[64]

(d) Automatism through intoxication

Although the Court of Appeal in *Quick* held that automatism arising from intoxication did not fall within the definition of insanity, this does not mean that a person who causes harm whilst in such an intoxicated state as to have significantly reduced consciousness or to be unable to control movements of the body should be acquitted. If the cause of the involuntariness is intoxication, then the case falls

---

[62] [1973] QB 910.   [63] [1984] AC 156.
[64] *Hennessy* (1989) 89 Cr. App. R 10.

within the ambit of the intoxication doctrine. It is rare for the evidence to be able to sustain a reasonable doubt that D was sufficiently intoxicated as to be in a state of automatism, but this seems to have been accepted in *Lipman* (1970),[65] where D had taken drugs and believed that he was fighting off snakes and descending to the centre of the earth, whereas he was actually suffocating his girl-friend. No defence of automatism was available: the case was treated as one of intoxication.[66] However, if D's condition appears to have arisen through intoxication and then through concussion resulting from a bump on the head, the court may have to establish the dominant cause of the condition and subsequent behaviour.[67]

(e) Prior Fault

The aim of the principle of prior fault[68] is to prevent D taking advantage of a condition amounting to automatism if it arose through D's own fault. In relation to automatism, the point was first made in *Quick* (1973),[69] where Lawton LJ held that this defence would not be available if the condition 'could have been reasonably foreseen as a result of either doing or omitting to do something, as, for example, taking alcohol against medical advice after using certain prescribed drugs, or failing to take regular meals whilst taking insulin'. According to this view, the question of prior fault is resolved by applying the test of reasonable foreseeability, the test of the reasonably prudent person in D's position. But in *Bailey* (1983)[70] the Court of Appeal held that a person should not be liable to conviction if the condition of automatism arose through a simple failure to appreciate the consequences of a failure to take sufficient food after a dose of insulin, even if the reasonably prudent person would have realized it. The defence of automatism should be available unless it can be shown that D knew that his acts or omissions were likely 'to make him aggressive, unpredictable and uncontrolled with the result that he may cause some injury to others'. Prior fault therefore requires awareness of risk, sometimes called subjective recklessness.[71]

---

[65] [1970] 1 QB 152. [66] On which, see below, Ch. 6.3.
[67] *Stripp* (1978) 69 Cr. App. R 318.
[68] Discussed below, Ch. 5.2(d).
[69] [1973] QB 910; for discussion of this development, see A. J. Ashworth, 'Reason, Logic and Criminal Liability' (1975) 91 LQR 102.
[70] (1983) 77 Cr. App. R 76.
[71] On which, see below, Ch. 5.3(c).

The principle of prior fault conflicts, as we shall see below,[72] with the principle of contemporaneity of fault and conduct. In some automatism cases an attempt has been made to avoid this conflict by convicting D in respect of an earlier point of time, when there was fault. Thus in *Kay v. Butterworth* (1945)[73] D fell asleep while driving home from night-work, and his car collided with soldiers marching down the road. It was held that he could be convicted of careless driving—not in respect of the collision (when he was asleep and therefore involuntarily omitting to exercise due care), but in respect of his earlier failure to stop driving when he felt drowsy. This approach is only possible where the offence is of a continuing nature, and even then depends on the charge being appropriately worded. Yet, impractical as it is as a solution to the conflict between the principles of prior fault and contemporaneity, it at least suggests some judicial recognition of the conflict.

(f) Reform

Even if it is accepted that cases of prior fault should continue to be excluded from automatism and that cases resulting from intoxication should be classified under the intoxication rules, one major unsatisfactory feature of the law on automatism is the line drawn between this defence and the defence of insanity. This will be discussed further in Chapter 6.2(c) where it is argued that if there is a broadened defence of mental disorder, with flexible powers of disposal (rather than the present requirement of mandatory committal to hospital), then at least cases of pathological automatism that is liable to recur should be taken into the mental disorder defence.[74]

4.6. CAUSATION

Once it has been established that D was not behaving involuntarily at the time of the act or omission, or that compliance with the law's demands was not impossible, the next point is to determine whether the result or other event was *caused* by D. Causation is the minimum requirement for attributing a specific result to D. In accordance with the principle of individual autonomy discussed in section 4.2 above, the law regards individuals as sovereign in most matters of causation, and thus tends to select the last human contribution as

---

[72] Ch. 5.2.(d).   [73] (1945) 173 LT 191.
[74] Law Com. No. 177, clause 34(c); see below, Ch. 6.2(c).

more important than all other events and effects. It will be suggested below that the courts have shown themselves willing to stretch causal arguments in order to ensure conviction for those who have acted with obvious culpability. It may be too much, then, to expect the principles of causation in the criminal law to emerge as a coherent doctrine.

(a) The General Principle

The definitions of many crimes require that D caused a result (e.g. murder, grievous bodily harm, criminal damage) or that he caused a result by certain means (e.g. obtaining property by deception). What is necessary in order to establish this causation? It is often not possible to identify a single cause of an event: often there are a number of contributory causes. But the criminal law's preoccupation with human agency narrows the question down to whether it may be said that D caused the result. This means that it will rarely be relevant to suggest that some coincidental event played a part,[75] or even that another person played a role (since concurrent causation is possible in law).[76] The principle of individual autonomy presumes that, where an individual who is neither mentally disordered nor an infant has made a sufficient causal contribution to an occurrence, it is inappropriate to trace the causation any further. This is taken to justify not only picking out D's conduct from other possible causes and regarding that conduct as operating on a 'stage already set',[77] but also declining to look behind D's conduct for other persons who might be said to have contributed to D acting as he or she did. The doctrine, then, is that voluntary conduct acts as a barrier in any causal enquiry in criminal law: by and large, D's voluntary conduct will usually be regarded as the cause of an act or an omission if it was the closest human conduct to the result. Any causal enquiry will be perfunctory if it is clear that D either intended to cause the result or knowingly risked causing it, for no court will see much merit in the argument that the result was highly unlikely in the circumstances and probably a coincidence. Thus the dictum 'intended consequences are never too remote' is one expression of the strong effect which

---

[75] Cf. above, section 4.6.

[76] e.g. *Attorney-General's Reference (No. 4 of 1980)* (1981) 73 Cr. App. R 40.

[77] See H. L. A. Hart and T. Honoré, *Causation in the Law* (2nd edn., 1985), Ch. 1 and *passim*, and the derivative discussions by S. Kadish, *Blame and Punishment* (1987), Ch. 8, and H. Beynon, 'Causation, Omissions and Complicity', [1987] Crim. LR 539; cf. also Williams, *Textbook of Criminal Law*, Ch. 14.

culpability has in hastening a finding of causation and overlooking restrictive policies which might otherwise be invoked.

Where the culpability element does not overshadow the issue—and particularly in crimes of strict liability, where no culpability may be required—the question arises of what minimum connection must be established between D's conduct and the prohibited result. It is, generally speaking, that the result would not have occurred *but for* D's conduct. Of course there may be many other 'but for' causes of the result, but an explanation has already been offered for the law's concentration on voluntary human behaviour—the principle of individual autonomy. Yet the 'but for' test does appear to be rather undemanding, and it may be consciousness of this which has led English courts to refer to further (though often uncertain) parameters. In *Cato* (1976),[78] for example, the Court of Appeal expressly stopped short of the 'but for' test. D had been convicted of the manslaughter of V, whom he had injected with a heroin compound at V's request. On the issue of whether D's injection of the heroin could be said to have caused V's death, the court stated that: 'As a matter of law, it was sufficient if the prosecution could establish that it was *a* cause, provided it was a cause outside the *de minimis* range, and effectively bearing upon the acceleration of the moment of the victim's death.'[79] The court later stated that the cause must be 'a cause of substance', although it recognized that the term 'substantial cause' would be putting the requirement too high.[80] Clearly, the court was reluctant to accept 'but for' causation here, fearing that the link between D's conduct and V's death might be too tenuous. But this was a case of manslaughter, and the court may have been using causal arguments to circumscribe the law of constructive manslaughter (see Chapters 5.2(*b*) and 7.5 below). It is unlikely that so restrictive a view of causal principles would have been taken if it had been a crime of intention in which D's intention had been proved.

Deception cases provide good example of the puissance of culpability over causality, for what has to be proved for offences such as obtaining property or services by deception, is that the obtaining was *caused* by the deception. A difficulty arises where V's mind plainly did not advert to D's deception. This may occur where D was trading on normal assumptions which were not true in his or her case, and where V acted on these normal assumptions without

---

[78] (1976) 62 Cr. App. R 41.   [79] Ibid. 45.   [80] Ibid. 46.

realizing that they were inapplicable. How does the 'but for' test apply here? According to the House of Lords decisions in *Metropolitan Police Commissioner v Charles* (1976)[81] and in *Lambie* (1982)[82], D's conduct in using a cheque card or credit card without mentioning that its use was unauthorized may be said to have caused V to hand over the goods (the obtaining), if V would have acted otherwise, had he or she known that D's use of the card was unauthorized. This type of case is complicated by the fact that the key element in D's conduct is an omission, the failure to alert V to the fact that the normal assumptions were untrue. This is not the place to discuss whether D has a *duty* to alert V to his or her lack of authority.[83] If such a duty is established for the purpose of criminal cases, then the causation issue becomes relevant to omissions.[84] Otherwise, these decisions might fairly be regarded as straining causal tests in order to secure the conviction of manifestly dishonest people. Culpability, once again, had the upper hand.

A further example of the interaction of causation and culpability is provided by the medical cases. At the celebrated trial of Dr Bodkin Adams, (1957), charged with murdering a patient by administering excessive doses of morphine, Devlin J stated the orthodox view that to shorten life by days and weeks is to cause death no less than shortening it by years, but he added that a doctor 'is still entitled to do all that is proper and necessary to relieve pain and suffering even if the measures he takes may incidentally shorten life'.[85] This direction to the jury might well be compatible with the principle subsequently espoused in *Cato*, that a *de minimis* contribution (i.e. a minimal cause which 'people of common sense would overlook'[86]) is not a sufficient cause in law. However, this probably does not capture the precise point of the *Adams* direction, which is rather that a doctor's conduct, founded upon clinical judgment, will not be regarded as a legal cause so long as it remains within reasonable bounds. In other words, treatment which is necessary, normal, and which does not substantially shorten the patient's life will not be regarded as a legal cause of death. This is really a narrowing of the doctrine of causation in cases of clinical judgment, and one might take the view that it would be better achieved

---

[81] [1977] AC 177.   [82] [1982] AC 449.
[83] See A. T. H. Smith, 'The Idea of Criminal Deception' [1982] Crim. LR 721, and below, Ch. 9.7.
[84] See Beynon, 'Causation, Omissions and Complicity'.
[85] [1957] Crim. LR 365; see Hart and Honoré, *Causation in the Law*, 344–5.
[86] Per Devlin J, at 375.

through a defence of medical justification than through distortion of the principles of causation.[87]

The principle of causation is that it is sufficient if D's conduct was a 'but for' cause which was more than minimal: it need not be a substantial cause, but it seems that a mere 'but for' cause will rarely be sufficient (the deception cases may be an exception here). The American Model Penal Code reaches a broadly similar position, stating that 'but for' causation is generally sufficient, apart from those causes which are too remote to have a just bearing on the case.[88] The requirement of 'but for' causation is sometimes termed 'factual causation', which is then contrasted with 'legal causation'— not only to suggest that the law requires something more than 'but for' causation, but also to indicate that there are other aspects of the doctrine to be considered.

(b) Interventions between Conduct and Result

What effect should be accorded to an intervention between D's conduct and the result specified in the definition of the crime? The principle is that a natural event should terminate D's causal responsibility if it is a coincidence, but not if it could reasonably be expected.[89] The contrast would be between D, whose assault victim catches scarlet fever in hospital and dies (which should be treated as a 'visitation of Providence' and as negativing any causal connection between D and the death), and E, who leaves the assault victim lying on a tidal beach, where he later drowns (this is within the risk which was reasonably foreseeable, and therefore not a sufficient coincidence to prevent causal responsibility for the death).

Where the intervening event is a human act, elaborate principles have to be developed to provide for the various eventualities. On the principle of individual autonomy, causal responsibility cannot be traced through a voluntary human act: thus, if A shoots B, inflicting a wound which would cause B's death within minutes, and then C arrives and kills B instantly, C's intervention relieves A of any causal responsibility for the death—A may be guilty of attempted murder or some other serious offence, but not for the death, even though one might be able to say that the death would not have occurred but for A's original shooting. The principle that causation cannot be traced through a voluntary intervening act has been tested in three distinct spheres—(i) the conduct of third

---

[87] See below, section 4.8(b).   [88] Model Penal Code, s. 2.03.
[89] Hart and Honoré, *Causation in the Law*, 342.

parties; (ii) the conduct of doctors; and (iii) the conduct of the victim—and the term 'voluntary' has not proved to be very helpful in setting the various boundaries.

(i) *Conduct of Third Parties.* The example in the previous paragraph shows that, generally, the intervening act of a third party relieves the original actor of causal responsibility. But there are exceptions to this, namely, in those cases where the third party's intervention would not be described as voluntary. If the third party is an infant or is mentally disordered, this lack of rational capacity may be regarded as sufficient to discount the third party's act in causal terms. The same applies if D sets out to use a responsible adult as an 'innocent agent', giving false information to that person in the hope that he or she will act upon it. The behaviour of the person who has been tricked is discounted as non-voluntary for these purposes. The case of *Michael* (1840)[90] illustrates the principles. D's child was in the care of a foster-mother, and D, wishing her child dead, handed a bottle of poison to the foster-mother, saying that it was medicine for the child. The foster-mother saw no need for the medicine and placed it on the mantelpiece, from which her own 5-year-old child later removed it and administered a fatal dose to D's child. The intended result was therefore achieved through the unexpected act of an infant rather than through the mistakenly 'innocent' act of an adult, but neither of these intervening acts was regarded as sufficient to relieve D of causal responsibility.[91]

A similar approach may be taken where the intervening act is one of compulsion, necessity, or duty. If the third party brings about the prohibited harm whilst under duress from D, then D may be regarded as the legal cause of the result.[92] The same analysis can be applied where D creates a situation of necessity, or where D's behaviour creates a duty to respond in the third party. These points may be illustrated by reference to *Pagett* (1983).[93] D was being pursued by the police and took his pregnant girl-friend hostage, holding her in front of him as a shield whilst he fired shots at the police. The police fired back at D, but killed the girl-friend. The Court of Appeal upheld D's conviction for the manslaughter of his girl-friend, even though the fatal shots were fired by the police

[90] (1840) 9 C & P 356; cf. G. Williams, '*Finis* for *Novus Actus*' [1989] Camb. LJ 391.

[91] Cf. *Cogan and Leak* [1976] 1 QB 217, on 'semi-innocent agency'. discussed in Ch. 10.6 below.

[92] (1952) 36 Cr. App. R 125; see also below, Ch. 10.6.

[93] (1983) 76 Cr. App. R 279; see Hart and Honoré, *Causation in the Law*, 330–4.

and not by him. The court offered two reasons in support of this conclusion: first, that the police-officer's conduct in shooting back at D was necessary for his self-preservation and therefore was not a voluntary act; and second, that the police-officer was acting from a duty to prevent crime and to arrest D. Both these reasons seem heavily imbued with formality and objectivity—Did a necessity exist? Was there a duty?—and yet they contain no reference to a duty to avoid harm to the person being held hostage. Surely a police-officer's duty to arrest D would conflict with his duty to safeguard the life of the hostage? And, arguably, the right to act in self-preservation might also be thus qualified. These points ought to have been explored at least. Perhaps the true rationale of this decision may be found in a doctrine of 'alternative danger': where D places a person in the position of having to choose between two drastic courses of action, one threatening self-danger and the other threatening danger to another, any response to such an emergency which is not totally irrational or unjustified ought to be treated as non-voluntary. That is, the emergency created may be regarded as depriving the third party of rational choice about the outcome, and the result may therefore be attributed causally to the creator of the emergency. This leaves open the possibility of finding that a trained police-officer ought to have acted with greater circumspection towards the hostage on the facts of *Pagett*, if that is a fair judgment on the facts of that case, since the law might justifiably expect more of a trained official than a hapless citizen caught up in extreme events.[94]

(ii) *Conduct of Doctors.* The decision in *Pagett* contains more than a hint that the court was far more concerned about convicting a morally culpable person than about the refinements of causation, and similar leanings may be found in cases involving doctors. There is rarely any doubt that medical intervention may properly be described as 'voluntary': doctors work under pressure, occasionally having to make rapid decisions, but they are trained and trusted to exercise clinical judgment in these circumstances. Perhaps doctors could be regarded as acting under a duty to treat patients, aligning their role with one of the formal reasons in *Pagett*? But the courts have not approached the cases by way of the concept of voluntariness. How have they dealt with cases where D alleges that medical

---

[94] See further Ch. 6.6 below; cf. the arguments of P. A. J. Waddington, '"Overkill" or "Minimum Force"?' [1990] Crim. LR 695, and pp. 120–122 below.

maltreatment of the victim caused the result, thereby negativing D's own causal responsibility?

A distinction has been drawn between cases where the wound inflicted by D remains a substantial and operating cause of death despite the subsequent medical treatment, in which case D remains causally responsible, and those where the original wound becomes merely 'the setting in which another cause operates', in which case D's responsibility is negatived.[95] The reference to an 'operating and substantial' cause might be regarded as more favourable to D than the general principle of causation, unless the term 'substantial', is read as meaning 'more than minimal'. On the other hand, the subsequent conduct of the doctor in treating the victim wrongly is ignored, and no clear reason is offered for discounting the voluntary intervening act of the doctor. If the doctor administers a drug to which the patient is known to be intolerant, or gives some other wrong treatment, should the inappropriateness of the medical treatment affect the causal enquiry? The courts have tended to avoid reasoning of this kind, focusing instead on whether the original wound was healing or not. This reluctance to discuss the causal significance of the medical treatment probably stems from a desire to ensure the conviction of a culpable offender. What is overlooked is that D, who inflicted the original wound which gave rise to the need for medical attention, will still be liable for attempted murder or a serious wounding offence even if the medical treatment is held to negative his causal responsibility for the ensuing death. A court which declares that it is not the doctor who is on trial but the original wrongdoer[96] may be trying to rationalize its failure to apply the ordinary causal principle that a voluntary intervening act which accelerates death should relieve the original wrongdoer of liability for the result. If that causal principle is unsuitable for medical cases, should we not look again at some limited doctrine of clinical medical necessity?[97]

(iii) *Conduct of the Victim.* The general principle that the law approaches causation by considering the effect of an autonomous individual's conduct upon a 'stage already set' is usually taken to extend to cases where the victim has some special condition which makes him or her especially vulnerable. This is sometimes known as the 'thin skull' principle, or the principle that defendants must take

[95] *Smith* [1959] 2 QB 35, distinguishing *Jordan* (1956) 40 Cr. App. R 152.
[96] Per Lord Lane CJ, in *Malcherek* (1981) 73 Cr. App. R 173.
[97] Section 4.8 below.

their victims as they find them. If D commits a minor assault on V, and V, who is a haemophiliac, dies from that assault, the principle applies to render D causally responsible for the death.[98] Now this principle of causation may have little practical effect on its own, since most of the serious criminal offences require proof of *mens rea* (proof that D intended or foresaw the risk of causing, say, serious injury), and it will usually be possible to show that the *mens rea* was lacking because D was unaware of V's special condition. However, in those systems of law which contain some offences of constructive liability (such as manslaughter in English and American law),[99] the 'thin skull' principle reinforces the constructive element by ensuring that there is no causal barrier to convicting D of an offence involving more serious harm than was intended or foreseen. If there is a problem here, it lies with the law of manslaughter rather than with the principles of causation.

What principles should apply to the causal effect of the victim's conduct after D's original act? Should V's conduct be subject to the normal rules of voluntary intervening acts? *Roberts* (1971)[100] was a case in which D, while driving his car, made suggestions to his passenger, making moves to remove her coat, at which point she opened the door and leapt from the moving car, suffering injury. The Court of Appeal upheld D's conviction for assault occasioning actual bodily harm, on the basis that a victim's 'reasonably foreseeable' reaction does not negative causation. Whether 'reasonable foreseeability' is an accurate way of expressing the point in question must be doubted; one might well say that the prospect of the woman jumping from the moving car was relatively unlikely. Surely it would be better to consider the principle of 'alternative danger': D's conduct had placed V in a situation of emergency in which she had to make a rapid choice about how to react. One might then say that any reaction which cannot be regarded as wholly abnormal or 'daft'[101] should remain D's causal responsibility. In this sense, V's reaction is non-voluntary.

What if the victim refuses to accept medical treatment for the injury inflicted by D? The question presented itself starkly in *Blaue* (1975).[102] D stabbed V four times, piercing her lung. V was advised

---

[98] A clear example, on these facts, is the American case of *State v. Frazier* (1936) 98 SW (2d) 707.

[99] See below, Chs. 5.2(*a*) and 7.7.   [100] (1971) 56 Cr. App. R 95.

[101] The word used by Stephenson LJ, ibid. 97.

[102] (1975) 61 Cr. App. R 271.

that she would die from the wounds unless she had a blood transfusion, but, adhering to her faith as a Jehovah's Witness, she
refused to undergo this treatment. She died. The Court of Appeal
held D to be causally responsible for her death. Her intervening
decision not to accept the 'normal' treatment did not negative D's
causal responsibility, because, the court argued, the situation was
analogous to that covered by the 'thin skull' rule. Stating that 'those
who use violence on other people must take their victims as they
find them', the court added that this 'means the whole man [sic], not
just the physical man. It does not lie in the mouth of the assailant to
say that his victim's religious beliefs which inhibited him [sic] from
accepting certain kinds of treatment were unreasonable.'[103] Is this
another example of a court stretching the principles of causation so
as to ensure the conviction of a wrongdoer? The 'thin skull' principle
applies only to pre-existing physical conditions of the victim. The
principle of individual autonomy suggests that, in general, any
subsequent act or omission by V should negative D's causal responsibility. Exceptions to this are where V's subsequent conduct
falls within the 'reasonable foreseeability' notion in *Roberts*[104] or,
perhaps, within the principle of 'alternative danger'. D's actions in
Blaue can certainly be said to have caused a situation of alternative
danger and emergency, and so then the question would be whether
V's reaction should be classified as wholly abnormal. In a statistical,
sense it surely was: it must be rare to refuse a blood transfusion
knowing that death will follow that refusal. But it could be argued
that the standard of normality should be informed by social values
rather than enslaved to statistical frequency, that religious beliefs
are a matter of conscience which should be respected, and therefore
that acts or omissions based on religious conviction should not be
set aside as abnormal.

So whilst it is possible to construct arguments in favour of D's
causal responsibility for the death, this may be more a question of
legalistic ingenuity that social appropriateness. It would have been
possible to convict Blaue of attempted murder or wounding with
intent to cause grievous bodily harm, both offences which carry a
maximum sentence of life imprisonment. There is much sympathy
and respect for the victim, courageously adhering to her religious
beliefs in the face of death, generating the argument that it would
not be appropriate to hold her causally responsible for her own

---

[103] Per Lawton LJ, ibid. 274.   [104] (1971) 56 Cr. App. R 95.

death. Pointing in the same direction is the principle of constructive liability, mentioned by Lawton LJ in *Blaue*,[105] namely, that anyone who does a wrongful act should take the conseqgences. But that principle, which will be discussed in Chapter 5.2(*b*), is relevant to the fault requirement of offences rather than to causation. If it were allowed as a principle of causation, then it would tend to render the original wrongdoer liable for all eventualities, despite the intervention of other voluntary actions. It is surely correct to retain the general principle that the intervening act of a third party will remove or displace the original wrongdoer's causal responsibility, and then to refine the exceptions to that principle. That has been attempted in the previous pages, and the principle of 'alternative danger' has been proposed as a possible approach.

(c) Causing Other Persons to Act

Can it ever be held that one person caused another to act in a certain way? The notion would seem to be inconsistent with the general principle of individual autonomy, emphasized above by reiterating the principle that a voluntary intervening act removes or displaces the previous actor's causal responsibility. Yet we have already noted one case in which a person can be said to cause another to act—the case of innocent agency, where the third party lacks rationality or has been tricked. Further cases arise in the law of complicity, that branch of the criminal law which holds people liable for helping or encouraging others to commit crimes, which will be discussed at length in Chapter 10.

One example of the type of case under discussion is where D goes to P and offers him money to injure or kill V:[106] the law will hold D liable for counselling and procuring P's subsequent offence, and one might say that D *caused* the offence, in some sense. Clearly, however, D did not cause P to act as an innocent agent: P was not, we assume, lacking in rational capacity, and so the general principle of individual autonomy regards P as causally responsible for the result. D cannot, therefore, be held to have caused that result in the usual sense, but one might follow Hart and Honoré in suggesting that D may be said to have 'occasioned' P's offence—in the sense that D provided P with a reason for committing it.[107] This is a dilution of the general approach to causation, aimed specifically at establishing the criminal liability of certain accomplices.

[105] (1975) 61 Cr. App. R 274.   [106] *Calhaem* [1985] QB 808.
[107] Hart and Honoré, *Causation in the Law*, 51.

But it is not only those who 'counsel or procure' who are brought within the English law of accomplice liability. It is also persons who 'aid and abet' others to commit offences. Advice, information, and other acts of assistance and encouragement may be great or small, and may be readily obtainable from others if this would-be accomplice had declined. So, as an element of causal contribution to P's offence, D's 'aiding' may be insignificant indeed—certainly well below the 'but for' threshold, even in the extended sense adopted by the notion of 'occasioning'. Many writers now acknowledge that the element of causation is absent from many cases of 'aiding and abetting', thus establishing one sphere of criminal liability without causation.[108] This does not mean that criminal liability is inappropriate for these persons: indeed, Chapter 10 will argue that there are better ways of ensuring it, by detaching the 'helper's' liability from that of the principal offender and creating a special offence of facilitating crime. But it does warn, at least, that any suggestion that causation is required throughout the criminal law is an exaggeration: at present, accomplices can be held liable for their principal's offence(s) without proof of causation.

4.7. JUSTIFIABLE CONDUCT

Many offences include a qualification such as 'without lawful excuse', 'without lawful authority or reasonable excuse', and so on. We are not concerned here with the different shades of meaning attached to such phrases,[109] nor with the legislature's frequent use of the word 'excuse' to refer to justifications, but rather with some general doctrines which operate as justifications for conduct which would otherwise be criminal. Self-defence is the best known of these justifications, but there are others concerned with the prevention of crime, the arrest of suspected offenders, the protection of property, and so forth. Lawyers frequently speak of these doctrines as defences, e.g. 'the defence of self-defence', but that may lead to a misunderstanding of their place in the criminal law. The theory is that every crime of violence (and probably all other crimes) has the word 'unlawful' implied within its definition. If there is evidence, usually raised by the defendant, that the conduct may have been justifiable,

---

[108] J. C. Smith, 'Aid, Abet, Counsel and Procure', in Glazebrook (ed.), *Reshaping the Criminal Law*; Kadish, *Blame and Punishment*, Ch. 8.

[109] See R. Card, 'Authority and Excuse as Defences to Crime', [1969] Crim. LR 359, 415.

the prosecution bears the burden of proving beyond reasonable doubt that the conduct was *not* justifiable or lawful.[110] Thus, justifiable force is a defence, in the sense that it may lead to an acquittal, but the defendant does not have to establish its elements— the prosecution has to negative them.

(a) Self-Defence and Individual Autonomy

It is hardly surprising that decisions on self-defence formed an important and frequent element in the development of the English common law in days when there was no organized policing and when the carrying of deadly weapons was common. The issues raised by such decisions are fundamental, since they concern the basic right to life and physical safety. An individual who is attacked or threatened with a serious physical attack must be accorded the legal liberty to repel that attack, thus preserving a basic right. A well-regulated society will provide a general protection, but it cannot guarantee protection at the very moment when an individual is subjected to sudden attack. The criminal law cannot respect the autonomy of the individual if it does not provide for this dire situation.

In terms of individual autonomy, one difficulty with this analysis is that these situations involve two individuals (at least). If the law gives the subject of the attack the liberty to wound or kill his aggressor, what happens to the aggressor's right to life and physical safety? One answer to this is that the aggressor forfeits those rights when he embarks on the attack, and that it is his misconduct in starting the conflict which justifies the law in giving preference to the liberty of his victim. This is the approach favoured by some legal systems, which maintain that an innocent person's rights are absolute and which recognize few limitations to those rights, even when that person is repelling a minor assault or defending property.[111] The common law accepted this approach at one time, and elements of it still remain, such as the liberty to defend one's home.[112] But the defect of an approach which allows the subject of an attack to stand fast and use whatever force is necessary to protect his rights of ownership and liberties of passage is that it assumes that the aggressor forfeits all rights when initiating a criminal act. Is this idea

---

[110] Among the many authorities are *Wheeler* (1967) 52 Cr. App. R 28, and *Beckford v. R* [1988] AC 130, at 144.
[111] G. P. Fletcher, *Rethinking Criminal Law* (1978), 862–3.
[112] See below, Ch. 4.7(c) (iii).

of forfeiture appropriate to modern society? Some might argue that it is, since it serves to deter would-be attackers and thereby to promote peace,[113] but that requires empirical proof. Is it not more concerned to vindicate honour than to protect basic rights?

(b) Social Justification and the Balancing of Harms

Rather than viewing cases of self-defence in terms of a conflict between an innocent individual and an aggressor, those cases and others involving justifiable force should be viewed in terms of the preservation of social values in situations of emergency. In Chapter 2 it was argued that life is the most basic value, and that physical violations are also high on the scale of harms.[114] The legal system should therefore be concerned to minimize such harms above all. For this reason there is a general prohibition on the use of force, and this should only be lifted in cases where the State is unable to provide protection (i.e. situations of emergency), and even then only to a limited extent. It is unsatisfactory to argue that the innocent subject of an attack may use whatever force is necessary to vindicate his threatened rights: that analysis assigns no value to the rights of the attacker (since it subscribes to the theory of forfeiture of rights). If the criminal law is committed to ensuring that harms are inflicted as rarely as possible, it cannot accept a vindication approach which seems to allow the infliction of gratuitous, or at least disproportionate, harm. The point is not quite taken in the drafting of the European Convention on Human Rights, article 2 of which provides that 'everyone's right to life shall be protected by law', but it goes on to declare that 'deprivation of life shall not be regarded as inflicted in contravention of this Article when it results from the use of force which is no more than absolutely necessary (a) in defence of any person from unlawful violence . . .'. The requirement of absolute necessity seems restrictive, but there might be cases in which a relatively minor attack could only be prevented by the infliction of a major harm: in that case the infliction of the major harm would be absolutely necessary, but should it be regarded as justifiable? A nineteenth-century Royal Commission remarked that a law whose only requirement was necessity 'would justify every weak lad whose hair was about to be pulled by a stronger one, in shooting the bully if he could not otherwise prevent the assault'.[115] The example is an extreme one, but its point is central.

---

[113] Kadish, *Blame and Punishment*, 117.   [114] See Ch. 2.4 above.
[115] Report of the Royal Commission on the Law Relating to Indictable Offences

The essence of justification lies in the fact that society regards the citizen's conduct as right on that occasion. It is right that a citizen should be at liberty to kill someone who launches a deadly attack upon him or her, it is right that a police-officer or other citizen should be at liberty to use force to apprehend an offender or to prevent a crime. But such conduct is only right if the prevented harm is not significantly less than the inflicted harm. The overall interest in the minimization of harm requires that a balance should be struck. There are those who reply that this is impossible, in view of the variety of circumstances and the suddenness with which they arise in real life. These are important points, but they are practical problems which can be discussed separately.[116] In terms of principle, it would be wrong to support a law which regarded it as justifiable for a police-officer to shoot a person suspected of stealing from a shop, or for a landowner to shoot a walker who was trespassing on his land. The only way to avoid such outcomes is to ensure that the doctrines of justifiable force are grounded firmly in a balancing of harms, a balancing from the point of view of the community at large, not a narrow weighing of the wrongdoing of the aggressor against the innocence or public-spiritedness of his victim.

(c) The Range of Justifications

The development of the common law has focused on self-defence, but there is also authority for the justifiable use of force in a range of other situations. The draft Criminal Code contains a useful statement of six circumstances in which force might be justified.[117] First, 'to prevent or terminate crime, or to effect or assist in the lawful arrest of an offender or suspected offender or of a person unlawfully at large'; second, 'to prevent or terminate a breach of the peace'; third, 'to protect himself or another from unlawful force or unlawful personal harm'—this is self-defence, broadened to cover defensive force in support of another citizen;[118] fourth, 'to prevent or terminate the unlawful detention of himself or another'; fifth, 'to protect property (whether belonging to himself or another) from unlawful appropriation, destruction or damage'; sixth, 'to prevent or terminate

---

(1879, C. 2345), note B, at 44; see p. 11 of the report for an assertion of the principle that 'the mischief done by, or which might reasonably be anticipated from, the force used is not disproportioned to the injury or mischief which it is intended to prevent'.

[116] See below, sections 4.7(c) (iii) and (iv).
[117] Law Com. No. 177, clause 44.
[118] See *Duffy* [1967] 1 QB 63, and *Devlin v. Armstrong* [1971] NI 13.

a trespass to his person or property'. It is obvious that the amount of physical force which may justifiably be inflicted on another in pursuit of any one of these purposes may vary considerably; much may turn on the purpose which D was pursuing when the force was used. But that variation of circumstances is not enough to warrant variation in the legal standard of justifiable force. At present, English law maintains two different standards: for the justifiable use of force in the protection of personal safety it requires reasonableness and necessity; whereas for the justifiable damaging of another's property it requires only that D believed that 'the means of protection adopted . . . would be reasonable having regard to all the circumstances'.[119] The latter rule is more indulgent to the defendant, and, indeed, it hardly embodies a legal standard at all. One feature of the draft Criminal Code is that it would abolish the special rule for property damage.

(d) The Rules and the Principles

A precise statement of English law on the justifications is difficult to locate. Section 3 of the Criminal Law Act 1967 states that 'a person may use such force as is reasonable in the circumstances in the prevention of crime . . .'. The section was not intended to supplant the common-law rules on self-defence,[120] and the courts have continued to develop those rules. It is true that in most situations of self-defence it could be said that the person was preventing crime (i.e. preventing an attack which constituted a crime), but that would still leave certain cases untouched—notably, attacks by a child under 10, by a mentally disordered person, or by a person labouring under a mistake of fact. Such aggressors would commit no offence, and so it is the law of self-defence, not the prevention of crime, which governs.

The law of self-defence, as it is applied by the courts, turns on two requirements: the force must have been necessary, and it must have been reasonable. In dealing with particular cases, however, the courts have, as we shall see, reached decisions which suggest certain sub-rules, but they have generally been reluctant to refer to them as such, preferring to make use of the broad flexibility of the concept of reasonableness. This indicates that the principle of maximum certainty is not followed in the English law on justifiable force.[121]

---

[119] Criminal Damage Act 1971, s. 5(2).
[120] A. Ashworth, 'Self-Defence and the Right to Life' [1975] CLJ 272, at 285.
[121] See above, Ch. 3.3(i).

Both the legislation and judicial decisions prefer to state the law in terms of what is 'reasonable' or 'reasonable and necessary'. It may be argued that this derogation from maximum certainty is not a serious matter; people who are attacked suddenly are unlikely to have time to reflect on the provisions of the criminal law before defending themselves. This argument is correct only on its own terms: people who are attacked suddenly may well respond without reflection,[122] but many cases in which justifiable force is raised concern either an expected attack or action by trained law enforcement officers. Moreover, legal certainty is important from the point of view of producing consistent and principled court decisions, as well as guiding the conduct of citizens. The approach of the draft Criminal Code in seeking to articulate some distinct principles and sub-rules is therefore to be welcomed.[123] The enactment of several sub-rules does not deprive courts of the flexibility to respond to new sets of circumstances, since the overall legal standards of reasonableness and necessity remain. The sub-rules merely deal with some recurrent issues which should be determined by principles rather than dealt with in an *ad hoc* fashion.

(c) The Proportionality Standard

The requirement that the use of force must be necessary should be limited, as it is in English law, by a further requirement that it must be reasonable in the circumstances. This flows directly from the notion that the doctrine of justifiable force requires a balancing of harms. The standard cannot be a precise one: probably the best way of defining it is in terms of what is reasonably proportionate to the amount of harm likely to be suffered by the defendant, or likely to result if the forcible intervention is not made. What is crucial is that it should rule out the use of considerable force to apprehend a fleeing thief, to stop a stolen car, etc. For offences against the person, it means that deadly force should only be justified for a life-threatening attack and, perhaps, for certain crimes of extreme seriousness. The American Model Penal Code provides that deadly force is not justified 'unless the actor believes that such force is necessary to protect himself against death, serious bodily harm, kidnapping or sexual intercourse compelled by force or threat'.[124] It

---

[122] See below, section 4.7(g).
[123] Law Com. No. 177, clause 44 and ii, paras. 12.24–12.37; for detailed argument in favour of this approach, see Ashworth, 'Self-Defence and the Right to Life'.
[124] Model Penal Code, section 3.04.

is debatable whether this goes too far in allowing the lawful sacrifice of a life to prevent certain non-fatal assaults, although actual cases of this kind may present great problems.[125] The reason for inserting the provision, however, was to try to narrow down the permissible use of force in a country which has often given primary weight to the autonomy of the subject of the attack and has therefore accepted deadly force with few limitations.

One aspect of the proportionality principle might be the limitation on the use of force against police-officers. A general provision covering the use of force to prevent false imprisonment might be thought to justify a citizen in using force to prevent the police from making an arrest which he or she knows to be mistaken. In fact, English law renders an arrest lawful if the police-officer has reasonable grounds for suspicion. There are English decisions which draw a distinction between resisting lawful—but mistaken—arrest (which is not justified), and repelling the unlawful use of violence by police (which is justified),[126] and this principle is to be found both in the Model Penal Code and the draft Criminal Code.[127] The point provides a good illustration of the difference between an autonomy-based system, which judges conflicts between individuals by reference to the culpability of those involved, and a more community-based approach, which considers the rights of the individuals in the light of a social ranking of harms and of the need for law enforcement. If one accepts that the police should be empowered to act on 'reasonable suspicion', then that should rule out the use of defensive force either by the suspect or by others acting on his or her behalf. There should be an accessible and effective mechanism for challenging police decisions through the civil courts or, where appropriate, through police disciplinary procedures, but there remains some reason for the criminal law to adopt a strict approach here.

(f) Aspects of the Necessity Requirement

The necessity requirement forms part of most legal regimes on justifiable force. The first question to be asked is: necessary for what? We have seen that force may be justified for any one of several lawful purposes. The necessity must be judged according to the lawful purpose which the defendant was trying to pursue: for

---

[125] J. C. Smith, *Justification and Excuse in the Criminal Law* (1989), 109 and Ch. 4, *passim*.
[126] *Fennell* [1971] 1 QB 428; *Ball* [1989] Crim. LR 579.
[127] Model Penal Code, s. 3.04(2)(a)(i); Law Com. No. 177, clause 44(4).

self-defence, purely defensive force will often be all that is necessary; in order to apprehend a suspected offender, on the other hand, a police-officer or citizen will need to behave proactively. These differences may become particularly important in cases where there is a suspicion or allegation that the force was used by way of revenge or retaliation rather than in pursuit of a lawful purpose. What was the defendant's purpose? Could the conduct be said to be necessary for that purpose?

It is in the sphere of necessity that the English courts have continued to develop the common law. A number of issues have been presented for decision.

(i) *Imminence*. It has been stated that the use of force can only be necessary if the attack is imminent or immediate.[128] Presumably the reasoning is that, if there is time to warn the police, then that is the course which should be taken, in preference to the use of force by a private individual. But this does not mean that it is unlawful to prepare or keep armaments for an anticipated attack. In the *Attorney-General's Reference (No. 2 of 1983)*[129] D's shop had been looted during rioting which the police had struggled to control; D made some petrol bombs, with which to repel any future attack, and the question was whether these were in his possession 'for a lawful object'. It was held that they were, if the jury accepted that D intended to use them only against an attack on his premises which the police could not control. Given the unusual circumstances of this case, this was an understandable extension of the concept of imminence: situations might arise in which the police would not be able to offer protection, and this chimes well with the rationale for justifiable force. But there are likely to be few situations in which objects so lethal as fire-bombs would be held to be a lawful means of defending property, as opposed to defending a home or human beings. This decision also leaves unresolved a problem about the lawfulness of carrying a gun or an offensive weapon in order to repel an anticipated attack: the authorities would seem to suggest that, although the use of the weapon might be lawful if an attack takes place, its possession beforehand remains an offence.[130]

(ii) *A Duty to Avoid Conflict?* One of the most technical but most significant elements in the common law of self-defence was the duty

---

[128] e.g. *Attorney-General for Northern Ireland's Reference* [1977] AC 105; *Chisam* (1963) 47 Cr. App. R 130. [129] [1984] QB 456.
[130] See Ashworth, 'Self-Defence and the Right to Life', 297–8, and Smith, *Justification and Excuse*, 117–23.

to retreat. Its technicality lay in its careful wording and its exceptions; its significance was that, from an early stage, the common law recognized limitations on the primacy of individual autonomy in these situations. The duty has now disappeared as such. In *Julien* (1969)[131] it was rephrased as a duty to demonstrate an unwillingness to fight, 'to temporise and disengage and perhaps to make some physical withdrawal'. In *Bird* (1985)[132] the Court of Appeal accepted that the imposition of a 'duty' is too strong. The key question is whether D was acting in self-defence or in revenge or retaliation. Evidence that D tried to retreat or to call off the fight might negative a suggestion of revenge, but it is not the only way of doing so. The modification of the law seems to derive from the suggestion in Smith and Hogan's textbook that the 'duty' as described in *Julien* is inconsistent with the liberty to make a preemptive strike.[133] It is not. The liberty to make a pre-emptive strike can easily be cast as an exception to the general duty to avoid conflict, and, as such, it is no more inconsistent with the rule than any other exception to a rule. The difficulty with regarding the duty to avoid conflict as merely one consideration to be borne in mind here is that it says nothing about the circumstances which might outweigh it. If the law is seriously to pursue the minimization of physical violation, it should at least state that the avoidance of conflict is in general the primary consideration.

(iii) *Protection of the Home.* One long-standing exception to the duty to retreat is that a person attacked at home has no duty to withdraw. This may be regarded as one remaining bastion of the autonomy-based view, regarding the individual's home as sacrosanct. Undoubtedly many citizens feel this way about their homes today, but there are two questions to be resolved. One is whether the use of force is reasonable in defence of one's home: there are several cases in which a firearm has been used to repel invaders, which raises questions about proportionality of harms.[134] The second question is whether an exception to the duty to avoid conflict should be recognised here: *should* there be any obligation to retreat if a person enters one's home unlawfully, manifesting an intent to steal property or to carry out an eviction? It could be argued that the autonomy argument should reassert itself here, combined with the

---

[131] [1969] 1 WLR 839.   [132] [1985] 1 WLR 816.

[133] J. C. Smith and B. Hogan, *Criminal Law*, (5th edn., 1983), 327, quoted by the Court of Appeal in *Bird* [1985] 1 WLR 816.

[134] D. J. Lanham, 'Defence of Property in the Criminal Law' [1966] Crim. LR 368, 426; and Smith, *Justification and Excuse*, 109–12.

value of privacy which extends to a person's home. This is not to deny that the balance may be a difficult one, for whilst it might be argued that the home is fundamental whereas a car is less so, there might well be several intermediate forms of property (business premises, a family heirloom) which cannot be classified so easily. But these may be regarded as questions of proportionality. The present question is whether there should be any duty to avoid conflict by withdrawing from one's home, and the answer should surely be not.

(iv) *Freedom of Movement*. English law also recognizes an exception to the duty to avoid conflict (if such a duty exists) in those cases where D is acting lawfully in remaining at, or going to, a place, realizing that there is a risk that someone will force a violent confrontation there. The authority for this is *Field* (1972),[135] where D was warned that some men were coming to attack him. D stayed where he was, the men came and made their attack, and in the ensuing struggle D stabbed one of them fatally. The Court of Appeal quashed his conviction, holding that he had no duty to avoid conflict until his attackers were present and had started to threaten him. The American case of *State v. Bristol* (1938)[136] takes the point further holding that D had no duty to avoid entering a bar where he knew his adversary (who had threatened him with attack) to be drinking. The American court declined to lay down a rule which might 'encourage bullies to stalk about the land and terrorize citizens by their mere threats'. These two decisions promote the value of freedom of movement above any duty to avoid conflict in advance. There are strong arguments in the opposite direction: should not the minimization of physical violation take precedence over mere freedom of movement? Is there not some analogy with omissions to assist in saving life, where a citizen's general liberty should also be outweighed by a specific social duty?[137] These remarks concern self-defence and the defence of property only; clearly, a person who acts with the purpose of preventing crime or arresting a suspected offender cannot be expected to avoid conflict, and is governed rather by the proportionality standard.

(v) *Pre-Emptive Strike*. The use of force in self-defence may be justifiable as a pre-emptive strike, when an unlawful attack is imminent.[138] This is a desirable rule, since the rationale for self-

---

[135] [1972] Crim. LR 435.
[136] (1938) 53 Wyo. 304. [137] See above, section 4.3.
[138] e.g. *Beckford v. R* [1988] AC 130, at 144.

defence involves the protection of an innocent citizen's vital interests (life, physical security), and it would be a nonsense if the citizen was obliged to wait until the first blow was struck. The liberty to make a pre-emptive strike is not inconsistent with a duty to avoid conflict (if it were recognized), but it should be read as being subject to that duty. In other words, it would be possible and desirable to have a law which imposed a general obligation to avoid conflict but, where this was not practical, authorized a pre-emptive strike.[139] A law which allows pre-emptive strikes without any general duty to avoid conflict runs the risk, as Dicey put it, of overstimulating self-assertion.[140]

(vi) *Necessity and Law Enforcement.* The point has already been made that a police-officer or citizen whose purpose is to prevent a crime or to apprehend an offender must behave proactively, and that the primary legal restriction on such conduct is the standard of proportionality. How serious an offence was being or had been committed? Is there a real danger of further offending? If there is to be a social policy of the minimization of force, it would seem to follow that any person pursuing such a purpose should not use force unless necessary, and should then use as little as possible. This is most clearly applicable to the use of force to prevent theft, or to arrest someone for minor criminal damage, or for taking a car without consent. It can be argued, however, that any policy of minimal force is not really practical. Increasingly, the police are issued with firearms; they are instructed to open fire only in conditions which would justify killing. Should they then shoot to kill, or try only to wound and disable? The policy of minimal force would suggest the latter, but in practice there are difficulties: (i) if the other person is armed, any failure to incapacitate totally may leave the opportunity for a gun to be fired or explosive to be detonated, resulting in the loss of innocent life; and (ii) it is far more difficult to shoot at and hit legs and arms than to shoot at and hit the torso, again making failure and the loss of innocent life more probable.[141] This argument, if sustained, might lead to the paradox that, in order to achieve minimal injury and loss of life, it would be best to shoot to kill as soon as the danger to life becomes apparent.

---

[139] See note 133 above, and accompanying text.
[140] A. V. Dicey, *Law of the Constitution* (8th edn., 1915), 489.
[141] Waddington, '"Overkill" or "Minimum Force"?'

(g) Justifiable Force and the Emotions

The numbered paragraphs in the previous section have considered principles which might produce consistent and socially acceptable outcomes in those varied situations in which a claim of justifiable force might arise. Some might regard those principles as too mechanical for the sudden and confused nature of many such situations. It is well known that a sudden threat to one's physical safety may lead to strong emotions of fear and panic, producing physiological changes which take the individual out of his or her 'normal self'.[142] According to this view, the most just law is the simplest: was the use of force an innocent and instinctive reaction, or was it the product of revenge or some manifest fault?

This simple approach may have the great advantage of recognizing explicitly the role of the emotions in these cases. It is surely right to exclude revenge attacks from the ambit of justifiable force.[143] It is also consistent with the doctrine of prior fault in construing the standards of reasonableness and necessity strictly against someone whose own fault originally caused the show of violence.[144] But how much indulgence should be granted to the innocent victim of sudden attack who reacts instinctively with strong force? In the leading case of *Palmer* (1971)[145] Lord Morris stated that it is 'most potent evidence' of reasonableness that the defendant only did what he or she 'honestly and instinctively thought necessary'. But it cannot be right for absolutely any reaction 'in a moment of unexpected anguish' to be held to be justifiable,[146] even if it is right for the courts to consider 'how the circumstances in which the accused had time to make his decision whether or not to use force and the shortness of the time available to him for reflection, might affect the judgment of a reasonable man'.[147] To the extent that in these cases the law moves away from objective standards towards indulgence to the emotions of innocent citizens, the rationale of justification becomes diluted by elements of excuse. This is also true of mistakes: when a

---

[142] For summaries of the scientific evidence on this point, see H. Grossman, *Physiological Psychology* (1967), 500–15, and, more descriptively, M. D. Vernon, *Human Motivation* (1969), Ch. 4.

[143] Cf. excessive force in manslaughter, discussed in Ch. 7.7 below.

[144] See Ashworth, 'Self-Defence and the Right to Life', 300, for references, and the draft Criminal Code (Law Com. No. 177), clause 44(6); the doctrine of prior fault is assessed in Ch. 5.2(e) below.

[145] [1971] AC 814, at 832.   [146] L. H. Leigh (1971) 34 MLR 685.

[147] Per Lord Diplock, in *Attorney-General for Northern Ireland's Reference* [1977] AC 105.

defendant misunderstands the situation (for example, by mistakenly believing V to be armed, or erroneously believing that V is about to strike), the law is that D should be judged as if the facts were as he or she believed them to be. These examples are discussed separately, as cases of excuse, in Chapter 6.6. But where D misjudges the amount of force which is reasonable or necessary, this is a mistake of law rather than of fact, and yet, in contrast to the strict approach to mistakes of law,[148] the courts have granted the wide indulgence signalled in *Palmer* towards the instincts of the innocent.

The fairness of this concession to what Blackstone termed 'the passions of the human mind'[149] is often supported by reference to the famous dictum of Holmes J, namely, that 'detached reflection cannot be demanded in the presence of an uplifted knife'.[150] This dictum is significant for its limited application: it concerns cases of an 'uplifted knife', i.e. typically, sudden and grave threats or attacks; it has no application to cases where the attack is known to be imminent and the defendant has time to consider his position. Nor should it necessarily be conclusive in relation to those who are trained to deal with extreme situations, such as the police and the army. As the element of sudden and unrehearsed emergency recedes, the social interest in the minimal use of force becomes a firmer precept again. In this type of situation, the law ought to give consideration to the relative importance of the sanctity of life and the physical safety of all persons, including offenders, when compared with such other interests as the free movement of citizens. The aphorism about the 'uplifted knife' should not be used to prevent principled discussion of cases to which it does not apply.

4.8. JUSTIFICATIONS, NECESSITY AND THE BALANCE OF INTERESTS

The discussion so far has focussed on self-defence and the justifications relating to law enforcement and the prevention of crime. Little has been said specifically about the use of force in defence of property,[151] although it might be expected that the proportionality requirements would be more strictly enforced in such cases. The extent to which English law justifies the use of force by a parent

---

[148] Ch. 6.7 below.   [149] *Commentaries on the Laws of England*, iii. 3–4.
[150] *Brown v. United States* (1921) 256 US 335, at 343.
[151] See Lanham, 'Defence of Property'.

when chastising a child is unclear in modern times,[152] but it is often mentioned in this context. Any underlying social justification, in these and other situations, should derive from a balancing of values and harms, not from an assertion of individual privacy or absolute freedom from molestation. If such balancing underlies the justifications for force already considered, might it not also be relevant to the defences of duress or necessity and in cases of medical necessity?

(a) Necessity as a Justification

English law contains limited defences of duress and necessity, which apply when a person commits an otherwise criminal act under threat or fear of death or serious harm. The law on this point is examined in a later chapter,[153] where it will become apparent that much of the argument about the ambit of the defences (especially in the courts) is ambivalent or even indiscriminate as to whether their basis lies in justification (it was right to use this force in the circumstances) or in excuse (it was wrong to use this force, but the defendant was not culpable). However, in rejecting duress as a defence to murder, the House of Lords held in *Howe* (1987)[154] that, even if D's own life is threatened, it cannot be justifiable to take another innocent life. The exclusion of duress from murder cases is therefore grounded in the absence of social justification. Whatever the weaknesses of this way of resolving the problem of choosing between two autonomous and 'innocent' lives,[155] the argument fails to cover those cases where the taking of one life will save two or more other lives. A recent example of this emerged from the inquest into the deaths caused by the sinking of the ferry *Herald of Free Enterprise*.[156] At one stage of the disaster several passengers were trying to gain access to the ship's deck by ascending a rope-ladder. On that ladder there was a young man, petrified, unable to move up or down. People were shouting at him, but he did not move. Eventually it was suggested that he should be pushed off the ladder, and this was done. He fell into the water and was never seen again, but several other passengers escaped up the ladder to safety. No English court has had to consider this situation,[157] and it is clear that only the

---

[152] *Hopley* (1860) 2 F&F 202.
[153] See below, Ch. 6.4.
[154] [1987] AC 417.
[155] See below, Ch. 6.4(*a*).
[156] Smith, *Justification and Excuse*, 73–9.
[157] Cf. *Dudley and Stephens* (1884). 14 QBD 273, the case in which two men saved themselves by killing and eating the weakest member of a threesome who had been

strongest Kantian prohibition on the taking of an innocent life would prevent a finding of justification here: in an urgent situation involving a decision between n lives and $n + 1$ lives, there is surely a strong social interest in preserving the greater number of lives. Naturally, the principle must be carefully circumscribed; it involves the sanctity of life, and therefore the highest value with which the criminal law is concerned. Although the provision in the Model Penal Code allows for a defence of 'lesser evil',[158] it fails to restrict the application of the defence to cases of imminent threat, opening up the danger of citizens trying to justify all manner of conduct by reference to overall good effects. This raises the moral problem of 'choosing one's victim', a problem which arises when, for example, a lifeboat is in danger of sinking, necessitating the throwing over-board of some passengers,[159] or when two people have to kill and eat another if any of the three is to survive.[160] To countenance a legal justification in such cases would be to regard the victim's rights as morally and politically less worthy than the rights of those protected by the action taken, which is clearly objectionable on a theory of individual rights. Yet it is surely necessary to make some sacrifice: a dire choice has to be made, and at least a fair method of resolving the problem must be chosen. But here, as with self-defence and the problem of 'uplifted knife' cases,[161] one should not obscure the clearer cases where there is no need to choose a victim: in the case of the young man on the rope-ladder, blocking the escape of several others, there was no doubt about the person who must be subjected to force, probably with fatal consequences.

(b) Medical Necessity

Is it ever a justification for a doctor to act contrary to the letter of the law 'in the best interests of the patient'? There has been little direct discussion of this by the courts or the legislature. The summing-up in *Bourne* (1939)[162] is sometimes cited as authority that a doctor

adrift in a boat for many days; but they were rescued the following day, and some have questioned the necessity of their act. See A. W. B. Simpson, *Cannibalism and the Common Law* (1984), and below, Ch. 6.4(a).

[158] Model Penal Code, s. 3.02; cf. G. P. Fletcher, *Rethinking Criminal Law* (1978), 788–98.

[159] *United States v. Holmes* (1842) 26 Fed. Cas. 360.

[160] *Dudley and Stephens* (1884) 14 QBD 273.

[161] See *Brown v. United States* (1921) 256 US 335, and the text accompanying n. 151 above.

[162] [1939] 1 KB 687.

may contravene the law (here, carry out an abortion) if it is necessary to save the life of the patient, but that particular area of the law is now subject to express statutory provisions.[163] More common in recent times has been the acceptance of 'concealed defences' of medical necessity, by means of stretching established concepts.[164] For example, we saw how Devlin J in the *Adams* trial modified the general proposition that any acceleration of death satisfies the conduct element for unlawful homicide.[165] And the next chapter will show how the House of Lords in *Gillick v. West Norfolk and Wisbech Area Health Authority* (1986)[166] deviated from the general proposition that intention includes foresight of virtual certainty. In both decisions the point was to produce a defence for a doctor who acted in the 'best interests' of the patient. The courts lacked the courage to develop a new ground of justification, even though the case of *Bourne* might have provided a starting-point, and chose instead to create special exceptions to established principles, for doctors actuated by sound clinical motives. This approach is not only juristically clumsy, in casting doubt on established doctrines of causation and intention,[167] but it also has the effect of suppressing open discussion about the proper limits of justification based on medical necessity and clinical judgment.

This chapter has dealt with a number of somewhat disparate issues relevant to criminal conduct. It began by considering the problems of establishing agency, looking at the principle of autonomy, at corporate liability, and subsequently at the concept of voluntary action; also discussed in this connection were the principles of causation. It has also dealt with some of the features of the kind of conduct typically specified in offences, such as the alleged preference for penalizing acts, and the supposed aversion to penalizing states of affairs or omissions. The latter parts of the chapter have examined the idea of justification, which may render lawful the infliction of harms which would otherwise be unlawful.

---

[163] Abortion Act 1967.   [164] Smith, *Justification and Excuse*, 64–70.

[165] See above, section 4.6 at n. 86; see also the 'medical' exception to the principle that a voluntary intervening human act negatives causal responsibility, in section 4.6(b) (ii) above.

[166] [1986] AC 112, discussed in Ch. 5.3(b).

[167] A further example is the manipulation of the act–omission distinction by courts and writers in relation to the treatment of dying persons by doctors and nurses: see Ashworth, 'The Scope of Criminal Liability for Omissions', 437, and Kennedy, *Treat me Right*, 167–74.

The full significance of the issues discussed in this chapter will not become apparent until Chapters 5 and 6, and some of the issues' reappear later in the book, but two points may be signalled at this stage. First, this chapter has provided ample evidence of the importance, in shaping the criminal law, of conflicts between an individualistic conception of autonomy and a broader social conception of co-operation and responsibility towards others. For example, even in relation to the principle of voluntary action—the veritable sanctum of individual autonomy—there are the marks of community-based limitations where the rules on insanity, intoxication and prior fault impinge. Similar conflicts are found in the legislative and judicial approaches to liability for omissions, and in the slow development of corporate criminal liability. Even in the justifications for force, the strong individualism which favours the 'innocent' defendant has occasionally come into conflict with the underlying social rationale for minimum force in these situations. A second general point is that most of the doctrines considered yield, at crucial junctures, to malleable terminology which leaves considerable discretion to those who apply the law. This is at its plainest with the ubiquitous term 'reasonable' in the justifications, although there is now evidence of a more closely principled approach. Discretion is also conceded by the proposition that the boundaries of omissions liability and of vicarious liability are governed by the interpretation of particular words in statutes, by various concepts in the sphere of causation (e.g. *de minimis*, 'voluntary'), and by such notions as prior fault and 'external factor' in automatism. The presence of these open-ended terms does not empty the rules of their significance, but it raises doubts about the law's commitment to the values upheld by the principle of maximum certainty outlined in Chapter 3.3 (*j*) above.

5
POSITIVE FAULT
REQUIREMENTS

5.1. THE ISSUES

Once it has been established that D is causally responsible for the act, omission, or state of affairs specified in the definition of an offence, it must also be shown that he fulfilled the fault requirements for the offence. It should not be assumed that there is a single fault requirement for each offence: the point may be illustrated by referring to the several different elements in the abduction offence contrary to section 20 of the Sexual Offences Act 1956, which consists of taking—without lawful authority or excuse—an unmarried girl under 16 out of the possession of her parent or guardian against his or her will. Clarity is assisted by analysing crimes such as these in terms of their separate elements rather than of a single *actus reus*, and then ascertaining what form of fault is required for each of these different elements.[1] The discussion in this chapter is confined to the positive fault requirements, in other words, the mental attitude specified in (or implied within) the offence—typically, intention, knowledge, and recklessness. Chapter 6 will discuss the negative fault requirements; these are not fault elements which the prosecution has to prove in every case, but various doctrines which suggest the absence of fault and which the prosecution has to negative (generally speaking) if they are raised by D. Thus, the fault elements involved in criminal liability go beyond the so-called mental elements required for each particular offence and extend to a range of other elements, each of which is assumed to be absent unless D adduces some evidence to the contrary.

The general approach of modern English text-writers has been to assert that subjective guilt should be proved in each case, and that therefore crimes should require proof of D's intention, knowledge, or recklessness. The orthodoxy is to criticize crimes of negligence

---

[1] P. H. Robinson and J. Grall, 'Element Analysis in Defining Criminal Liability: The Model Penal Code and Beyond' (1983) 35 *Stanford LR* 681.

and, even more powerfully, crimes of strict liability for their departure from these standard requirements. The courts, on the other
hand, have tended to pursue more variable approaches, upholding
subjective principles on some occasions and giving way to objective
or 'public policy' arguments on others. One of the aims of this
chapter and Chapter 6 is to examine the foundations of these
various approaches and to attempt to disentangle some of the
principles which are at play beneath the banner of 'subjective
liability' and some of the policies claimed to be in the 'public
interest'.

5.2. SOME GENERAL PRINCIPLES

(a) Choice and the Subjective Principles

What might be termed 'subjective' principles have had a considerable effect on criminal-law scholarship and on the form of English
criminal law. The implication of these principles, sometimes summarized as 'the doctrine of *mens rea*', is that criminal liability should
be imposed only on persons who are sufficiently aware of what they
are doing, and of the consequences it might have, that they can
fairly be said to have *chosen* the behaviour and its consequences.
The element of choice is grounded in the liberal theory of individual
rights, as developed by such writers as Hart and Dworkin.[2] Individuals are regarded as autonomous persons with a general capacity
to choose from alternative courses of behaviour, and they are
entitled to equal concern and respect in exercising that capacity. By
regarding them as criminally liable only when they can be said to
have chosen a particular act or consequence, and by ensuring that
any punishment is in proportion to that choice, the criminal law
would ensure that 'each person is guaranteed a greatest liberty,
capacity and opportunity of controlling and predicting the consequences of his or her actions compatible with a like liberty,
capacity and opportunity for all'.[3] What this liberal view rejects is
an approach which holds people criminally liable solely on the
ground that liability and punishment would have a general deterrent
effect in preventing further harms. That approach, associated with

[2] See H. L. A. Hart, *Punishment and Responsibility* (1968), Chs. 2 and 5, and
R. M. Dworkin, *Taking Rights Seriously* (1977), Ch. 1.
[3] D. A. J. Richards, 'Rights, Utility and Crime', in M. Tonry and N. Morris
(eds.), *Crime and Justice: An Annual Review*, iii (1981), 274.

utilitarian theories,[4] looks to the probable social effects of liability and punishment, denying the individual defendant any special status in the matter: if the punishment of people in D's position would have an overall deterrent effect, then D should be punished, even though he or she cannot be said to have *chosen* to cause the harm. Liberal theories, on the other hand, regard respect for the autonomy of each individual citizen as capable of overriding general calculations of social utility—especially in relation to criminal liability and punishment, with its condemnatory elements.

What it means to describe these liberal theories as 'subjective' is that they place the emphasis on the viewpoint of the individual defendant: criminal liability should, in principle, be grounded in, and linked to, the choice and control of that person. Only in those circumstances does D deserve conviction. This yields what we may term 'the principle of *mens rea*' and 'the belief principle'.[5] The principle of *mens rea* is that defendants should only be held criminally liable for events or consequences which they intended or knowingly risked. This ties liability to awareness of possible consequences; at a minimum, it requires a fault element of either intention or (subjective) recklessness. This ensures that defendants may be said to have chosen to cause, or to risk causing, the outcome, and rejects liability for events or consequences when defendants were unaware of the possibility of their occurrence. Similarly, according to the belief principle, criminal liability is established on the basis of what defendants *believed* they were doing or risking, not on the basis of actual facts which were not known to them at the time. Once again, the emphasis is upon the element of choice in what D actually thought was, or might be, the true situation. The principle of *mens rea* looks to D's awareness of the possible consequence of the act or omission; the belief principle looks to D's awareness of the circumstances at the time of the act or omission.

A third principle, closely connected with the principle of *mens rea* and the belief principle, is what we will term 'the principle of correspondence': the fault element for a crime should correspond to the conduct element in that crime. Thus, if the conduct element is 'causing serious injury', then the fault element ought to be 'intention

---

[4] For discussion, see K. Greenawalt, 'Punishment', in S. Kadish (ed.), *Encyclopaedia of Crime and Punishment* (1984), and J. Bentham, *Introduction to the Principles of Morals and Legislation* (1789).

[5] See further, A. Ashworth, 'Belief, Intent and Criminal Liability', in J. Eekelaar and J. Bell (eds.), *Oxford Essays in Jurisprudence: Third Series* (1987), 1.

or recklessness as to causing serious injury'; a lesser fault element, such as 'intention or recklessness as to a mere assault', would breach the principle of correspondence. The important point here is that the fundamental notion of choice is not an abstract phenomenon, but should in principle be linked to the circumstances or consequences specified in the definition of the crime.

The aim of these three subjective principles is therefore to heighten the relationship between criminal liability and the defendant's choices, thereby reducing the effect of chance and luck. Value is placed on the ability to predict one's liabilities as a factor which shows respect for, and maximizes, individual autonomy.

(b) 'Desert' and Resulting Harm

The subjective principles sketched above may be linked to the idea of deserved punishments outlined in Chapter 1.4. The argument would be that people only deserve criminal liability and punishment when, and to the extent that, they *choose* to engage in certain conduct or to cause certain consequences: liability for unforeseen consequences stands as a prime example of undeserved punishment. There are, however, other ways of applying the rationale of 'desert' to the question of criminal liability. One way is to argue that it should be influenced more by the actual consequences than by the mental state of the defendant at the time. This need not be an argument in favour of universal strict liability for harm caused: a more sophisticated version, which has shaped various rules of English law over the centuries, is that anyone who knowingly commits an offence against another's interests should be held liable for all the consequences. This doctrine has a Latin tag, *versari in re illicita*,[6] but it is more recognizable here as the principle of constructive liability. Its most powerful manifestation was the felony-murder rule, which rendered anyone who caused death whilst committing a felony liable for the murder of his victim, even though the death was accidental. The felony-murder rule was abolished in England in 1957, but it remains law in many American states.[7] Its spirit survives in modern English law in the law of manslaughter: if D commits a criminal offence which produces a risk of some harm to another person, and death results from that offence, the crime may

[6] J. Hall, *General Principles of Criminal Law* (2nd edn., 1960), 6.
[7] For discussion, see P. Robinson, *Fundamentals of Criminal Law* (1989), Ch. 9, and Crump and Crump, 'In Defence of the Felony Murder Doctrine' (1985) 8 Harv. JLPP 359.

be manslaughter. This is so, even though D merely intended to commit a minor assault, and the victim, by chance, fell awkwardly. The law of manslaughter takes the criminal intention or reckless-ness (as to a minor offence), couples it with the harm caused (which is major), and constructs liability for a serious offence. Even though the sentence may be relatively light,[8] the label (manslaughter) is serious. The doctrine may be supported by arguing that, though the death may be accidental, it is a direct result of D's fault in committing the minor crime, and so D should bear the legal responsibility for it. But this goes too far: if the fault in committing minor crimes is so great, why not regard them all as serious because of their potential to cause death? Surely one can separate D's fault in committing the minor crime from the accidental consequence of death?[9] One response to this might be that it is the significance of death which is crucial here: life is valued so highly that a person who destroys it in these circumstances should be labelled accordingly. A similar approach is taken to the offence of causing death by reckless driving, which differs from reckless driving only in respect of an outcome which may be regarded as a matter of chance,[10] but which it is thought symbolically important to mark. Constructive liability may also be found in lesser offences against the person, as we shall see in Chapter 8.3(c) and (d) below. The principle of constructive liability is in direct conflict with the principle of correspondence, and runs counter to the notion of individual choice which underlies all three subjective principles. Whether elements of constructive liability are justifiable where the harm resulting is serious remains open to debate. There are those who would argue that an important social function of the law is to denounce the causing of such harms by the use of constructive liability and, more especially, that to move away from a law which has long embodied this form of denunciation might be regarded as reducing the law's concern for these serious harms. The argument is unacceptable, in that it neglects the importance of 'desert', proportionality, and fair labelling in the structure of offences, but it does point to a real political problem in the symbolism which may attach to legal reforms.

---

[8] But see e.g. *Hughes* (1988) 10 Cr. App. R(S) 169, for a strong example of the aggravating effect on sentence of accidental death following an assault; the relevant law is discussed in Chapter 7.5(a).

[9] See L. L. Weinreb, 'Desert, Punishment and Criminal Responsibility' (1986) 49 *L&CP* (No. 3), 64–7.

[10] See the discussion of causing death by reckless driving, Ch. 7.6 below.

(c) Policies of Social Defence

The philosophical basis of the three subjective principles seems to lie in Kant's famous principle that no person should be treated as a means only, but as an end in himself or herself.[11] Yet, careful attention to that principle demonstrates how individualistic, even atomistic, are the assumptions implicit in the liberal theory which underlies the subjective principles. It seems to be assumed that individuals should never suffer disadvantages or coercive measures for the good of society as a whole. Would this rule out taxation? Of course, there is a line of argument which reasons that we choose to be taxed—and, indeed, to be punished for offences—in the sense that we choose to remain in the country and therefore to participate in (or at least, not openly to reject) its political system. It is not difficult to find counter-arguments to this somewhat idealistic model,[12] and it will not be pursued here. More important is the argument that these constraints and judgments are not individually chosen but rather represent the kinds of restrictions which one can expect to suffer in a society based on mutual co-operation. In other words, what is wrong with the Kantian maxim is its implication that societies consist of a large number of individuals operating atomistically; in fact, belonging to a society involves certain restrictions on autonomy in order to have access to the benefits of social co-operation.[13]

It is therefore not surprising that the extreme individualism of the subjective principles has been mitigated as a result of conflict with policies which may broadly be described in terms of 'social defence' (although we saw in Chapter 3.2(b) and 3.3(j) that the notion must be analysed with care). These conflicts have produced a mass of criminal offences of 'strict liability', which require hardly any fault element at all, to be discussed in section 5.3(a) below. Even beyond those offences, however, the effects of 'social defence' have come to be felt. One manifestation is that, where the harm to be prevented is a fundamental one (such as death), the tendency is for the criminal law to go beyond the principle of *mens rea* and to introduce liability for negligence. The more serious the social harm, the greater care it is fair to expect citizens to take to avoid it. Another manifestation

---

[11] See J. Raz, *The Morality of Freedom* (1987), 145–8.

[12] N. Lacey, *State Punishment* (1988), 22–5.

[13] See the careful argument by Raz, *The Morality of Freedom*, Chs. 10 and 15, and above, Ch. 4.4 on omissions.

has been the recent extension of the concept of 'recklessness', previously confined to an assessment of subjective awareness, to cover situations where D failed to see an obvious risk—an extension which, in part at least, challenges the moral basis of subjective recklessness in the notion of choice. The essence of the argument is that there may be just as much culpability in failing to think about an 'obvious' risk as in being aware of it, since part of living in a society is that citizens ought to be conscious of the potential of harm to others of their activities. These issues will be considered in great detail below, in sections 5.3(c)–(g).

(d) The Principle of Contemporaneity

It is often stated that the fault element must coincide in point of time with the conduct element in order to amount to an offence. This is the principle of contemporaneity. It forms part of the ideology that the function of the criminal law is not to judge a person's general character or behaviour over a period of time; its concern is only with the distinct criminal conduct charged. According to this view, whether or not criminal conviction is deserved depends on D's conduct and mental attitude at the relevant time. But this narrow statement of the principle, if indeed it ever represented a complete statement of the law,[14] has been progressively abandoned in the face of intuitions to the contrary exemplified in leading cases. In the famous case of *Fagan v. Metropolitan Police Commissioner* (1969)[15] D accidentally drove his car on to a policeman's foot, and then deliberately left it there for a minute or so. The defence to a charge of assault was that the conduct element had finished before the fault element began; the act and the intent never coincided. The Divisional Court held that D's conduct in driving the car on to the foot and leaving it there should be viewed as a continuing act, so that the crime was committed when the fault element arose (by D deciding to leave the car there). This is not the only occasion on which the courts have invoked the notion of a 'continuing act' to expand the time-frame of a crime,[16] clearly diluting the application of the contemporaneity principle to a considerable extent.

[14] An early general statement was that of Lord Kenyon CJ in *Fowler v. Padget* (1798) 7 Term. Rep. 509.
[15] [1969] 1 QB 439.
[16] e.g. in rape (*Kaitamaki v. R* [1985] 1 AC 147) and in theft (on appropriation, *Hale* (1978) 68 Cr. App. R 415); for a general critique, see M. Kelman, 'Interpretive Construction in the Substantive Criminal Law' (1981) 33 *Stanford LR* 591.

A somewhat similar approach has been taken in two homicide cases. In *Thabo Meli v. R* (1954)[17] the plan was to kill V in a hut and then throw his body over a cliff: this was what D believed he was doing, but in fact V died from the fall down the cliff and not from the beating in the hut. The argument for the appellant was based on the lack of contemporaneity (this time it was intent first, death later), but the Privy Council rejected this, holding that the beating and the disposal over the cliff formed part of a planned series of acts which should be regarded as a single course of conduct. That reasoning was extended in *Church* (1966)[18] to cover a series of acts which had not been planned but which simply followed one after the other. Both these cases could have resulted in convictions for other offences (attempted murder and causing grievous bodily harm, respectively), but the courts apparently took the view that since the end results—death—were directly attributable to D's fault, they ought to yield homicide convictions. A similar analysis would be possible in non-homicide cases. The decisions therefore have a substantial element of constructive liability[19] in them: they could be regarded as exceptions to the principle of contemporaneity or as extensions of it, but they certainly suggest that the principle is far from absolute (in its narrow form).

(e) The Doctrine of Prior Fault

Behind the narrow application of the principle of contemporaneity lies the insistence that the criminal law is concerned only with the prohibited event itself, not with its antecedents or its sequels. Tensions have led not only to the extension of the contemporaneity principle noted above, but also to the development of a doctrine which expressly refers back to the antecedents of certain events and personal conditions. This is the doctrine of prior fault, which is, broadly stated, that a person should not be allowed to take advantage of any defence or partial defence to criminal liability if the relevant circumstances or condition were brought about by his or her own fault. Two examples will suffice here. First, a person who deliberately drinks to excess in order to stoke up the courage to do a certain act will not be allowed to rely on that intoxication by way of defence

[17] [1954] 1 WLR 228.
[18] [1966] 1 QB 59.
[19] Cf. the felony-murder rule and constructive manslaughter, section 5.2(c) above.

because it arose from prior fault.[20] Second, if D taunts another in the hope of inducing the other to attack him, D will not be able to rely on provocation or self-defence as defences to a charge of murder, because the attack on D will be regarded as self-induced.[21] Examples of the doctrine of prior fault in operation were noted in Chapter 4, in relation to automatism and self-defence, and will be seen in abundance in Chapter 6 (on intoxication, duress, necessity, etc.).

One remaining question concerns the amount of 'fault' required for the doctrine to take effect. A study by Robinson has shown considerable diversity of provisions in the Model Penal Code and in American laws generally,[22] and a similar diversity appears in England.[23] Should *any* causal contribution by D make the defence unavailable, or should it be a lack of proper care (for example, drinking alcohol when its possible effects are widely known,[24] joining a gang which is known to use violence[25]), or should it require proof that D foresaw the possibility that certain conduct might follow? The differences between these approaches ought not to be regarded as unimportant, since the withdrawal of a *defence* simply on the grounds of some small amount of fault on D's part is equivalent to a principle of constructive liability for *offences*. One way of avoiding this difficulty would be to devise a range of offences to cover 'faulty' acts (e.g. excessive consumption of alcohol), and then convict D of that offence—whilst not removing any defence which might otherwise be open. This would introduce further complexities into the law, but at least it shows recognition of an otherwise neglected issue.[26]

5.3. VARIETIES OF FAULT

(a) Strict Liability.

There is no clear convention about when criminal liability should be classified as 'strict'. We will use the term here to indicate those

---

[20] See *Attorney-General for Northern Ireland v. Gallagher* [1963] AC 349, and below, Ch. 6.3.

[21] Cf. *Edwards v. R* [1973] AC 648, with *Johnson* (1989) 89 Cr. App. R 148; below, Ch. 7.4(*b*).

[22] P. H. Robinson, 'Causing the Conditions of One's Own Defense: A Study in the Limits of Theory in Criminal Law Doctrine' (1985) 71 *Virginia LR* 1.

[23] Cf. the different wording in the draft Criminal Code (Law Com. No. 177) on automatism (clause 33(1)(b)) and on duress (clause 42(5)), for example.

[24] See below, Ch. 6.3(*c*).   [25] *Sharp* [1987] QB 853, and below, Ch. 6.4(*c*).

[26] Robinson, 'Causing the Conditions of One's Own Defense'.

offences for which a person may be convicted without proof of intention, knowledge, recklessness, or negligence. Some of the most powerful writings on the subject seem, at times, to muddy the waters. Baroness Wootton campaigned strongly in favour of the extension of strict liability to the major types of offence, but when one looks carefully at one statement of her argument, it seems to be advocating liability for negligence rather than strict liability:

in the modern world as much and more damage is done by negligence, or by indifference to the welfare or safety of others, as by deliberate wickedness . . . The time has come for the concept of legal guilt to be dissolved into a wider concept of responsibility . . . in which there is room for negligence as well as purposeful wrongdoing.[27]

Similarly, among the reasons given in the landmark decision in *Sweet v. Parsley* (1970)[28] for not imposing strict liability were that Parliament did not intend to make criminals of persons who were not blameworthy;[29] that Parliament did not agree with the conviction of those who, by all reasonable and sensible standards, were without fault;[30] and that it was wrong to penalize someone who had taken all proper care to inform herself of any facts which would make her conduct lawful.[31] The House of Lords decided that it was beyond its powers to impose liability for negligence in this case, preferring to present the choice as lying between strict liability and a requirement of *mens rea* (knowledge or reckless knowledge). The arguments adduced, however, were arguments in favour of negligence liability, not in favour of the *mens rea* which they decided to require.

Some offences allow the defendant to avoid liability on proof of 'due diligence', and there is dispute about whether offences with such provisos are properly termed 'strict liability' offences.[32] For our present purposes such offences will be included within the concept of strict liability. This corresponds with the Canadian approach, which separates strict liability (where a defendant can avoid liability by establishing that there was no negligence) from absolute liability (where the only defences available are the basic ones of insanity, automatism, or necessity).[33] The term 'absolute liability' has its own difficulties, in fact, since one can argue that

[27] B. Wootton, *Crime and the Criminal Law* (2nd edn., 1981); 50.
[28] [1970] AC 132.   [29] Per Lord Reid, at 148.
[30] Per Lord Morris, at 153.   [31] Per Lord Diplock, 163.
[32] L. H. Leigh, *Strict and Vicarious Liability* (1982).
[33] See E. Colvin, *Principles of Criminal Law* (1986), 22.

liability should only be described as absolute where there is no defence available at all to someone who is proved to have caused the prohibited event. What this shows, above all, is the inadequacy of common terminology to give simple expression to the numerous permutations of conditions for liability. If one takes account of the device of shifting the burden of proof on to the defendant, then the permutations range from requiring *mens rea*—with the burden of proof on the prosecution—to defining special defences or provisos with an evidential burden on D, defining special defences or provisos with a legal burden of proof on D, requiring proof of negligence by the prosecution, creating a no-negligence defence to be proved by D, imposing liability with no due diligence defence at all, and even to a dispensation from proving an element of the offence.[34]

Let us leave aside the complexities introduced by changes in the burden of proof, and formulate a central question: what are the arguments for imposing criminal liability with no due diligence defence available? The main argument is a form of protectionism or 'social defence'. It maintains that one of the primary aims of the criminal law is the protection of fundamental individual and social interests. Why should this function be abandoned when the violation of those interests resulted from some accident or mistake by D? Surely, Wootton argued, 'mens rea has got into the wrong place': it should be relevant not to the actual conviction, but to the appropriate means of dealing with the offender after conviction. 'If the object of the criminal law is to prevent the occurrence of socially damaging actions, it would be absurd to turn a blind eye to those which were due to carelessness, negligence or even accident. The question of motivation is in the first instance irrelevant.'[35] At a time when victims' interests are receiving greater recognition, arguments of this kind may find considerable support. The infliction of the prohibited harm would become the trigger for state action, aimed at minimizing the risk of the harm being repeated.

The strength of the argument lies in its concern for the welfare of citizens. Its weakness is to suggest that this is a justification for using the *criminal law* in *this* way. There are two major questions to be answered here: Would it be fair? Would it be effective? The fairness issue is one which runs through this chapter and, indeed, through the whole book. The criminal law is society's most condemnatory

[34] A. Ashworth, 'Towards a Theory of Criminal Legislation', (1989) 1 *Criminal Law Forum* 41.
[35] Wootton, *Crime and the Criminal Law*, 47.

instrument, and, as argued above in the context of the principle of *mens rea* and the belief principle, respect for individual autonomy requires that criminal liability be imposed only where there has been choice by D. A person should not be condemned (as distinct, perhaps, from being held civilly liable) for wrongdoing without proof of choice. This is a fundamental requirement of fairness to defendants.[36] But this can be dismissed as a mere matter of convention—and outmoded convention at that. The criminal law could simply be regarded as an efficient social resource for the prevention of harm, with conviction carrying no special moral connotations of 'guilt' or 'blame'. Is there not something incongruous in allowing citizens to die or to be injured whilst the State meticulously observes the 'intent' and 'belief' principles, the presumption of innocence, and other fairness principles so as to facilitate the acquittal of clumsy, ignorant, but nevertheless dangerous people?[37] One answer to this challenge is to reassert that the prevention of harm is neither the sole nor the overriding aim of the criminal law, and that the criminal law is not the only official means of preventing harm. Even Bentham, whose general approach was to transcend individual considerations and to weigh the social benefits against the social disadvantages of criminal liability, argued that criminal punishment is an evil which should be reserved for the worst cases, and that legislators should turn first to education, regulation, and civil liability as means of preventing harms.[38]

This dialogue, however, is rooted in a form of individualism. The principles of fairness have been developed out of respect for the autonomy of individual citizens, whereas many of the harms which afflict, or threaten to afflict, citizens today are the result of the acts or omissions of corporations. Pollution, defective products, food and drugs, safety at work, transport systems—all these sources of danger are dominated by corporate undertakings.[39] The traditional doctrines of the criminal law are not appropriate when it comes to dealing with corporate decision-making and responsibility. The implications for corporate criminal liability were discussed in the last chapter.[40] In the present context it is the standard of liability which is at issue, and the proposition is that some corporations operate in spheres of such potential social danger, and wield such

---

[36] See above, Ch. 5.2.
[37] J. Braithwaite, *Corporate Crime in the Pharmaceutical Industry* (1984), Ch. 9.
[38] *Introduction to the Principles of Morals and Legislation*, Ch. XIII.
[39] See above, Ch. 2.4, and below, Ch. 4.3.   [40] Ch. 4.3(*b*).

power (in terms of economic resources and influence), that there is no social unfairness in holding them to higher standards than individuals when it comes to criminal liability, In short, the conflict between social defence and fairness to defendants should be resolved differently according to whether the defendant is a private individual or a large corporation.

Moving to the second question, whether criminal liability without fault is a particularly efficacious means of preventing harm, it is important to keep in mind the differences between individual behaviour and corporate activity. At least two aspects of efficacy arise: the ease of enforcing no-fault offences; and the preventive effects of liability without fault. Ease of enforcement may be thought to be a simple matter: clearly, it is less trouble to prepare a prosecution in which fault does not have to be proved than to prepare one in which proof of fault is needed. For the more serious offences, however, fault will have to be established for the courts to pass sentence on a proper basis.[41] This means that the prosecution will have to prepare some evidence on the point, which in turn diminishes any procedural benefit of strict liability. But there may still be benefits to the prosecutor in not having to prove fault for minor offences, and there may also be indirect benefits as a result of being able to use the threat of prosecution and conviction in order to secure compliance. Many of the regulatory agencies with the power to invoke 'strict liability' offences adopt what may be termed a 'compliance strategy' towards law enforcement—that is, aiming to secure conformity to the law without the need to process and penalize violators.[42] Their activities focus on obtaining compliance, and prosecution is reserved for the few cases where either the violator is recalcitrant or the violation is so large that public concern can only be assuaged by a prosecution. This may also mean that prosecutions tend to be brought only in cases where there is fault: indeed, there are regulatory agencies which pursue such a policy, even though they have no-fault offences at their disposal.[43] There is little evidence among the regulatory agencies of a 'deterrence strategy', using criminal prosecutions as a primary means of

[41] See *Lester* (1975) 63 Cr. App. R 144.
[42] A. Reiss, 'Selecting Strategies of Social Control over Organizational Life', in K. Hawkins and J. M. Thomas (eds.), *Enforcing Regulation* (1984).
[43] See e.g. G. Richardson, A. Ogus, and P. Burrows, *Policing Pollution* (1982), B. Hutter, *The Reasonable Arm of the Law* (1988), and the review by G. Richardson, 'Strict Liability for Regulatory Crime: The Empirical Research' [1987] Crim. LR 295. Cf. R. Baldwin, "Why Rules Don't Work", (1990) 53 MLR 321.

preventing breaches of the law. This approach to law enforcement is more typical of the police, who rarely occupy themselves with the so-called regulatory offences dealing with commercial and industrial safety etc. Part of the explanation for this may be that the number of police-officers has steadily increased in recent years, whereas the staffing and funding of regulatory agencies has been strictly controlled.[44]

With regard to assessing the efficacy of no-fault liability as a means of prevention, then, it is difficult to reach a firm conclusion. It is probably an overstatement to regard it as a 'means of prevention', since the no-fault offence usually forms one part of a broad regulatory scheme. Some argue that the availability of a no-fault offence strengthens the regulator's hand in ensuring compliance and, therefore, prevention. Others argue that no-fault offences which are followed by low penalties on conviction are almost counterproductive, resulting in the imposition of derisory fines on large organizations. Indeed, if regulation in such spheres as industrial safety had been harnessed to relatively serious offences requiring proof of fault, then those offences might now be taken much more seriously, integrated into people's thinking about offences against the person rather than being regarded as 'merely regulatory' and 'not real crime'.[45] This is, of course, part of a much wider issue about the conventional concepts of crime (as now embodied, for example, in the draft Criminal Code)[46] and about conventional approaches to enforcement which regard some offences as police matters and some not. Thus the issues here turn on the agency through which enforcement takes place, the style of enforcement adopted, and the elements of discretion in choosing and following a style of enforcement.

Before considering the approach of English criminal law to no-fault offences, it is worth giving separate consideration to the question of offence-seriousness. Is it an argument in favour of, or against, strict liability that the offence is a minor one or a grave one? The English courts have used both triviality and gravity as arguments in favour of strict liability. Many offences with low penalties are, or

---

[44] S. Box, *Recession, Crime and Unemployment* (1987), 98–102.
[45] Ibid.
[46] Cf. the justifications for confining the English codification initiative to 'traditional' offences by the Code Team (Law Com. No. 143, paras. 2.10–2.13 and Appendix A) and by the Law Commission (Law Com. No. 177, paras. 3.3–3.6), with the critical remarks of C. Wells, 'Restatement or Reform' [1986] Crim. LR 314.

have been held to be, offences requiring no proof of fault.[47] This reasoning derives some justification from an economic argument based on ease of prosecution: such trivial offences are not worth the public expenditure of prosecution and court time in proving fault. There is hardly any stigma in being convicted of such offences, and so it is thought to be in the public interest to dispose of them quickly. But none of this can apply to grave offences. Principles of individual fairness, even if overridden by economic considerations in respect of minor offences, should surely be central to the question of conviction for grave offences. One clear bench-mark here is the availability of imprisonment as a punishment. The American Model Penal Code proposes that imprisonability should be a conclusive reason against strict liability.[48] In practice, the American Supreme Court has been less principled, imposing strict liability for the offence of possession of an unregistered hand-grenade (maximum penalty, ten years' imprisonment).[49] No strong presumption against the imposition of no-fault liability for imprisonable offences has been enunciated in this country; indeed, English law contains several examples of courts using the seriousness of the offence as an argument for strict liability—a course of reasoning which inevitably results in no-fault liability for some imprisonable crimes. The nadir of such judicial reasoning was probably reached in *Howells* (1977),[50] where D was charged with possessing a firearm without a certificate, an offence contrary to section 1 of the Firearms Act 1968, with a maximum penalty of three years' imprisonment. D sought to rely on section 58 of the Act, which exempted 'an antique firearm which is . . . possessed as a curiosity or ornament'. When evidence was given that the gun was not an antique but a reproduction, the defence then argued that D believed it to be an antique, since it had been sold to him as such. This would only be a defence if some requirement of knowledge or belief could be read into the statute. The Court of Appeal ruled this out and upheld strict liability:

First, the wording would, on the face of it, so indicate. Secondly, the danger to the community resulting from the possession of lethal firearms is so obviously great that an absolute prohibition against their possession without proper authority must have been the intention of Parliament when

---

[47] *Alphacell Ltd. v. Woodward* [1972] AC 824, following the notion of 'quasi-crimes' outlined by Lord Reid in *Sweet v. Parsley* [1970] AC 132.
[48] Model Penal Code, s. 6.02(4).
[49] *U.S. v. Freed* (1971) 401 U.S. 601.
[50] [1977] QB 614.

considered in conjunction with the words of the section. Thirdly, to allow a defence of honest and reasonable belief that the firearm was an antique and therefore excluded would be likely to defeat the clear intentions of the Act.[51]

This decision is illustrative in a number of ways. The powerful expression of the second point, the danger to the community, gives no weight at all to the argument against rendering a person liable to imprisonment without proof of fault; indeed, the argument seems not to have been mentioned. The 'danger to the community' argument is surely questionable in itself. Is it really being contended that, the more serious the offence, the stronger the argument for strict liability? Moreover, it is linked here to an assertion about the original intention of Parliament: and yet there is no reference in the judgment to the origins of the Firearms Act. The third point in the quotation merely restates the assertion. Everything depends on whether Parliament, by failing to include any fault terms in the relevant section of the Act, did intend to exclude fault, or whether it was merely leaving the issue to be determined by the courts.[52] This brings us back to the first point, that the wording 'on the face of it' favours strict liability. This is a monumentally unhelpful statement, which calls for some discussion of the respective functions of the legislature and the courts in these matters.

Part of Parliament's function in defining offences should be to state any fault requirements for liability. It discharges this function in many cases, but in many others it remains silent, merely enacting a provision which appears to penalize an act or an omission without any reference to fault. Over the years the courts have had to 'interpret' these provisions on many occasions, deciding whether or not to insert a fault requirement. It has been estimated that over half of the 7,000 offences in English criminal law require no proof of fault.[53] The courts' approach to interpretation has not been a model of consistency. In some cases they regard it either as a linguistic matter or as something to be resolved by looking at the structure of the Act as a whole. In others they make high statements of principle, which may briefly raise hopes that a consistent framework is to be established; but those hopes are usually dashed, as the supposed principle is progressively whittled away or, more damningly, simply ignored. The relevant decisions of the courts are legion, covering an

---

[51] Per Browne LJ, at 626.
[52] P. Devlin, *Samples of Lawmaking*, esp. 71–3.
[53] JUSTICE, *Breaking the Rules* (1980).

enormous variety of offences (including many within the field of road traffic), and the paragraphs which follow aim merely to give the flavour of the main judicial approaches.

One of the earliest statements of principle was that of Wright J in *Sherras v. de Rutzen* (1895),[54] who stated that 'There is a presumption that mens rea . . . is an essential ingredient in every offence; but that presumption is liable to be displaced either by the words of the statute creating the offence or by the subject-matter with which it deals, and both must be considered.' Thus, in his view, the reason why both bigamy and the abduction of a girl under 16 are offences of strict liability is to be found in the wording of the statutes. What 'subject-matter' displaces the presumption? One example given by Wright J is 'acts which are not criminal in any real sense', where the criminal penalty is attached to acts which are not regarded as morally wrong. This was a reference to offences involved in regulating the sale of tobacco, food, alcohol, and so forth. There were a number of judicial decisions in the 1960s which held persons liable for quite serious drug offences without proof of any fault, in the belief that public policy demanded this, but this trend was arrested in what is probably the leading case, *Sweet v. Parsley* (1970).[55] The case involved a schoolteacher who was prosecuted for being concerned in the management of premises used for the purpose of smoking cannabis; she had rented her farmhouse to a group of students who, unbeknown to her, smoked cannabis there. The case went up to the House of Lords on the question of whether any fault had to be proved. If one takes the language 'on its face', to refer back to the quotation from *Howells*,[56] it suggests liability without fault. But their Lordships were unanimous in holding that the statute should be construed in the light of the presumption that *mens rea* is required. They regarded it as improper for the courts to impose negligence liability in such cases: the choice lay between *mens rea* and strict liability, and the presumption should be in favour of the former.

This presumption did not fare well during the next decade. It was soon held to be displaced in another House of Lords case, *Alphacell Ltd. v. Woodward* (1972)[57], where a company was convicted of causing polluted matter to enter a stream. One reason was linguistic: the word 'cause' was thought to favour strict liability; the maximum penalty was low, and pollution offences were probably regarded as

---

[54] [1985] 1 QB 918.   [55] [1970] AC 132.
[56] See n. 51 above.   [57] [1972] AC 824.

not being criminal in a real sense. We have already seen that the decision in *Howells* is also hard to reconcile with *Sweet v. Parsley*, but it is not the only one. In *Pharmaceutical Society of Great Britain v. Storkwain Ltd.* (1986)[58] the House of Lords held that a person may be liable to conviction for selling drugs without a valid prescription, contrary to the Medicines Act 1968, without proof of fault. The decision was reached by analysing the statute, with scant reference to general principle and without giving weight to the fact that the offence carried a maximum sentence of two years' imprisonment.

It is manifest that the courts have not confined strict liability to offences which may be described as 'not criminal in any real sense', since they have extended it to several imprisonable crimes.[59] A final and powerful example of this is *Gammon v. Attorney-General for Hong Kong* (1985)[60]. Following the collapse of a building, the defendants were charged with offences against the construction regulations which carried high fines and a maximum prison sentence of three years. Lord Scarman, giving the opinion of the Privy Council, reaffirmed the presumption of *mens rea* laid down in *Sweet v Parsley*, and added that 'the presumption is particularly strong where the offence is "truly criminal" in character'. He went on:

the only situation in which the presumption can be displaced is where the statute is concerned with an issue of social concern; public safety is such an issue . . . Even where a statute is concerned with such an issue, the presumption of mens rea stands unless it can also be shown that the creation of strict liability will be effective to promote the objects of the statute by encouraging greater vigilance to prevent the commission of the prohibited act.

The last few words make it clear that the courts still abide by the principle that strict liability should not be imposed where there is nothing more a defendant could reasonably be expected to do in order to avoid the harm.[61] However, the earlier part of the quotation demonstrates how muddy the waters still are. The courts say that strict liability is appropriate for minor offences which are not truly

---

[58] (1986) 83 Cr. App. R 359.
[59] See e.g. the decisions in *Storkwain* (above, n. 58), *Gammon v. Attorney-General for Hong Kong* [1985] AC 1, and *R v. Wells Street Magistrates' Court and Martin, ex p. Westminster City Council* [1986] Crim. LR 695; cf. the Canadian decision, under the Charter of Rights and Freedoms (1982), section 7, in *Reference re Section 94(2) of Motor Vehicle Act, RSBC 1979* (1986) 48 CR (3d) 289.
[60] [1985] AC 1.   [61] See *Lim Chin Aik v. R* [1963] AC 160.

criminal. Yet they also seem to hold, as in *Howells*[62] and in *Gammon*, that it is appropriate where offences relate to public safety or social concern—a description which could extend to large areas of the criminal law. On some occasions the courts seem to focus on a linguistic analysis of the statute, without reference to general principle. High-sounding declarations in such cases as *Sweet v. Parsley* become hollow when strict liability is imposed for imprisonable offences. The courts have not explicitly discussed the idea of adopting different approaches for individual and corporate defendants: indeed, there has been an unwillingness to debate the issues at a general level. It is not that the decisions have lacked principles: it is rather that there are too many principles and policies being used by the courts, with no attempt to draw them together into a single coherent pattern. The subject is more appropriate for legislative resolution than judicial decision making. But parliamentary abstention has left a wide area of judicial discretion as to the approach to be taken, with corresponding diminution of the 'rule of law' value of maximum certainty.

This discussion of strict liability as a basis for criminal conviction has raised questions not only about effectiveness of enforcement, but also about the use of 'social defence' concepts such as public protection and social concern. If 'desert', proportionality, and fair labelling are to be respected as primary aims, then it is important to ensure that powerless individuals are not treated more severely, in law or in practice, than powerful corporations. This calls for an appraisal of the relative seriousness of the harms involved: where the harm is relatively high, then—at least where individuals are involved—there should be some fault requirement, out of respect for individual autonomy. Exactly what that fault requirement should be is discussed in the following sections of this chapter.

(b) *Intention*

As noted above, the term *'mens rea'* has conventionally been used to connote four fault requirements: intention or recklessness as to the specified consequence, and knowledge of, or recklessness as to, the specified circumstance. In discussing offences of strict liability, we have considered the main arguments in favour of requiring *mens rea* as a condition of criminal liability, arguments of choice and control deriving from respect for individual autonomy. Now

[62] [1977] QB 614.

we move to the more detailed and specific question of drawing distinctions between the four main forms of fault which generally fall under the umbrella of *mens rea*. The task is important, because this is one way in which the law seeks to differentiate among crimes. Intent alone is sufficient for offences of attempt, offences defined in terms of 'doing X with intent to do Y' (such as burglary: entering as a trespasser with intent to steal),[63] and the crimes of murder and wounding with intent to do grievous bodily harm. The last two crimes are examples of the law using intention as the main method of grading offences: both the murder–manslaughter distinction and the dividing line between wounding under section 18 of the Offences against the Person Act 1861 (maximum penalty of life imprisonment) and wounding under section 20 (maximum penalty of five years' imprisonment) turn on the presence or absence of intention.

It is quite possible—indeed, quite normal—to do things with more than one intention in mind. I can demolish a fence with the simultaneous intentions of making way for a new fence, providing wood for the fire, pleasing my spouse (who has repeatedly asked me to demolish the fence), and so on. The approach of the criminal law, however, is generally not to ask with what intentions D committed the act, but to ask whether one particular intention was present when the act was committed. The policy, generally speaking, is for the law to be interested in the presence or absence of one particular intention—that specified in the definition of the offence charged—and not to conduct a general review of D's reasons for the behaviour in question. Did D intend to kill the crew of the aircraft on which he placed a bomb, as well as intending (as he admits) to claim the insurance money on the cargo? Did D intend to assist the enemy by his actions, as well as intending (as he admits) to save his family from a concentration camp?[64]

The law's approach in selecting one intention, and then abstracting it from D's other reasons and beliefs at the time, calls for careful consideration. It is essential to keep in mind the particular intent required by the definition of the offence. It is quite possible to say 'D pulled the trigger of the gun intentionally', without implying that D intended to kill V when he pulled the trigger. The offence of murder turns (broadly)[65] on the presence or absence of an intention

---

[63] Burglary is discussed below, Ch. 9.5. For a general discussion of offences defined in an inchoate mode, see A. Ashworth, 'Defining Criminal Offences without Harm', in P. F. Smith (ed.), *Criminal Law: Essays in Honour of J. C. Smith* (1987).
[64] See the discussion of *Steane* below, p. 152.   [65] See below, Ch. 7.3(c).

to kill; whether the trigger was pulled intentionally or accidentally may be an important part of the case, but the legally required intention is that D *intended to kill* V. Loose references to whether D 'acted intentionally' can blur this distinction: it is the intent specified in the indictment which must be proved. Reference to the relevant consequence also avoids the idea that intentions are some kind of entity in the human mind which the court must try to identify. Some statements by lawyers tend to give the impression of human action involving two distinct entities, the mind and the body. It is much more realistic to regard mental states as inextricably bound up in behaviour, rather than as detached phenomena which have to be tracked down. One way of ensuring that 'intention' is not thus detached is to define it in terms of whether D acted 'in order to bring about' the specified result.[66]

This definition of intention may avoid some philosophical errors, but is it sufficient? The proper definition of intention has been the subject of theoretical debate and judicial disagreement for many years. The core of 'intention' is surely aim, objective, or purpose: whatever else 'intention' may mean, a person surely acts with intention to kill if killing is the aim, objective, or purpose of the conduct causing death. In *Mohan* (1976)[67] James LJ defined intention as 'a decision to bring about [the proscribed result], insofar as it lies within the accused's power, no matter whether the accused desired that consequence of his act or not'. This definition has the advantage of stating that desire is not essential to intention (one may act out of feelings of duty, for example, rather than desire); it has the disadvantage of referring to a 'decision', whereas in many offences of violence and other crimes the events happen so suddenly and rapidly that a fleeting realization of what one is doing may be the most that time allows. Yet it is well established that this fleeting realization is enough for intention, rendering the term far less concrete than it is in ordinary speech.[68]

The *Mohan* case involved an attempted crime, and intention is thought to be crucial to attempts, because one cannot be said to *attempt* to produce a result unless one *intends* to produce it (see below, Chapter 11.3(*a*)). The decision in *Mohan* goes some way

---

[66] This point is elaborated in various writings by R. A. Duff: see his 'The Obscure Intentions of the House of Lords' [1986] Crim. LR 771, and his 'Codifying Criminal Fault', in I. Dennis (ed.), *Criminal Law and Criminal Justice* (1987).

[67] [1976] QB 1.

[68] R. Cross, "The Mental Element in Crime' (1967) 83 LQR 215.

towards stating the core of the concept of intention: how much further should its meaning be taken? Many writers have assumed that intention includes not only purpose but also foresight of certainty; or, to phrase it properly, that D can be said to have intended a result if he or she realized that the result was certain to follow from the behaviour in question. An early example of this may be found in Bentham's writings, and his distinction between direct and oblique intention is one way of expressing the point.[69] One might say that a consequence is *directly* intended if it is D's purpose or desire to produce it, and that it is *obliquely* intended if it is a foreseen but undesired consequence.[70] Modern writers have often used 'foresight of certainty' to capture the latter point. It is crucial to examine what is happening at this stage in the argument. It is not a question of language: it is not being asserted that common English usage would describe D as having *intended* a result if he *foresaw* that it was certain to follow the behaviour in question. In all probability linguistic usage on the point would differ, and many people would not describe this as a case of D 'intending' the result. The step which *is* being taken is to assert that behaviour of this kind should be classified as falling within intention rather than the lesser category of recklessness—and that step is being taken in the knowledge that it will result in some killings being classified as murder rather than manslaughter, some woundings being described as 'with intent' rather than merely unlawful, and so on.

It follows from this that anyone who wishes to classify these cases within the ambit of intention rather than recklessness has to establish not that all cases of foresight of certainty are socially or morally as bad as all cases of purpose, but that it is more appropriate to classify them thus. Moreover, the shorthand phrase 'foresight of certainty' is perhaps too brief in this context. Few future events in life are absolutely certain, and a reference to consequences as 'certain to follow' would generally mean 'practically certain to follow' or 'certain, barring some unforeseen intervention'[71]. A familiar example is D, who places a bomb on an aircraft with the aim of blowing it up in mid-flight in order to claim the insurance money on the cargo. D knows that it is practically certain that the crew of the

---

[69] Bentham, *Introduction to the Principles of Morals and Legislation*, Ch. VIII, on direct and oblique intent. Bentham's definition of oblique intent was wider than that described here, a point discussed by Glanville Williams, 'Oblique Intent' [1988] CLJ.

[70] Ibid.

[71] The phrase of Lord Lane CJ, in *Nedrick* (1986) 83 Cr. App. R 267.

aircraft will be killed as a result of the explosion. One might say that D's *purpose* is to claim the insurance money, but if the charge is murder, that is irrelevant. The key question is whether D intended *to kill*. Since it was *not* D's purpose to kill, that aspect of the definition of intention is not fulfilled. Should the law extend the definition to cover D's awareness of the practical certainty that the crew would be killed? The argument in favour of this is that D's behaviour shows no respect for the value of human life at all: D knows that the crew will die, and yet he still pursues the purpose of blowing up the aircraft. There is little social or moral difference between that and planning the explosion in order to kill the crew. It is sometimes thought that the 'test of failure' argues against this:[72] since D would not regard the explosion as a failure if the cargo were destroyed but the crew were not killed, this serves to differentiate him from someone whose purpose is to kill. But to establish a philosophical distinction between D and the purposeful killer is not to conclude the case in favour of a legal distinction. Another counter-argument is that the ordinary meaning of 'intention' is unclear on the point, and it is wrong for the law to use ordinary terms in unusual senses;[73] yet it is surely true that ordinary language is not sufficiently refined for many legal purposes, and it would be asking too much for the law to invent a whole new vocabulary. Fundamentally, it is a question of social judgment whether D should be bracketed with the purposeful killer or regarded as merely reckless. The draft Criminal Code has it right, surely, in defining intention so as to cover the person who acts 'being aware that [the prohibited consequence] will occur in the ordinary course of events'.[74]

There is at present no legislative definition of intention, and the pronouncements of the courts have not been a model of consistency. The leading decisions concern the crime of murder, to be discussed in a later chapter,[75] but the recent developments can be summarized here. The first of the leading cases is *Moloney* (1985),[76] in which the House of Lords held that judges should generally avoid defining the term 'intention', beyond explaining that it differs from 'desire' and 'motive'. Only in exceptional cases should the judge depart from

[72] R. A. Duff, 'Intention, Recklessness and Probable Consequences' [1980] Crim. LR 404.

[73] Lord Goff, 'The Mental Element in the Crime of Murder' (1988) 104 LQR 30.

[74] Law Com. No. 177, clause 18, and J. C. Smith, 'A Note on Intention', [1990] Crim. LR 85.

[75] Ch. 7.3(c).   [76] [1985] AC 905.

this golden rule, notably, where the essence of the defence is that D's purpose was only to frighten, not to harm, the victim. Here the jury should be instructed to decide whether D foresaw the prohibited consequence as 'a natural consequence' of the behaviour: if the answer was yes, they could infer intention from that. In the course of his speech Lord Bridge gave hints of the sort of cases he meant to include—cases where the consequence was a 'little short of overwhelming', or 'virtually certain'—but unfortunately the centrepiece of his speech was the term 'natural consequence'. When this was used by the judge to direct the jury in *Hancock and Shankland* (1986),[77] it was held to be unsatisfactory. The House of Lords overruled its own test of 'natural consequence', and Lord Scarman held that juries should be told that 'The greater the probability of a consequence the more likely it is that the consequence was foreseen, and that if that consequence was foreseen the greater the probability is that that consequence was also intended.'

These decisions left unclear the precise legal meaning of intention and the proper approach to directing a jury, and Lord Lane CJ attempted to synthesize the House of Lords decisions in *Nedrick* (1986):[78]

Where the charge is murder and in the rare cases where the simple direction is not enough, the jury should be directed that they are not entitled to infer the necessary intention, unless they feel sure that death or serious bodily harm was a virtual certainty (barring some unforeseen intervention) as a result of the defendant's actions and that the defendant realised that such was the case.

Removed from the context of murder, this means that the courts are entitled to infer intention from foresight of virtual certainty. But if they are only entitled to *infer* intention in these cases, then that means that, logically, intention does not include foresight of virtual certainty. What, then, is the definition of intention? This question has not received a clear answer, although, extrajudicially, Lord Lane has given the obvious one[79]—that intention does include foresight of virtual certainty, and that the reference to 'inferring' is not strictly accurate here. What the courts probably meant to say is that intention includes both purpose and foresight with regard to a particular consequence occurring in the ordinary course of events. Since most of these cases involve defendants who deny that they

---

[77] [1986] AC 455.   [78] (1986) 83 Cr. App. R 267.
[79] In a House of Lords debate on murder: HL Deb. 512, col. 480 (Nov. 1989).

intended such a result, it is inevitable that the jury will be left to draw inferences from the surrounding circumstances. But the evidential process of drawing inferences—which is basic to every case where D does not confess, since one cannot see into another person's mind—should not be confused with the legal definition of intention.[80]

It will be noted that one effect of the recent decisions has been to promote the term 'virtual certainty' instead of 'certainty' or 'practical certainty'. Does this represent a lowering of the requirement, and a broadening of the definition of intention? It is worth recalling that, before the recent decisions, the leading case was *Hyam v. DPP* (1975),[81] which suggested that a person could be held to intend a result which he had foreseen as probable (or highly probable) to occur. This is much wider than 'virtual certainty', and consequently much further from ordinary language. The argument in its favour would be that, if D realizes that a consequence probably will occur if a particular act is done, and, when the act is done, the consequence does occur, D should be rendered criminally liable for that consequence. There are various difficulties with this. First, it swallows up a large part of the species of fault known as recklessness, which typically involves the realization that a given consequence may ensue. Second, it does so in a rather vague way, so that the distinction between intention and recklessness falls short of the principle of maximum certainty. If the law is to draw the distinction between intention and recklessness, as a major device of classification, it should be clearly done. The *Hyam* test of probability or high probability fails to achieve this. It might be argued that foresight of 'virtual certainty' also leaves room for an element of doubt, and that the draft Code's formulation of 'being aware that it will occur in the ordinary course of events' is preferable.[82] At bottom, the terminology must surely leave room for a small element of doubt—absolute certainty is rare in human affairs. To revert to the example of the bomb on the aircraft, the *Guinness Book of Records* states that a person has survived an aircraft explosion some 37,000 feet in the air: should this freak statistic be sufficient to remove the act of placing the bomb out of 'intention' and into 'recklessness'? The answer should surely be no: it is so unusual for a person to survive a mid-air explosion that it should be practically discounted. The sceptic may

---

[80] See E. Griew, 'States of Mind, Presumptions and Inferences', in Smith (ed.), *Criminal Law*, and R. A. Duff and A. Norrie [1990] Crim. LR 637–44.

[81] [1975] AC 55.   [82] See above, n. 74.

wonder, however, to what extent this particular example is loaded by the fact that it involves a bomb—and only wicked people plant bombs. Might it not be true that, wherever the law incorporates an uncertain term such as 'virtual', the flexibility thus granted to the courts is exercised according to moral judgments of D's behaviour rather than according to supposed predictions of the degree of probability?[83]

It is at this stage that we might reflect further on the law's approach in selecting *one* intention and declining to conduct a general review of D's reasons for behaving in a particular way. Is it not unjust to confine the enquiry so narrowly? It is not enough, critics might contend, to point out that the defendant can raise any defence for which there is evidence—self-defence, duress, mistake of law, and so forth. The law should not regard a person as intending a result unless it is D's purpose to produce that result. According to this view, the Court of Criminal Appeal in *Steane* (1947)[84] was right to hold that the broadcasts D made to save his family from a concentration camp were not sent out 'with intent to assist the enemy', even though he knew full well that they would assist the enemy. And the House of Lords was right in *Gillick v. West Norfolk and Wisbech Area Health Authority* (1986)[85] to hold that a doctor who prescribes contraceptives to a girl under 16 does not intend to aid and abet the offence of unlawful sexual intercourse with a girl under 16; the purpose was to prevent unwanted pregnancy, even though the doctor knew full well that the offence would take place.

It may be argued, however, that these decisions are wrong. Steane *did* intend to assist the enemy, since he knew that his acts would inevitably have this effect; the law should provide him with a defence of duress, because of the threats to his family, rather than distorting the meaning of intention.[86] The doctor in the *Gillick* case *did* intend to aid and abet the offence of unlawful sexual intercourse, because he knew that the offence would follow; the law should provide a defence based on clinical judgment or medical necessity, rather than distorting the meaning of intention.[87] What these decisions show, surely, is the tension which underlies attributions of 'intention'. Since intention is the key element in several offences, and since the range of excuses and justifications in English law is

---

[83] Cf. A. Norrie, 'Oblique Intention and Legal Politics' [1989] Crim. LR 793.
[84] [1947] KB 997.   [85] [1986] AC 112.
[86] G. Williams, *The Mental Element in Crime* (1965).
[87] See above, Ch. 4.8(*b*).

limited, it is hardly surprising that where the court feels that there is a compelling social reason for acquitting D but no available defence, it should try to narrow the meaning of intention so as to achieve the desired outcome. It is, however, far more conducive to consistency for the courts to allow the meaning of key terms to continue unaltered, creating new and circumscribed defences instead. This course has now been taken in relation to duress of circumstances,[88] but not for medical necessity or, for example, human compassion. This leaves us with a paradox. The criminal law often uses the distinction between intention and recklessness as a means of grading the seriousness of offences. But since the definition of recklessness includes the requirement that the risk be socially unjustified (see below)[89], whereas the definition of intention includes no reference to social justification, there are cases of recklessness which may well be adjudged more heinous than cases of intention.

(c) Recklessness

Much of the preceding discussion about the proper limits of the concept of intention in the criminal law has inevitably concerned the dividing line between recklessness and intention. The argument was that there are some cases in which D knows the risk of the prohibited consequence to be so very high (i.e. practically certain) that it is more appropriate to classify his mental attitude within the highest category of culpability (intention) rather than in the lesser category of recklessness. There are some who would draw the dividing line lower, arguing that if D foresaw the prohibited consequence as a *probable* result, this should be classified as intention, leaving only the lesser degrees of risk within the category of recklessness.[90] We will now move on from these arguments, but they do remind us that the boundaries of the concept of recklessness are open to debate, and that this debate should concern ways of grading culpability so as to reflect social and moral distinctions. This is equally true of the dividing line between recklessness and negligence, a line which assumes great importance, because recklessness is traditionally held to lie inside, and negligence to lie outside, the concept of *mens rea*.

---

[88] See below, Ch. 6.4(c).   [89] Section 5.3(c).
[90] This was one of the views expressed in *Hyam v. DPP* [1975] AC 55, by Lord Diplock (not dissenting on this point); see J. Buzzard, 'Intent' [1978] Crim. LR 5, with reply by J. C. Smith at [1978] Crim. LR 14; cf. also Bentham, *Introduction to the Principles of Morals and Legislation*.

An abiding difficulty in discussing the legal meaning of reckless-ness is that the term has been given several different shades of meaning by the courts over the years. In the law of manslaughter, 'reckless' was long regarded as the most appropriate adjective to express the degree of negligence needed for a conviction:[91] in this sense, it meant a high degree of carelessness. In the late 1950s the courts adopted a different meaning of recklessness in the context of *mens rea*, referring to D's actual awareness of the risk of the prohibited consequence occurring:[92] we shall call this 'common-law recklessness'. Controversy was introduced into this area in the early 1980s, when the House of Lords purported to broaden the meaning of recklessness so as to include those who failed to give thought to an obvious risk that the consequence would occur:[93] we shall call this *Caldwell* recklessness. The law of manslaughter will be left for discussion later:[94] here we will focus on the last two meanings of recklessness.

(i) *Common-Law Recklessness.* It was in 1957 that the Court of Criminal Appeal held that, in a statute, the term 'malicious' denotes intention or recklessness, and that recklessness means that 'the accused has foreseen that the particular kind of harm might be done and yet has gone on to take the risk of it'.[95] There are essentially three elements in this definition, and they are the same ones found in the Model Penal Code's definition of recklessness as 'the con-scious taking of an unjustified risk'.[96] First, it requires D's actual awareness of the risk; this is why it is often referred to as 'subjective recklessness', and it is regarded as the key element in bringing recklessness within the concept of *mens rea*. A person should only be held to have been reckless about a particular result if the court is satisfied that he or she was aware of the risk at the time. The second element is that a person may be held to have been reckless if he or she was aware of any degree of risk: we have seen that when the risk is so high as to be a practical certainty, D may be classed as intending the consequence, but any risk, however slight, may be sufficient at the lower end, so long as D is aware of it and it materializes. The third element is that the risk which D believes to

---

[91] See *Andrews v. DPP* [1937] AC 576, discussed below in Ch. 7.5.

[92] *Cunningham* [1957] 2 QB 396, adopting the definition offered by C. S. Kenny, *Outlines of Criminal Law* (1st edn., 1902; 16th edn., 1952).

[93] *Caldwell* [1982] AC 341, and *Lawrence* [1982] AC 510.

[94] Ch. 7.5(*b*).

[95] See above, n. 92   [96] Model Penal Code, section 2. 02(2)(c).

be present must be an unjustified or unreasonable one. This element in the definition does not usually raise any problems—there is rarely any social justification in taking risks with other people's safety or property. But one can think of cases where the element of unreasonableness is relevant: someone who risks another's death by playing 'Russian roulette' cannot claim social justification, whereas the surgeon who attempts a difficult operation may well be justified in doing so even if there is a significant risk of failure. This issue of social justification is to be decided objectively by the court—which is why it is not really accurate to refer to this form of recklessness as 'subjective'—but it appears that this judgment should be based on the degree of risk which D *believed* to exist (where that differs from the degree of risk which actually existed).[97]

The justification for the common-law definition of recklessness is grounded in the element of choice which underlies the fairness principles outlined above.[98] The distinction between recklessness and negligence turns on D's awareness or unawareness of the risk. In both cases there is an unreasonable risk taken, but D should only be held to have been reckless if he or she was aware of the risk. A person who is aware of the risk usually chooses to create it, and therefore chooses to place his or her interests above the well-being of those who may suffer if the risk materializes. Choosing to create a risk of harmful consequences is generally much worse than creating the same risk without realizing it. Moreover, holding a person reckless despite unawareness of the risk would result in a conviction in a case like *Stephenson* (1979).[99] D, a schizophrenic, made a hollow in a haystack in order to sleep there; he felt cold, and so lit a small fire, causing the whole haystack to go up in flames, and resulting in damage of some £3,500. The defence relied on medical evidence that D may not have had the same ability to foresee the risk as a mentally normal person. The Court of Appeal, quashing D's conviction, held that the definition of common-law recklessness clearly turned on what this defendant actually foresaw, and the medical evidence should have been taken into account on this point. This decision, then, clearly affirms the element of individual fairness in the common-law definition. An entirely objective test of negligence would exclude this.

Does concentration on the element of awareness always produce decisions in accord with fairness? There are at least two types of

---

[97] Compare *Watson* [1989] Crim. LR 733, with *Ball* [1989] Crim. LR 730.
[98] See above, section 5.2(*a*).   [99] [1979] QB 695.

awkward case for a test of liability which requires the court to be satisfied that the defendant actually saw the risk, however briefly. One is where a person acts impulsively in the heat of the moment. This is often expressed in ordinary speech by saying 'I acted without thinking', or 'I just didn't think'. D denies that he or she was aware of the risk at the time of acting. In *Parker* (1977)[100] D tried unsuccessfully to make a telephone call from a kiosk; in his frustration he slammed down the receiver and it broke. The Court of Appeal upheld his conviction for causing criminal damage recklessly, despite his defence that it did not occur to him that he might damage the telephone, on the basis that he must have known that he was dealing with breakable materials, even if that fact was not at the forefront of his mind when he slammed the receiver down. He had 'closed his mind to the obvious', or suppressed this knowledge at the time of acting.[101] It is quite evident that this decision involves some stretching of the awareness element which is thought to be central to common-law recklessness. In effect, it broadens the time-frame from the moment of the act itself to an earlier and calmer time, when D would almost certainly have answered the question: 'What might happen if you slammed down a telephone receiver?', by saying: 'It might break'. The reason for thus broadening the time-frame is presumably to prevent bad temper resulting in an acquittal, since this would be socially undesirable: people should control their tempers. But it does sully the subjective purity of this part of common-law recklessness. The second problem is the 'couldn't care less' attitude: D might not have thought about a particular consequence, because it was irrelevant to his interests. This might be described as an attitude of 'practical indifference' to that consequence,[102] and might be illustrated by a person who sets fire to a shop without thinking of the possible danger to people living above, and who says that he was not really interested in what happened to them. It is an attitude which might be called 'callous' in everyday language. Strictly speaking, like actions in a fit of temper, the actions of a callous and indifferent person are not reckless if in fact D did not think about the risk at the time the acts were done. Yet it may be argued that the person who fails to advert to the risk because

---

[100] [1977] 1 WLR 600.
[101] See the discussion by Lane LJ, in *Stephenson* [1979] QB 69, and M. Wasik and M. P. Thompson, 'Turning a Blind Eye as Constituting Mens Rea' (1981) 32 NILQ 328, at 339.
[102] R. A. Duff, 'Recklessness' [1980] Crim. LR 282.

it means nothing to him or her is far more blameworthy than the person who fails to advert to the risk simply through oversight or error. There is a problem, once one reaches this point, in establishing the reason for non-advertence in each particular case.[103] But the law is accustomed to dealing with difficult issues of proof, and they should not be allowed to distract attention from the social or moral conclusions. Those conclusions are that there are at least two types of situation in which the 'awareness' requirement, the centre-piece of common-law recklessness, may fail to yield an acceptable grading of blameworthiness. One is the person who acts impulsively or in a temper, 'without thinking'. The other is the person who fails to think about the consequences out of callous indifference to them. A third possibility would be where D states that he was so preoccupied with other aspects of what he was doing as to give no thought to a particular consequence (although the courts might be reluctant to accept such a defence).[104]

(ii) *Caldwell Recklessness.* It may or may not be true historically that the *Caldwell* test grew out of dissatisfaction with the limitations of the common-law definition, but it certainly succeeds in encompassing both the situations just discussed (acts during loss of temper, and acts due to callous indifference). In the House of Lords decision in *Caldwell* (1982)[105] Lord Diplock formulated the following model direction: a person is guilty of causing damage recklessly if

(i) he does an act which in fact creates an obvious risk that property would be destroyed or damaged and (ii) when he does the act he either has not given any thought to the possibility of there being any such risk or has recognised that there was some risk involved and has nonetheless gone on to do it.

It will be noticed that this definition includes the common-law test (by referring to the person who recognizes the risk and takes it), but then goes further, extending to all those who fail to give any thought to the possibility of a risk which may be described as obvious. Lord Diplock's speech was unclear on the question of to whom the risk must be obvious. At one stage he suggested that it was necessary to

---

[103] This was one of the justifications advanced by Lord Diplock for making no distinction: *Caldwell* [1982] AC 341, at 352: see generally R. A. Duff, '*Caldwell* and *Lawrence*: The Retreat from Subjectivism', (1983) 3 *Oxford JLS* 77.

[104] See G. Williams, 'The Unresolved Problem of Recklessness' (1988) 8 *Legal Studies* 74, at 82.

[105] [1982] AC 341.

show that it would have been obvious to D if D had stopped to think:[106] this version of *Caldwell* might have allowed the acquittal of a person such as *Stephenson*,[107] whose mental disturbance meant that he might not have been able to see a risk which other people would regard as obvious. But subsequent decisions have confirmed that the proper interpretation is whether the risk would have been obvious to a reasonable person.[108] The *Caldwell* test therefore treats as reckless not only those who act in temper or out of indifference, but anyone who fails to foresee an obvious risk. In this respect, it is akin to negligence as a standard.

What is the justification for this extension of recklessness beyond the common-law definition? Lord Diplock offered three reasons. One was that the dividing line between awareness and unawareness of risk is so narrow and so difficult to prove that juries and magistrates should not be required to labour over it. The factual basis of this must be accepted: it may be virtually impossible to know whether or not a person was fleetingly aware of the consequences of his action. The same is true of intention, mistake, and other questions which turn on the contents of another person's mind at some time past. But it does not follow from this that the distinction must be abandoned; it is right to persist with it, if it is regarded as crucial to the grading of culpability—that is the question. Another reason given by Lord Diplock was that, in ordinary speech, the term 'reckless' is wider than awareness of risk, and includes lack of care and lack of thought. That may be true, but it does not solve the question of how wide the law's definition should be. The third reason given by Lord Diplock is the only one worthy of being called a justification: that it may be no less blameworthy for a person to fail to foresee an obvious risk than it is to see the risk and knowingly to take it. In other words, Lord Diplock challenged the common-law distinction between recklessness and negligence on the ground that it fails to draw the line in the right place. It will be observed that Lord Diplock did not appear to be altering the balance between individual responsibility and social protection. He did not argue that the definition of recklessness should be widened

---

[106] See G. Williams, 'Recklessness Redefined' [1981] *CLJ* 252; E. Griew, 'Reckless Damage and Reckless Driving: Living with *Caldwell* and *Lawrence*' [1981] Crim. LR 743; G. Syrote, 'A Radical Change in the Law of Recklessness?' [1982] Crim. LR 97; R. A. Duff, 'Professor Williams and Conditional Subjectivism' [1982] CLJ.

[107] See above, n. 99 and accompanying text.

[108] *Elliott v. C* (1983) 77 Cr. App. R 103; *Stephen Malcolm R* (1984) 79 Cr. App. R 334.

because a person who fails to give thought to an obvious risk is just as *dangerous* as the person who realizes the risk. Rather, he attacked fundamental conceptions of responsibility by arguing that the idea of *mens rea*, as encompassing intention and common-law recklessness, is unsatisfactory because it omits some equally culpable cases. As we have seen, some of its supporters admit that it is underinclusive, and have attempted to stretch it to include actions during fits of temper and actions out of indifference. The question now is whether *Caldwell* is not over-inclusive, in that it covers cases where there is little culpability at all.

One criticism which must be faced at the outset is that *Caldwell* recklessness cannot properly be termed *mens rea*, because it is not a state of mind. A person who fails to give thought to a consequence does not have a state of mind in relation to that consequence. But this presupposes that the only proper ground for ascribing blame for serious offences is advertence, in other words, that the minimum requirement for criminal culpability should be that the harmful consequence passed through D's mind. This is exactly what *Caldwell* is attacking, and this substantive challenge cannot be defeated by the procedural or linguistic device of saying that this is not *mens rea*. '*Mens rea*' is just a Latin term which is used as a shorthand reference to the requirements of intention, recklessness, knowledge, and reckless knowledge which have generally been thought to set the appropriate conditions for liability for serious offences. That could be changed if it were agreed that *Caldwell* is a more accurate representation of social judgments of blame.

A true objection is that, whereas common-law recklessness is under-inclusive, *Caldwell* recklessness is over-inclusive. Its standard of what would have been obvious to the reasonable person admits of no exceptions, and therefore sweeps into the definition of recklessness some defendants whose personal inadequacies indicate that they should not be convicted at all. The argument could be rested on the decision in *Stephenson* (1979),[109] which was overruled as a decision on the Criminal Damage Act by *Caldwell*. This means that Stephenson would now be convicted despite his inability, stemming from schizophrenia, to foresee a risk which others would have foreseen. If he is not within the defence of insanity, then he must be judged by the standard of mentally normal people. But the point emerges even more strongly from *Elliott v. C* (1983).[110] Here, a

---

[109] See above, n. 99 and accompanying text.
[110] (1983) 77 Cr. App. R 103.

backward girl of 14 who had not slept all night wandered into a shed, poured white spirit on to the the floor, and dropped lighted matches on to it. The shed was destroyed; apparently D did not know about the inflammable properties of white spirit. The Divisional Court held that she should none the less be convicted of criminal damage, since she should be judged on the basis of whether the risk would have been obvious to the reasonable adult. The court held that it was bound by precedent, unable to modify the test either for her age or for her mental condition. There is ample evidence from this decision and others[111] that some judges are unhappy with *Caldwell*, or at least with this aspect of *Caldwell*, but the model direction in that case remains unaltered. The objection here could be accommodated within *Caldwell*—without destroying its central thrust of responsibility for the thoughtless and careless—by introducing an exception based on diminished capacity, which would exempt those whom it would be unfair to judge by the standard of the normal adult.[112]

Another difficulty with *Caldwell* is that the model direction makes no mention of the person who recognizes the risk but believes that it can be eliminated. This has led commentators to argue that there is a gap or loophole which may be exploited to gain an acquittal in appropriate cases: if D has recognized the risk, he is not in Lord Diplock's category of failing to give thought to it; and if D believes the risk has been eliminated, he has not gone on to take the risk. The argument was run before the Divisional Court in *Chief Constable of Avon and Somerset v. Shimmen* (1987), [113] where D, an exponent of a martial art, was showing his friends how close to a shop-window he could kick without damaging it. In fact, he broke the window. The Divisional Court did not gainsay the loophole argument, but they directed that D should be convicted because he had said in evidence that he 'thought [he] had eliminated as much risk as possible'. This means that he did not think he had eliminated *all* risk, which in turn means that he knew there was a slight risk, and that is enough for common-law recklessness (without the need to rely on the *Caldwell* extension).[114] If the loophole argument is

---

[111] Goff LJ expressed doubts in *Elliott v. C*, ibid., as did Ackner LJ in *Stephen Malcolm R* (1984) 79 Cr. App. R 334.

[112] Cf. H. L. A. Hart, 'Negligence, Mens Rea and Criminal Responsibility', in his *Punishment and Responsibility*.

[113] (1987) 84 Cr. App. R 7.

[114] See D. J. Birch, 'The Foresight Saga: The Biggest Mistake of All?' [1988] Crim. LR 4, and *Goodfellow* (1986) 82 Cr. App. R 23.

viewed on a social plane, however, can it be maintained that there is less culpability in erroneously believing that one has eliminated all risk than in failing to give thought to the risk at all? The difference is merely that between mistake and accident: in the former case D is under a misapprehension which leads to harm; in the latter case D fails to consider the consequences of actions and causes harm. The former amounts to an omission to discover the true nature of the risk; the latter amounts to an omission to think about the existence of the risk. It is by no means clear that the *Caldwell* test is logically consistent in excluding the former and including the latter.

Finally, the *Caldwell* extension might be more acceptable if it were limited to cases of gross negligence, i.e. where a reasonable person would avoid the risk by taking elementary precautions, rather than covering cases where there is merely a risk to which D failed to advert when a reasonable person would advert.[115] In its present form it casts the net very wide, without reference to the degree of risk or the type or amount of harm risked, both of which may be relevant to culpability.

(iii) *Application of the Two Tests.* So far the *Caldwell* definition has been applied only to the crimes of criminal damage, reckless driving, and manslaughter.[116] The courts have shown little enthusiasm for extending it further, despite encouragement from the House of Lords in the early 1980s.[117] It is quite clear that common-law recklessness still applies to offences which use the term 'maliciously'.[118] There is doubt, however, about the meaning of recklessness in rape[119] and, now, about recklessness in assault.[120] The respective merits of the two tests are discussed again in section 5.3(*g*).

(d) Knowledge and Belief

In general terms, the requirement of knowledge is regarded as having the same intensity as that of intention, except that knowledge relates to circumstances forming part of the definition of the crime, and intention relates to the consequences specified in the definition

---

[115] See Williams, 'The Unresolved Problem of Recklessness', 87.

[116] In *Lawrence* [1982] AC 510, and *Seymour* [1983] 2 AC 493, respectively.

[117] Lord Roskill stated in *Seymour*, ibid., that 'recklessness' should be interpreted in its *Caldwell* sense unless Parliament ordained otherwise.

[118] e.g. *W v. Dolbey* [1983] Crim. LR 681 and *Rainbird* [1989] Crim. LR 505.

[119] See *Satnam S and Kewal S* (1983) 78 Cr. App. R 149, and below, Ch. 8.5(*d*).

[120] See *DPP v. K* (1990) 91 Cr. App. R 23, overruled by *Spratt* (1990) 91 Cr. App. R 362, and by *Parmenter* (1990) 92 Cr. App. R 68. For a note on these decisions, see A. Ashworth and K. Campbell (1991) 107 LQR.

of the crime. In fact, the distinction between circumstances and consequences is not without difficulty when applied to the many definitions of offences, but as a pragmatic dividing line it has some utility.[121] If we take the basic definition of the offence of criminal damage: a person is guilty if he or she damages property belonging to another with intent to damage property belonging to another (Criminal Damage Act 1971, section 1(1)).[122] One can argue, of course, that the only fault element required here is intention—does D intend to damage property belonging to another? But it is also possible to divide the fault element into two: Does D intend to damage property? Does D know that the property belongs to another? The knowledge relates to a fact or circumstance: although it will usually be relevant to D's reasons for acting, it may be separated analytically from the result which D intends. Such an analysis is essential for those crimes which require no result or conduct, such as possessing a controlled drug, where knowledge becomes the key element in the crime.[123] The matter is absolutely clear in the many offences which include the term 'knowingly' in their definition, such as being knowingly concerned in the importation of prohibited goods into the country.[124] There are also some offences in which the requirement is extended slightly, such as handling stolen goods knowing or believing them to be stolen, where the reference to 'believing' is taken to include people who may not *know* that the goods are stolen but may have no substantial doubt that they are.[125]

It is at this point, however, that a significant difference opens up between intention and knowledge as fault requirements. One can intend a result, whether or not it actually occurs: D can intend to kill by, say, shooting at V; if D's shot missed, then D still intended to kill and may be convicted of attempted murder. If the intention fails to come to fruition, it is none the less an intention. But this does not apply to knowledge. If we return to the basic offence of criminal damage as described above, we can consider the facts of *Smith*

---

[121] For discussion of the potential problems, see G. Williams, 'The Problem of Reckless Attempts' [1983] Crim. LR 365, and R. J. Buxton, 'Circumstances, Consequences and Attempted Rape' [1984] Crim. LR 25.

[122] This is a truncated definition: see further, D. W. Elliott, 'Criminal Damage' [1988] Crim. LR 403.

[123] *Warner v. Metropolitan Police Commissioner* [1969] 2 AC 256.

[124] Customs and Excise Management Act 1979, s. 170; see e.g. *Taaffe* [1984] AC 539.

[125] See *Hall* (1985) 81 Cr. App. R 260, and the discussion below, Ch. 9.6.

(D. R.) (1974):[126] D was renting a flat, and during the course of his tenancy he fixed some panelling to the walls to conceal the wires of his stereo equipment. When his tenancy ceased, he took down and destroyed the panelling—which he had put up for his own convenience. He was charged with criminal damage, on the basis that, in law, the panelling became the property of the landlord once it was fixed to the walls. The Court of Appeal quashed his conviction for criminal damage, pointing out that although he did intend to damage property, he believed that the property was his own, and therefore he lacked the fault element for the crime. If D had been asked whether the panelling was his own, he would surely have replied: 'Yes'. In that sense, he *knew* that it was his own. Yet it would be inaccurate to say that he knew something which was not in fact true. It is more accurate to say that he *believed* the panelling to be his own; this belief should not be described as knowledge, because it does not accord with the true position. Therefore, although one can intend something which does not come to fruition, one cannot know something which is not in fact (or in law) true.

It is relatively unusual for the element of 'knowledge of circumstances' to be contested in serious crimes. Neither murder nor manslaughter is committed if D does not know that the object against which he uses force is a human being, but there are few cases of defendants arguing that they thought their target was a theatrical dummy.[127] In some cases of rape the defendant argues that he believed that the victim was consenting, even though it subsequently transpires that she was not. Absence of consent is an element in the definition of rape, and so it must be proved either that D knew that the victim was not consenting or that he was reckless[128] as to the absence of consent. Where D argues that he mistakenly believed her to be consenting, and the jury is left in reasonable doubt about this, he should be acquitted of rape as the law stands, because the prosecution has failed to prove that he had the requisite knowledge of absence of consent. This is what is sometimes called 'the defence of mistake', but it should be clear from our discussion that it cannot properly be termed a defence. A defendant who argues that he was mistaken about consent may succeed in creating a reasonable doubt in the minds of the jury, but the defendant does not have to prove anything: the prosecution has to establish knowledge or reckless

---

[126] [1974] QB 354.
[127] See G. Williams, 'Homicide and the Supernatural' (1949) 65 LQR.
[128] For the relevant meaning of recklessness, see below, Ch. 8.5(*d*).

knowledge as to the absence of consent, as the House of Lords held in the landmark case of *DPP v. Morgan* (1976).[129] Lawyers tend to refer loosely to 'the defence of mistake', but in most cases this means, strictly speaking, that it will be argued that the prosecution has failed to prove that D had the required knowledge of the elements in the definition of the crime. It is not a defence in the sense that D must prove anything; and mistaken belief is simply an explanation of why knowledge was lacking.

Although it is rare in offences against the person for the defendant to claim that he did not know he was striking another human being, mistaken beliefs are occasionally raised in these cases in a different way. Offences of assault and wounding are defined not just in terms of the use of force against another, but the *unlawful* use of force. As we saw in Chapter 4.7, force may be lawful if it is used in self-defence or the prevention of crime, for example. If D used force in the belief that he was preventing a crime, when in reality this was not so, D would lack the knowledge that the use of force was unlawful and should therefore be acquitted of the offence. An example here is *Williams* (1984):[130] V saw a man, X, snatch a bag from a woman in the street; V ran after X and forcibly detained him; D then came upon the scene and asked V why he was punching X; V said, untruthfully, that he was a police-officer; D asked V for his warrant card, and when V failed to produce the card, D struck V. D was charged was assaulting V, and his defence was that he had mistakenly believed that his actions were justifiable in the prevention of crime. It is plain that his actions were not in fact justified, since V was acting lawfully in trying to detain X. But the law requires the prosecution to satisfy the court that D was aware of the facts which made his action unlawful, and he was not. He was mistaken. The Court of Appeal held that his conviction should be quashed: 'The mental element necessary to constitute guilt is the intent to apply unlawful force to the victim. We do not believe that the mental element can be substantiated by simply showing an intent to apply force and no more.'

What is the situation, then, if the defendant is labouring under a mistake of fact as to the circumstances? What if he believes, but believes mistakenly, that the victim is consenting, or that it is necessary to defend himself, or that a crime is being committed which he intends to prevent? D must then be judged on the

---

[129] [1976] AC 182.   [130] (1984) 78 Cr. App. R 276.

mistaken facts *as he believes them to be*. If, judged on those facts or circumstances, the prosecution fails to establish guilt, then D is entitled to be acquitted.[131] This may be seen as an unambiguous endorsement of the 'belief principle', and as a general principle, it is strongly related to the principle that D must be proved to have been aware of all the facts or circumstances specified in the defence—a principle which includes a reference to defences with a justificatory element, incorporated into the definitions of offences expressly or impliedly by the word 'unlawfully'.

The emphasis thus far in the discussion of knowledge and mistake has been upon the 'inexorable logic', as Lord Hailsham put it,[132] that if an offence requires knowledge of a given circumstance, a person who is mistaken about that circumstance should be acquitted for lack of knowledge. Logic it may be, but that should not be taken to mean that there is no place for objective requirements of reasonableness in this realm of the law. There are some offences which expressly require a mistake to have been reasonable if it is to excuse: for example, offences under the Misuse of Drugs Act 1971, to which section 28 provides defences which require proof that D had 'no reason to suspect' certain facts alleged by the prosecution.[133] It can also be argued that the very offence with which the leading decision of *DPP v. Morgan*[134] was concerned—rape—should incorporate a requirement of reasonable grounds for the belief in consent; the two parties are so physically close that there is every opportunity for D to find out whether or not the woman is consenting by asking her.[135] The result of *DPP v. Morgan* is that the English offence of rape includes no such requirement, but there are other spheres in which a mistake is required to be on reasonable grounds if it is to exculpate. One decision which still stands is *Tolson* (1889),[136] where D's conviction for bigamy was quashed on the ground that she reasonably believed that her first husband was dead and that, if he had been dead, this would have prevented conviction for the offence. There has also been a requirement of reasonableness in relation to some of the defences to crime other than self-defence and prevention of crime. Thus, where the defence is duress or

---

[131] Per Lord Lane CJ, at 280; see further, Ch. 6.6.

[132] In *DPP v. Morgan* [1976] AC 182, at 214.

[133] For discussion, see R. Ribeiro and J. Perry, 'Possession and Section 28 of the Misuse of Drugs Act 1971', [1979] Crim. LR 90, at 99–107.

[134] [1976] AC 182.

[135] See A. Ashworth, 'Towards a Theory of Criminal Legislation'.

[136] (1889) 23 QBD 168.

necessity, the courts have required D's belief that dire threats were being made or that circumstances of necessity had arisen to be based on reasonable grounds if it is to excuse.[137]

It is significant that the insistence on reasonableness of beliefs in duress and necessity occurred during the same decade (1980s) as the establishment of the principle that mistakes in relation to self-defence and prevention of crime must be genuine but need not be reasonable. Whilst it is possible to discern theoretical differences between the two kinds of defence, the difference of legal approaches is more likely to reflect ambivalence about the proper treatment of mistakes. This may be similar to the ambivalence about the para-meters of culpability shown by *Caldwell* and the ensuing debate.[138] Just as one might argue that a person who fails to give thought to an obvious risk of harm is sufficiently blameworthy for criminal liability, so one might argue that a person who acts on an unreasonable belief about facts or circumstances may also deserve criminal conviction.

(e) Reckless Knowledge

'Reckless knowledge' bears the same relation to knowledge as recklessness to intention. Thus, the general, common-law meaning of reckless knowledge is that D believes that there is a risk that the prohibited circumstance exists, and goes on to take that risk. Where *Caldwell* applies, reckless knowledge is extended to cover those who fail to give thought to the existence of the prohibited circum-stances, when a reasonable person would have done so. An example might be provided by the facts of *Smith (D. R.)*, discussed above.[139] The Criminal Damage Act 1971 penalizes anyone who damages property either intending to damage property belonging to another or who is reckless as to whether property belonging to another is damaged. When the case was decided in 1974, the common-law meaning applied and D would have been found reckless if he realized the risk that the panelling now belonged to his landlord: he did not. If the case arose now, *Caldwell* would apply, and he would be convicted if he failed to give any thought to the possibility that his landlord owned the panelling and if a reasonable person would have seen that risk. In fact, D would not be convicted, since he falls into the *Caldwell* gap:[140] he had thought about the matter and believed that the panelling belonged to him.

---

[137] See Ch. 6.6 on putative defences.   [138] See above, section 5.3(c).
[139] See above, n. 126 and accompanying text.
[140] See above, nn. 113 and 114, and accompanying text.

The tendency in the modern cases has been to draw no distinction between circumstances and consequences, and therefore to regard recklessness as something which applies in the same way to all elements of the offence. Thus in *Kimber* (1983)[141] D was convicted of indecent assault on a woman. His defence had been that he believed she was consenting, but the court did not accept this. The question then was whether the court could find that he was reckless as to the fact that she was not consenting, and the Court of Appeal held that 'his attitude to her was one of indifference to her feelings and wishes. This state of mind is aptly described in the colloquial expression, "couldn't care less", In law this is recklessness.' The court did not say that it was dealing with reckless knowledge, but clearly this is what the crime of indecent assault requires—that D was reckless as to the woman's non-consent. The use of the phrase 'couldn't care less' is somewhat equivocal as between common-law recklessness and *Caldwell*.

One other point on reckless knowledge is the proper approach to what is termed 'wilful blindness'. This is a description of the situation in which D knows that there is a risk that a prohibited circumstance exists, but refrains from checking it. An example is *Westminster City Council v. Croyalgrange Ltd.* (1986),[142] where D was charged with knowingly permitting the use of premises as a sex establishment without a licence. The House of Lords held that:

it is always open to the tribunal of fact, when knowledge on the part of a defendant is required to be proved, to base a finding of knowledge on evidence that the defendant had deliberately shut his eyes to the obvious or refrained from enquiry because he suspected the truth but did not want to have his suspicion confirmed.[143]

It will be seen that Lord Bridge used the language of inference here, suggesting that a court might infer knowledge from wilful blindness in the same way as he suggested that intention might be inferred from foresight of virtual certainty.[144] The true meaning of the passage is surely that wilful blindness is treated as actual knowledge, which has long been the law.[145] Although, strictly speaking, D does

---

[141] (1983) 77 Cr. App. R 225.
[142] (1986) 83 Cr. App. R 155; see also the draft Criminal Code, Law Com. No. 177, clause 18(a).
[143] *Westminster City Council v. Croyalgrange Ltd.* (1986) 83 Cr. App. R 155; see generally Wasik and Thompson, 'Turning a Blind Eye'.
[144] See *Moloney* [1985] AC 905, and above, n. 80.
[145] The classic statement is that of Devlin J, in *Roper v. Taylor's Garages Ltd.* [1951] 2 TLR 284, at 288.

not *know*, since he has refrained from finding out, he has an overwhelmingly strong belief (he believes it is virtually certain) that the prohibited circumstance exists. Thus, wilful blindness may be treated not as reckless knowledge, but as a form of actual knowledge.

(f) Negligence

Traditionally, books dealing with English criminal law afford an extremely brief discussion to negligence as a standard of liability. Among the common-law crimes, only manslaughter rests on liability for negligence (even that is now in doubt),[146] and careless driving is perhaps the only common offence based on negligence. Yet there are many offences of negligence among the statutory offences regulating various commercial and other activities, often taking the form of an indictable offence of doing an act 'with intent' to contravene the regulations, supported by a summary offence of negligence in committing an act in such a way as to 'have reason to believe' that the regulations will be contravened.[147] Moreover, other systems of law tend to have a larger group of offences of negligence, and might look askance at a set of laws which penalizes negligence where death is caused but does not penalise it where serious injury or suffering is caused or risked.

One reason for the opposition of modern English text-writers to criminal liability for negligence is that it is regarded as a gross derogation from the primary principle of criminal responsibility, that is, the principle of subjective choice.[148] The doctrine of *mens rea*, as expressed in the requirements of intention and recklessness (before *Caldwell*),[149] makes liability depend on proof that D chose the harm, in the sense of intending it or at least being aware that it might result. These elements are missing where mere negligence is admitted; there is no need to prove that D adverted to the consequences at all, so long as the court is satisfied that a reasonable person would have done so. To have negligence as a standard of liability would therefore move away from personal choice as the foundation of criminal responsibility. It would dilute the element of personal guilt which justifies the public condemnatory element in a criminal conviction, as distinct from a judgment of damages in tort or contract.

---

[146] See below, Ch. 7.5(c).
[147] Some examples are collected at [1980] Crim. LR 1.
[148] See above, Ch. 5.2(a).   [149] Discussed above, Ch. 5.3(c).

The counter-argument to this might be a form of 'capacity theory', the origins of which might be found in the proposition that human actions are sufficiently free, rather than determined, as to make blame and punishment defensible. This proposition underlies most of the criminal law.[150] Its relevance here is that we are justified in convicting a person who caused another person's death, and intended to do so, on the basis of that intention and of the assumption that the person could have done otherwise—he could have refrained from killing if he had had a change of mind. From that position, it might be argued that a person who negligently causes harm could have done otherwise—he could have taken the care necessary to avoid the harm. Now this is not advanced as an analytic proposition— that it is invariably possible to change one's mind or to behave in a different way, unless one is suffering from some kind of compulsion or disease. That would be an argument for strict liability rather than negligence liability. No, the argument is that individuals have the capacity to behave otherwise, and that it is fair to impose liability in those situations where there are sufficient signals to alert the reasonable citizen to the need to take care.

Three features of this counter-argument should be noted. First, its focus on capacity should not be dismissed as 'objective', for that would be an undiscriminating use of the term. As Hart has shown, it is no less possible than desirable to make exceptions for those who cannot be expected to attain the standard of foresight and control of the reasonable citizen. One only has to supplement the question, 'Did D fail to attain a reasonable standard of care in the circumstances?', with the further question; 'Could D, given his mental and physical capacities, have taken the necessary precautions?'.[151] Negligence liability need be 'objective' only insofar as it holds liable those who fail to take precautions when they could reasonably have been expected to do so. Second, negligence liability may also derogate from any principle of contemporaneity, in the sense that the culpable failure to take precautions often pre-dates the causing of the harm: the railwayman failed to check the signals or the track, so that a crash occurred later; D misunderstood the mechanism of the gun, so that when he later pulled the trigger it killed someone. The enquiry into capacity and opportunity necessitated by negligence liability widens the time-frame of the criminal law, giving precedence

---

[150] Discussed above, Ch. 4.2.
[151] This is the argument of Hart, *Punishment and Responsibility*, Chs. 2 and 5.

to the doctrine of prior fault over the principle of contemporaneity.[152] Third, the great difference between negligence liability and strict liability is that the former only arises where there is reason to suppose that precautions were necessary. The reason may have been the obligations of D's work, particularly applicable to those operating systems of public transport; or the obligations of driving a motor vehicle; or the obligations of owning or managing a factory; or the obligations of engaging in a particular trade or business. Many such enterprises have their own legislation or codes which lay down standards of care. Where they do, there is little difficulty in establishing prior fault.

The discussion thus far should have established that people who cause harm negligently may be culpable, in the sense that they fail to take reasonable precautions when they have the capacity to do so. What it does not establish is that negligence is an appropriate standard for criminal liability, for it must be borne in mind that criminal liability is the law's most condemnatory form, and it should be reserved for serious wrongs. How might it be argued that the English tradition of drawing the line of criminal liability below intention and recklessness, and above negligence (at least for 'conventional' crimes, such as those in the draft Criminal Code),[153] is ill-founded? One approach would be to establish that some cases of negligence manifest greater culpability than some cases of common-law recklessness. Thus it could be claimed that a person who knowingly takes a slight risk of harm is less culpable than another person who fails to think about or recognize a high risk of the same harm: D, a shot-gun champion, fires at a target, knowing that there is a slight risk that the bullet will ricochet and injure a spectator, which it does; E, who rarely handles guns, is invited to participate in a shooting-party and fires wildly into bushes, failing to consider the possibility of others being there, and one is injured. Is D manifestly more culpable than E? A different comparison would be between someone who knowingly takes the risk of a small harm occurring and someone who fails to recognize the risk of a serious harm occurring: a criminal law which convicts the former and not the latter could be said to be transfixed by the notion of a 'consistent' general part. Why maintain that negligence is never an appropriate standard of criminal liability, even where the harm is great and the risk obvious?

[152] See above, section 5.2(d).
[153] See above, nn. 39 and 40, and accompanying text.

The argument is therefore moving towards the conclusion that negligence may be an appropriate standard for criminal liability where: (i) the harm is great; (ii) the risk is obvious; and (iii) the defendant has the capacity to take the required precautions. This opens up further debates on various points. The thesis is that negligence may be an appropriate standard where there are well-known risks of serious harm. This argues in favour of negligence as a standard of liability for serious offences against the person, including some serious sexual offences,[154] and also for some serious offences against the environment and property. Critics would be able to attack decisions to draw the line at certain levels of seriousness, but these would be essentially practical criticisms which would not undermine the argument in favour of negligence liability. The spread of negligence liability would not have to result in the broadening of the traditional category of *mens rea*, and would not mean that intention, recklessness, and negligence would henceforth be bracketed together. It would be perfectly possible for a criminal code to provide separate offences of negligence, with lower maximum sentences, at appropriate points in the hierarchy of offences. This, in turn, raises possibilities of defendants who foresaw the risk of the harm (and were therefore subjectively reckless) pleading guilty to the lesser offence of negligence, whereas if there were no such offence, they would be duly convicted of the 'intentionally or recklessly' higher offence. But this is a systemic problem in criminal justice, and cannot be a conclusive argument against spreading the net of the criminal law in respect of serious harms. A further issue is whether the offences of negligence should be in the inchoate mode, 'failing to take reasonable precautions', or should be tied to the occurrence of the particular harm. Careless driving is of the former type, manslaughter of the latter, and this point will be pursued further in connection with crimes of endangerment.[155]

Even granted this argument in favour of criminalizing certain instances of negligence, what would be the point of doing so? This takes us back to the aims of the criminal law, discussed earlier.[156] It might be tempting to maintain that the general preventive aim of the criminal law cannot be served by offences of negligence; the notion of deterrence presupposes rational reflection by D at the time of offending, whereas the distinguishing feature of negligence is that D failed to think (when a reasonable person would have

---

[154] See the discussion of rape in Ch. 8.5.
[155] See Chs. 7.6, 7.7, and 8.3(*j*).   [156] See Ch. 1.3.

done). However, it can be argued that crimes of negligence may exert a general deterrent effect, by alerting people to the need to take care in certain situations. The practical prospects of deterrence here seem no less propitious than in relation to offences requiring intention or recklessness. The principal justification, however, would be that negligent harm-doers deserve criminal conviction because they are sufficiently culpable. This is a question of degree and of judgment, on which views may differ. But it is certainly not resolved by stating that persons found to have acted with the form of *mens rea* known as recklessness are always more culpable than those who act negligently. Once the falsity of this proposition is demonstrated, the argument about the appropriate level of culpability for criminal conviction cannot be concluded simply by drawing a line based on *mens rea*, awareness, and 'choice'.

(g) Objective versus Subjective

Much of the above discussion might be characterised as an 'objective v. subjective' debate within the criminal law. Such a description could be misleading, however, for all forms of recklessness have an objective element (was the risk an unjustified one?)[157] and it has been shown that liability for negligence can be adapted so as to take account of the capacities of each individual defendant (would that be labelled objective or subjective?). The real debate has been over the assumption that criminal liability is only appropriate, at least for 'traditional offences', where D is proved to have adverted to the prohibited consequence and to have been aware of the relevant circumstances. That assumption was challenged by the House of Lords in *Caldwell* (1982),[158] where it introduced the extended notion of recklessness to include those who failed to think about a risk which would have been obvious to a reasonably prudent person. Clearly this amounted to the incorporation of some cases of negligence, previously not criminalized, into the *mens rea* concept of recklessness. The outcry from traditionalists was great, amplified by subsequent decisions which refused to modify the test to take account of capacities diminished through youth, tiredness, and mental backwardness.[159] Yet, as the discussion of negligence liability in the previous section has suggested, it is important to separate the clearly objectionable from the less contentious. There is surely room for argument about whether the law is justified in criminalizing

---

[157] See above, p. 155.   [158] [1982] AC 341, discussed above, p. 157.
[159] See above n. 111.

someone who fails to be sufficiently alert in circumstances where there is a risk of serious harm which would be obvious to ordinary citizens with normal capacities. What is objectionable about *Caldwell* is that it criminalizes all such people, even those whose capacities are significantly diminished.

5.4. THE REFERENTIAL POINT OF FAULT

To say that a certain crime should require intention, or intent or recklessness, is not enough. One must enquire: intention (or recklessness) as to what? It might be said loosely that 'the crime of manslaughter requires proof of intention or recklessness': the reason why this is a loose statement is that the intent or recklessness required is the same as that for assault or some other criminal act, whereas the liability imposed is that for homicide. Close analysis of the elements of the crime will show that the required fault and the result specified in the definition fail to correspond. This is the burden of the principle of correspondence, outlined above.[160] Whenever one is discussing intent or recklessness, it is a good idea always to establish its referential point.

(a) Fault, Conduct, and Result

The argument may be carried further by considering the breadth or narrowness of the definitions of offences. If the law included a general offence of intentionally causing physical harm to another, it would be far easier to establish the intent than if the law had a series of graded offences, such as causing serious injury intentionally, causing injury intentionally, and so forth. Similarly, a law which includes a general offence of intentionally causing damage to property belonging to another makes it far easier to establish the intent than a law with a series of offences differentiated according to the type of property damaged. Do these different legislative techniques have significant implications for the subjective doctrines of fault? Surely they do: if these doctrines rest on the view that persons should only be labelled and punished according to what they chose to do, one could argue that a single broad offence of 'intentionally causing physical harm to another' obliterates the distinction between intending a minor assault and intending a major injury, and that a single broad offence of 'intentionally damaging property belonging

---

[160] See above, Section 5.2(*b*).

to another' obliterates the distinction between intending damage to a cheap item and intending damage to an expensive item. The trend towards broader offence definitions, evident in criminal damage[161] but not in offences against the person in England,[162] gives greater weight to the principle of taking the consequences of any wrong-doing (section 5.2(b) above) than to the principle of correspondence (section 5.2(a) above). To that extent, it detracts from the elements of choice and control which are fundamental to the subjective approach. But how should this problem be solved?[163] It is hardly practical to allow each person to nominate those factors which he or she regarded as significant in any particular event: who is to say whether fidelity to individual choice and control requires two or twenty grades of criminal damage, or two or four grades of offences of violence? At least, the implications for fault principles of these labelling decisions[164] should be kept firmly in mind.

The argument may be taken still further, for there are cases where, as everyone agrees, D intended to cause a different result from the one which actually occurred. How ought the law to deal with such cases? Should it respect D's choice, and provide for a conviction of attempting to do X (which was what D intended to do)? Or should it regard the result as the dominant factor, ignore the difference in D's intention, and convict on the basis of 'sufficient similarity' between the intention and the result? English law adopts the latter, more pragmatic approach. The Law Commission, in introducing a provision into the draft Criminal Code which follows the traditional approach, confirms the emphasis on results by stating that a conviction for attempt would be 'inappropriate as not describing the *harm done* adequately for labelling or sentencing purposes'.[165] The traditional English approach rests on three doctrines—unforseen mode, mistaken object, and transferred fault.

[161] See Law Com. No. 29, *Offences of Damage to Property* (1970), and the Criminal Damage Act 1971; also above, n. 122.

[162] See Criminal Law Revision Committee, 14th Report, *Offences against the Person* (1980, Cmnd. 7844), discussed below, Ch. 8.3(k).

[163] See A. Ashworth, 'The Elasticity of Mens Rea', in C. Tapper (ed.), *Crime, Proof and Punishment* (1981), and M. Moore, 'Intentions and Mens Rea', in R. Gavison (ed.), *Issues in Contemporary Legal Philosophy* (1987).

[164] See the discussion of the principle of fair labelling in Ch. 3.3(l).

[165] Law Com. No. 177, ii, para. 8.57 (my italics).

(b) Unforeseen Mode

When D sets out to commit an offence by one method but actually causes the prohibited consequence in a different way, the offence may be said to have been committed by an unforeseen mode. Since most crimes penalizing a result (with fault) do not specify any particular mode of commission,[166] it is easy to regard the difference of mode as legally irrelevant. D intended to kill V; he chose to shoot him, but the shot missed; it hit a nearby heavy object, which fell on V's head and caused his death. Any moral distinction between the two modes is surely too slender to justify legal recognition. To charge D with *attempting* to kill V when he *did* kill him seems excessively fastidious. Pragmatism is surely the right approach here.[167]

(c) Mistaken Object

When D sets out to commit an offence in relation to a particular victim but makes a mistake of identity and directs his conduct at the wrong victim, the offence may be said to have been committed despite the mistaken object. The same would apply if D intends to steal one item of property but mistakenly takes another. So long as the two objects fall within the same legal category, it may be said that any moral distinction between them is too slender to justify legal recognition. Two questions may be raised here, however. First, there is one other area of criminal law where a change in the identity of the victim is regarded as crucial, namely, the law of complicity.[168] Is there really no moral significance in the plea: 'I intended to kill my enemy, X, and never meant any harm to the poor innocent, Y'? Second, much depends on the breadth of definition of the relevant offence: there is surely some moral significance in the plea: 'I thought the picture I damaged was just a cheap copy; I had no idea that a valuable painting would be kept in that place.'[169]

(d) Transferred Fault

When D sets out to commit an offence in relation to a particular person or a particular property but his conduct miscarries and the

---

[166] The offences of obtaining by deception form an exception: see below, Ch. 9.7.
[167] See Ashworth, 'The Elasticity of Mens Rea', 46–7.
[168] See Law Com. No. 177, ii, para. 8.31, and below, Ch. 10.5(a).
[169] See Ashworth, 'The Elasticity of Mens Rea', 47.

harm falls upon a different person or a different property, D's intent may be said to have been transferred and the offence to have been committed against the actual victim or property. When the fault is transferred, any defence which D might have is transferred with it.[170] As with unforeseen mode and mistaken object, the fault may only be transferred within the same offence.[171] Thus, if D throws a brick at some people, intending to hurt them, and the brick misses them and breaks a window, the intent to injure cannot be transferred to the offence of damaging property:[172] the possibilities are an attempt to cause injury, and recklessly damaging property. As with the doctrine of mistaken object, the breadth of definition of the offence has some importance here. It is one thing to accept that D, who swung his belt at W and struck V, should be convicted of injuring V; it is quite another thing, in moral terms, to accept that E, who threw a stone at a window, should be convicted of intentionally damaging a valuable painting which, unbeknown to him, was hanging inside. Yet English law would convict E, probably by reliance on the broad wording of the Criminal Damage Act 1971 (any 'property belonging to another'), without expressly invoking the doctrine of transferred fault.[173]

(e) Establishing the Referential Point

A system of criminal law which succeeded in reflecting the varying degrees of importance which people attribute to aspects of their intentions (the mode of execution, the identity of the victim, the value of the property) might be a 'law professor's dream', but it is clearly not practical. The law is right to regard some aspects as relevant and others as irrelevant. But that does not establish that the traditional English approach is the most appropriate. It is certainly pragmatic, and the draft Criminal Code ensures that this will continue.[174] Does its pragmatism stretch too far? Would it not be better to analyse some of these cases in terms of an unfulfilled intention, combined with an accidental (or perhaps reckless) causing of harm? Some would argue that the present law of inchoate

---

[170] *Gross* (1913) 23 Cox CC 455.

[171] See A. Ashworth, 'Transferred Malice and Punishment for Unforeseen Consequences', in P. Glazebrook (ed.), *Reshaping the Criminal Law* (1978); see also M. Moore, *Criminal Law Theory* (1991).

[172] *Pembliton* (1874) 12 Cox CC 607.

[173] See Ashworth, 'Transferred Malice and Punishment', 89–93.

[174] In effect, clause 24 of the draft Criminal Code is a 'deeming' provision: see Law Com. No. 177, ii, para. 8.59.

offences would not ensure a conviction in all these cases of mis-carried intent and miscarried recklessness:[175] according to this view, the three doctrines are not merely simpler for prosecutors, and not merely consistent with the traditional emphasis of English law on results, but also necessary if justice is to be done in all cases. There is, it may be argued, no serious distortion of 'desert' or proportionality involved in the three doctrines, since the doctrines depend on what D set out to commit. Yet there remains the law's ambivalence about the importance of a victim's identity: if this really is significant to offenders and people's judgments of them, should not more use be made of the law of attempts, where it is clearly applicable?

This chapter has outlined only part of the picture of fault require-ments in criminal law, since the negative fault requirements (to be discussed in Chapter 6) have a significant bearing on general conceptions of 'desert', responsibility, and culpability. However, it may be worthwhile to give an interim selection of issues.

First, there is the importance of analysing the elements of each offence, so as to be clear about their various fault requirements and thus about the referential point of fault. Second, there is the manifest flexibility of the borderlines between the various gradations of fault: the penumbra of vagueness in the extent to which 'intent' goes beyond purpose, in the distinction between recklessness and negligence, and even in the notion of strict liability, not only breaches the principle of maximum certainty but also places some discretion in the hands of the courts. Thirdly, and most importantly, warnings have been sounded about the indiscriminate use of social defence arguments to justify restrictions on the pursuit of subjective principles respecting individual autonomy. There are, it is evident, decisions to be reached about the priority given to conflicting principles of subjective liability and social defence. Courts and some writers are unaccustomed to articulating or even referring to the principles, but take refuge readily in assertions about public protection. It was questioned whether too much emphasis had been placed on social-defence arguments in relation to strict liability and too little emphasis in relation to the debate about liability for recklessness or negligence. Moreover, the assumption appears to be that the same standard of liability should operate as widely as

---

[175] G. Williams, 'Convictions and Fair Labelling' [1983] CLJ 85.

possible, that standard being intention, knowledge, and subjective recklessness. If the potential harm is great and the precautions needed to avoid it are either well-known (or should be known to someone engaged in the particular activity), the argument for departing from the supposed orthodoxy is a powerful one.

6

NEGATIVE FAULT
REQUIREMENTS

6.1. GROUNDS OF EXCUSE

Criminal lawyers sometimes speak and write as if criminal guilt consists of the presence of *mens rea*, but observations in previous chapters have already hinted that matters are not so simple. The notions of fault and culpability go beyond *mens rea* and require a discussion of other doctrines which are sometimes referred to as 'excuses' or 'defences'. It is technically incorrect to use the term 'defence' when referring to the 'defence of mistake' or the 'defence of accident', since these (along with intoxication and insanity, to some extent) are simply 'failure of proof' arguments; 'mistake' or 'accident' is merely a way of explaining why the prosecution has failed to prove knowledge, intention, or recklessness.[1] Beyond these, there is a range of possible excuses which contain elements which do not correspond to the positive requirements of criminal liability (e.g. duress, mistake of law), and they are discussed here with a view to assessing whether they have any general characteristics in common. They are termed 'negative fault requirements' in order to indicate that they are generally matters which the prosecution does not have to disprove unless the defence raises some credible issue on one or more of them. In other words, it is assumed that D has no excuse on any of these grounds unless some evidence of it is adduced in court. It therefore follows that many of these excuses are not inconsistent with *mens rea:* duress and mistake of law, for example, may be perfectly compatible with an intention to commit the prohibited act. But it should not be assumed that all these excuses are compatible with *mens rea*. Indeed, the first two conditions

---

[1] See Paul Robinson, 'Criminal Law Defenses: A Systematic Analysis' (1982) 82 *Columbia LR* 199, and his *Criminal Law Defenses* (1984), for a fivefold classification of defences: (i) failure of proof defences; (ii) offence modifications (e.g. withdrawal in complicity); (iii) justifications; (iv) excuses; and (v) non-exculpatory public-policy defences (e.g. time limitations). This chapter is concerned with (iv) and with some forms of (i).

to be discussed—insanity and intoxication—might well exclude *mens rea* in particular cases, but the law has evolved doctrines which prevent or restrict the avoidance of liability by this means. As we shall see, the law takes such a serious view of harm caused by an insane or intoxicated person that not only does it invoke social-defence arguments to justify special provisions for these cases, but it also goes some way towards ensuring that these special provisions also apply to other conditions created by insanity or intoxication (e.g. automatism, mistake).

6.2. MENTAL DISORDER

One of the fundamental presumptions of the criminal law and criminal liability is that the defendant is 'normal', i.e. is able to function within the normal range of mental and physical capabilities. We have seen that many of the principles of individual fairness presuppose an individual who is rational and autonomous: otherwise he does not deserve to be liable to criminal punishment. A person who is mentally disordered may fall below these assumed standards of mental capacity and rationality, and this may make it unfair to hold him responsible for his behaviour. It is for this reason that most systems of criminal law introduce tests of 'insanity' which result in the exemption of some mentally disordered persons from criminal liability. However, uneasiness and ambiguity abound here, since there is also a belief that those exempted on grounds of insanity are dangerous, and therefore ought to be detained at the State's discretion. The result is that what is usually described as a 'defence of insanity' (implying an arrangement to the defendant's advantage) may become an instrument of social protection (since the 'defence' results in indefinite detention).

(a) Unfitness to Stand Trial

Before considering the defence of insanity, some attention should be devoted to the procedural provisions for dealing with persons who are unfit to stand trial through mental disorder or (in some cases) through being deaf mute. The key question is whether the person is capable of giving, receiving, and understanding communications relating to a criminal trial—on matters such as challenging jurors, deciding on a plea, understanding the evidence, instructing counsel, and so forth.[2] This question is decided by a jury, after

---

[2] See *Pritchard* (1836) 7 C & P 303, and *Robertson* [1968] 1 WLR 1767.

hearing medical evidence. If the jury decides that the person is 'unfit to plead', the judge must order him to be admitted to a hospital and detained there until the Home Secretary or a Mental Health Review Tribunal decides on his release.[3]

The contrast between the reasons of individual fairness—which lead to the exemption of the person from criminal trial—and the reasons of social protection—which lead to indefinite detention—is all too apparent. Indeed, the contrast begins to approach confusion when one reflects that it is not only the defence but also the prosecution and the judge who may raise the issue. The judge does have a power to postpone the issue of 'fitness to plead' until the prosecution case has been presented, thereby avoiding indefinite commitment in a case where the prosecution evidence would not have been strong enough for conviction anyway.[4] The Butler Committee recommended that there should be a trial of the facts in every case, taking account of both the prosecution and defence arguments; this would avoid the indefinite detention of someone who would receive a complete acquittal if the defence evidence could be presented—which it now cannot be.[5] The Committee also advocated flexible powers of disposal for the judge, rather than mandatory commitment to indefinite hospitalization.[6] This discretion would go some way towards redressing the balance in favour of individual fairness, especially in a case where the charge against a defendant is theft of £5 and three light bulbs.[7] It is surely wrong that a person too disordered to stand trial should be compulsorily detained under criminal powers for a period well beyond that appropriate to the gravity of the alleged (or indeed, proven) offence. If longer compulsory detention is thought necessary, this should be based on civil powers of commitment and detention. The significance of the crime ought not to outlast the period of detention which would have been proportionate to that offence in the case of a 'normal' person.

(b) The Special Verdict of Insanity

If the defendant is thought fit to stand trial, then the issue of mental disorder may also be raised as a defence; namely, that at the time of

---

[3] Criminal Procedure (Insanity) Act 1964, s. 5. [4] Ibid., s. 4(2).
[5] *Report of the Committee on Mentally Abnormal Offenders* (chairman: Lord Butler; 1975, Cmnd. 6244), para. 10.24; see R. D. Mackay, 'The Decline of Disability in Relation to the Trial' [1991] Crim. LR 87. [6] Ibid., Ch. 3.
[7] See C. Emmins, 'Unfitness to Plead: Glenn Pearson's Case', [1986] Crim. LR 604.

the alleged offence D was too disordered to be held liable. Medical evidence will be crucial in determining this, but it is for the law to lay down the appropriate test. Mental disorder is a broad concept under the Mental Health Act 1983,[8] and few would maintain that all those who fall within one of the four classes of disorder under that Act should be exempted from criminal liability. The criminal law has settled on a much narrower conception of 'insanity', proof of which should lead to a verdict of 'not guilty by reason of insanity', followed by an order committing the defendant to indefinite hospitalization at the discretion of the Home Secretary or a Mental Health Review Tribunal.[9] In about one-fifth of cases the patient is released within nine months,[10] so it cannot be said that the consequences of an insanity verdict are always Draconian. But release is a discretionary matter, unrelated to the gravity of the offence involved. The general structure of the insanity defence combines the basic idea that it is unfair to hold a person criminally liable for conduct whilst insane, with a fear that such a person may be so dangerous as to require indefinite detention. A further paradox is that many mentally disordered defendants, aware of the possible consequences of the insanity defence, plead guilty to the charge, seeking only to raise their mental condition in mitigation of sentence. The special verdict certainly cannot be regarded as effective in singling out the most dangerous mentally disordered harm-doers. In practice, about a thousand convicted offenders a year receive a hospital order or a psychiatric probation order at the sentencing stage, and it is likely that in a completely fair system, some of them would not be burdened with a criminal conviction but would be granted a defence of mental disorder instead.

The tension between considerations of individual fairness and policies of social protection is also manifest in the evidential and procedural provisions. Insanity is the only general defence where the burden of proof is placed on the defendant, a paradox when one reflects that the consequence of a successful defence favours social protection (indefinite commitment) rather than the defendant's own interests. The prosecution may raise insanity if the defendant pleads diminished responsibility in response to a murder charge,[11]

[8] See s. 1 of the Act, discussed by A. Ashworth and L. Gostin, 'Mentally Disordered Offenders and the Sentencing Process', [1984] Crim. LR 195, at 195–8.
[9] Criminal Procedure (Insanity) Act 1964, s. 5.
[10] R. D. Mackay, 'Fact and Fiction about the Insanity Defence' [1990] Crim. LR 247.
[11] Criminal Procedure (Insanity) Act 1964, s. 6.

and, according to one view, can do so in all cases where D puts state of mind in issue.[12] The prosecution bears the burden of proving insanity here, which is much more appropriate given the consequences of the verdict of 'not guilty by reason of insanity'.

The requirements of the defence of insanity were laid down by the judges in *M'Naghten's Case* as long ago as 1843.[13] The defence applies where D was labouring under such a defect of reason, due to disease of the mind, as either not to know the nature and quality of the act or, if D did know this, not to know that he or she was doing wrong. A 'defect of reason' means the deprivation of reasoning power, and does not apply to temporary absent-mindedness or confusion.[14] The phrase 'disease of the mind' has been construed broadly, so as to encompass any disease which affects the functioning of the mind—whether its cause be organic or functional, and whether its effect be permanent or intermittent—so long as it was operative at the time of the alleged offence.[15] But the phrase 'disease of the mind' has been held to exclude conditions arising from some external factor, such as drugs or hypnosis: such cases may fall within the ambit of automatism.[16] Where it is established that there was a defect of reason due to disease of the mind, it is then necessary to show that it had one of two effects. First, the defence is fulfilled if D did not know the nature and quality of the act—in other words, did not realize what he was doing. In most cases this would show the absence of intention, knowledge or recklessness; but since this mental state arises from insanity, considerations of social protection are held to require the special verdict rather than an ordinary acquittal. Second, the defence is fulfilled if D did not know that he was doing wrong. In English law 'wrong' has been given the narrow meaning of 'legally wrong'[17] although in practice it seems that some cases veer towards the Australian interpretation of 'failure to appreciate that the conduct was morally wrong' (usually, where D believes that he must, for some distorted reason, do the act).[18]

---

[12] Per Watkins LJ, in *Dickie* (1984) 79 Cr. App. R 213, at 219.
[13] (1843) 10 Cl. & Fin. 200; see generally N. Morris, *Madness and the Criminal Law* (1982), and I. Potas, *Just Deserts for the Mad* (1985).
[14] *Clarke* (1972) 56 Cr. App. R. 225.
[15] Per Lord Diplock, in *Sullivan* [1984] AC 156.
[16] *Quick* [1973] QB 910 above, p. 97.
[17] *Windle* [1952] 2 QB 826, followed by the majority of the Supreme Court of Canada in *Schwartz* (1979) 29 CCC (2d) 1.
[18] *Stapleton v. R* (1952) 86 CLR 358.

Judicial interpretation of the M'Naghten Rules has generally been driven by considerations of social protection. The main features have been twofold. First, it is clear that evidence of mental disorder may only be used to negative *mens rea*, and thereby to lead to an ordinary acquittal, if the mental disorder falls outside the M'Naghten Rules. Judges have the power to rule that a defendant is raising the defence of insanity if the substance of the evidence given supports all the elements required for that defence,[19] even though D was trying to secure an ordinary acquittal. In these circumstances D will usually be advised to change the plea to guilty in order to avoid the special verdict. Second, the courts have used the broad concept of 'disease of the mind' to ensure that some types of case which might appear to fall within automatism are brought within the insanity verdict and its protective consequences. In *Sullivan* (1983)[20] epilepsy was included, and in *Hennessy* (1989)[21] diabetes was included. Neither condition would ordinarily be regarded as a form of insanity. But, since they resulted in violent behaviour, and since they were diseases which affected the functioning of the mind, social-protection arguments led the courts to ensure that they fall within insanity.

(c) Reform

It is not difficult to argue that the M'Naghten Rules are outmoded. Medical science has advanced enormously in the last 150 years. The Rules refer only to mental disorders which affect the cognitive faculties, i.e. knowledge of what one is doing, or of its wrongness, whereas some forms of mental disorder impair the power of control over actions. This is now recognized in the 'diminished responsibility' doctrine in manslaughter,[22] which includes cases of 'irresistible impulse', and it should clearly be recognized as part of a reformed mental-disorder defence. The Model Penal Code accomplishes this by referring to mental disorders which result in D lacking 'substantial capacity either to appreciate the wrongfulness of his conduct or to conform his conduct to the requirements of the law'.[23] The Butler Committee proposed to take this into account in a different way— by ensuring that one ground for a mental-disorder verdict is that, at

[19] e.g. *Kemp* [1957] 1 QB 399, *Clarke* (1972) 56 Cr. App. R 225.
[20] [1984] AC 156.
[21] (1989) 89 Cr. App. R 10; cf. cases of diabetes where the loss of consciousness results from the taking of insulin rather than from the failure to take it: above, Ch. 4.5(c).
[22] Homicide Act 1957, s. 2; see below, Ch. 7.4(e).
[23] Model Penal Code, s. 4. 01.

the time of the alleged offence, D was suffering from severe mental illness or handicap.[24] In other words, if the mental disorder was severe in degree, there is no need to establish that it affected D's cognition: so long as the court is satisfied that the conduct was attributable to that disorder, the special verdict should be returned. It therefore includes both cognitive and volitional incapacity. The other limb of the Butler proposals, also to be found in a revised form in the draft Criminal Code,[25] concerns cases where evidence of mental disorder is used to show that D lacked the mental element for the crime. This includes cases of 'pathological automatism that is liable to recur', again classifying diabetes and epilepsy within mental disorder for reasons of social defence.[26]

These proposals show that both individual fairness and social defence would have a distinct influence on the reformed law, although some would argue that fairness to the 'mad' requires more than this.[27] The English approach appears to be that it is unfair to hold persons who lack sufficient rationality liable to criminal punishment, for they do not deserve it. But there are some mentally disordered persons who cause serious harm and may be regarded as 'dangerous':[28] some measure of social protection is clearly needed. Thus, one crucial issue is the consequence of a verdict of 'not guilty by reason of mental disorder'. The Butler Committee was firmly of the opinion that there should be discretion in disposal here.[29] If this were the case, the law would have a radically different effect: there would be no need for D to change his plea to guilty if the judge ruled that the defence was one of mental disorder; and no need for the judge to commit D indefinitely to hospital. The new special verdict might attract less stigma than the present insanity verdict, and fairness principles might have an influence on disposals, disturbing the present assumption that all such persons are so dangerous as to require indefinite commitment.

---

[24] Butler Report, para. 18.30.

[25] Law Com. No. 177, clauses 34–40.

[26] Ibid. ii, para. 11.28.

[27] Morris, *Madness and the Criminal Law*.

[28] This opens up a wide area of debate. What amounts to evidence of future dangerousness? Would this evidence be acceptable in the case of a 'normal' person? How accurate are predictions of dangerousness? See e.g. J. Monahan, *Predicting Violent Behaviour* (1981), and J. Floud and W. Young, *Dangerousness and Criminal Justice* (1981), esp. Appendix B.

[29] Butler Report, para. 18. 42.

6.3. INTOXICATION

Research confirms that many of those who commit crimes of violence and burglary (at least) have taken some kind of intoxicant beforehand.[30] Alcohol is probably the most widely used of intoxicants, but narcotic or hallucinogenic drugs are involved in some cases, too, and our discussion will relate to those who have taken alcohol, drugs, or a combination of the two. The usual effects are a loosening of inhibitions and, perhaps, a feeling of well-being and confidence. It is well known that people who have taken intoxicants tend to say or do things which they would not say or do when sober, and, in that sense, intoxicants may be regarded as the cause of certain behaviour. But, as we saw in Chapter 5 and in the discussion of the insanity defence, the criminal law's conception of fault has tended to concentrate on cognition rather than on volition. One would therefore expect the law to be more concerned with the question of whether D's intoxicated state negatived *mens rea* than with the question of whether D's power to choose to cause the prohibited harm was substantially reduced, and this is so. However, as with insanity, arguments of social defence have been used to prevent the simple acquittal of those who cause harm and who lack awareness at the time because of intoxication. And this, as we shall see, has caused various doctrinal difficulties for English criminal law.

(a) The English Intoxication Rules

The 'inexorable logic'[31] of the doctrine of *mens rea* still has some force in this sphere of English law, but not much. If D becomes intoxicated involuntarily—where a drink is laced without D's knowledge, for example, or where a drug is medically prescribed and no warning of possible incapacitating effects is given—D should be acquitted of any offence if the required *mens rea* was absent.[32] Where D becomes intoxicated 'voluntarily' (i.e. where there is no reason to regard it as 'involuntary'), D may rely on that intoxication to establish that he lacked intention if the crime charged is an offence of specific intent. This is the rule established by the decision in *DPP v. Majewski* (1977),[33] which divides crimes into

---

[30] See the circumspect findings of R. Walmsley, *Personal Violence*, Home Office Research Study No. 89 (1986), 15–17.

[31] The phrase of Lord Hailsham in *DPP v. Morgan* [1976] AC 182, at 214.

[32] This was recognized in *DPP v. Majewski* [1977] AC 443.   [33] Ibid.

'offences of specific intent' and 'offences of basic intent', and allows intoxication as a 'defence' to the former not to the latter. Murder and wounding with intent are crimes of specific intent, and there is no great loss of social defence in allowing intoxication to negative the intent required for those crimes when the amplitude of the basic intent offences of manslaughter and unlawful wounding lies beneath them—ensuring D's conviction and liability to sentence. Various theories have been advanced in an attempt to explain why those offences (together with theft, handling, and all crimes of attempt, for example) are crimes of 'specific intent' whereas others are not, but they need not detain us here.[34] The central point is that the courts have restricted the operation of the 'inexorable logic' of *mens rea* to this narrow sphere in which no great loss of social defence can occur. Eleswhere, they have pursued a policy of preventing evidence of intoxication being adduced to negative intention or recklessness.

This policy was expressed in *DPP v. Majewski* through the idea of 'offences of basic intent', and was expressed slightly differently in *Caldwell* (1982)[35] in terms of 'recklessness'. Thus, where recklessness is sufficient *mens rea* for the crime, evidence of intoxication is irrelevant because anyone who was intoxicated is deemed to have been reckless. The justification for this sweeping rule, as we shall see below, is grounded in the widespread knowledge that alcohol and narcotics can have incapacitating effects. One exception has recently been allowed, to deal with cases where D was unaware of the effects of a medically prescribed drug[36] or where D believed, and people generally believe, that the drug is of a sedative or soporific kind which would not lead to aggressive or unpredictable behaviour (in this case, valium).[37] Apart from this exceptional category, the courts have taken a strong line in restricting the legal relevance of evidence of intoxication. Thus, where it is alleged that intoxication induced a state of automatism, the case is treated as one of intoxication (the cause) rather than automatism (the effect);[38] a similar approach has been taken in some cases of intoxicated mistake, bringing them under the rules of intoxication (the cause) rather than mistake (the effect).[39] Even in cases of diminished

---

[34] Their inadequacy is demonstrated by G. Williams, *Textbook of Criminal Law* (2nd edn., 1983), 428–30, and A. Ward, 'Making Some Sense of Self-Induced Intoxication' [1986] CLJ 247.

[35] [1982] AC 341.   [36] *Bailey* [1983] 1 WLR 760.

[37] *Hardie* [1984] 1 WLR 64.   [38] *Lipman* [1970] 1 QB 152.

[39] Cf. *O'Grady* (1987) 85 Cr. App. R 315 and *O'Connor* [1991] Crim. LR 135, with *Jaggard v. Dickinson* [1981] QB 527.

responsibility, which is merely a qualified defence to murder and results in conviction for manslaughter, the courts have striven to separate the effects of intoxication from those of mental disorder.[40]

(b) The Attack on the English Approach

The approach of the English courts has been attacked on several grounds. The absence of a definition of 'specific intent' which enables lawyers to assign offences to that category or to 'basic intent' is a familiar source of criticism.[41] Nor has the approach of deeming intoxicated persons to be reckless been any better received. Any 'deeming' is plainly a fiction, and the attempts of Lord Elwyn-Jones in *DPP v. Majewski* to argue that intoxicated persons really are reckless because 'getting drunk is a reckless course of conduct'[42] involve a manifest confusion between a general, non-legal use of the term 'reckless' and the technical, legal term, which denotes (in most offences against the person)[43] that D was aware of the risk of the result which actually occurred. In most cases it is far-fetched to argue that a person who is getting drunk is aware of the type of conduct he or she might later indulge in.

These criticisms of the courts' attempts to stretch the established meaning of 'intent' and of 'recklessness' in order to deal with the problems of intoxication have been joined by other arguments. Some have held that the intoxication rules are inconsistent with section 8 of the Criminal Justice Act 1967, which requires courts to take account of all the evidence when deciding whether D intended or foresaw a result:[44] but the effect of *DPP v. Majewski* is to deny that evidence of intoxication is relevant unless the crime is one of specific intent, and section 8 extends only to legally relevant evidence.[45] Another argument is that the intoxication rules are inconsistent with the principle of contemporaneity, in that they base D's conviction (of an offence of basic intent) on the antecedent fault of voluntarily taking intoxicants:[46] but the principle of contemporaneity itself conflicts with the doctrine of prior fault, as we have

---

[40] Cf. *Gittens* [1984] QB 698, with *Tandy* (1988) 87 Cr. App R 45.

[41] See above n. 33.   [42] [1977] AC 443, at p. 475.

[43] See above, 5.3(c), for discussion. Where *Caldwell* recklessness is the standard, as in manslaughter (below, Ch. 7.5(b)), subjective awareness is not required.

[44] See J. C. Smith, 'Intoxication and the Mental Element in Crime', in P. Wallington and R. Merkin (eds.), *Essays in Honour of F. H. Lawson* (1987).

[45] [1977] AC 443, at 475; see C. Wells, 'Swatting the Subjectivist Bug' [1982] Crim. LR 209.

[46] Voiced by majority judges in the High Court of Australia, in *O'Connor* (1980) 54 ALJR 349.

noted,[47] and there seems no reason why contemporaneity should be an absolute principle. The question is whether it is appropriate to apply the rival doctrine of prior fault to intoxication cases.

Whatever the merit of these criticisms, it is undeniable that the intoxication rules in English law rest on fictions and apparently illogical legal devices. Is it the policy of restricting the defence of intoxication which is wrong, or merely the legal devices used to give effect to the policy?

(c) Intoxication, Culpability and Social Policy

One may concede that, in fact, a person may be so drunk as not to know what he or she is doing when causing harm to others or damage to property, and yet maintain that there are good reasons for criminal liability. What might these reasons be? At the root of the 'social defence' or 'public protection' arguments is the proposition that one of the main functions of the criminal law is to exert a general deterrent effect so as to protect major social and individual interests, and that any legal system which allows intoxication to negative *mens rea* would present citizens with an easy route to impunity. Indeed, the more intoxicated they became, the less likely they would be to be held criminally liable for any harm caused. As a matter of human experience, it is far from clear that this argument is soundly based. There are several common-law jurisdictions which have declined to follow the English approach and which allow intoxication to negative *mens rea*,[48] and yet there do not appear to have been untoward social effects in those countries. Two comments might be made here. First, these jurisdictions can be taken to be reinforcing the important and often neglected point that it is extremely rare for a defendant to be able to raise even a reasonable doubt that he was unaware of what he was doing. All that is required for proof of intent or recklessness is a momentary realization that property is being damaged or that a person is being assaulted, etc. Thus, even if evidence of intoxication were relevant, it would not usually be acute enough to prevent conviction. Second, the extreme rarity of acquittals based on intoxication in these jurisdictions may simply be because juries and magistrates are applying a normative test rather than a purely factual test. Thus the confidence of the majority judges in the High Court of Australia that juries and magistrates

---

[47] See Ch. 5.2(*d*) and (*e*).
[48] See *Keogh* [1964] VR 400, and *O'Connor* (1980) 54 AJLR 349, in Australia, and a minority of three judges in the Canadian case of *Leary* [1978] 1 SCR 29.

will not be too readily persuaded to acquit in these cases[49] might derive less from the rarity of total intoxication than from a belief that the courts will simply decline to return verdicts of acquittal where D is regarded as unworthy or culpable in some general way. This might suggest that the English doctrine is socially acceptable, even if legally inelegant.

There remains the question of individual culpability. What distinguishes evidence of intoxication from many of the other explanations for D's failure to realize what most ordinary people would have foreseen is the element of prior fault. It was D's fault for taking drink or drugs to such an extent as to lose control over his behaviour. Does this mean that, in order to support a finding of culpability, it must be established that D knew of the likely effects of the intoxicants upon behaviour? Probably not, for it would be regarded as perfectly fair to assume that all people realize the possible effects of taking alcohol or drugs (apart from the exceptional situations discussed above):[50] 'It is common knowledge that those who take alcohol to excess or certain sorts of drugs may become aggressive or do dangerous or unpredictable things.'[51] This is plainly an objective standard, but it is so elementary that it should not be regarded as unfair on anyone to assume such knowledge. This suggests that there is an element of culpability in these intoxication cases which serves to distinguish them not only from insanity cases (which arise without fault) but also from many other cases of absence of *mens rea*.[52]

But on what is the culpability based? Specifically, is it for becoming intoxicated or for causing the proscribed harm? It is fairly simple to establish culpability for becoming intoxicated if there is no evidence that it was 'involuntary'. It is fairly difficult to establish culpability for causing the proscribed harm if we follow normal principles: we must assume acute intoxication at the time of the act, and if we look back to the period when D was becoming intoxicated, it is unlikely that one could establish actual foresight of the kind of harm eventually caused. Perhaps some people who regularly assault others when drunk might realize that there is a risk of this occurring, but in order to encompass the majority of cases, it would be necessary to rewrite

---

[49] *Keogh* [1964] VR 400, and *O'Connor* (1980) ALJR 349.

[50] See above, nn. 35 and 36, and accompanying text.

[51] *Bailey* [1983] 1 WLR 760, at 864.

[52] One case in which this was the defence was *Attorney-General for Northern Ireland v. Gallagher* [1963] AC 349, but the House of Lords used the prior fault doctrine (here, prior intention) to affirm the conviction.

the proposition about 'common knowledge' so as to maintain that people realize that, when intoxicated, they are likely to cause damage or to assault others. The culpability, in other words, is somewhat unspecific—as in many instances where prior fault operates to bar a defence.[53] Sentencing decisions suggest that intoxication might mitigate on the first occasion it is raised, so that the offence can be portrayed as 'out of character', but it will not mitigate any subsequent offences committed in an intoxicated state.[54]

(d) Finding a Legal Solution

The simplest solution is to regard evidence of intoxication as relevant on issues of *mens rea*, as the courts in the non-Code states of Australia do.[55] There will only rarely be acquittals, and these may be regarded as part of the price of a liberal theory which rests on individual autonomy and choice—like acquittals of clumsy and thoughtless individuals.[56] The objection to this is that it does seem to yield the anti-social maxim 'more alcohol, less liability', and gives no weight to the elements of choice and risk involved in getting drunk. The choice is to loosen one's self-restraint rather than to commit a crime, let alone a particular kind of crime, but the retention of control over one's behaviour might fairly be regarded as a social duty. This argument is considerably weakened where D is addicted to alcohol or drugs, since the element of choice may have been exhausted long ago.[57]

There is a strong argument of social defence for restricting the relevance of intoxication to *mens rea*, and yet for trying to improve upon the structure of the English rules. One basic issue in all this concerns the relevance of the resulting harm: should the conviction of an intoxicated person reflect the harm done? Does D deserve to be labelled as that kind of harm-doer, or only as a person who became drunk and dangerous? The criminal law manifests considerable ambivalence on this kind of issue. It punishes reckless harms, but not generally recklessness which happens not to result in

---

[53] See P. H. Robinson, 'Causing the Conditions of One's Own Defence' (1985) 71 *Virginia LR* 1, at 50–1, discussed above, in Ch. 5.2(*e*).

[54] A typically resolute Court of Appeal decision against allowing intoxication to mitigate is *Bradley* (1980) 2 Cr. App. R(S) 12.

[55] *Keogh* [1964] VR 400, and *O'Connor* (1980) 54 ALJR 349.

[56] See above, Ch. 5.2(*a*) on the subjectivist principles.

[57] Cf. H. Fingarette, 'Addiction and Criminal Responsibility' (1975) 84 *Yale LJ* 413.

harm.[58] It punishes driving with excess alcohol, but not simple drunkenness except in the form of a summary offence of public drunkenness.[59] Since the culpability in most intoxication cases lies in becoming drunk, perhaps in the knowledge that there is a risk of harmful behaviour, it might be logical to criminalize the drunkenness irrespective of whether any harm actually results. But this would be a widely resented law; it would be thought to be unduly restrictive of individual liberty, unduly oppressive in terms of police power, and unnecessary in terms of the relative infrequency of harm caused by people who are completely intoxicated. The compromise, then, is to impose criminal liability only where harm results.

The Butler Committee recommended the creation of an offence of being 'drunk and dangerous', to come into operation whenever a defendant was acquitted of a 'dangerous' offence for lack of *mens rea* due to intoxication.[60] The Criminal Law Revision Committee rejected this because it fails to reflect the type and magnitude of the harm actually caused by D. The Committee therefore proposed what was essentially the continuation of the present English approach, imputing 'recklessness' to anyone who caused harm whilst drunk. A minority of the Committee preferred a special verdict of 'guilty of doing the act while in a state of voluntary intoxication',[61] which has the advantage of avoiding the imputed variety of recklessness. However, both the majority and the minority of the Committee took the view that the conviction must refer to the harm done, even though D was unaware of the nature of the harm being caused. The Butler proposal is to be preferred on this score, although it leaves open the proper approach to sentencing in these cases. The Butler Committee proposed a maximum prison sentence of one year for a first offence, and three years for a subsequent offence: just as the present law may encourage over-severity in directing attention to the resulting harm, so the Butler proposals may encourage undue leniency in directing attention away from the known risks.

6.4. DURESS AND NECESSITY

This part of the chapter deals with cases in which D's behaviour fulfils the conduct element in an offence, but in which D acted as a

---

[58] See above, Ch. 5.2(*b*), on resulting harm.
[59] Cf. A. Ashworth, 'Intoxication and the General Defences' [1980] Crim. LR 556.   [60] Butler Report, para. 18.56.
[61] Criminal Law Revision Committee, 14th Report, *Offences against the Person* (1980, Cmnd 7844), paras. 263–72.

result of threats from another person (sometimes called 'duress *per minas*') or in order to avert dire consequences (called 'necessity' or 'duress of circumstances'). Some cases of necessity might be regarded as justifications for causing harm, and they were discussed briefly in Chapter 4.8. What we will find below is that the development of the common law on duress and necessity is characterized by the interplay of reasons of excuse and justification, and by conflicts between recognizing the pressure to which D was subject and upholding the rights of victims.

(a) Some Illustrative Cases

Before exploring the foundations and the limits of the doctrines of duress and necessity, it may be instructive to consider three of the leading English cases. In *Hudson and Taylor* (1971)[62] two teenage girls were prosecution witnesses at a trial for wounding. They gave evidence that they did not know the man charged and could not identify him as the culprit. The man was acquitted but the girls were charged with perjury. They admitted that they gave false evidence, but said that they were under duress, having been threatened with violence by various men, one of whom was in the public gallery at the original trial. The Court of Appeal quashed their convictions because the defence of duress had been wrongly withdrawn from the jury—the trial judge had ruled that the threats were not sufficiently immediate, since the girls were in the safety of the courtroom at the time they committed the perjury, but the Court of Appeal regarded this as too narrow a concept of immediacy, given that the threats could be carried out later that night.

In *Howe* (1987)[63] the two defendants had been involved in two killings, one as aiders and abettors and the other as principals. Their defence was that they did the acts because they had been threatened with violence by two other men, who were present and who were the principals in the first killing. The main point of appeal to the House of Lords was whether the defence of duress was available in murder cases; the House held that it should not be available either to principals or to secondary parties in the crime of murder.

In *Conway* (1989)[64] two men approached D's car, whereupon D, urged on by his passenger, drove off at great speed and in a reckless manner. D's explanation was that he knew that his passenger had recently been threatened by two men who had fired a shot-gun. D

---

[62] [1971] 2 QB 202.   [63] [1987] AC 417.   [64] [1989] 3 All ER 1025.

feared that these two men intended harm, and his driving was in response to that emergency. The Court of Appeal quashed the conviction for reckless driving because the trial judge had failed to leave the defence of duress of circumstances to the jury.

These three cases give some idea of the defences under consideration. The key element in duress is threats from another person. The key element in necessity is usually either impending physical harm or a natural occurrence, such as a flood, a hurricane, or a fire.

(b) Theoretical Foundations for the Defences

These three cases suggest that persons who act under threat of violence or in fear of violence may have a defence to crimes other than murder. Before we explore the limits of these defences in English law, what are the reasons for allowing them at all? One argument is that acts under duress or necessity are justified in the sense that they constitute a lesser evil than the carrying-out of the threat: the credentials of such a justification were discussed in Chapter 4.8. The courts, as we shall see, seem to mix arguments of justification with those of excuse, without noticing the distinction. How strong are the arguments for excusing D rather than justifying the act? It is fairly clear that duress and necessity do not negative intent, knowledge, or recklessness: D will know only too well the nature and consequences of the conduct. It also seems unlikely that they negative the voluntary nature of D's conduct: the elements of unconsciousness and uncontrollability of bodily movements which are regarded as the hallmark of involuntary behaviour[65] are not typically to be found in duress cases. Yet it might be possible to argue that conduct in response to duress or necessity is *non*-voluntary, even if it is not *in*voluntary. It could be said that there is a significantly lower degree of choice and free will in these cases than in the normal run of actions. The phrases used by the Court of Appeal in *Hudson and Taylor*—'effective to neutralise the will of the accused', and 'driven to act by immediate and unavoidable pressure'—show that the courts also have this in mind, although 'neutralising the will' puts it rather too strongly.

If the defence of duress is based on 'pressure' which is 'immediate and unavoidable', why should these factors be regarded as so powerful? Surely people frequently act in a certain way because they feel under intense pressure, but that does not mean that we

---

[65] See Ch. 4.5.

treat them as not responsible for those actions. Moreover, the criminal law generally presumes free will and disregards the possibility that our acts are determined to any significant degree. Perhaps one element which marks out circumstances of duress and necessity is that they cast D as the innocent—often, chance—victim, and another person or some natural phenomenon as the primary causal force. Emotional, financial, or social pressures may be felt just as intensely by certain people at certain times, and the resulting acts might be equally 'determined', but perhaps it is regarded as difficult to treat D as entirely innocent in their production,[66] and there may be no other person who can be identified as the cause of the wrongdoing (as in duress). Some of this may be implicit in Lord Morris's explanation that 'the law would be censorious and inhumane which did not recognise the appalling plight of a person who perhaps suddenly finds his life in jeopardy unless he submits and obeys'.[67]

Thus, what distinguishes duress and necessity from other acute pressures is that D is presented with an urgent and threatening situation, not of his own making, and D's actions may therefore be regarded as an understandable response to those extreme pressures. This analysis is consistent with the test of whether a person of reasonable firmness would have withstood the threats: if the answer is no, then the grounds for a defence are laid, since it is unfair to expect D to resist pressure which a reasonably steadfast citizen would not have resisted.[68] The test is sufficient to establish that D's freedom of choice was so severely restricted that he does not deserve criminal conviction and punishment. But the test also has the effect of ensuring that the defence is not based purely on the degree of pressure subjectively experienced, and is confined by objective standards of reasonableness.

This argument concedes that acts under duress or necessity are not justified, and contends that D should be excused because the pressure placed on him was such that 'a person of ordinary firmness' would not have resisted. But this reasoning does depend on a question of degree, and one might enquire about the dividing line between a complete defence and matters in mitigation of sentence.

---

[66] The proposal for a defence based on 'social deprivation' is discussed below, Ch. 6.9(*b*), text at n. 157.

[67] In *DPP for Northern Ireland v. Lynch* [1975] AC 653.

[68] See J. Dressler, 'Reflections on Excusing Wrongdoers: Moral Theory, New Excuses and the Model Penal Code' (1988) 19 *Rutgers LJ* 671, at 708–15, and below, Ch. 6.9(*c*).

As a defence, duress is restricted to cases involving threats of death and serious injury, as we shall see. It seems to be assumed that only such dire threats should exclude all criminal liability; other threats (e.g. to set fire to one's house or business premises) are appropriate merely for mitigation of sentence. But it might be argued that, since there are so many questions of degree in duress and necessity cases (degree of threat, degree of immediacy, seriousness of crime), they are much more appropriate for the sentencing stage than the liability stage.[69] At present the answer of English law (except in murder cases) is that there is a point at which the threat or emergency may place so much pressure on an individual that it is unfair to attribute criminal responsibility. The defences are narrowly circumscribed in order to try to identify these extreme cases.

For those who argue that deterrence should be the primary aim of the criminal law, these cases present a particular problem. The general approach is to maintain that the stronger the temptation or pressure to commit a crime, the stronger the law's threat should be in order to counterbalance it.[70] The law and its penalties should be used to strengthen the resolve of those under pressure. Yet Bentham also accepted that criminal liability and punishment are inefficacious where a person is subject to such acute threats (e.g. death, serious injury) that the law's own threat cannot be expected to counter-balance it: in these cases, he said, there should be a complete defence.[71] The difficulty with this analysis is that the point at which duress becomes a complete defence seems to betoken the difference between acquittal and a substantial deterrent sentence. There is, however, a sliding scale of intensity of duress and necessity, and 'desert' theory can reflect the gradations by providing a complete defence, perhaps a qualified defence (e.g. murder to manslaughter), and variable mitigation of sentence.

(c) Requirements of the Defences in English Law

Keeping in mind the idea that the defences of duress and necessity are founded chiefly on the belief that it is unfair to expect persons to resist extreme pressure from threats or circumstances of emergency, let us examine the conditions for the defences which have evolved at common law.

---

[69] See below, Ch. 6.9(a), and M. Wasik, 'Duress and Criminal Responsibility' [1977] Crim. LR 453.
[70] J. Bentham, *Introduction to the Principles of Morals and Legislation*, Ch. XIV, para. 9.   [71] Ibid, para. 11.

The defence of duress may be restricted to cases where the threat is to cause death or serious injury.[72] There was a dictum in *Steane* (1947)[73] that a threat of false imprisonment would suffice, and this raises the question of whether it is necessary for the courts to place such a tight objective restriction as 'threats of death or serious injury alone' upon the defence. In principle, it could be argued that the further and more general requirement, that the threats must be such that 'a sober person of reasonable firmness' would not have resisted them, is sufficient to prevent the defence being used by the weak-willed to excuse a serious offence by relying on a trivial threat—which is presumably the 'public policy' factor to which the court in *Graham* (1982)[74] adverted. Of course, the 'death or serious injury' test is vastly superior in terms of certainty, but that raises the question of whether the boundaries of a defence like duress need to be certain. Is it practical to suggest that reliance is ever placed on them by persons under duress? Surely it is far more realistic to suggest that a court should be permitted to apply a general standard (the person of reasonable firmness) in considering both the threat and the act committed. Yet this standard could operate harshly against relatively timorous people caught up in a desperate situation, and it is important that any standard should be modified to deal with defendants incapable of attaining it.[75]

Among the other requirements of the defence of duress, it is established that the threat need not be against D personally:[76] it may be against D's family, or friends, or perhaps anyone. The threat must be 'present' and not a remote threat of future harm; but, as *Hudson and Taylor*[77] showed, it is not necessary to show that the threat would be carried out immediately, so long as its implementation was imminent. That case also raised the question of whether the defence is barred if D failed to take an opportunity to alert the police. The Court of Appeal thought that a rule of that kind would be too severe a restriction, and held that D loses the defence by failing to 'avail himself of some opportunity which was reasonably open to him to render the threat ineffective . . . having regard to his

---

[72] See *DPP for Northern Ireland v. Lynch* [1975] AC 653.
[73] [1947] KB 997.   [74] (1982) 74 Cr. App. R 235.
[75] See the discussion of negligence above, Ch. 5.3(*f*). On duress itself, see P. Alldridge, 'Developing the Defence of Duress' [1986] Crim. LR 433, and K. J. M. Smith, 'Must Heroes Behave Heroically?' [1989] Crim. LR 622.
[76] *Gill* (1963) 47 Cr. App. R 166, and Law Com. No. 83, *Defences of General Application* (1977), 2–3.
[77] See above, n. 61, and accompanying text.

age and circumstances, and to any risks to him which may be involved in the course of action relied upon'. This test, with its mixture of objective factors and subjective elements, ensured that the two young women in that case did not forfeit the defence by failing to notify the police.[78]

For many years the defence of necessity was said not to be recognized by the common law, following the notorious case of *Dudley and Stephens* (1884)[79] in which two shipwrecked mariners who had killed and eaten a cabin-boy were denied a defence to murder. But it has recently become established under the name 'duress of circumstances'. The two elements required are: first, that D was impelled to do the acts because he had good cause to fear that death or serious injury would result otherwise (presumably, to D or to anyone else); and second, that a sober person of reasonable firmness, sharing D's characteristics, would have responded to the situation in the same way.[80] Once again the courts insist on two objective elements—not merely the 'person of reasonable firmness' test but also the 'death or serious injury' restriction. Thus far, the doctrine of 'duress of circumstances' has been applied only to victimless crimes such as reckless driving and driving whilst disqualified, but it has a wider potential application.

Both duress and necessity are subject to the doctrine of prior fault. In *Sharp* (1987)[81] D joined a gang of robbers, participating in crimes where guns were carried, but when he tried to withdraw, he was himself threatened with violence. The Court of Appeal held that the defence of duress is unavailable to anyone who voluntarily joins a gang 'which he knows might bring pressure on him to commit an offence and was an active member when he was put under such pressure'. Although this is phrased subjectively, 'which he knows . . .', the principle here is surely an objective one. In the later case of *Shepherd* (1987)[82] it was added that 'There are certain kinds of criminal enterprises the joining of which, in the absence of any knowledge of propensity to violence on the part of one member, would not lead another to suspect that a decision to think better of the whole affair might lead him into serious trouble.' Phrased again

[78] For criticism, see A. Ashworth, 'Reason, Logic and Criminal Liability' (1975) 91 LQR 102.
[79] (1884) 14 QBD 273; see A. W. B. Simpson, *Cannibalism and the Common Law* (1984).
[80] *Conway* [1988] 3 All ER 1025, *Martin* [1989] 1 All ER 652, discussed by D. W. Elliott, 'Necessity, Duress and Self-Defence' [1989] Crim. LR 611.
[81] [1987] QB 853.   [82] (1988) 86 Cr. App. R 47.

in subjective language, the possibility of running a defence of duress should remain open in such cases.

(d) Duress, Necessity, and the Taking of Life

Although most of the elements of the defences seem to be based on a rationale of excusing a person's understandable submission to the threat, the troubled issue of whether the defences should be available to murder has led the courts to draw on justification-based rationales. The tone was set in the late nineteenth century with *Dudley and Stephens*,[83] where the shipwrecked mariners killed and ate a cabin-boy after seventeen days adrift at sea. Lord Coleridge CJ held that no defence of necessity was available in a case of taking another person's life. In the first place, he argued, there is no *necessity* for preserving one's own life, and there are circumstances in which it may be one's duty to sacrifice it. Then, secondly, if there were ever to be a similar case, who would judge which person is to die? (This point might be overcome by drawing lots.) So he concluded that, terrible as the temptation might be in this kind of case, the law should 'keep the judgment straight and the conduct pure'. The sentence of death was later commuted to six months' imprisonment, thus exhibiting the obvious conflict between the desire to reaffirm the objective standards of the sanctity of life and the widely felt compassion for people placed in an extreme situation.

In *DPP v. Lynch* (1975)[84] the House of Lords accepted, by a majority of three to two, that duress by threats should be available as a defence to an accomplice to murder, reflecting the law's compassion towards a person placed under such extreme pressure. But then the Privy Council in *Abbott v. R* (1977)[85] held that duress was unavailable as a defence to the principal in murder, and in *Howe* (1987)[86] the House of Lords had to decide whether to perpetuate this distinction between principals and accomplices. Their Lordships decided not to do so, unanimously favouring a rule which renders duress and necessity unavailable as defences in all prosecutions for murder and attempted murder. The primary reason for their decision was that the law should not recognise that any individual has the liberty to choose that one innocent citizen should die rather than another. All duress cases involve a choice between

---

[83] (1884) 14 QBD 273.   [84] [1977] AC 653.
[85] [1977] AC 755; cf. I. Dennis, 'Duress, Murder and Criminal Responsibility' (1980) 96 LQR 208.
[86] [1987] AC 417; see above, n. 62 and accompanying text.

innocents, D and the intended victim, and the law should not remove its protection from the victim. Thus D is required to make a heroic sacrifice. A secondary argument, similar to that employed a century earlier in *Dudley and Stephens*, was that executive discretion could take care of deserving cases—either by releasing D on parole at an early stage or even by refraining from prosecution.[87]

Both these arguments are open to criticism. The argument based on protection for the innocent victim seems to assume that duress is being advanced as a justification for killing: this enables the judges to assume that, because the killing of an innocent person is unjustified, duress should not be a defence. Surely the claim is not that the killing was justified, but that it should be excused because of the extreme pressure under which D was placed by the threats? There are other situations in which a killing may be excused in whole or in part (e.g. mistaken self-defence, intoxication, insanity), without being justified.[88] Utilitarians might argue that a rule denying duress as a defence to murder is preferable because it might achieve a net saving of lives:[89] this not only fails to take the defendant's interests into account, but also assumes that persons under duress will know of the law's approach and will be influenced by it, an assumption which may have force in some terrorist cases. The second argument, in favour of convicting the person under duress and then invoking executive clemency to reduce the punishment, also smacks of an unrealistic utilitarian solution. If we are satisfied that D was placed under extreme pressure, we ought to declare that publicly either by allowing a defence or, if not, by allowing a qualified defence to murder on an analogy with provocation.[90] The argument in favour of merely a qualified defence should not be understated: as Chapter 7.4(c) will confirm, the sanctity of life is a fundamental value to which the law should give high recognition.

One remaining point is that *Howe* concerns only the one-to-one situation: what if the threats or necessity mean that one person is to be killed in order to save a greater number from death? This was discussed in Chapter 4.8, under the heading of 'Justifications, Necessity, and the Balance of Interests'.

---

[87] Per Lords Griffiths and Mackay, at 446 and 457.

[88] P. Alldridge, 'The Coherence of Defences' [1983] Crim. LR 665.

[89] A. Kenny, *Freewill and Responsibility* (1978), 38.

[90] Cf. the argument to the contrary by the House of Lords Select Committee on Murder and Life Imprisonment (1988–9, HL Paper 78), criticized by A. Ashworth, 'Reforming the Law of Murder' [1990] Crim. LR 75, at 82–3.

6.5. PROVOCATION

Should the criminal law provide a defence of provocation in certain circumstances? The context of the question differs from mental disorder, intoxication, and duress, since provocation is not generally regarded as a defence to criminal liability.[91] Many legal systems allow it as a qualified defence to murder which reduces the crime to manslaughter or culpable homicide, and provocation will be discussed in this connection below, in Chapter 7.4(*b*). Here the questions are whether it should ever be a complete defence, or, if not, how it differs from those conditions which are admitted as complete defences. The details of provocation in English law are reserved for Chapter 7: it is enough to state that provocation is generally taken to include both a subjective condition (was D provoked to lose self-control?) and an objective condition (was the provocation enough to cause any reasonable person in D's position to lose self-control?).

(a) Elements of Excuse in Provocation

One way of enquiring whether provocation should be regarded as negativing the fault element is to ask whether it excludes either *mens rea* or voluntariness. It is generally assumed that loss of self-control does not negative intention: indeed, this is part of the logic of provocation as a qualified defence to murder, since no such defence might be required if it simply negatived intention. One might argue, however, that in some cases D would act in such a blind rage, after being provoked, that he would be unaware of what he was doing. Such an extreme condition might be difficult to prove, as distinct from lesser degrees of anger, but that is a quite separate argument for refusing to admit a defence. This is merely a manifestation of the general assumption that people who are not drunk or mentally disordered know what they are doing and cannot be heard to say otherwise.

Might loss of self-control negative voluntariness? Since unconscious behaviour is not an issue here, the question is whether behaviour during loss of self-control is 'uncontrollable' rather than simply 'uncontrolled'. There is ambiguity in the law at this point: the law clearly does not require *total* loss of self-control as a precondition of allowing provocation as a partial defence to murder,

[91] In the Code states of Australia provocation is a defence to assault: see Queensland Criminal Code, s. 269.

but quite what it means by 'loss of self-control', and how great a loss is required, remains uncertain. It is not difficult to conceive of conditions of extreme rage in which a person would find it virtually impossible to control his actions, although, again, it would be difficult to prove this. Provocation may therefore be one of those areas in which elements of determinism substantially limit the normal presumptions of free will.[92] Probably there is enough in the argument that loss of self-control may occasionally negative *mens rea* or voluntariness to suggest that it should be *capable* of amounting to a complete defence.[93] But, as we saw in relation to intoxication, this may not be sufficient to conclude the issue. As a matter of social policy it might be decided that citizens have a duty to learn to control their passions and tempers to the extent of not inflicting criminal harms, and thus the law might adopt the view that loss of self-control should never be allowed to negative the fault requirements for an offence. This would be a strong policy, presumably exempting only the mentally disordered, and not those who have abnormal difficulty in controlling themselves. Indeed, in English law the policy seems to be stronger than that in intoxication cases, since intoxication is allowed as a defence to the wider (though illogical) category of 'specific intent' crimes, whereas provocation is currently a defence only to murder. Is there not a case, based on fairness to individual defendants, for arguing that extreme loss of self-control should be capable of acting as a defence to crimes of specific intent, at least? Would not the response to this argument be based on practicalities, such as the dangers of making trials even more complex, rather than principle?

(b) Elements of Justification in Provocation

There are cases in which D pleads provocation on a charge of murdering a bullying father or husband and receives so light a sentence as to suggest that the court regards the killing as not far short of justifiable.[94] The analogy with self-defence or prevention of crime in such cases is necessarily diluted, since there is usually no

---

[92] See above, Ch. 4.2, and A. Ashworth, 'The Doctrine of Provocation' [1976] CLJ 292.

[93] Cf. F. McAuley, 'Anticipating the Past: The Defence of Provocation in Irish Law' (1987) 50 MLR 133, and J. Dressler, 'Provocation: Partial Justification or Partial Excuse?' (1988) 51 MLR 467, at 472–3.

[94] M. Wasik, 'Cumulative Provocation and Domestic Killing' [1982] Crim. LR 29, and J. Horder, 'Sex, Violence and Sentencing in Domestic Provocation Cases' [1989] Crim. LR 546.

immediate threat to D at the time of the killing, but they serve to raise the question of whether there is a significant element of justification in provocation cases. The answer may be sought in various directions. The objective condition in the provocation defence to murder is whether the provocation was enough to cause a reasonable person to lose self-control. The element of reasonableness may be discerned in the paradigm of provocation as a wrongful act towards D, and in the assumption that lawful acts should not be regarded as provocation.[95] Indeed, Aristotle argued that anger is a socially respectable emotion which may, within limits, be a proper response to certain behaviour by others.[96] It is therefore necessary to consider both D's feelings and the moral basis: the principle is that culpability is reduced where D acts in anger towards the victim, and has good reason for being angry in virtue of some apparent wrong or impropriety suffered at the victim's hands.[97] A further way of answering the question would be to argue that a provoked offence is caused by the provoker rather than by D, which suggests that D's responsibility for the outcome is less than it would otherwise be.[98]

None of these arguments is sufficient to establish that provocation should be a complete justification. It is one thing to state that the victim 'asked for it' by what he or she did; it is quite another thing to suppose that the victim asked to die.[99] But the element of wrongdoing by the victim (or another)[100] which typifies provocation cases is surely significant in assessing whether, and to what extent, D deserves punishment. Thus we must return to the discussion about the excusing elements in provocation, and consider whether the combination of loss of self-control (in its broad, undefined sense) with an element of partial justification might provide grounds for a defence. The point now is not merely that D lost control at the time of the offence, but that D was understandably and with some

[95] See A. Ashworth, 'Self-Induced Provocation and the Homicide Act' [1973] Crim. LR 483.

[96] Aristotle, *Nicomachean Ethics*, Bk. V. 8; cf. the discussions by Ashworth, 'The Doctrine of Justification', and Dressler, 'Provocation'.

[97] This adapts the 'principle of resentment' proposed by A. von Hirsch and N. Jareborg, 'Provocation and Culpability', in F. Schoemann (ed.), *Responsibility, Character and the Emotions* (1988); the adaptation is the insertion, following Aristotle, of the word 'apparent'.

[98] Dressler, 'Provocation', 477–80.

[99] Ashworth, 'The Doctrine of Justification'.

[100] See R. S. O'Regan, 'Indirect Provocation and Misdirected Retaliation [1968] Crim. LR 319.

justification *provoked* to lose self-control at the time of the offence. Is there an analogy here with duress and necessity as defences? It is certainly true that duress, though predominantly an excuse, contains elements of justification. A person under duress is presented with an urgent situation, not of his or her own making, and then acts in an understandable response to these extreme pressures. The analogies between provocation and duress cases are: (i) that the situations are not of D's own making; and (ii) that the acts are not regarded as freely willed. The differences are: (i) that there is no element of necessity in D's reactions to provocation; and therefore (ii) that the severe restrictions on choice of action found in duress cases are not present in provocation. D will not suffer serious physical harm if he fails to respond to the provocation. The argument is that, whilst it is unfair to expect citizens to withstand threats sufficient to affect even a person of reasonable firmness, it is not unfair to expect citizens to control their behaviour when provoked. We might recognize that such control is abnormally difficult in certain extreme situations by allowing a circumscribed defence of provocation to reduce the grade of offences (murder to manslaughter; but why not also 'causing serious injury with intent' to 'causing serious injury recklessly'?[101]), but still maintain the general social proposition that citizens who are not mentally disordered can be expected to control their tempers. The difficulties which people encounter in provocative circumstances may be recognized by reducing the grade of offence and by mitigation of sentence, but they are not, on this reasoning, so strong as to suggest that fairness demands no criminal liability at all.

(c) Extreme Mental or Emotional Disturbance

In its Model Penal Code the American Law Institute includes a partial defence of 'extreme mental or emotional disturbance . . . for which there is reasonable explanation or excuse'.[102] The defence is confined to murder, like provocation and diminished responsibility in English law, and seeks to cover broadly the same conditions (together with duress) in a single doctrine. It dispenses with any technical definition of what might amount to adequate provocation by simply requiring 'reasonable explanation', a formulation which

---

[101] One direct counter-argument is that a provoked wounding might be intentional rather than reckless, and so conviction for the recklessness offence would be a mislabelling. The proper label should perhaps be 'wounding in the second degree'.

[102] S. 210.3.1(b); see Robinson, *Criminal Law Defenses*, and Dressler, 'Reflections on Excusing Wrongdoers', 704–5.

retains some normative element. Like provocation, it directs atten-tion to earlier or pre-existing circumstances by way of exculpation rather than adhering strictly to the principle of contemporaneity. It covers cases of cumulative provocation,[103] since there is no specifi-cation of the origin of the disturbance: so long as the court finds a reasonable explanation or excuse, that is sufficient. It channels the mentally abnormal and the mentally normal into a single doctrine, by focusing on the element of disturbance, but, in so doing, it obscures the element of partial justification which at present separates provocation cases. Two points may be made in the present context. First, is it preferable to forgo the labelling distinctions which would be achieved by separate qualified defences to murder of provocation, diminished responsibility, and duress in favour of a test which might prove simpler for trial courts to deal with? Second, if there is a case for such a broadly drawn partial defence based on emotional or mental disturbance, is it right that it should only be available in murder cases, and not available to reduce the grade of other offences in the same way as the 'specific intent' rule in intoxication?

6.6. PUTATIVE DEFENCES

What if D mistakenly believes in the existence of circumstances which, if they did exist, would form the basis for one of the defences or partial defences? It is not those defences which are purely excusatory but those which have a greater or lesser degree of justification in them which are relevant here—self-defence, pre-vention of crime, provocation, duress, and necessity. If the required circumstances do not exist, the defence cannot, properly speaking, be said to arise: there is actually no threat of immediate force, for example. But if D *believes* that the required circumstances exist, the solution might seem to lie in a direct application of the belief principle, that D should be judged on the facts as he believed them to be.[104] If D believed that V had a gun in the plastic bag he was pointing at D, whereas in fact it was a cucumber, D's conduct should be judged on the basis of the believed threat. As outlined in the previous chapter,[105] this is the answer given by English courts in cases of mistaken or putative self-defence and prevention of crime. The logic is that: (i) unlawfulness is an element in all crimes; (ii) intent,

---

[103] This refers to provocative behaviour which occurs over a period of time: see Wasik, 'Cumulative Provocation'.

[104] See above, Ch. 5.2(*a*).   [105] See above, Ch. 5.3(*a*).

knowledge, or recklessness must be proved as to that element; and therefore (iii) a person who mistakenly believes in the existence of circumstances which would make the conduct lawful should not be criminally liable.

English law now seems settled that, where D acts in the belief that force is necessary in self-defence or prevention of crime, D should be judged on the believed facts and not the actual facts.[106] The question has not recently come up for decision in connection with provocation as a partial defence to murder, but the authorities favour the view that D should be judged on the facts as he believed them to be.[107] However, this has not been the courts' approach in duress cases: in *Graham* (1982)[108] the Lord Chief Justice held that, if D is mistaken about the existence or nature of a threat, the mistake must be a reasonable one if the defence of duress is to be available; and in *Conway* (1989)[109] the Court of Appeal held that 'A defence of duress of circumstances is available only if from an objective standpoint the defendant can be said to be acting in order to avoid a threat of death or serious injury.' The reasoning in these two cases appears to be that, since defences of duress and necessity are available only where a person of *reasonable* steadfastness would have yielded to the threat, it follows that mistakes must be based on *reasonable* grounds if they are to excuse.

Is this a sound course of reasoning? Surely the 'person of reasonable firmness' standard is, like the limitation of 'reasonable force' in self-defence cases,[110] a form of words designed to ensure some proportionality between threat and response. It sets the legal standard for the magnitude or quantum of threat or response. The issue of mistaken belief concerns perception, and we have seen that English law's general approach to questions of perception embodies the belief principle—a subjective enquiry, not an objective standard. Once the confusion between issues of proportionality and perception has been dispelled, there remains the question of whether the belief principle should be regarded as the absolute doctrinal solution to these cases. It focuses on D's attitude of mind at the time, but includes no reference to the circumstances of the act, to D's responsibilities, or to social expectations of conduct in that situation. It

---

[106] *Gladstone Williams* (1983) 78 Cr. App. R 276, and *Beckford v. R* [1988] AC 130.
[107] *Letenock* (1917) 12 Cr. App. R 221; see also *Wardrope* [1960] Crim. LR 770.
[108] (1982) 74 Cr. App. R 235.
[109] [1988] 3 All ER 1025.   [110] See above, Ch. 4.7(*e*).

was argued earlier that in rape cases those considerations militate in favour of a requirement of reasonable grounds for any mistake;[111] and a similar argument might be developed in relation to the responsibilities of a police-officer with firearms training, as in *Beckford v. R* (1987).[112] Of course, any such infusion of objective principles must reflect the exigencies of the moment, and must not expect more of D than society ought to expect in that particular situation. The general point, however, is that there may be good reasons for society to require a certain standard of conduct if the conditions were not such as to preclude it, particularly where the potential harm involved is serious. Whether these arguments are strong enough to support a 'reasonable grounds' requirement for putative defences in cases of duress and necessity, which usually impinge suddenly and by chance upon ordinary people, must be open to doubt.

Lastly, the use of the word 'reasonable' to designate the amount of force which is lawful in self-defence, and the magnitude of the threat necessary to give rise to a defence of duress, does sow some seeds of confusion for mistake cases. What if D shoots at and wounds a trespasser in his garden, believing that he is entitled to do this? His mistake, one as to the legal standard, is classified technically as a mistake of law: there was no misunderstanding of facts, simply an erroneous view of the law.[113] This situation will be discussed in the section below.

6.7. IGNORANCE OR MISTAKE OF LAW

(a) The English Rules

English criminal law appears to pursue a relatively strict policy against those who act in ignorance of the true legal position, but the maxim *ignorantia juris neminem excusat* (ignorance of the law excuses no one) is too strong as a description. Ignorance or mistake as to civil law, rather than criminal law, is capable of forming the basis of a defence; indeed, the crimes of theft and criminal damage explicitly provide for defences where D believes that he has a legal right to take or to damage property.[114] But it would be unsafe to

---

[111] See above, Ch. 5.3(*d*).
[112] [1988] AC; cf. J. Horder, 'Cognition, Emotion and Criminal Culpability' (1990) 106 LQR 469.
[113] A. Ashworth, 'Excusable Mistake of Law' [1974] Crim. LR 652.
[114] Theft Act 1968, s. 2(1)(a); Criminal Damage Act 1971, s. 5(2) (a).

state the rule by reference to a distinction between matters of civil law and criminal law, because offences are often defined in such a way as to blur the two. Whether goods are classified as 'stolen' for the purposes of the offence of handling stolen property seems to be a question of criminal law, so if D knows all the facts but misunderstands their legal effect this is irrelevant. Whether an auditor is disqualified from acting for a certain company seems to be a question of civil law, so where D was unaware of the relevant law, his conviction for acting as an auditor knowing that he was disqualified was quashed.[115] One difference between these two offences is that the latter contains the word 'knowingly', whereas the crime of handling includes the words 'knowing or believing'; it is certainly true that a number of English decisions have allowed mistake or ignorance of the law to disprove 'knowingly',[116] but this cannot explain all the decisions.[117] There are also some well-established exceptions, even if the policy is expressed as 'ignorance of the criminal law is no excuse': the fact that a Statutory Instrument has not been published will usually afford a defence to any crime under that Instrument to a person unaware of its existence,[118] and failure to publish a government Order in respect of a particular person will also afford a defence to that person if he or she is unaware of the Order.[119]

(b) Individual Fairness and Public Policy

It could be argued that individual fairness demands the recognition of ignorance or mistake of law as an excuse: a person who acts in the belief that conduct is non-criminal, or without knowing that it is criminal, should not be convicted of an offence. In order to support such a fairness principle, one might wish to argue that ignorance or mistake as to the law should be recognized as an excuse in the same way (though for different reasons) as duress. It may not negative the fault requirements of a particular offence, but there are reasons of fairness which support the excuse in its own right: a person who chooses to engage in conduct without knowing that it is criminal makes a choice which is so ill-informed as to lack a proper basis. The counter-arguments are ones of policy. One is the utilitarian argu-

---

[115] *Secretary of State for Trade and Industry v. Hart* [1982] 1 WLR 481.
[116] Williams, *Textbook of Criminal Law*, Ch. 20.
[117] *Grant v. Borg* [1982] 1 WLR 638.
[118] Statutory Instruments Act 1946, s. 3(2).
[119] *Lim Chin Aik v. R* [1963] AC 160.

ment that it is desirable to encourage knowledge of the law rather than ignorance, and any rule which allowed ignorance as a defence would therefore tend to undermine law enforcement.[120] This does not establish that ignorance of the law is wrong, merely that it is socially harmful. Another is the argument that, if we judged defendants on their *conception* of the law rather than the law as it is, we should be contradicting the essential objectivity of the legal system.[121] This is, to say the least, an exaggeration: so long as the court stated what the law is, the law's objectivity would remain unimpaired. It would also seem to suggest that for a court to allow any excuse amounts to a denial of the offence. This not only confuses the element of excuse with the element of wrongdoing,[122] but also overlooks the value of a publicized trial, where reasonable mistake of law is allowed, as a means of public education.

What is needed here if the policy is to be supported, is an argument that it is wrong to be ignorant or mistaken about the law. This can be found in the conception of duties of citizenship. Thus, to argue that a person might be convicted despite ignorance of the law is not to attack the principles of choice and individual autonomy which were identified earlier as fundamental to the principles of fairness;[123] it is to forsake the atomistic view of individuals in favour of a recognition of persons as social beings, with both rights and responsibilities within the society in which they live.[124] This line of argument might therefore support a duty on each citizen to take reasonable steps to acquaint himself with the criminal law. The duty should not be an absolute one, however. First, there is often uncertainty in the ambit of the law. Sometimes the legislature acknowledges the difficulty of stating the law by allowing D's own standards as a bench-mark of lawfulness, as in the crime of blackmail.[125] Sometimes it resorts to a broad standard such as 'reasonable' or 'dishonest', leaving it to the courts to apply after each event. There is a clear link here with the principle of maximum certainty and the 'thin ice' policy.[126] This is not to suggest that every case in which the courts change the law should inevitably raise a defence in favour of D; but it does at least recall the issues of principle and

---

[120] O. W. Holmes, *The Common Law* (1881), 48.
[121] J. Hall, *General Principles of Criminal Law* (2nd edn., 1960), 388.
[122] G. P. Fletcher, *Rethinking Criminal Law* (1978), 734, and above, Ch. 4.1.
[123] See above, Ch. 5.2(*a*).
[124] J. Raz, *The Morality of Freedom* (1987), 206–7, and above, Ch. 4.9.
[125] Theft Act 1968, s. 21(1), discussed below, Ch. 9.4.
[126] See above, Ch. 3.3(*h*).

policy which had to be resolved in the case of *Shaw v. DPP* (1962).[127] A second reason for not making the policy absolute is the possibility that the State has not fulfilled its duties in respect of making a new offence known and knowable. This state duty is obvious where the criminal law seeks to impose liability for an omission,[128] and applies also to publishing a law. At present, non-publication is an exception to the so-called rule, but it would surely be preferable to leave the ambit of exceptions open by referring to 'ignorance or mistake of law based on reasonable grounds'. This would not blunt the efforts of legislatures to increase the number of offences aimed at reinforcing regulatory schemes in industry and commerce—there is surely a well-recognized duty on anyone engaged in a particular trade to keep abreast of regulations—nor would it impair the efficacy of the rules of the road, where new laws are coming into force each year—again, it is a road-user's duty to keep abreast of changing rules and regulations—but it would allow an individual to argue that there were reasonable grounds for the ignorance or mistake which led to the offence. To rebut the claim that such an excuse might be raised so often as to impede the administration of the criminal law, one has only to refer to the lengthy experience of Scandinavian countries in allowing defences of this kind.[129]

So far the discussion has focused on ignorance or mistake of criminal law as an excuse; yet it functions in some English cases as a simple negation of *mens rea*, particularly in offences which include the word 'knowingly'[130] Is this compatible with a general policy of restricting the effect of ignorance or mistake of criminal law to cases in which it is based on reasonable grounds? The answer is surely no. The legislature has not pursued a consistent policy in deciding whether or not 'knowingly' should form part of the definitions of offences, and it certainly cannot be assumed that Parliament has considered the conflict between a 'literal' interpretation and the application of the policy against allowing unreasonable ignorance or mistakes of criminal law as a defence. In recent years courts have

---

[127] [1962] AC 220, discussed above, in Ch. 3.3(*g*).

[128] See the American case of *Lambert v. California* (1957) 355 US 225, and above, Ch. 4.4(*c*).

[129] J. Andanaes, '*Error Juris* in Scandinavian Law', in G. Mueller (ed.), *Essays in Criminal Science* (1961); cf. generally P. Brett, 'Mistake of Law as a Criminal Defence' (1966) 5 *Melb. U. LR* 179.

[130] See *Secretary of State for Trade and Industry v. Hart* [1982] 1 WLR 481, and Williams, *Textbook of Criminal Law* Ch. 20.

veered between allowing ignorance of law to negative 'knowingly' and declaring that this approach would be 'wholly unacceptable'.[131] Surely the courts should interpret all statutes in the light of general principles of the criminal law, as they have been accustomed to do in cases of insanity and intoxication. The same approach should be adopted where the offence includes a phrase such as 'without lawful excuse' or 'without reasonable excuse'.[132]

(c) The Reliance Cases

Another benefit of moving away from the relatively strict English policy against defences based on mistake or ignorance of criminal law towards a 'reasonable grounds' defence is that the 'reliance' cases could also be accommodated. In *Cooper v. Simmons* (1862)[133] an apprentice absented himself from his apprenticeship after the death of his master, having sought the advice of an attorney and having been counselled that he was no longer bound. The court nevertheless convicted him of unlawfully absenting himself from his apprenticeship, and Pollock CB stated that 'it would be dangerous if we were to substitute the opinion of the person charged . . . for the law itself'. In *Arrowsmith* (1974)[134] D had on occasions distributed leaflets urging British soldiers not to serve in Northern Ireland. In the past the Director of Public Prosecutions had declined to prosecute her under the Incitement to Disaffection Act 1934, but now she was charged with an offence under that Act. One line of defence was that she reasonably believed, as a result of a letter from the Director, that her conduct did not contravene the Act. The Court of Appeal upheld her conviction, stating that 'a mistake as to the law would not avail the appellant except perhaps in mitigation of sentence'. Both these cases would surely be better analysed in terms of reasonable reliance. If it is established that D relied on advice from officials with regard to the lawfulness of the proposed conduct, that ought to be sufficient to support reasonable grounds for the mistake of law. Arguably, this ought also to extend to reliance on a

---

[131] Cf. *Secretary of State for Trade and Industry v. Hart* [1982] 1 WLR 481, with *Grant v. Borg* [1982] 1 WLR 638, two decisions of the House of Lords in the same year; see generally A. T. H. Smith, 'Error and Mistake of Law in Anglo-American Criminal Law' (1985) 14 *Anglo-American LR* 3.

[132] See R. Card, 'Authority and Excuse as Defences to Crime' [1969] Crim. LR 359 and 415.

[133] (1862) 7 H & N 707, discussed by Brett, 'Mistake of Law as a Criminal Defence'.

[134] (1974) 60 Cr. App. R 211.

lawyer's advice, although the Model Penal Code stops short of this.[135] Confusion may arise about the entitlement of a particular agency or official to advise a member of public about the law, as one English case vividly demonstrates,[136] but since reasonable mistake of law would be an excuse, the key question is whether D reasonably assumed that the person giving the advice was duly authorized. In the element of reliance, these cases can call upon a kind of estoppel reasoning—the State and the courts should not convict a person whom they or their officers have advised otherwise.[137] Also, D's effort to ascertain the legal position is surely a strong indication against conviction. The Control of Pollution Act 1974, section 3(4), specifically creates a defence to the crime of unlicensed waste-disposal where D 'took care to inform himself from persons who were in a position to provide information'. This ought to fore-shadow wider recognition of these grounds for a defence. Indeed, one reason why the defence is so rarely raised in English courts is the prevalence of crimes of strict liability in some fields: such offences leave no more room for a mistake of law defence than for a mistake of fact.

6.8. ENTRAPMENT

There are cases in which the police arrange for either one of their own officers or for some other person to approach D and tempt him to commit an offence. If D commits the offence, should there be a defence of entrapment? Many American jurisdictions admit such a defence, within limits, but English law has always rejected it. What are the main arguments?[138]

No such defence would be available if it were a private individual who, on his or her own initiative, incited D to commit the offence: the fact that one person incites another does not relieve the other of criminal liability, since the law regards each of them as autonomous individuals who are able to choose what to do. Yet one might wish to argue that, if the person incited was an ordinary citizen, and not someone predisposed to committing such offences, that person's offence might fairly be said to have been caused by the temptations proffered by the *agent provocateur*. This would seem to shift the

---

[135] Model Penal Code, s. 2. 04(3).
[136] *Cambridgeshire and Isle of Ely CC v. Rust* [1972] 2 QB 426.
[137] Ashworth, 'Excusable Mistake of Law'.
[138] J. D. Heydon, 'The Problems of Entrapment' [1973] CLJ 268.

cnquiry back towards the character and previous record of the person incited—and, perhaps, into dangerous ground, in the sense that persons with previous convictions would be unable to take advantage of any defence of entrapment. This is the course which American law has taken: persons held to be 'predisposed' towards the offence may not avail themselves of the defence of entrapment.[139]

Is it the involvement of the State, through its law-enforcement officers or their agents, which alters the complexion of the event? Can it be said that this state involvement affects D's culpability, when incitement by a private individual would not? In one sense there is no difference at all. But since many defences involve a compromise between principles of fairness to the individual and social-defence policies, it might be argued that the State should not stultify itself by creating the very offences which it then goes on to punish. If it is granted that D would not have committed this offence on this occasion had it not been for the entrapping conduct of the State's agents, the element of entrapment may be said to create a potential contradiction in criminal justice which can only be prevented by excluding D from criminal liability. A counter-argument to this is that techniques amounting to entrapment are sometimes necessary if the police are to make significant progress towards detecting certain forms of crime, particularly so-called 'victimless' crimes such as drug offences. The police should be controlled in these activities, but that is a separate matter from the question of D's liability to conviction. So the counter-argument is that there is sufficient social justification for entrapment to outweigh the alleged 'contradiction' reasoning, and that there is insufficient injustice to individual defendants to warrant a defence to liability.

That provides, incidentally, some support for the English position whereby entrapment is unavailable as a defence, and does not provide a conclusive reason for the exclusion of evidence thereby obtained,[140] but it may be taken into account in mitigation of sentence if appropriate. The English debate has been preoccupied with arguments of a kind not mentioned above, such as the problems of controlling entrapment practices. This raises important issues of controls upon police operational methods, and has led the Law

---

[139] Cf. *Sorrells v. US* (1932) 287 US 435, with *Sherman v. US* (1958) 356 US 369.
[140] *Sang* [1980] AC 402; see now s. 78 of the Police and Criminal Evidence Act 1984, discussed by A. A. S. Zuckerman, *The Principles of Criminal Evidence* (1989), Ch. 16.

Commission to propose the creation of an offence of entrapment.[141] But it leaves untouched the question of whether fairness to individuals requires the admission of a defence of entrapment; whether there are sufficient social-defence arguments in the other direction; and whether the sentencing discretion is a sufficient response to bad cases.

6.9. FAULT AND THE EXCUSES

This chapter and Chapter 5 have discussed the fault requirements for criminal liability, both the positive ones which the prosecution must establish in order to fulfil the definition of the offence, and the negative ones which may be raised by evidence and which the prosecution then (with the exception of insanity) bears the burden of disproving. Voluntariness, discussed in Chapter 4.5 on automatism, may also be regarded as a fault requirement. It has been noted that, although some of the excuses, such as insanity and intoxication, have their basis in the negation of fault, others, such as duress and mistake of law, do not correspond to any of the positive fault requirements. There is, for example, no express requirement that a person should have acted 'unconstrained by threats' as a condition of criminal liability; the issue only arises when there is evidence of threats which affected D. The fact that the 'negative fault requirements' do not all correspond to, or amount to a negation of, the positive fault requirements has led some commentators to regard these excuses as a separate group from cases where there is a negation of a positive fault requirement, such as a mistake of fact. However, no such distinction is drawn here, for it is argued that the principles and policies which bear on *mens rea* have sufficient similarity and relation to those which bear on 'defences' such as those considered in this chapter—insanity, intoxication, duress, necessity, provocation, mistake of law, and entrapment.

This concluding section will raise some general issues about fault and the excuses. First, we shall examine the implications of the threshold question: should a suggested excuse be recognized as a defence or merely as a mitigating factor in sentencing? Then we consider the roots of fault and the excuses in conceptions of individual responsibility, from which we go on to examine the arguments in favour of elements of social responsibility and policies of social

---

[141] Law Com. No. 83, *Defences of General Application* (1977), Ch. 5; see A. Ashworth, 'Entrapment' [1978] Crim. LR 137.

defence. Whether it is possible to travel beyond a demonstration of the conflicting policies and principles and to achieve a unifying theory is then the question which remains.

(a) The Recognition of the Excuses

One issue which has been present throughout this chapter and which should be noted before embarking on the theoretical discussion is the range of alternative ways in which excuses can be recognized in the criminal-justice system. Even within the criminal law itself it is not simply a question of whether there is a defence or not. Provocation and diminished responsibility[142] are available as qualified defences to murder, reducing the crime to manslaughter, and there is no procedural reason why they and other qualified defences should not be granted a wider application—wherever there is a gradation of offences, the qualified defence might serve to reduce the higher to the lower.[143] There are obvious counter-arguments, grounded in the increased complexity and length of trials of cases where the unique stigma of 'murder' is not present,[144] but these concede rather than weaken the moral/social arguments for allowing the reduced culpability in, say, provocation cases to be signified by a reduction in the offence of conviction. This may be regarded as an example of fair labelling,[145] reflecting the reality that there is a 'scale of excuse, running downwards from excusing conditions, through partial excuses to mitigating excuses'.[146]

In their consideration of the various alleged excuses, the courts have often been conscious of the conflicting pressures of low individual responsibility and strong social policies, and have sometimes resorted to the sentencing discretion as a possible means of reconciliation. This is the solution in cases of entrapment,[147] and for many years it was the courts' answer to excuses based on necessity.[148] Indeed, the House of Lords recently went further and invoked executive discretion as a desirable way of mitigating the effective punishment of those who kill under duress.[149] This approach raises

---

[142] See below, Ch. 7.4(b) and (e), and above, Ch. 6.5.

[143] This was proposed by the Criminal Law Revision Committee in its 1976 Working Paper, 'Offences against the Person'.

[144] Cf. M. Wasik, 'Partial Excuses in the Criminal Law' (1982) 45 MLR 515, with S. Morse, 'Undiminished Confusion in Diminished Capacity' (1984) 75 J. Crim. Law and Criminology 1, and reply by J. Dressler, ibid. 953.

[145] See above, Ch. 3.3(l).   [146] Wasik, 'Partial Excuses', 524.

[147] See above, Ch. 6.8.   [148] See above, Ch. 6.4(c).

[149] Howe [1987] AC 417; see above, Ch. 6.4(a).

various difficulties. It would be possible to deal with all excuses, and, indeed, with all fault requirements, in this way: as we saw in Chapter 5.2(a), one could create a system in which proof of conduct and causation was sufficient for conviction, and fault would then be considered as a pointer to the most appropriate means of state intervention to ensure any repetition. The objection to this is that a criminal conviction is rightly regarded as condemnatory, an indication of fair labelling which, in turn, should rule out liability altogether in cases where D's absence of fault is so high on the 'scale of excuse' that there should be no formal blame. On Baroness Wootton's theory, however, conviction might not carry such a stigma, since it would not imply culpability.[150] Under 'desert' theory, the sentencing discretion would remain important as a means of 'fine tuning' the 'desert' of a particular defendant who fails to fulfil an excusing condition.[151] This is not to deny the difficulty of drawing an uncontroversial line between excuses which do, and excuses which do not, reach such a high level as to justify a complete acquittal. The point, rather, is that the line ought to be drawn so as to reflect the defendant's 'desert'; it ought not to be abandoned simply because this involves awkward judgments of degree.

Another way of approaching the matter which does prevent conviction is to exercise the discretion not to prosecute, and the English Code for Crown Prosecutors indicates several sets of personal circumstances (e.g. old age or infirmity of the offender, mental illness, or stress) which should weigh against prosecution.[152] Important as this approach is in sparing some persons the trauma of a court appearance, it cannot be regarded as a suitable approach for all excuses, since the discretion appears not to be subject to review, and it even dispenses with the enquiry in open court which takes place before sentencing.[153] Discretion allows flexibility for individual circumstances of defendants, but it may also allow decisions to be made on irrelevant or discriminatory criteria. Moreover, it leaves no room for one element in the defences which is an important manifestation of the social-defence element—the possibility of an enforceable court order. This is assured by the 'special verdict'

---

[150] The views of Baroness Wootton are discussed above, Ch. 5.3(a).

[151] See M. Wasik, 'Excuses at the Sentencing Stage' [1983] Crim. LR 450.

[152] Crown Prosecution Service, *Code for Crown Prosecutors* (1986), para. 8, discussed by A. Ashworth, 'The "Public Interest" Element in Prosecutions' [1987] Crim. LR 595.

[153] Procedures to ensure proper fact-finding on matters relevant to sentencing are still developing: see D. A. Thomas, *Current Sentencing Practice*, L2.

in insanity cases, and by conviction in intoxication cases. Non-prosecution prevents such intervention—although some mentally disordered persons would be admitted to hospital informally or as civil patients with the concurrence of the police.[154] Where the alleged offence is serious, however, it should be for a court to determine whether compulsory measures are required.

(b) Individual Responsibility

It was shown in Chapter 5.2(a) that the roots of the conception of individual responsibility which underlies the principle of *mens rea* lie in respect for the autonomy of the individual, which indicates criminal liability only where D chose the conduct and had the capacity and a fair opportunity to choose otherwise. As is invariably the case in these formulas, it contains at least one word which imports value judgments, namely, 'fair'. What are the measures of fairness of an opportunity? The test which seems to emerge, particularly from the excuses of duress and necessity, is whether a person of reasonable firmness might have been expected to withstand the pressures placed on D. Now in one sense this might be thought to be indulgent to D—there is no requirement that he should have felt totally deprived of his freedom of action, merely that a reasonably steadfast citizen would have found the pressure intolerable.[155] But in another sense the standard of reasonable firmness precludes actual enquiry into the pressures experienced by this defendant: even if D felt totally overwhelmed by the pressures, the law would not allow a defence of duress unless a reasonably steadfast person would also have been seriously affected. By this means, the idea of individual responsibility (how impaired was the choice and freedom of this person?) is compromised—perhaps for fear of false defences if the law were totally subjective, perhaps for fear of a significant loss in the deterrent effect of the law, or perhaps for other social reasons. One way of preventing harsh convictions of weak or vulnerable defendants would be to allow an exception to the standard for those lacking the capacity to conform, as Chapter 5.3(d) and (g) proposed above.

We have also noted that the notions of choice and free will do not retain their full vigour within the excuses. In the extreme cases of

---

[154] D. Carson, 'Prosecuting People with Mental Handicap' [1989] Crim. LR 87.
[155] See the decisions in *Graham* (1982) 74 Cr. App. R 235, and *Conway* [1988] 3 All ER 1025, and the theoretical discussion by A. Brudner, 'A Theory of Necessity' (1987) 7 *Oxford JLS* 339.

duress and necessity, the admission of defences is a clear recognition that D's behaviour was determined to a considerable degree by the circumstances. Behaviour in these cases is not *in*voluntary, as in cases of automatism,[156] but it can certainly be described as *non*-voluntary. The same might be said of acts done during a provoked loss of self-control.[157] Most of these cases arise suddenly and place D under pressure of an emergency, but it may be asked whether the law should recognize excuses in other cases where behaviour is substantially determined. One example of this is the proposal for a defence of 'social deprivation', based on the assertion that many offenders drift into crime because society fails to provide the conditions, facilities, and resources for their proper moral and social development. In arguing this case in the United States, Judge Bazelon referred to such individuals as 'the ignorant, the ill-educated and the unemployed and often unemployable', adding, in connection with their offending: 'I cannot believe that this is coincidental.'[158] The argument is that some of these people are trapped in a criminal life-style, with scarcely more freedom of action than the person under duress. They have not had a fair opportunity to conform their behaviour to the law. Critics suggest that this confuses explanation with excuse: research may demonstrate a causal link between social deprivation and offending behaviour, but this does not deny a fair opportunity to behave otherwise.[159] Not all persons from these backgrounds commit serious offences, and many other citizens from different circumstances suffer from personality problems which make it difficult for them to do the right thing at the right time. There are other arguments against a social-deprivation defence (it would be difficult to define and administer, for example; it might weaken the general deterrent effect of the law), and there is a widespread view that the excuse, where applicable, is more appropriately considered at the sentencing stage than at trial.[160] This seems to be a response not so much to difficulties of proof as to the view that social deprivation cannot be bracketed with duress and similar excuses; its effect is less urgent and more diffuse, and

---

[156] See above, Ch. 4.3.   [157] See above, Ch. 6.5(*a*).

[158] D. Bazelon, 'The Morality of the Criminal Law' (1976) 49 *S. Cal. LR* 385.

[159] M. Moore, 'Causation and the Excuses' (1985) 73 *Cal. LR*, 1091; S. Kadish, *Blame and Punishment* (1987), 102–6; Dressler, 'Reflections on Excusing Wrong-doers'.

[160] References to social deprivation and similar background factors are often found in the social enquiry reports submitted to sentencers by probation officers: see J. Thorpe, *Social Inquiry Reports*, Home Office Research Study No. 48 (1978).

political means should ideally be used to alleviate it.[161] Cases might arise where a particular person's upbringing has been so heavily determined by social circumstances as significantly to diminish his responsibility, but the expectation here is that all citizens who are not mentally disordered have the ability to overcome such influences.

Together with lack of 'fair opportunity' the other criterion of excuse was lack of 'capacity'. The examples here are children under the age of criminal responsibility (10, in Britain), and those classified as insane. In the case of the insane, it is mental disorder in the sense of a 'disease of the mind' which forms the basis of the excuse. In English law the insanity defence is tied firmly to cognitive criteria, whereas other jurisdictions have extended it to volitional deficiencies. One approach is to regard the matter rather as a question of status: mentally disordered persons lack the capacity for rational thought and direction of behaviour which normal citizens generally have, and they should therefore not be subjected to criminal liability and punishment.[162] But the tendency in English law has been to try to link the insanity defence with the positive fault requirements, such as *mens rea*, and this poses the question of whether other personal conditions might form the basis of a defence. One such question would be whether pre-menstrual syndrome should be accepted as a defence. It has been contended that hormonal imbalance can so unhinge a woman for a few days every month as significantly to impair her capacity to conform her conduct to the law. If the medical credentials of this condition and its effects are established, then there would seem to be good reason for recognizing an excuse in those cases where its effects reach an appropriate level of incapacitation.[163]

(c) Social Responsibilities and Social Defence

This chapter can have left little doubt about the influence of considerations of social defence on the shaping of the law relating to excuses. Fear that individuals will raise, and succeed with, false defences is never far from the minds of judges and legislators, and goes some way towards explaining the presence of restricting conditions in duress and necessity (the 'person of reasonable

---

[161] On political obligation, cf. N. Lacey, *State Punishment* (1988), Chs. 4 and 6.

[162] See M. Moore, *Law and Psychiatry* (1985); R. A. Duff, *Trials and Punishments* (1986).

[163] Taylor and Dalton, 'Pre-Menstrual Syndrome: A New Criminal Defense?' (1983) 19 *Cal. WLR* 269; *Sandie Smith* [1982] Crim. LR 531; and Dressler, 'Reflections on Excusing Wrongdoers', 707.

firmness'), in intoxication (the restriction to crimes of 'specific intent'), and in ignorance or mistake of law (the virtual denial of such a defence). Whether these fears should be accorded weight is debatable: much of the criminal law depends for its operation on proof of awkward matters, such as a person's intention, and if this were used as a general argument, the law would take a radically different shape. There are, however, other social arguments for restrictions, apart from 'fear of false defences'. One is the importance of taking compulsory measures against persons shown to be capable of causing harm in their condition. This is a major plank of the 'special defence' in insanity cases, where absence of capacity leads to a defence which, in turn, attracts compulsory measures of social protection.[164] Yet the terms of the defence are not designed to demonstrate that D is a dangerous person, likely to cause further serious harm if given a simple acquittal. At present, with compulsory and indefinite committal to mental hospital, dangerousness is assumed from the presence of mental disorder of a particular kind, together with one act of (usually serious) criminal harm. The fragility of all predictions of dangerousness is well known; the present English system depends on the conscientiousness of Mental Health Review Tribunals, and the reformed system suggested by the draft Criminal Code would depend on the discretion of the trial judge.[165]

Prediction of future dangerousness may also play some part in the prevailing English approach to intoxication as a defence, but probably the chief reason for restricting the defence is the belief that people who do harm whilst intoxicated are blameworthy. This is a strong application of the doctrine of prior fault. Australian and other jurisdictions reject both the dangerousness and the prior-fault reasoning in intoxication cases, maintaining an approach based on pure individual responsibility at the time of the act. No loss of social defence appears to have resulted.[166] This may be nothing more than a demonstration of the rarity of truly acute intoxication, or of the intolerance of juries for drunken harm-doers, but it does raise questions about the need for vigorous policies of social defence and about the propriety of a concept of *mens rea* which is compatible with advanced states of intoxication.

But the restrictive approach of English and American law towards excuses based on intoxication may be supported on a different and

[164] See above, Ch. 6.2.   [165] Ibid., and Law Com. No. 177, clause 39.
[166] See above, Ch. 6.3(*a*).

more general ground: namely, that the view of criminal responsibility as essentially 'subjective', and as concerned only with D's state of mind at the time of the act, treats the individual as an abstracted and isolated person rather than as a member of society in a particular situation. The subjective principles and the contemporaneity principle,[167] ingrained as they are in much academic writing in the common-law world and in some judicial pronouncements,[168] seem premised on an atomistic view of individual behaviour. An alternative approach would spell out certain duties of citizenship which should form part of membership of a legal community and which might have some bearing on issues of criminal responsibility. One such duty might be to keep one's behaviour under control at all times. This might be combined with the general social proposition that persons who take large amounts of alcohol or certain drugs constitute a greater risk of causing harm to establish the basis of a restrictive approach to intoxication and criminal responsibility. Whether this takes the form of some restrictive and artificial rules relating to 'specific intent' or 'recklessness', or results in the creation of a new special defence or offence for the intoxicated, is a separate (though important) question.[169] The foundation is the duty to keep control over one's behaviour. That duty may also be used to justify the refusal to admit provocation as a general defence—if we are satisfied that no exceptions should be admitted to the principle that citizens should control their tempers. However, some of the arguments examined above have shown that certain provocation cases contain strongly exculpating elements, which at the very least make a strong case for provocation as a qualified defence.[170]

This line of reasoning may also be applied, in a critical fashion, to mistake cases. Citizens may surely be expected to make reasonable efforts to acquaint themselves with the contours of the criminal law, but this does not support the refusal of the English courts and legislature to recognize a general excuse based on ignorance or mistake of law. On the contrary, the citizen's duty is fulfilled by reasonable enquiries, and this would support a defence of reasonable ignorance or mistake of law (including reasonable reliance on official advice).[171] Citizenship duties also have relevance to the

---

[167] See above, Ch. 5.2(a) and (d).
[168] M. Kelman, 'Interpretive Construction in the Substantive Criminal Law' (1981) 33 Stanford LR 591.
[169] See above, Ch. 6.3(d).
[170] See above, Ch. 6.5(b).   [171] See above, Ch. 6.7(b) and (c).

controversy over mistake of fact: the reasoning here is less a matter of general duties than of a proper sensitivity to the rights of others in particular situations which ought to alert the citizen. Thus, rather than regarding the defendant in a rape case as abstracted from the situation of close proximity to a woman and subject only to the momentary and 'inexorable' logic of the question: 'did he at that time realise that there was a risk that she was not consenting?', the law might fairly ask whether he took care to ensure that his sexual partner was willing.[172] Similarly, rather than regarding a police-officer as abstracted from his or her training and knowledge of alternative means of resolving a situation and subject only to the momentary and 'inexorable' logic of the question: 'did he at that time believe that his life was in danger from V?', the law might perhaps ask whether he took care to ensure that V was armed, before taking another person's· life.[173]

The drift of this argument is towards the idea of duties of citizenship which relate in part to control of one's own passions or 'vices'[174] and in part to one's respect for the rights of others in situations which obviously concern those rights (e.g. sexual inter-course, the use of deadly force). Strict compliance with the principle of contemporaneity gives way here to the doctrine of prior fault, as the various duties tug the enquiry away from the momentary conduct towards a broader consideration of the situation and its antecedents. Those wedded to traditional theory will doubtless regard this as the spread of negligence liability, and so it is. In this sense, it is compatible with much of what was said by Lord Diplock in *Caldwell*,[175] in that failure to give thought to those matters which the reasonable citizen might regard as obvious may be just as culpable as momentary advertence to such matters. But the idea of duties of citizenship does not require full adherence to the *Caldwell* doctrine. Two modifications are particularly important. First, the general notion that citizens with ordinary powers of perception and self-control should exercise those powers must be subject to an exception in favour of persons incapable of attaining that general standard. *Caldwell* recklessness is too inflexible in this respect.[176] Second, a full-blown notion of individual responsibility in a social

[172] C. Wells, 'Swatting the Subjectivist Bug' [1982] Crim. LR 209 and below, Ch. 8.5(c).
[173] Horder, 'Cognition, Emotion and Criminal Culpability'.
[174] Fletcher, *Rethinking Criminal Law*, 514.
[175] [1982] AC 341, discussed above, Ch. 5.3(c).
[176] See above, Ch. 5.3(c).

context should lay greater emphasis on the avoidance of greater harms. The paradox of *Caldwell* is that it applies to an offence which is, in most instances,[177] well down the scale of seriousness. A socially sensitive doctrine would impose greater duties of care on citizens in situations where harm is widely known to be possible (e.g. use of firearms, fire-raising, irregular driving), where great harm is a possibility (e.g. the operation of transport systems, sports stadiums), and particularly where the means of avoiding harm are relatively simple (as in sexual intercourse, enquiring about the other's willingness). It will be evident that these arguments do not promise a simplified system of fault and excuses, but Chapters 5 and 6 should have demonstrated that the present system is far from simple. Conflicts between 'pure' individual responsibility and questions of social responsibility are endemic in this sphere: they must be recognized, examined, and constantly reappraised.

In order to avoid the arguments for social responsibility being seen as placing too great an onus on individuals, it is important not to neglect the duties of the State in these matters. The obligation to publicize new criminal laws is obviously one such duty, particularly strong in respect of duties to act. The obligation not to entrap citizens into committing offences might be another.[178] And then there is the more general issue of the State's responsibility for social conditions which foster crime. This is not an outrageous notion: the preamble to the European Convention on Compensation for Victims of Crimes of Violence refers to the idea that the State has a duty to provide compensation through its failure to prevent crimes,[179] and this suggests at least an obligation to take reasonably determined measures to reduce crime. One such measure is to relieve those criminogenic social conditions of poverty, bad housing, unemployment, lack of social facilities, and so forth which have an established link with law-breaking.[180] Even if we are not prepared to go so far as to accept social deprivation as an excuse for crime,[181] it may be regarded as significantly reducing an offender's 'desert',

---

[177] Cf. criminal damage by fire (arson), which is often serious.

[178] See above, Ch. 6.8.

[179] Council of Europe, *European Convention on Compensation for the Victims of Crimes of Violence* (1984).

[180] Cf. S. Box, *Recession, Crime and Unemployment* (1987), 30–1, with J. Q. Wilson and R. Herrnstein, *Crime and Human Nature* (1983), esp. Pt. VI. See also S. Field, *Trends in Crime and their Interpretation*, Home Office Research Study, No. 119 (1990).

[181] See above, n. 157 and accompanying text.

and thus as an example of state neglect of a duty towards its citizens.[182]

(d) Fault, Excuse, and 'Desert'

Modern writings on the criminal law have made substantial advances in uncovering and criticizing the reasons for admitting, rejecting, and shaping the various fault requirements in criminal liability. Interest in the distinction between justification and excuse has brought greater clarity to the analysis of the so-called 'defences'[183] although such analysis is still not common practice among English writers and has failed to avert confusions in the courts.[184] It is doubtful, however, whether a defence can be said to be incoherent simply because it draws on strands of both excuse and justification, so long as the reasons for doing so are convincing.[185]

The search for a unifying theory of excuses has been less productive. Proposed theories of excuse seem to offer conclusory descriptions rather than criteria which may be used to admit or reject possible excuses. Hart's doctrine of fair opportunity has been particularly influential, and yet it leads us into uncharted waters. His argument that a person should only be held criminally liable if he or she had the capacity and a fair opportunity to act in conformity with the law[186] rests, to a large extent, on conceptions of what is and what is not a 'fair' opportunity. In disputed areas such as ignorance and mistake of law, the cutting edge of this theory is rather blunt.[187] The same might be said of 'desert' theory, in either of its two modern manifestations. One is the character theory, which argues that D's 'desert' is 'gauged by his character' and therefore that 'a judgment about character is essential to the just distribution of punishment'.[188] Behaviour should be excused when it does not reflect on D's character, but D should be held responsible whenever the behaviour can be regarded as genuinely expressive of his dispositions.[189]

---

[182] See Lacey, *State Punishment*, Ch. 3, and 140–1.

[183] Notably Fletcher, *Rethinking Criminal Law* Ch. 10, K. Greenawalt, 'The Perplexing Borders of Justification and Excuse' (1984) 84 *Columbia LA* 1897; J. Dressler, 'Justifications and Excuses: A Brief Review of the Concept and the Literature' (1987) 33 *Wayne LR* 1155; G. Williams, 'The Theory of Excuses' [1982] Crim. LR 732.   [184] See the discussion of *Howe* above, Ch. 6.4(*d*).

[185] Alldridge, 'The Coherence of Defences'.

[186] H. L. A. Hart, *Punishment and Responsibility* (1968), Chs. 2 and 7.

[187] Cf. Dressler, 'Reflections on Excusing Wrongdoers', 703–715.

[188] Fletcher, *Rethinking Criminal Law*, 800.

[189] M. Bayles, 'Character, Purpose and Criminal Responsibility' (1982) 1 *Law and Philosophy* 5, and Lacey, *State Punishment*, 65–78.

There are several difficulties with this approach, one of which is the breadth of the conception of character it employs, and another its lack of sharpness in distinguishing between acceptable and unacceptable excuses.[190] Fletcher's attempt to limit the theory to the particular act charged, by reference to the principle of legality and the value of privacy, is unconvincing.[191] It also brings the theory close to the second manifestation of 'desert' theory, which focuses more explicitly on the act or omission charged, and argues that liability is undeserved where D's practical reasoning capacities were impaired.[192] Again, it is unclear whether this provides a sufficient criterion for dealing with controversial areas such as mistake of law and provocation. Moreover, there is a difficulty with such a momentary conception of 'desert'. It is one thing to join with Nozick in asserting that 'desert' does not have to go 'all the way down',[193] so that it is unnecessary to investigate whether every element of the situation can be said to be deserved; it is quite another to abstract D's 'desert' from the situation which confronted him at that time, which may have been 'determined causally and (therefore) not according to desert'.[194] However, all arguments about 'desert' must assume some limitations on individual freedom to determine the conditions of behaviour, whilst asserting sufficient residual autonomy to make sense of responsibility.

Underlying these various theories, there are slightly differing rationales for admitting excuses at all. Having demonstrated the inadequacy of the utilitarian argument that the law should excuse those who were not susceptible of deterrence,[195] Hart argued that the justification for requiring fault and admitting excuses is that this enables citizens to predict when they are liable to be subjected to sanctions and, thereby, to decide whether or not to avoid them.[196] This places the criminal law on a strangely neutral basis, rather like shopping decisions in a supermarket, and a stronger justification is that respect for individual autonomy requires deference

---

[190] Dressler, 'Reflections on Excusing Wrongdoers', 692–701.
[191] See Fletcher, *Rethinking Criminal Law*, 800, criticized by Brudner, 'A Theory of Necessity', 344–7.
[192] Moore, 'Causation and the Excuses'.
[193] R. Nozick, *Anarchy, State and Utopia* (1974), 225, quoted by Weinreb, 'Desert, Punishment and Criminal Responsibility' (1986) 49 *Law and Contemporary Problems* (No. 3), 47.
[194] Weinreb, 'Desert, Punishment and Criminal Responsibility', 75.
[195] Bentham, *Introduction to the Principles of Morals and Legislation* Ch. XIII.
[196] Hart, *Punishment and Responsibility* Ch. 2.

to individual choice and control.[197] Broader references to principles of justice and moral blame seem to stem from this. Although these arguments from respect for autonomy should be accepted as the reason for contemplating the admission of excuses, the diversity of the social arguments considered in this chapter shows that some of the key operational questions—whether to require fault and at what level, whether to admit an excuse at all, what conditions to place on that excuse—ought to be set in a wider context of social obligations. References to the 'moral' basis of excuses, which take no account of the social and political factors which also impinge on questions of the proper ambit of the law, encourage this neglect. The idea of 'desert' can certainly be made to comprehend these notions of social responsibility, but, like the idea of 'fairness', it does not lead directly to them without some more specific reflection on the relationship between individuals and society.

[197] R. Dworkin, *Taking Rights Seriously* (1977), 8–11; see further above, Ch. 5.2(*a*).

7

HOMICIDE

This chapter deals with the approach of the criminal law to behaviour which causes or risks causing death. Murder, manslaughter, and several other offences are discussed, and one recurrent issue here is whether English law responds proportionately to the different degrees of culpability manifested in cases where death is caused.

7.1. DEATH AND FINALITY

For practical purposes, the culpable causing of another person's death may fairly be regarded as the most serious offence in the criminal calendar. There is an argument that treason is a more serious offence, since it strikes at the very foundations of the State and its social organizations, but treason is so rare that it is surely permissible to treat homicide as the most serious form of crime. The reason for this is not difficult to find: the harm caused by many other crimes is remediable to a degree, whereas the harm caused by homicide is absolutely irremediable. Even in crimes of violence which leave some permanent physical disfigurement or psychological effects, the victim retains his or her life and, therefore, the possibility of further pleasures and achievements, whereas death is final. This finality makes it proper to regard death as the most serious harm that may be inflicted on another, and to regard a person who chooses to inflict that harm as the most culpable of offenders, in the absence of some excuse or justification.

Although many deaths arise from natural causes, and many others from illnesses and diseases, each year sees a large number of deaths caused by 'accidents', and also a number caused by acts or omissions which amount to some form of homicide in English law. For 1987 the statistics show that there were some 20,000 accidental deaths, of which some 7,000 occurred in the home, 6,000 at work, and 5,000 on the roads.[1] By comparison, the number of deaths recorded as criminal homicide was 600, which includes all the

[1] *Social Trends 1987* (HMSO, 1988).

murders and manslaughters.[2] This figure is relatively small when compared with many American cities, but that is no cause for satisfaction. There are still awkward questions to be confronted. For example, are we satisfied that the 600 deaths recorded as homicide are in fact more culpable than all, or even most, of the deaths recorded as accidents? In other words, does English criminal law pick out the most heinous forms of killing as murders and manslaughters, or are the boundaries frozen by tradition? Another question is whether the criminal law ought not to be wider in its application to activities which carry some risk of causing death than in other spheres. Thus, even if it would be excessive to sweep large numbers of the deaths now recorded as 'accidents' into the law of homicide, there may be sufficient justification for creating or enforcing offences designed to ensure safe conditions of work, safe goods, safe buildings, and so on. It was argued in Chapter 2 that the criminal law ought to spread its net wider where the potential harm is greater. It will be seen that English law does this up to a point, and in the process seems to accept social-defence arguments as reasons for departing from several of the principles set out in Chapter 3.

7.2. REQUIREMENTS OF CRIMINAL HOMICIDE

English law distinguishes between the offences of murder and manslaughter, as we shall see, but the two crimes do have certain common elements. It must be proved that the defendant's act or omission caused the death of the victim within a year and a day.[3] (The requirements of causation in the criminal law are discussed elsewhere.[4]) The 'year and a day' rule is a legacy of times when medical science was so rudimentary that, if there was a substantial lapse of time between injury and death, it was unsafe to pronounce on whether the defendant's conduct or some other event caused the death. Nowadays the problem is quite the reverse: medical science is generally able to determine whether D's conduct caused the death, and innovations such as life-support machines mean that life can be prolonged for months and years in some instances.[5] In one recent case the victim of a stabbing died two and a half years after

---

[2] *Criminal Statistics 1987* (1988, Cmnd 498), Table 4.2.

[3] Rule affirmed in *Dyson* [1908] 2 KB 454, and in *R v. West London Coroner, ex p. Luca* [1988] Crim. LR 541; see D. E. C. Yale, 'A Year and a Day in Homicide' [1989] CLJ 202.

[4] See above, Ch. 4.6.

[5] See Ian Kennedy, *Treat Me Right* (1989), Ch. 18.

the incident, having been kept on a life-support machine for almost the entire time.[6] In principle, it seems unjust that a homicide conviction should not be possible in such a case, if all the other elements can be established and only the 'year and a day' rule stands in the way. But the rule was confirmed by the Criminal Law Revision Committee in 1980,[7] on the ground that a defendant should not be left in peril of a homicide conviction indefinitely. Surely prosecutorial discretion should be enough to prevent unfair convictions years after the event. The rule itself is out of accord with modern medical conditions and should be abolished.

7.3. DEFINING MURDER: THE INCLUSIONARY QUESTION

(a) The Procedural Context

If causing death is to be regarded as the most serious harm that can be inflicted, it would seem to follow that the most blameworthy form of homicide should result in the highest sentences imposed by the courts. Indeed, many systems of criminal law impose a mandatory sentence for murder (or whatever the highest form of homicide is called in that system). In some jurisdictions this is a mandatory sentence of death. In others, such as those in the United Kingdom, it is the mandatory sentence of life imprisonment. Why should this penalty be mandatory, and not at the discretion of the court as in other offences? One argument in favour of the mandatory sentence of life imprisonment is that it amounts to a symbolic indication of the unique heinousness of murder. It places the offender under the State's control, as it were, for the remainder of his or her life. This is often linked with a supposed denunciatory effect—the idea that the mandatory life sentence denounces murder as emphatically as possible—and with a supposed general deterrent effect, in declaring that there is no mitigation of sentence available for this crime. It might also be argued that the mandatory life sentence makes a substantial contribution to public safety.

None of these arguments is notably strong, let alone conclusive. The mandatory penalty does indeed serve to mark out murder from other crimes, but whether the definition of murder is

---

[6] *Oxford Times*, 17 Mar. 1989.
[7] Criminal Law Revision Committee, Fourteenth Report, *Offences against the Person* (1980, Cmnd 7844), paras. 39–40. The Law Commission now takes the opposite view: see its evidence to the House of Lords Select Committee on Murder and Life Imprisonment (1988–9, HL Paper 78), para. 32.

sufficiently refined to capture the worst killings, and only the worst killings, remains to be discussed below. Whether the life sentence is regarded as a sufficient denunciation in society depends on the public's perception of what life imprisonment means: if it is widely believed that it results in an average of nine years' imprisonment, the effect will be somewhat blunted. The same applies to the general deterrent argument: its effectiveness depends on whether the penalty for murder affects the calculations of potential killers at all, and, if it does, whether life imprisonment is seen as significantly more or less severe than the alternative of a long, fixed-term sentence. As for public protection, this depends on executive decisions with regard to release; it fails to take into account whether it is necessary for public protection to keep 'lifers' in for so long.[8]

This brings the discussion to a crucial point: what does the sentence of life imprisonment mean in practice, and what would be the alternative? What it means is that the time of release from prison is determined by the Home Secretary, on the advice of the Parole Board and the Lord Chief Justice, rather than by the judge at the trial. In procedural terms, therefore, the life sentence involves a transfer of function: normally it is the judge who determines the sentence (or at least its upper limit, since earlier release on parole may be possible), whereas a life sentence entrusts that function to the executive, who must first ascertain the opinions of the Lord Chief Justice and the trial judge. The Home Office is not bound by those opinions, and appears to depart from them frequently.[9] In 1983 the Home Secretary imposed restrictions on the release of persons serving life for murders of police- and prison-officers, terrorist killings, murder during robbery, and the sadistic or sexual murder of young children, fixing a minimum of twenty years' imprisonment for these offenders.[10] Whatever the justifications for introducing this policy, it serves to underline the fact that sentencing in murder cases is enacted without each case being considered in- dividually, after hearing representations from the offender's counsel, and without a sentence announced in court and subject to appeal.

At present, the executive takes decisions to release some murderers after only a few years and to keep others in prison for extremely long periods. Should those decisions not be taken by the courts, in

---

[8] On this, see the cautious words of S. Brody and R. Tarling, *Taking Offenders out of Circulation*, Home Office Research Study No. 64 (1980), 33.

[9] HL Select Committee on Murder etc., paras. 154–6.

[10] Ibid., and [1983] Crim. LR 761.

the same way as other sentencing decisions? The answer sometimes given is that murderers should be treated differently because they are particularly dangerous: anyone who chooses to kill once can choose to kill again. But this argument will seem less persuasive when we have discussed cases of manslaughter by reason of diminished responsibility: where a murder is reduced to manslaughter, the judge has a wide sentencing discretion and may, according to the facts of the case, select a determinate prison sentence, a hospital order, or life imprisonment. Those who kill and are convicted of manslaughter by reason of diminished responsibility are no less dangerous than those convicted of murder, and yet the judge has sentencing discretion in one case and not in the other. Considerations of this kind have led the House of Lords Select Committee on Murder and Life Imprisonment to recommend the abolition of the mandatory sentence for murder.[11] In its place would be a sentencing discretion, which judges would use, in many cases, to mark the relative heinousness of the murder by a determinate prison sentence. In cases where life imprisonment was thought to be the appropriate sentence, the trial judge would still specify—in open court—the number of years to be spent in prison, taking the gravity of the offence into account, and release would be determined by a judicial tribunal. Such a reform would bring improvements in natural justice without loss of public protection.

(b) Degrees of Homicide

English criminal law has two degrees of homicide, murder and manslaughter. Many American jurisdictions have three degrees of murder—first-degree murder, requiring premeditation, and second- and third-degree murder, covering lesser shades of culpability.[12] In England there has been a proposal that we should do away with all these distinctions, leaving a single offence of criminal homicide.[13] That proposal, if implemented, would shift almost all the decision-making in homicide cases from the trial to the sentencing stage: the

[11] HL Select Committee on Murder etc., paras. 101–22, adopting the reasoning of D. A. Thomas, 'Form and Function in Criminal Law', in P. R. Glazebrook (ed.), *Reshaping the Criminal Law* (1978); cf. also M. D. Farrier, 'The Distinction between Murder and Manslaughter in its Procedural Context' (1976) 39 MLR 414. However, the government was swift to signal its rejection of this proposal: Home Office, *Crime, Justice and Protecting the Public* (1990, Cm 965), para. 6.15.

[12] See further P. Low, J. Jeffreys, and R. Bonnie, *Criminal Law, Cases and Materials* (2nd edn., 1986), Ch. 6.

[13] Per Lord Kilbrandon, in *Hyam v. DPP* [1975] AC 55, at 98.

only issue of any consequence in most cases would be the sentence to be imposed, and all the distinctions now drawn at the stage of criminal liability would be reflected in the sentence alone. The jury would have no role in most homicide cases, since a plea of guilty would be the norm. Contrast this with the position in jurisdictions where there are three or more degrees of homicide: pleas of guilty to first- and second-degree murders would be less frequent, since there would be the possibility of argument in court (if no bargain was struck beforehand between prosecution and defence), and the defence might succeed in persuading the jury to reduce the degree of the killing. Moreover, the borderlines between the various degrees would raise questions of law, which would provide much opportunity for legal argument and for appeals. The result would be that killings were classified and labelled in a more refined way, but at the cost of lengthy trials and mounting legal-aid bills. That cost is not difficult to justify where capital punishment is the penalty for first-degree murder. Where there is no capital punishment, how-ever, the question of how many degrees of homicide it is desirable to have calls for careful weighing of the principle of fair labelling (see Chapter 3.3 (l)) against the cost and time arguments mobilised by the policy of efficient administration (see Chapter 3.3 (m)).

The structure of the English law of homicide is rather strange. Although there are two offences, murder and manslaughter, the latter includes two distinct varieties: 'voluntary' manslaughter (killings which would be murder but for the existence of defined extenuating circumstances); and 'involuntary' manslaughter (killings for which there is no need to prove any awareness of the risk of death being caused, but for which there is thought to be sufficient fault to justify criminal liability). The arguments therefore tend to focus on three borderline questions: What is the minimum fault required for con-viction of murder? What conditions are needed to reduce murder to manslaughter? And what is the minimum fault required for a conviction of manslaughter?

(c) Requirements for Murder

In English criminal law there are now two alternative fault require-ments for murder: an intent to kill, or an intent to cause grievous bodily harm. What do these requirements mean? Do they extend the definition of murder too far, or are they too narrow?

Intent to kill may be regarded as the most obvious and indisputable form of fault element for murder, but to some extent that depends on the meaning of 'intent'. This has been the subject of a number of House of Lords decisions,[14] and yet the definition is still not clear and settled. Probably the most accurate statement would be that a person *intends* to kill if it is his or her purpose to kill by the act or omission charged, or if he or she foresees that death is practically certain to follow from that act or omission. In this way, both purpose and foresight of practical certainty are regarded as part of the definition of intent, although there are other statements suggesting that foresight of practical or 'virtual' certainty is merely evidence from which intent may be inferred.[15] How would this test be applied? In many cases the word 'intent' is used without elaboration, but there are some for which a full explanation of the meaning of intention is necessary. A fairly typical set of facts is provided by *Nedrick* (1986),[16] where D had a grudge against a woman and had threatened to 'burn her out'. One night he went to her house, poured paraffin through the letter-box and on to the front door, and set it alight. One of the woman's children died in the ensuing fire. When asked why he did it, D replied: 'Just to wake her up and frighten her.' A defence of this kind, a claim that the purpose was only to frighten and not to cause harm, requires the full definition to be put to the jury. The question is: granted that D's purpose was to frighten, did he nonetheless realize that it was practically certain that his act would cause death or grievous bodily harm to someone? The jury should answer this by drawing inferences from the evidence in the case and from the surrounding circumstances.

What about the alternative element in the definition, an intent to cause grievous bodily harm? This has considerable practical importance, since this is all that the prosecution has to prove in order to obtain a verdict of guilty of murder. It must be shown that the defendant intended (which, again, includes both purpose and awareness of practical certainty) to cause really serious injury to someone. The House of Lords confirmed this rule in *Cunningham* (1981):[17] D struck his victim on the head a number of times with a chair, causing injuries from which the victim died a week later. D maintained throughout that he had not intended to kill, but there was evidence from which the jury could infer—and did infer—that he intended to cause grievous bodily harm. The House of Lords

[14] Apart from *Hyam* (ibid.), now overruled, there is *Moloney* [1985] AC 905, and *Hancock and Shankland* [1986] AC 455, both discussed in Ch. 5.3(*b*) above.
[15] Such statements are to be found in all three decisions listed above, n. 14.
[16] [1986] 3 All ER 1.   [17] [1982] AC 566.

upheld D's conviction for murder: an intent to cause really serious injury is sufficient for murder, without any proof that the defendant intended, or even contemplated, the possibility that death would result.

Does the 'grievous bodily harm' rule extend the definition of murder too far? If the point of distinguishing murder from manslaughter is to mark out the most heinous group of killings for the extra stigma of a murder conviction, it can be argued that the 'grievous bodily harm' rule draws the line too low. In terms of principle, the rule requires justification because it departs from the principle of correspondence (see Chapter 5.2(a)), namely that the fault element in a crime should relate to the consequences prohibited by that crime. By allowing an intent to cause grievous bodily harm to suffice for a murder conviction, the law is violating a general principle, turning the most serious of its offences into a constructive crime. Why should it be necessary to 'construct' a murder conviction out of this lesser intent? There are arguments in favour of this: death is final, murder is the gravest crime, and there is no significant moral difference between someone who chooses to cause really serious injury and someone who sets out to kill. No one can predict whether a serious injury will result in death—that may depend on the victim's physique, on the speed of an ambulance, on the distance from the hospital, and on a range of other medical and individual matters. If one person chooses to cause serious injury to another, it should be presumed that he or she realizes that there is always a risk of death, and such cases show a sufficiently wanton disregard for life as to warrant the label 'murder' if death results. The counter-arguments, which would uphold the principle of correspondence, are that breach of that principle is unnecessary when the amplitude of the crime of manslaughter lies beneath murder, and also that the definition of grievous bodily harm includes a number of injuries which are most unlikely to put the victim's life at risk. In the leading case of *Cunningham* Lord Edmund-Davies (dissenting) gave the example of breaking someone's arm: that is a really serious injury, but one which is unlikely to endanger the victim's life.[18] So in practice the 'grievous bodily harm' rule goes further than the arguments of its protagonists would support.

Would it be right, then, to confine the fault element in murder to an intent to kill? That would have the merit of simplicity, but would

---

[18] [1982] AC 582; see also *Donnelly* [1989] Crim. LR 739.

it strike the right note socially? There are powerful arguments in favour of saying that there are other killings where an intent to kill cannot be established, and yet where the moral or social culpability is equal to that in most intentional killings. Of course, one cannot be adamant about whether they merit the label 'murder', because that is a question of drawing the line between murder and manslaughter, which is not susceptible of any precise resolution. It is hard to argue conclusively that the category of murder should be smaller or larger (unless the death penalty or a mandatory life sentence follows); it is a question of social judgment.

Let us briefly consider some of the possibilities. The fault element for many serious offences is intent or recklessness: why should this not suffice for murder? The question is whether all killings in which the defendant is aware of the risk of death are sufficiently serious to warrant the term 'murder'. One answer sometimes given is that they are not, because a driver who overtakes on a bend, knowingly taking the risk that there is a car travelling in the opposite direction, should not be labelled a murderer if a collision and death happen to ensue.[19] This example assumes that a sympathy for motorists will overwhelm any tendency to logical analysis. One might ask whether motorists are ever justified in knowingly taking risks with other people's lives. Yet if the example is modified a little, so that the overtaking is on a country road at night and the risk is known to be slight, it becomes questionable whether the causing of death in these circumstances should be labelled in the same way as intentional killings. This is not to suggest that motorists should be treated differently. The point is rather that, even though knowingly taking risks with other people's lives is usually unjustifiable, taking a slight risk is less serious than intentionally causing death. In discussing the boundaries of murder, we are concerned with classification, not exculpation.

To classify all reckless killings as murder might be too broad, but the point remains that some reckless killings may be thought no less heinous than intentional killings. Can a satisfactory line be drawn here? One approach would be to draw the line by reference to the degree of probability. Murder is committed in those situations where D caused death by an act or omission which he knew had death as the probable or highly probable result. A version of this test of foresight of high probability is used in several other European

---

[19] One of the examples given by Lord Goff, 'The Mental Element in the Crime of Murder' (1988) 104 LQR 30, at 48.

countries;[20] it was introduced into English law by the decision in *Hyam v. DPP* (1975),[21] but abandoned in *Moloney* (1985)[22] on grounds of uncertainty.

A second approach is to frame the law in such a way as to make it clear that the court should make a moral judgment on the gravity of the defendant's conduct. Section 210.2 of the Model Penal Code includes within murder those reckless killings which manifest 'extreme indifference to the value of human life'. Scots law treats as murder killings with 'wicked recklessness', a phrase which directs the court's attention to the circumstances of the killing.[23] Both the Model Penal Code test and the Scots test may be reduced to circularity, however, for when one asks how extreme or how wicked the recklessness should be, the only possible answer is: 'wicked or extreme enough to justify the stigma of a murder conviction'. Admittedly, the Model Penal Code does contain a list of circumstances which may amount to extreme indifference, which assists the courts and increases the predictability of verdicts in a way that Scots law does not, but the essence of both approaches is that there is no precise way of describing those non-intentional killings which are as heinous as intentional killings. Their protagonists argue that the law of murder is so important socially that derogation from the principle of maximum certainty should be allowed in favour of more accurate labelling by the courts; opponents argue that the principle of maximum certainty is needed here specifically to reduce the risk of verdicts based on discriminatory or irrelevant factors, such as distaste for the defendant's background, allegiance, or other activities.[24]

A third, more precise formulation derives from the recommendations of the Criminal Law Revision Committee in 1980, namely, that a killing should be classified as murder in those situations where there is an intention to cause serious injury coupled with awareness of the risk of death.[25] Neither an intention to cause serious injury

---

[20] See the formulations listed by HL Select Committee on Murder etc., App. 5.
[21] [1975] AC 55.　　　　　　　　　　　　[22] [1985] AC 905.
[23] For discussion, see G. H. Gordon, *Criminal Law of Scotland* (2nd edn., 1978), 736–41.
[24] This is particularly relevant to killings resulting from the activities of terrorist, or allegedly terrorist, groups. HL Select Committee on Murder etc., para. 76, concluded that 'It is neither satisfactory nor desirable to distort [general principles] in order to deal with the reckless terrorist and other "wickedly" reckless killers, who will, in any event, be liable to imprisonment for life [i.e. for manslaughter].'
[25] 14th Report (1980), para. 31, adopted in the draft Criminal Code, clause 54(1), and supported by HL Select Committee on Murder etc., para. 71.

nor recklessness as to death should be sufficient on its own, but together they restrict one another, producing a test which both satisfies the criterion of certainty and marks out some heinous but non-intended killings.

A fourth approach, adopted by English law until 1957 and still in force in many American jurisdictions, is some form of felony-murder rule: anyone who kills during the course of a felony (or, more restrictively, a serious crime of violence) or whilst resisting arrest should be convicted of murder.[26] Thus stated, there is no reference to the defendant's intention or awareness of the risks: the fact that D has chosen to commit rape, robbery, or another serious offence, and has caused death thereby, is held to constitute sufficient moral grounds for placing the killing in the highest category. Plainly, this is a form of constructive criminal liability: the murder conviction is constructed out of the ingredients of a lesser offence. Presumably the justification is that D has already crossed a high moral/social threshold in choosing to commit such a serious offence, and should therefore be held liable for whatever consequences ensue, however unforeseeable they may be. The objections would be reduced if awareness of the risk of death was also required: in other words, if the test were the commission of a serious offence of violence plus recklessness as to death. The effect of that test would be to pick out those reckless killings which occurred when D had already manifested substantial moral and legal culpability, and to classify them as murder.

Four alternative approaches have been described, and many others could be listed. The point is that the traditional concepts of intention and recklessness do not, of themselves, appear to be sufficiently well focused to mark out those killings which are the most heinous. The law must resort to some kind of moral and social evaluation of conduct if it is to identify and separate out the most heinous killings. Many people might think that a person who causes death whilst using an unlawfully held firearm or explosives ought to be convicted of murder because there is, generally speaking, no excuse for using such dangerous equipment. Some of the people thus covered would be armed robbers, others would be terrorists. The armed robber might say that he had no intention of using the firearm, that he carried it with him simply to frighten the victim, and

---

[26] For discussion of American formulations, see G. P. Fletcher, *Rethinking Criminal Law* (1978), Ch. 4.4, and P. Robinson, *Fundamentals of Criminal Law*, Ch. 5, s. 19.

that it went off accidentally:[27] if the jury believes that, should he be convicted of murder? The terrorist might say that he gave sufficient warning of the bomb for the area to be cleared, and that it was unforeseeable that a deaf person should remain on the premises and be killed in the explosion, which was intended only to cause damage. If the jury believes that, should he be convicted of murder?[28] It is possible that juries would prefer to convict of murder in such cases so as to register their abhorrence of the defendant's activities in general. If so, this would suggest a social preference for regarding killings of these kinds as among the worst because of the circumstances in which they occur, rather than because of the defendant's awareness of the possible consequences. However, the Royal Commission on Capital Punishment, which reviewed the matter thoroughly in the early 1950s, and later law-reform committees have accorded preference to the 'general principle' that 'persons ought not to be punished for consequences of their acts which they did not intend or foresee'.[29] A conviction for manslaughter would be sufficient to mark the gravity of those cases in which D was not aware of the risk of death, and the court would have ample discretion in sentencing to reflect the blameworthiness of D's conduct. However, there would have to be clear parameters of sentencing in order to avoid the intrusion of discriminatory or irrelevant factors at this stage.

To summarize: the existing English law classifies as murder those killings where there was an intent to kill or an intent to cause grievous bodily harm. The reason for distinguishing between murder and manslaughter must be to identify and to label the most heinous killings as murder, and it has been questioned whether English law succeeds in this. There are issues of general principle at stake, but it is also true to say that there can be no *absolutely right* place in which to draw the line. The issue assumes special significance when conviction for murder carries a mandatory penalty, particularly when that penalty is death.

---

[27] In *Donnelly* [1989] Crim. LR 739, the defence was that D used the gun to strike V on the head, and never intended to fire the gun, but it went off accidentally.

[28] See the discussion by Lord Goff, 'The Mental Element in Murder', and Glanville Williams, 'The *Mens Rea* for Murder: Leave it Alone' (1989) 105 LQR 387.

[29] Report of the Royal Commission on Capital Punishment (1953, Cmd. 8932), para. 76.

7.4. DEFINING MURDER: THE EXCLUSIONARY QUESTION

Even in a legal system which had the narrowest of definitions of murder—say, premeditated intention to kill—there would still be an argument that some cases which fulfil that criterion should have their label reduced from murder to manslaughter because of extenuating circumstances. Just as the discussion of the *inclusionary* aspect of the definition of murder travelled beyond the concepts of intent and recklessness, so the discussion of the *exclusionary* aspect (i.e. which killings fulfilling the definition should be classified as manslaughter rather than murder?) must consider the circumstances in which the killing took place and the culpability of the killer.

(a) The Mandatory Penalty

It is sometimes argued that the main reason for allowing such matters as provocation to reduce murder to manslaughter is to avoid the mandatory penalty for murder. Thus, if the mandatory penalty were abolished, it would be sufficient to take account of provocation when sentencing for murder. This argument neglects the symbolic function of the labels applied by the law and by courts to criminal conduct. Surely it is possible that a jury might decline to convict of murder a person who intentionally killed under gross provocation, even though they knew that the judge could give a lenient sentence, because they wished to signify the reduction in the defendant's culpability by using the less stigmatic label of man-slaughter. Since there are two offences—and particularly in juris-dictions where there arc three or more grades of homicide—surely it is right and proper to use the lesser offence to mark significant differences in culpability. This may be seen as an application of the principle of fair labelling. The lesser verdict may also assist the judge in sentencing, and help the public to understand the sentence imposed.[30] However, this reasoning is not accepted in English law for non-homicide offences, and provocation is not generally allowed to reduce a more serious offence to a less serious offence—probably for reasons associated with the policy of efficient administration (see Chapter 3.3(*m*)), which the significance of death is thought to outweigh in homicide cases.

---

[30] This was the view taken by HL Select Committee on Murder etc., paras. 80–3, agreeing with the CLRC, 14th Report (1980), para. 76.

(b) Manslaughter upon Provocation

Provoked killings are generally thought to be less heinous than un-
provoked killings, and provocation has long been accepted as a ground
for reducing to manslaughter a killing which would otherwise fulfil the
definition of murder.[31] From time to time there are cases where the
provocation is so gross and so strong that a court imposes a very short
prison sentence or even a suspended sentence for the manslaughter—
typically, cases where a wife, son, or daughter kills a persistently
bullying husband or father—and such cases raise the more general
question of whether provocation should ever be a complete defence to
homicide or to other crimes. That question was discussed in Chapter
6.5 above. The issue here is whether provocation should remain a
qualified defence to murder, and, if so, how far it should extend.

  In English law the doctrine of provocation has two main elements,
both of which are laid down in section 3 of the Homicide Act 1957.
First, there must be evidence that D was provoked to lose self-
control and kill. Second, the jury must decide whether the provocation
was enough to make a reasonable man do as D did. D is not required
to prove any of this: in a murder trial, if there is sufficient evidence
that D was provoked to lose self-control, the judge is bound to leave
provocation to the jury, and the burden of disproving it beyond
reasonable doubt lies upon the prosecution.

  (i) *The Subjective Requirement.* The first requirement of the
qualified defence of provocation is predominantly subjective—evidence that D was provoked to lose self-control and kill. This
requirement contributes to the excusing element in the provocation
doctrine, the idea being that a person who has lost self-control is less
responsible for subsequent conduct. Without this element, there
would be no way of excluding planned revenge killings, and the
argument is that they should be excluded from the defence because
a person who plans a response to an affront or a wrong ought to
ensure that the response conforms with the law. The genuinely
provoked killer, on the other hand, is in such a disturbed state of
mind that such calculation does not occur.

  How disturbed does this state of mind have to be? The concept of
loss of self-control has received little close attention from lawyers.[32]
Such phrases as 'loss of temper' or 'heat of passion' are treated

---

[31] See A. J. Ashworth, 'The Doctrine of Provocation' [1976] *Camb. LJ* 262.
[32] Compare P. Brett, 'The Physiology of Provocation', [1970] Crim. LR 634, with
Ashworth, 'The Doctrine of Provocation' [1976] CLJ 303–6.

as useful synonyms, for which angry or apparently uncontrolled reactions may be treated as evidence. One matter which is viewed as significant is a short space of time between the provocation and the killing, and there are some judicial statements which treat this as a matter of law: the loss of self-control must, it is sometimes held, be 'sudden and temporary'. Thus in *Ibrams* (1982)[33] there had been considerable ill-treatment and violence by the deceased towards D and his girlfriend, and this led them eventually to plan and carry out a night-time raid on the deceased's flat, during which they attacked and killed him. The Court of Appeal confirmed that the defence of provocation was unavailable; even if D had lost his self-control at the time, it was hardly a sudden and temporary response to an act of the deceased, who was asleep when D struck him. Differing slightly from *Ibrams* are the many cases where 'cumulative provocation' has been directed towards D over a period of time, and then some minor act sparks off the loss of self-control and killing.[34] In cases of this kind (which rarely come before the Court of Appeal except on appeal against sentence), the last act of the provoker, even though minor in itself, may be placed in the context of the previous provocation, and may itself be treated as sufficient to show that the loss of self-control was 'sudden and temporary'. However, there is no reference to a requirement of 'suddenness' in the Homicide Act 1957, and the courts have in effect restricted the defence to people with certain kinds of temperament. It is one thing to exclude cases like *Ibrams* from the defence—the gap of some five days between provocation and killing savours of considered revenge; it is another thing to exclude defendants with slow-burning temperaments, who do not react straight away to an insult or wrong, but go away and then react after hours of festering anger. Should a court be prevented from hearing and acting on evidence that, despite the lapse of a few hours, a defendant's temperament was such that it is fair to say that he or she was provoked to lose self-control, and that it was not calculated revenge?

The Homicide Act requires evidence that D was *provoked* to lose self-control: this is wide enough to include things said or done by persons other than the deceased, and acts done against persons other than D (e.g. where D is provoked to kill someone who has just committed a sexual offence upon D's son, daughter, wife, etc.). But

---

[33] (1982) 74 Cr. App. R 154.
[34] See M. Wasik, 'Cumulative Provocation and Domestic Killing', [1982] Crim. LR 29, and *Burke* [1987] Crim. LR 336.

the word 'provoked' does seem to require a human act rather than a natural event which leads D to lose self-control. Thus, in *Doughty* (1986),[35] the crying of a 17-day-old child was held to be sufficient to fall within the requirement (even though such an infant is not aware of the significance of what he or she is doing), whereas someone who loses self-control after a storm or explosion has destroyed his property would be outside the requirement. These restrictions show that the subjective element is merely preparing the ground for the objective element; it is not part of a broader defence of emotional pressure of the kind discussed in Chapter 6.5(c) above.

(ii) *The Objective Condition.* Once the court is satisfied that there is evidence that D was provoked to lose self-control, it must go on to consider the second requirement: was the provocation enough to make a reasonable man do as D did? This is English law's rather clumsy attempt to reflect the element of partial justification in the doctrine of provocation. The clumsiness is evident in the standard of 'the reasonable man', an anthropomorphic (and male) standard which might be taken to suggest a paragon of virtue if it were not for the context of partially exculpating a killing by such a person. The underlying point is that it is not every act of provocation which should be allowed to reduce murder to manslaughter, but only those serious enough to unbalance the behaviour of a person with reasonable self-control.

In earlier times the judge would rule on the sufficiency of the provocation, and the result of this was rather narrow and legalistic categories of sufficiency (e.g. violence or finding a spouse in adultery were enough, but words or a confession of adultery were not). The Homicide Act 1957 deprived judges of their power to give authoritative rulings on the sufficiency of provocation, and the question must now be left to the jury, which should apply the test of the 'reasonable man' to everything said or done before the killing which might amount to provocation. There appears to be no time-limit on the matters to be considered, so that not only the final act but a whole course of conduct may be taken into account. If this is correct, it goes some way towards dealing with cases of 'cumulative provocation', and towards a broader defence of emotional pressure.

How has the 'reasonable man' test been interpreted by the courts? In *Bedder v. DPP* (1954)[36] D, who was sexually impotent,

---

[35] (1986) 83 Cr. App. R 3l9, on which see J. Horder, 'The Problem of Provocative Children' [1987] Crim. LR 654.
[36] [1954] 2 All ER 201.

was taunted about his impotence and kicked in the groin by a prostitute with whom he had been attempting to have sexual intercourse, whereupon he lost self-control and killed her. The House of Lords held that the jury should consider the effect of these acts on a reasonable man, without regard to the sexual impotence. The court seemed to be afraid that if it allowed the jury to take account of one characteristic, such as sexual impotence, then it would be illogical to direct them not to take account of another characteristic, such as irascibility or bad temper. It is no less illogical, however, to ask a jury to consider the effect of taunts of impotence on a reasonable person who is *not* impotent, and the *Bedder* approach was overruled by the House of Lords in *DPP v. Camplin* (1978).[37] A court should now consider the effect of the provocation on 'a person having the power of self-control to be expected of an ordinary person of the sex and age of the accused, but in other respects sharing such of the accused's characteristics as they think would affect the gravity of the provocation to him'.

This test demonstrates that the illogicality alleged in *Bedder* does not exist: some characteristics of each individual defendant must be considered by the jury in assessing the gravity of the provocation, but the level of self-control must be kept constant. Bad temper could not be taken into account, for that is plainly inconsistent with the standard of reasonable self-control. Mental imbalance should also be excluded, since that seems inconsistent with the idea of an 'ordinary person', and the defence should be one of diminished responsibility. Intoxication is plainly outside the test: if the provocation was not enough to lead an ordinary sober person to do as D did, then the essence of D's defence is intoxication rather than provocation. The criteria adopted by the Court of Appeal in *Newell* (1980)[38] were that courts should only take account of characteristics with which the provocation was concerned; permanent characteristics such as race and, probably, religion may be taken into account, but transient conditions such as intoxication and exhaustion may not.

The underlying idea is that citizens are expected to keep control over their behaviour, but that in circumstances where even a person of normal self-control might be provoked, the offence may be reduced from murder to manslaughter. The required standard of self-control is kept fairly constant, but in order to assess the strength of the provocation, it is necessary to consider the relevant personal

---

[37] [1978] AC 705.
[38] (1980) 71 Cr. App. R 331, on which see A. T. H. Smith (1980) 43 MLR 441.

characteristics. This demonstrates the interaction between the excusing elements in provocation (not just the loss of self-control, but the degree of provocation experienced) and the justificatory elements (to an extent, D was right to react angrily to what had been said or done, unless the alleged provocation was self-induced or was a legally justified act). The interaction between these elements is a complex one, as we saw in Chapter 6.5. Thus, the standard of self-control is not constant but may vary, according to *Camplin,* with the age and sex of the defendant. To modify the standard where D is very young (Camplin was 15) is understandable: it is not fair to expect a youth to show the same level of self-restraint as an adult. The idea of having different standards for males and females has not been elaborated by the English courts. Clearly, sex may be a relevant characteristic in some cases, for some provocations are specific to one sex, but is there an argument for different standards of self-control for males and females? Does the plight of battered wives who kill after a spate of ill-treatment warrant special treatment by the law?[39]

(iii) *A Further Requirement?* At common law the famous case of *Mancini v. DPP* (1942)[40] held that the retaliation must bear a reasonable relationship to the provocation. The idea was that only an extremely grave provocation ought to mitigate a killing with a deadly weapon, whereas a lesser provocation might be allowed to mitigate other killings. This rule seemed to be modelled on the proportionality requirement in self-defence, and was criticized as quite unsuitable for cases of provocation, where loss of self-control intervenes between the provocation and the retaliation. Is it not both illogical and unreasonable to require a person who has lost self-control to ensure, none the less, that his response is not disproportionate? This counter-argument has been given some recognition by the courts, in that the 'reasonable relationship rule' is no longer a rule of law.[41] But traces of it remain, since a jury must still be asked not merely whether the reasonable man would be provoked to lose self-control, but also 'whether he would react to the provocation as the accused did'.[42] The precise meaning of this formulation is unclear—does it mean 'lose self-control and kill', or

---

[39] See F. Rosen, 'The Excuse of Self-Defense: Correcting a Historical Accident on behalf of Battered Women who Kill' (1986) 36 *Amer. U. LR* 11.

[40] [1942] AC 1.   [41] *Brown* [1972] QB 229.

[42] This phrase follows from the wording of s. 3 of the Homicide Act 1957, and forms part of the model direction set out by Lord Diplock in *Camplin* [1978] AC 705.

'lose self-control and kill in the way D did'?—but it seems to derive from the notion that there are degrees of loss of self-control. If that is the underlying proposition, it is important to dissociate it from the unacceptable idea that a person's acts after loss of self-control should still be measured on an objective scale.

(iv) *Provocation and Murder.* The two key questions here are: first, whether provocation ought to reduce murder to manslaughter; and, second, how wide the qualified defence should be. The answer to the first question is closely related to issues of stigma, labelling, and widely held opinions about culpability. It was argued above that it is unacceptable to claim that the mandatory penalty for murder supplies the *raison d'être* for the qualified defence of provocation: the label 'murder' should be reserved for the most heinous of killings, and there is a widely held belief that provoked killings are not in this group.

The second question, the proper ambit of the provocation defence, is more troublesome. It would be possible to absorb provocation into a wider notion of 'extreme emotional disturbance', as the American Model Penal Code does, so that the key to mitigation would be the extent of the defendant's psychological disturbance at the time of the killing rather than the reasons for it.[43] One way of accomplishing this in English law would be to merge provocation into a widened doctrine of diminished responsibility. However, a central element in the common-law doctrine of provocation is the *reason* for the loss of self-control. If the explanation for the violent outburst lies in something which might understandably lead a person to be so angry as to lose self-control, then this supplies an added reason for mitigating the offence and the sentence. Thus the court must first ascertain the gravity of the provocation experienced by the defendant, and then consider whether this provides some excuse for the loss of control. This does not gainsay the fundamental proposition that it is every citizen's duty to retain self-control—at least to the extent of not violating other people's interests—but it does open the way to a manslaughter verdict and to sentences which are rarely longer than eight years' imprisonment (less than half as long as the time served by many convicted of murder) and may be considerably shorter. However, the significant reduction in sentence is probably connected with the normative elements in the provocation doctrine, the elements of 'partial justification'. In the existing law

[43] Model Penal Code, s. 210.3.1(b); see above, Ch. 6.5(c).

this is shown by the requirement of reasonable self-control, and by the (probable) exclusion of conduct known to be legally justified from the category of sufficient provocation. Surely it is the combination of the elements of partial excuse and partial justification (see Chapter 6.5 above) which raises sufficient exculpation to warrant a reduction to manslaughter.

(c) Duress as a Qualified Defence

In 1987 the House of Lords (in *Howe*[44]) held that duress should not be available as a defence to murder. Their Lordships devoted little of their speeches to the possibility of allowing duress to function as a qualified defence to murder, reducing the crime to manslaughter and leaving the judge to pass an appropriate sentence. This would preserve the principle that a person who is threatened must be prepared to undergo heroic self-sacrifice rather than take the life of a third party, just as the provocation doctrine preserves the principle that citizens ought always to retain self-control. However, the House of Lords preferred to see a conviction for murder in these cases, with the use of executive discretion to secure an early release from the mandatory sentence of life imprisonment for offenders who killed when under duress, and thus appear to have reduced culpability.[45] This is surely an unsatisfactory way of dealing with these cases, where the degree of emotional disturbance is likely to be no less than that involved in most provocation cases. The normative requirements of the defence of duress (discussed in detail in Chapter 6.4) ensure that it is restricted to dire and realistic threats which a citizen of reasonable firmness could not be expected to resist. The degree of emotional pressure on the defendant can almost be taken for granted in these cases. 'If murder is to be reserved for those homicides which are most deserving of stigma, this does not seem to be one of them.'[46] If duress is not to be allowed as a complete defence to murder, the reduction in culpability should surely be reflected by reducing the conviction to manslaughter.

(d) Killings by the Use of Excessive Force on a Justified Occasion

Just as it seems strange and unnecessary that the law should have to choose between duress as a complete defence to murder, and duress

[44] [1987] AC 417, above, p. 199.
[45] See particularly the speeches of Lord Hailsham and Lord Griffiths.
[46] HL Select Committee on Murder etc., para. 88; the remark referred to cases of excessive defence, but its force is surely general.

as no defence at all, so it seems strange and unnecessary that a killing which narrowly fails to come within the requirements of self-defence or other justifiable force should then be classified as murder.

The Australian case of *McKay* (1957) [47] involved a chicken farmer who, when he found an intruder stealing chickens, shot at him five times, killing him. The farmer's defence was that he intended only to wound the thief, and thought he was entitled to do so. In another Australian case, *Howe* (1958),[48] D was attacked by a man, in an isolated place, whom he believed was trying to force him to commit sodomy. D took a gun and, fearing that this stronger man would renew his attack, shot and killed him. In both these cases it was held that the alternative of a manslaughter verdict ought to be left to the jury where the occasion justifies action in self-defence, or to prevent a crime, or to apprehend an offender, but where the defendant acts beyond the necessity of that occasion. Three reasons may be advanced for labelling these cases as manslaughter rather than murder. First, cases of 'excessive defence' have a grounding in legal justification, in that the occasion was one which justified the use of some force, and this places them on a higher social plateau than killings with no element of justification at all. Second, the defendant has what one might term the 'lawful motivation', believing that the actions taken were right and proper. This is a subjective, motivational factor which corresponds to the objective moral distinction identified as the first reason. Third, in some cases the defendant acts instinctively in response to an unexpected situation, completely misjudging the proper reactions in the heat of the moment: this is a similar reason to the second, but adds the element of emotional disturbance, which may explain the over-reaction in certain cases. Both the second and, more strongly, the third reason show that the doctrine of excessive defence may include a substantial element of excuse in its rationale,[49] even though its theoretical foundation lies unmistakably in the concept of legal justification.

The Australian initiative was rejected both by the Privy Council and the English courts,[50] largely on the grounds that the common-law precedents were not compelling, that the full defence of self-defence should be applied indulgently in favour of those who use such force as they instinctively think necessary, and that the doctrine

---

[47] [1957] VR 560.   [48] (1958) 100 CLR 448.

[49] See the discussion above, Ch. 4.7(*g*), on justifiable force and the emotions, and also Ch. 6.6 on putative defences.

[50] See *Palmer v. R* [1971] AC 814, and *McInnes* (1971) 55 Cr. App. R 551.

of provocation might be used to accommodate other cases. The Criminal Law Revision Committee disagreed, recommending that a verdict of manslaughter should be possible where the use of some force was justified by the occasion and where D honestly believed that the force he used was reasonable in the circumstances.[51] History then took a strange twist, for in *Zecevic v. DPP* (1987)[52] the Australian High Court denounced the doctrine of excessive force as too complicated for juries and removed it from Australian law.

There is surely a strong social argument for regarding those who kill by using *excessive* force on an occasion which justifies the use of *some* force as less culpable than the ordinary run of murderers. Whether this moral–social distinction should be reflected in the law by introducing a doctrine of manslaughter by excessive defence depends on the importance attached to the principle of fair labelling (see Chapter 3.3(*l*)). It is assumed here that juries and others do attach considerable importance to the label when it is a question of homicide, and therefore that the excessive use of force in self-defence is a matter which is properly reflected by a separate qualified defence, rather than being left to sentencing (which means executive discretion, if the mandatory penalty for murder remains) or forced artificially into the doctrine of provocation (when there may be no real evidence of loss of self-control). The problem encountered in Australia, of the doctrine being too complicated for juries, was the result of a six-stage direction which the courts developed; surely the essence of the doctrine can be conveyed more simply than that, rather than destroying it entirely.[53]

(e) Manslaughter by Reason of Diminished Responsibility

Of the qualified defences to murder in English law, diminished responsibility is the most frequently used. From 1977 to 1986 there were about half as many convictions for manslaughter on grounds of diminished responsibility as there were murder convictions. The phenomenon is a relatively recent one, since diminished responsibility was only introduced into English law in 1957, in response to long-standing dissatisfaction with the insanity defence. Insanity was, and still is, a complete defence to crime, as we saw in Chapter 6.2 above, but its confines are narrow, and some persons

---

[51] 14th Report (1980), para. 288.   [52] (1987) 61 ALJR 375.
[53] Cf. clause 59 of the draft Criminal Code with the complexity of the Australian position revealed in *Zecevic* (ibid.) and discussed by D. J. Lanham, 'Death of a Qualified Defence?' (1988) 104 LQR 239.

obviously suffering from mental disorder came to be sentenced to death for murder before 1957. Diminished responsibility has a wider ambit, but its effect is merely to reduce murder to manslaughter, giving the judge discretion on sentencing or other disposal.

The wording with which section 2 of the Homicide Act 1957 introduced diminished responsibility is rather unsatisfactory, but judges, counsel, doctors, and juries have approached it with a compassionate pragmatism rather than with the rarefied verbal analysis too frequently encountered in English criminal law. The mainstay of section 2 is a wide concept of 'abnormality of mind', interpreted in the leading case of *Byrne* (1960)[54] as

a state of mind so different from that of ordinary human beings that the reasonable man would term it abnormal. It appears to us to be wide enough to cover the mind's activities in all its aspects, not only the perception of physical acts and matters and the ability to form a rational judgment whether an act is right or wrong, but also the ability to exercise will-power to control physical acts in accordance with that rational judgment.

Section 2 does require that the abnormality of mind should be one 'arising from a condition of arrested or retarded development of mind or any inherent causes or induced by disease or injury', but this range of admissible causes is sufficiently general to encourage a broad construction of the defence. The court must, lastly, be satisfied that the mental abnormality 'substantially impaired his [D's] mental responsibility' for the killing. The formulation is strange, since it suggests that one can measure a person's ability to conform to the law. In practice, it has been taken as allowing the jury to assess whether the mental abnormality was such a significant factor in the killing as to reduce D's culpability to the extent that the offence should be reduced from murder to manslaughter. In most cases it is not the jury who takes this decision but the prosecution, who, with the judge's agreement, accepts the defendant's plea of guilty to manslaughter under section 2. Some 80 per cent of diminished-responsibility defences are accepted by the prosecution, and only in around 13 per cent of cases does the prosecution contest the defence evidence and thus require the jury to apply section 2.[55]

What is the practical effect of a successful section 2 defence? In the three years from 1984 to 1986 there were some 229 such cases, of which almost half were dealt with by a hospital order under the

[54] [1960] 2 QB 396.
[55] See the excellent study by Suzanne Dell, *Murder into Manslaughter* (1984) 25–7.

Mental Health Act 1983 (with or without restrictions). Ten per cent received life imprisonment, 15 per cent were given determinate prison sentences of between four and ten years, 10 per cent were given prison sentences below four years, and 15 per cent were given probation orders (with or without a condition of psychiatric treatment). These figures show the diversity of the cases dealt with under section 2, and they also represent a significant shift from policy in the 1960s, when around 70 per cent of diminished-responsibility offenders were given hospital orders. The decline in hospital orders and the rise of prison sentences are traceable formally to the practice of modern psychiatrists of recommending fewer hospital orders, and in reality to the more restrictive policy on admission to special hospitals being pursued by the DHSS, and also to the higher proportion of defendants who are declared to have 'recovered' by the time of the trial. No hospital order will be made where the defendant is said to have recovered, and the courts often feel it necessary to impose a prison sentence in such cases. Delays before trial can therefore affect the result, for a defendant who is committed to hospital and recovers there would usually be released back into the community fairly swiftly. Also receiving determinate prison sentences are those whose offence is reduced to manslaughter on a combined plea of provocation and diminished responsibility. Among those receiving probation orders will be those for whom the section 2 defence is used to mitigate a mercy killing.[56]

Should the qualified defence of diminished responsibility be retained? In answering this question, one has to contend with two muddles in English law, a general muddle about mental disorder and criminal responsibility, and a specific muddle about murder and manslaughter. The general muddle was discussed in Chapter 6.2(c) above: in principle, a person whose conduct was caused by mental disorder should not be liable to criminal conviction, but in practice the narrow and antiquated defence of insanity is rarely invoked in England (a handful of cases each year), and the courts normally proceed to conviction and then select a medical disposal where appropriate. The muddle could—and should—be cleared by introducing a workable mental-disorder defence, along the lines recommended by the Butler Committee in 1975.[57] If such a defence were

---

[56] See Dell, *Murder into Manslaughter*, 35–6.
[57] For discussion, see S. Dell, 'Wanted: An Insanity Defence that Can Be used' [1983] Crim. LR 341, and E. Griew, 'The Future of Diminished Responsibility' [1988] Crim. LR 75.

available in murder cases—and the consequence of a successful plea would be to give the court a limited discretion as to the order to be made—the case for a separate doctrine of diminished responsibility would be weak.

The second muddle concerns murder and manslaughter specifically, namely, that since there is no workable defence of insanity, it is often assumed that the existence of the mandatory penalty for murder is the essential reason for the section 2 defence. The Butler Committee argued that relatively minor mental disorders may be regarded as falling within section 2 simply because this outcome is thought to be preferable to mandatory life imprisonment. 'The medical profession is humane', commented the Butler Committee, 'and the evidence is often stretched.'[58] That may be so, but it may be suggested that as much depends on the surrounding legal rules as on the mandatory penalty. If there is no workable defence of insanity, it is surely wrong to convict a grossly disordered killer of murder when the less stigmatic offence of manslaughter is at hand. And if the law of homicide makes no special provision for mercy killings (see Chapter 7.4(h) below) or for killings during extreme emotional disturbance, despite a widely held view that such cases ought to be treated as less culpable than 'ordinary' murders, is there not an argument for a fairly broadly defined qualified defence?

(f) Infanticide

This is a separate offence from manslaughter, but it is relevant here because of its close links with diminished responsibility. By the Infanticide Act 1922 Parliament mitigated the application of the law of murder to mothers who killed their new-born babies whilst suffering from the effects of childbirth. Doubts arose over the length of time which might elapse before the child ceased to be regarded as 'newly born', and the Infanticide Act 1938 extended the definition to the killing of a child within twelve months of its birth by a mother whose mind is disturbed either by reason of her not having fully recovered from the effect of giving birth to the child or by reason of the effect of lactation consequent upon the birth of the child. Infanticide is a defence to murder, but it is more usual to charge infanticide in the first place. The maximum penalty remains

[58] Report of the Committee on Mentally Abnormal Offenders (1975, Cmnd. 6244), para. 19.4.

life imprisonment, although almost all the cases each year (twenty or so) are dealt with non-custodially, usually by a probation order.[59]

Three interconnected criticisms of the law may be considered here. First, the definition of infanticide is limited to the killing of the child most recently born, which means that when a mother in a disturbed state kills both her last-born child and another slightly older child, the one killing is infanticide and the other may be murder, whereas the defendant's culpability is surely the same in both cases. If the essence of infanticide lies in the effects of the stresses consequent upon recent childbirth, then it is this, and not the age of the victim, which should be the basis of the law. Second, the law is gender-specific, singling out women for more lenient treatment. Some people take exception to this on the ground that it may imply that women generally have weaker characters and are less responsible for their behaviour. There is also the argument that the fathers of children may kill whilst overwhelmed by the stress consequent upon the arrival of a new child, and they should be not be left outside the law of infanticide.[60] The third criticism is that the medical basis of the Infanticide Act 1938 is now discredited: the reference to the effect of lactation is without foundation, and it is acknowledged that the social pressures consequent upon the arrival of a new child (such as financial demands, unsuitable housing, effects on family relationships) may be just as likely to lead to the mental disturbance manifest in these cases as any condition linked specifically with the event of giving birth. In their evidence to the Criminal Law Revision Committee, the Royal College of Psychiatrists pressed for legal recognition of these wider social and situational factors. The Committee was equivocal on this, but recommended a formulation which would be broad enough to encompass these wider factors—'the balance of the woman's mind was disturbed by reason of the effect of giving birth or circumstances consequent upon that birth'.[61]

Would it not be preferable to absorb infanticide into the doctrine of diminished responsibility and allow the prosecution to charge manslaughter in such cases? This would have the advantage of removing both the restriction as to the victim and the limitation to

---

[59] See the decisions in *Sainsbury* and *Lewis*, [1990] Crim. LR 348.

[60] The case of *Doughty* (see above, n. 35 and accompanying text) might be an example here; see generally, K. O'Donovan, 'The Medicalisation of Infanticide' [1984] Crim. LR 259.

[61] 14th Report (1980), paras. 100–14.

women, but the Criminal Law Revision Committee thought that this would lead to an effective narrowing of the scope of infanticide. There might be cases of killings by mothers burdened by 'social and emotional pressures' which could not be brought within the definition of mental disorder which would be the basis of a reformed defence of diminished responsibility.[62] Of course, doctors might be prepared to stretch those definitions in order to bring such cases within diminished responsibility, but that is an unsatisfactory basis on which to reform the law, and it provides the defendant with no legal protection against a murder verdict. The Committee's solution was to persist with a separate offence of infanticide. Would it not be preferable to broaden the defence of diminished responsibility so as to convert it into a defence of extreme emotional disturbance, applicable to both sexes?

(g) Killing in Pursuance of a Suicide Pact

Section 4 of the Homicide Act 1957 provides that a person who kills another in pursuance of a suicide pact is guilty of manslaughter not murder. A suicide pact exists where two or more people, each having a settled intention of dying, reach an agreement which has as its object the death of both or all. This may be said to amount to a mutual exercise of the individuals' rights of self-determination. Cases are infrequent, tending to occur in circumstances which evoke compassion rather than condemnation. The Criminal Law Revision Committee recommended that killings in pursuance of a suicide pact should be a separate offence, on the ground that the stigma and maximum penalty for manslaughter are inappropriate in these cases.[63]

Suicide and attempted suicide ceased to be a crime when the Suicide Act 1961 became law, in recognition of the right to self-determination, but there remains an offence of aiding, abetting, counselling, or procuring the suicide of another which carries a maximum penalty of fourteen years' imprisonment. Many of the cases involve compassionate assistance, of the kind which may be necessary and justifiable if the right to self-determination is to have any meaning for those who are weak or bedridden (e.g. responding to a request to bring pills), but not all are like this. In McShane (1977)[64] a woman was convicted of an attempt to counsel her

---

[62] Ibid., para. 102.   [63] Ibid., para. 132.
[64] (1977) 66 Cr. App. R 97.

mother's suicide by repeatedly encouraging her to take an overdose, and it was shown that the mother's death would greatly alleviate the defendant's financial problems. It is for cases of this kind, where the evidence shows that there was active persuasion rather than compassionate assistance to someone already determined to commit suicide, that a substantial maximum penalty is thought necessary. For this offence and for the proposed suicide-pact offence, the Criminal Law Revision Committee (CLRC) recommended a maximum of seven years' imprisonment.[65] This grading of the offences may be seen as a compromise between the compassionate elements in the offences, which are related to the right to self-determination, and the need to protect the vulnerable from persuasion on such a crucial matter as the ending of life, an argument also derived from the right to self-determination.

(h) Mercy Killing

This concept has no special significance in English criminal law. Where a clear case of mercy killing emerges in practice, the usual response is that 'legal and medical consciences are stretched to bring about a verdict of manslaughter by diminished responsibility'.[66] The Criminal Law Revision Committee regarded this bending of the law as unsatisfactory, and tentatively proposed a new offence of mercy killing where a person, out of compassion, unlawfully kills another who is, or is believed by him to be, permanently helpless or in great pain. The proposal attracted strong opposition, some arguing that it might withdraw legal protection from the weak and vulnerable, others arguing that the fundamental ethical problems could not be satisfactorily resolved by legal definition. The difficulty with the counter-arguments is that the practice of 'stretching' diminished responsibility gives a *de facto* defence to mercy killers already. Thus, in Dell's sample of diminished responsibility cases there were some ten cases with a mercy-killing element. Most of them involved 'killings committed impulsively with whatever means were at hand', usually by 'men in their 60s or 70s [who] had reached breaking point under the continuing strain of looking after wives with severe mental or physical illness'.[67] In some of these cases the

---

[65] 14th Report (1980), paras. 136–7.
[66] Ibid., para. 115; cf. *Cocker* [1989] Crim. LR 740.
[67] Dell, *Murder into Manslaughter*, 35–6.

defendant appeared mentally normal when examined by the doctor, but the doctor was none the less willing to infer from the circumstances that there had been abnormality of mind at the time of the killing, and to write a report which brought this within section 2. Practitioners seem to accept that worthy cases of mercy killing invariably have this outcome, but this informal approach provides the defendant with no legal basis for a defence—he or she is truly at the mercy of the psychiatrists, the prosecutor, and the judge. Thus, to return to the arguments mobilized against the CLRC's proposal: the chief difference in protection of the vulnerable between the present system and the CLRC's is that the latter had a maximum penalty of two years' imprisonment, whereas life imprisonment is available where a defence of diminished responsibility succeeds; and the fundamental ethical problems are now swept under the carpet by a combination of a stretched diagnosis of 'abnormality of mind' and the ample judicial sentencing discretion, whereas the CLRC's proposal attempted to make the issues justiciable. If, however, the CLRC's proposal were altered so as to make mercy killing into a new qualified defence to murder, with the normal maximum sentence of life imprisonment, the central plank of the opposition to an explicit recognition of this mitigation in English law would disappear.[68]

Beneath these arguments about legal form lie the wider issues of self-determination. English law might be said to recognize a right to self-determination, inasmuch as suicide is no longer a crime, but that right does not yield a clear answer to the present difficulty. The right to self-determination might realistically be extended to cover those who desire their own death but lack the resources or the strength to accomplish it: this is a strong argument for a mercy-killing defence or offence. Yet, recognition of that extension might at the same time open up the possibility that vulnerable people who do not desire death, despite their suffering, might be killed by others for reasons of their own: this would subvert the right to self-determination, and is an argument against a mercy-killing defence or offence. It seems probable that some doctors carry out mercy killings by administering large doses of pain-killing drugs which shorten life significantly, and the law may well protect them from

---

[68] Such a proposal was put to the HL Select Committee by the Law Commission, but the Committee made no recommendation on the subject: see HL Select Committee on Murder etc., paras. 94–100.

liability.[69] However, such trust is not shown towards relatives and friends who assist suffering people in this way: they must run the gauntlet of a legal process which accords no formal recognition to the circumstances under which they killed.

(i) Conclusion: The Murder–Manslaughter Boundary

The basic legal distinction between murder and manslaughter lies in the mental element, but English law has now developed qualified defences to murder which mark out cases where, despite the presence of the mental element for murder, culpability is thought to be sufficiently reduced to warrant a reduction in the class of offence. Our discussion has taken a broad view of qualified defences, commenting also on some qualified defences which might be recognized but which do not feature in contemporary English law. Various reasons have been advanced for recognizing qualified defences to murder. Some regard the mandatory penalty for murder as the chief, even the sole, reason for these doctrines. It has been suggested here that the mandatory penalty is relevant but not critical. The key issues are, on the one hand, the proper legal classification of an offence which contains some exculpatory features, and, on the other, the distribution of decision-making power between the judge, the jury, and the executive. The label 'murder', and the stigma thought to accompany it, should be reserved for the most heinous group of killings; there is a well-recognized offence of manslaughter beneath murder, and this should be used for offences where the culpability is significantly lower. The mandatory penalty of life imprisonment for murder makes issues of relative culpability non-justiciable at present, since the length of imprisonment is 'determined or partly determined behind the scenes by someone who has not heard any representations by or on behalf of the prisoner on grounds which the prisoner does not know'.[70] If, on the other hand, Lord Kilbrandon's suggestion of a single offence of unlawful homicide were adopted, the crucial questions of culpability would be decided solely at the sentencing stage by the judge. The jury would have no role in this; the judge would derive no assistance from their verdict.

What, then, should be the proper division of functions between judge and jury in homicide cases? The arguments in favour of some

[69] See the summing up of Devlin J, in *Adams* [1957] Crim. LR 365, discussed above, Ch. 4.6(a) and 4.8(a).

[70] The words of the Lord Chief Justice, Lord Lane, giving evidence to the HL Select Committee on Murder etc., para. 151.

seven qualified defences have been considered above. Since it is possible that more than one defence might be raised in each case, sometimes in combination with a defence of lack of intent, a system of criminal law which offers seven qualified defences to murder risks undue complication and confusion in contested cases. The merit of separate qualified defences is that they focus the evidence and the legal argument, giving the jury (in contested cases) an opportunity to assess the defence, and giving the judge fairly precise guidance on the basis for sentencing: this might be thought to ensure that each defendant is dealt with more fairly, but the risk of confusing the jury in a contested case might tend to erode that protection. One approach would be to consider amalgamating some of the defences. This is not to condone 'stretching' defences, using diminished responsibility to cover mercy killing, for example, or provocation to cover excessive defence, but rather to examine whether the defences have common rationales which can be drawn together. Three of the qualified defences discussed above have an element of justification—provocation, excessive defence, and some cases of duress. Most of the qualified defences have an element of excuse—provocation, diminished responsibility, most duress cases, infanticide, mercy killing, and suicide pacts.

One possibility would be to evolve a qualified defence of killing under extreme emotional disturbance, following the lead of the Model Penal Code. This might encompass all those qualified defences with an element of excuse in them. A provoked loss of self-control could fall within this new doctrine—as, indeed, could losses of self-control stemming from non-human sources such as a natural disaster or financial ruin. Diminished responsibility could also be accommodated, although a general defence of mental disorder remains a better way of labelling and dealing with cases of clinical mental disorder. Cases now treated as infanticide often involve extreme emotional disturbance, as do mercy killings, suicide pacts, and cases of duress. One advantage of this amalgamation might be that there would be less potential for the jury to become confused, and yet the jury would still be empowered to reduce murder to manslaughter in appropriate cases. One disadvantage of the change might be that the more precise moral distinctions currently incorporated within the law would become submerged within the sentencing discretion, where the signposts are less clear and the arguments less structured. This might be the case with provocation, for example: there may be objections to some of the distinctions now drawn by the law of provocation, but a broader defence of extreme emotional disturbance might provide for reduction of the offence in cases of loss of self-control when caring for a baby or when arrested by a police-officer known to be acting lawfully, and some might feel that there are strong arguments against this.[71] However, such disadvantages could be minimized by elaborating the definition of extreme emotional disturbance so as to clarify its extent and its limitations, and by evolving sentencing guidelines which set out the major determinants of culpability. This would attribute some weight to the principle of maximum certainty (see Chapter 3.3(i)) in this important area of the law. Yet there would undoubtedly remain a considerable amount of discretion, both for judges and juries applying the law, if the words 'sufficient to reduce the offence from murder to manslaughter' were retained, and at the sentencing stage, in response to the particular combination of factors in each case. Such a reformulated qualified defence would not encompass cases of excessive self-defence, since they may involve a genuine and unhurried misjudgment of the amount of force permissible, and so they would have to be the subject of a separate qualified defence. But the question remains whether, in practice and in theory, it would not be fairer to retain several separate qualified defences which labelled the circumstances of each mitigated killing more accurately.

7.5. 'INVOLUNTARY MANSLAUGHTER'

The category of killings which has come to be known as involuntary manslaughter has nothing to do with involuntariness, properly so called. These are not cases where the accused has caused death while in an involuntary state.[72] These are cases where death has been caused with insufficient fault to justify labelling it as murder, but with sufficient fault for a manslaughter verdict. The word 'involuntary' is therefore used merely to distinguish these killings from ones which have the necessary intent for murder but which are reduced to manslaughter by one of the doctrines just considered, such as provocation or diminished responsibility. The legal debate in involuntary manslaughter is over the lower threshold of homicide liability—where to draw the line between manslaughter and killings which should be ascribed to mere accident. There is, however, a large variety of killings which lie above that line but

---

[71] See Ashworth 'The Doctrine of Provocation'.
[72] Discussed in the context of automatism in Ch. 4.5 above.

below the line demarcating murder: a killing in which D knew there was a risk of death, but was held not to have intended death or grievous bodily harm, would fall within involuntary manslaughter and might justify a high sentence; whereas a killing in which D pushed a person during an argument in the street and the person fell backwards, cracking his head on the kerb and dying from a brain haemorrhage, might also fall within involuntary manslaughter and might justify a low sentence. The offence, as now defined in English law, covers a wide spectrum of culpability.

Beneath the law of involuntary manslaughter lie some deep issues of general principle. For example, the offence includes a species of constructive liability, which was criticized in Chapter 5.2(b). Can this be justified by reference to the magnitude of the harm resulting, i.e. death? Or would it be fairer to convict the harm-doer of a lesser offence, thus ignoring the chance result? Another problem is the more general one of liability for negligence: as we saw in Chapter 5.3(f), this is regarded as insufficient for liability for most serious offences, and yet it may be sufficient for manslaughter. Is it right that liability for the second most heinous crime in English law, which carries a maximum penalty of life imprisonment, should be satisfied by this relatively low grade of fault? These questions will be discussed in more detail once the elements of the offence have been outlined.

(a) Manslaughter by Unlawful and Dangerous Act

This species of involuntary manslaughter is based upon constructive liability. In broad terms, the law constructs liability out of the lesser crime which D was committing, and which happened to cause death. In fact, the courts have progressively narrowed this species of manslaughter over the last century or so:[73] there was a time when the mere commission of a tort or civil wrong sufficed as the 'unlawful act', and when there was no additional requirement of 'dangerousness' to be satisfied. What the prosecution must now prove is that D was committing a crime (not being a crime of negligence or a crime of omission), that in committing this crime he caused V's death, and that what he did when committing this crime was objectively dangerous. Let us examine each of these requirements in turn.

First, D must have been committing a crime. In many cases the crime which constitutes the 'unlawful act' will be a battery or an

[73] R. J. Buxton, 'By Any Unlawful Act' (1966) 82 LQR.

assault occasioning actual bodily harm, arising from a push, a punch, or a kick. The prosecution must establish that all the elements of the crime relied upon as the unlawful act were present, and this includes the mental elements of intent or recklessness in assault or battery. To that extent there may be said to be a mental element required for this variety of manslaughter, but it is a manifestly low mental element compared with the death which results. If the unlawful act is arson (criminal damage by fire), the fault element will be intention or *Caldwell* recklessness, and the latter does not require any subjective awareness on the defendant's part.[74] Where D was intoxicated when committing the 'unlawful act', it is likely that he would be liable to conviction for that offence despite his intoxicated state.[75] If so, the offence is sufficient to fulfil the 'unlawful act' requirement for manslaughter.

There are two types of crime which will not suffice as the unlawful act: crimes of negligence and crimes of omission. The reasons for excluding crimes of omission are examined in section 7.5(*d*) below. The reasons for excluding crimes of negligence were stated in. *Andrews v. DPP* (1937),[76] where a driver had killed a pedestrian whilst overtaking another car. There was little dispute that D had committed the offence of dangerous driving, but did that automatically make him guilty of manslaughter when death resulted? The House of Lords held that it did not: since the essence of dangerous driving was negligence, a driver should only be convicted of manslaughter if his driving was so bad as to amount to the gross negligence required under the third head of involuntary manslaughter (see below). Whether or not the decision was motivated by tenderness towards motorists is hard to tell, but there was certainly some logic in keeping offences of negligence out of the 'unlawful act' doctrine when a separate head of manslaughter by gross negligence already existed.

Once it has been established that D was committing a criminal offence, the second step is to establish that this caused the death. In most cases of battery or actual bodily harm the causal connection will be plain, but cases involving drugs have presented difficulties. In *Cato* (1976)[77] the Court of Appeal was prepared to hold that the offence of possessing controlled drugs was sufficient, together with the act of injecting another with these drugs, even though it is difficult to see how mere possession (which is the offence) can cause

---

[74] See above, Ch. 5.3(*c*).   [75] *Lipman* [1970] 1 QB 152.
[76] [1937] AC 576.   [77] [1976] 1 WLR 110.

death. In *Dalby* (1982)[78] the unlawful act was the supplying of controlled drugs to V, who then took them. The Court of Appeal held that the supplying was insufficient as an unlawful act because it was not 'directed at' V. Subsequent decisions are unclear whether the 'directed at' test remains good law,[79] and a better approach to the facts of *Dalby* would be to hold that the supplying of drugs did not cause the death because V took them himself.

The third requirement is that the defendant's conduct in committing the crime must have been objectively dangerous. This was seen as a slight restriction of the doctrine when it was imposed in *Church* (1966)[80], where the court held that 'The unlawful act must be such as all sober and reasonable people would inevitably recognize must subject the other person to, at least, the risk of some harm resulting therefrom, albeit not serious harm.' The House of Lords has declined to narrow this requirement by demanding that D recognized the risk,[81] and it has also been held that the dangerousness should be judged on the actual circumstances, ignoring D's mistaken belief about the facts.[82] The *Church* test therefore appears to be broad and readily fulfilled, but the phrase 'some harm . . . albeit not serious harm' has been construed restrictively in one sense. In *Dawson* (1985) D, wearing a mask and carrying a pickaxe handle, approached a petrol-station attendant and demanded money; D fled when the attendant pressed the alarm bell, but the attendant then suffered a heart attack and died.[83] The Court of Appeal held that the unlawful act would only be regarded as 'dangerous' if it was likely to cause physical harm, not if mere emotional shock (unaccompanied by physical harm) was foreseeable.

(b) Manslaughter by Recklessness

The most recent development in the law of involuntary manslaughter is the doctrine of manslaughter by recklessness. Although the word 'reckless' had been used many times before in the context of manslaughter, a distinctive doctrine was established in *Seymour* (1983).[84] After an argument with the woman with whom he had been living, D drove his lorry into her car and crushed her to death.

---

[78] [1982] 1 WLR 425.
[79] See *Goodfellow* (1986) 83 Cr. App. R 23, and *Ball* [1989] Crim. LR 730.
[80] [1966] 1 QB 59.　　　　[81] *DPP v. Newbury and Jones* [1977] AC 500.
[82] *Ball* [1989] Crim. LR 730, interpreting *Dawson* (1985) 81 Cr. App. R 150.
[83] (1985) 81 Cr. App. R 150; cf. the strange interpretation of this decision in *Ball* [1989] Crim. LR 730 and in *Watson* [1989] Crim. LR 733.
[84] [1983] 2 AC 493.

The House of Lords held that this was manslaughter if there was an obvious and serious risk of causing physical injury to some other person, and D had either failed to give any thought to this risk or, having recognised the risk, nonetheless went on to take it. It will be seen that this is the *Caldwell/Lawrence* formula for recklessness (analysed in Chapter 5.3(*c*)), and is virtually the same as the test for the separate offence of causing death by reckless driving. The House of Lords accepted that the definitions of the two offences are the same, merely adding that the prosecutor should charge manslaughter when the maximum penalty for the offence of causing death by reckless driving (five years) might be insufficient.

In *Seymour* the House of Lords seemed to be principally concerned with manslaughter committed with a motor vehicle, but subsequent cases establish that the test of 'obvious and serious risk of physical injury to some person' is applicable to offences using different methods, such as fire.[85]

(c) Manslaughter by Gross Negligence

Although the authorities conflict, it has been laid down that the new doctrine of reckless manslaughter supersedes the older doctrine of manslaughter by gross negligence.[86] Many of the old cases could indeed be subsumed within the new doctrine, but it does not cover them all. In the case of *Finney* (1974)[87], where an attendant at a mental hospital caused the death of a patient by releasing a flow of boiling water into a bath, the test was whether he was grossly negligent. In *Bateman* (1925)[88], where a doctor had attended the confinement of a woman who died whilst giving birth, the Court of Criminal Appeal held that there must be negligence over and above that which is sufficient to establish civil liability, and which shows 'such disregard for the life and safety of others' as to deserve punishment. Both these cases might be decided similarly on the *Seymour* test, but that cannot be said of *Lamb* (1967).[89] Here two young men were joking with a gun; D pointed it at V and pulled the trigger, believing that it would not fire because neither bullet was opposite the barrel. The gun was a revolver, however, and it did

[85] *Goodfellow* (1986) 83 Cr. App. R 23.
[86] *Kong Cheuk Kwan v. R* (1986) 82 Cr. App. R 18, at 26, approving a statement of Watkins LJ in the Court of Appeal in *Seymour* (1983) 76 Cr. App. R 211, at 216. However, the Court of Appeal approved the use of the gross-negligence doctrine in *Ball* [1989] Crim. LR 730.
[87] (1874) 12 Cox CC 625.
[88] (1925) 94 LJKB 791.   [89] [1967] 2 QB 981.

firc, killing V. The Court of Appeal held that D might properly be convicted if his belief that there was no danger of the gun firing was formed in a criminally negligent way. However, under the test derived from *Caldwell*, a person is not reckless if he thinks about the possible risk but decides that it does not obtain. This is the *Caldwell* gap, and *Lamb* is a case which might have fallen into it. It therefore follows that, if the courts have indeed replaced manslaughter by gross negligence with manslaughter by recklessness, they have narrowed the law slightly. It is more likely, however, that manslaughter by gross negligence remains in addition to reckless manslaughter.

(d) Manslaughter by Omission

The courts have been reluctant to bring omissions cases within the above categories, manifesting once again their belief in the separate moral and legal status of omissions. This was not always so: in *Senior* (1899)[90] a man who belonged to a religious sect called the Peculiar People refused to call a doctor to his child, who subsequently died; he was held guilty of manslaughter on the ground that he had committed an unlawful act (wilful neglect of the child) which caused death. However, this very reasoning was abjured in *Lowe* (1973)[91], where D failed to ensure that medical help was summoned to his child, and it died. The Court of Appeal held that a manslaughter verdict would not necessarily follow from a conviction for wilful neglect:

if I strike a child in a manner likely to cause harm it is right that if the child dies I may be charged with manslaughter. If, however, I omit to do something with the result that it suffers injury to health which results in death, we think that a charge of manslaughter should not be an inevitable consequence, even if the omission is deliberate.

This passage suggests that the law should, and does, draw a distinction between the blameworthiness of acts and omissions, even where the omission is deliberate. And yet the connection between withholding medical aid and subsequent death is surely closer than that between striking a child once and subsequent death. The father's duty in *Senior* and in *Lowe* is manifest and incontrovertible. If the 'unlawful act' doctrine is thought sound, these cases should fall squarely within it. If the doctrine is thought unsound, both the omissions

---

[90] [1899] 1 QB 283.   [91] [1973] QB 702.

cases and the act cases should be taken out of it. A distinction between them is morally untenable.

Omissions cases falling within manslaughter by recklessness or gross negligence have also been set apart from cases of positive acts. The leading modern case is *Stone and Dobinson* (1977)[92], where two people were convicted of manslaughter for allowing a sick relative, whom they had permitted to live in their house, to die without medical attention. The Court of Appeal's grounds for finding a duty of care in this case are scrutinized elsewhere.[93] Once the duty is established, the fault element required was expressed as recklessness, and defined thus: 'a reckless disregard of danger to the health and welfare of the infirm person. Mere inadvertence is not enough. The defendant must be proved to have been indifferent to an obvious risk of injury to health, or actually to have foreseen the risk but to have determined nevertheless to run it.' This passage is rendered ambiguous by the use of the word 'indifferent': if that connotes failure to realize an obvious risk, the test is similar to *Caldwell* but probably inconsistent with the earlier assertion that 'mere inadvertence is not enough'. If the *Caldwell* test of recklessness does indeed apply, then this form of omissions liability could be assimilated within the general doctrine of manslaughter by recklessness. The only difference would be that *Seymour* required an obvious risk of physical injury to another, whereas *Stone and Dobinson* required a risk of injury to health, and the difference may be more apparent than real.

(e) The Contours of Manslaughter

The English law of manslaughter exhibits a tension between various principles of fairness to the defendant and the significance of the harm caused. It is the resulting harm (death) which still dominates, as is evident from the fact that many forms of conduct fall within the law of manslaughter if death happens to result, whereas they would not even amount to a serious offence if a consequence less than death had ensued. Thus 'unlawful act' manslaughter, which can be committed by virtue of a mere assault or battery, is an example of constructive liability (see Chapter 5.2 (*a*) and (*b*)); it is only luck which makes the difference between the summary offence of common assault (maximum, six months' imprisonment) and the grave

---

[92] [1977] QB 354.
[93] A. Ashworth, 'The Scope of Criminal Liability for Omissions' (1989) 105 LQR 440–5.

offence of manslaughter (maximum, life imprisonment). 'Reckless' manslaughter is also an example of constructive liability; even if *Caldwell* recklessness is justifiable as a standard,[94] it is only an obvious risk of injury which must have been foreseeable. Can these derogations from principle be justified? Reasons can only be found in the unique significance of human life and in the need to mark out, and to prevent, conduct which causes its loss.

In considering whether these reasons are strong enough, we should not neglect the fact that some offences of manslaughter lie well above the lower boundaries of liability and fall little short of murder. There is no doubting the substantial culpability of the person who embarks on a course of conduct knowing that there is a risk of death to another (e.g. the man who administered chloroform in *Pike*)[95], and the person who foresees the risk of really serious harm to another from the course of conduct being pursued. The offence of murder is restricted to intent, and it would seem natural that recklessness as to the same consequences should amount to the lesser offence of manslaughter. The Criminal Law Revision Committee, which found much of the English law of manslaughter unsupportable, argued that there is a need for a homicide offence beneath murder to encompass those who cause death when reckless as to death or serious injury.[96]

But what about the lower threshold of manslaughter, where its minimum requirements form the boundary with accidental (non-criminal) homicide? Surely, to apply the label 'manslaughter' to the conduct of a person who envisaged no more than a common assault, e.g. by a single punch, is both disproportionate and unfair. It grossly exaggerates the amount of subjective culpability. And, viewed objectively, the risk of death from a single punch is far too remote to enter into one's reasonable contemplation. The present law attributes too much weight to chance: 'the offender's fault falls too far short of the unlucky result. So serious an offence as manslaughter should not be a lottery.'[97]

To support manslaughter liability in these cases one would have to espouse the draconian principle that a person should be held liable for all the consequences of any wrongful act.[98] A refusal to espouse that principle is perhaps the only ground on which the omissions cases (see 7.5(*d*) above) can be defended, since their

[94] For discussion see above, Ch. 5.3(*c*) and (*g*).
[95] [1961] Crim. LR 547.
[96] 14th Report (1980), paras. 123–4.
[97] Ibid., para. 120.
[98] See the discussion above, Ch. 5.2(*b*).

distinction between acts and omissions is unconvincing. Different considerations press forward, however, when we move on to the various situations in which known risks ought to be guarded against: bad driving of a motor vehicle may carry an obvious risk of causing death or serious injury, as may bad navigation of a ship or an aircraft, bad driving of a train, setting fire to a residential building, and the handling of firearms. These risks are widely known, distinguished as much by the possibility of one or several deaths occurring as by the frequency with which the risk materializes. Those who deal with firearms are generally aware of the attendant risks, and the days when those involved in motoring and other forms of transport could make light of the risks to life have now long passed, as various air, sea, rail, and road disasters have occurred. In spheres of conduct such as these, where the risks are widely known, there are strong reasons for broadening the basis of criminal liability so as to encompass negligence.

This still falls well short of supporting the English law of manslaughter, where the 'unlawful act' doctrine allows a manslaughter conviction if death results from a mere assault or battery. It also fails to substantiate the claim that death-causing acts or omissions in these situations of known danger should fall within the law of manslaughter rather than some other offence. Thus it remains for discussion whether it would not be preferable to criminalize them by means of special 'endangerment' offences. One advantage of that approach would be to direct attention to the particular source of danger, thus labelling the offence in a way which both describes the circumstances of the offence and serves an educative or even deterrent purpose. A possible disadvantage is that, since such offences may lack the stigma of the word 'manslaughter', they may tend to underplay the gravity of the behaviour involved. On the other hand, the social significance of the offences is likely to be set as much by prosecution policy and sentencing policy as by the label of the offence.

These tensions behind the law of manslaughter are evident in the decisions of the courts during this century, many of which have narrowed the offence, but some of which have extended it. However, only the legislature can create new offences of endangerment. What progress has it made towards this?

7.6. ENDANGERMENT ON THE ROADS

English law contains a number of offences which penalize the driving of a car on a road in a manner which may cause harm. There is the offence of driving recklessly (contrary to section 2 of the Road Traffic Act 1972), and there are also the lesser offences of driving without due care and attention, and driving without reasonable consideration for other persons using the road (contrary to section 3 of the 1972 Act). Clearly, the difference between reckless driving and careless driving is one of degree. In the leading case of *Lawrence* (1981)[99] it was held that reckless driving consists of driving which creates an obvious and serious risk of causing physical injury to some other person who might be happening to use the road or of doing substantial damage to property, and that the fault element is that the driver either failed to give any thought to the possibility of such a risk or, having recognized the existence of a risk, went on to take it. Many of the cases falling within this offence may involve serious fault—where there is racing on the highway, for example, or a prolonged course of very bad driving, or bad driving in order to avoid apprehension.[100] Some less culpable forms of bad driving might also be labelled 'reckless', such as a momentary dozing-off at the wheel, or the failure to notice a pedestrian on a crossing.

In addition to these two offences, there is a homicide offence of causing death by reckless driving (contrary to section 1 of the 1972 Act). The elements of the offence are exactly the same as for reckless driving, with the extra element of causing death. It will readily be noticed that the elements of causing death by reckless driving are virtually the same as those of 'reckless manslaughter': indeed, in *Seymour* (1983)[101] the House of Lords held that they are the same, and the only doubt arises over the reference to 'substantial damage to property' in the *Lawrence* test. An obvious risk of property damage alone is insufficient for manslaughter, but may suffice for the driving offences.[102]

The driving offence of 'causing death' was first introduced in 1956, largely because juries were unwilling to convict culpable motorists of such a serious-sounding offence as manslaughter. The

---

[99] [1982] AC 510.
[100] See the sentencing guidelines case of *Boswell* (1984) 79 Cr. App. R 277.
[101] [1983] 2 AC 493.
[102] In *Kong Cheuk Kwan v. R* (1986) 82 Cr. App. R 18, Lord Roskill made it clear that references to property damage should merely be incidental to the main test of an 'obvious and serious risk' of causing injury.

position now seems to be that the two offences have the same legal definition, and that the prosecution should prefer the charge of manslaughter when the case is a bad one which might merit a sentence in excess of the five-year maximum for causing death by reckless driving. Ever since the offence of causing death by reckless driving was introduced (it formerly included causing death by dangerous driving, too), there have been those who have pointed to its 'illogicality'. The difference between an offence of reckless driving (maximum penalty of two years) and one of causing death by reckless driving (maximum penalty of five years) may simply be one of chance. Bad driving may or may not lead to an accident, depending on the chance conjunction of other factors and other people's behaviour. And an accident may lead to death (in which case the more serious offence is committed) or merely to serious injuries or to minor damage. The response to this 'illogicality'—which is, of course, the very problem with the law of involuntary manslaughter too—has varied in recent English proposals. Both the James Committee in 1976[103] and the Criminal Law Revision Committee in 1980[104] recommended the abolition of the offence of causing death by reckless driving, thereby accepting the 'illogicality' argument. This accords with the CLRC's proposal that both 'unlawful act' manslaughter and reckless manslaughter should be abolished.[105] However, the report of the Road Traffic Law Review has reversed this trend. The Review accepts the general principle that persons should be judged according to the intrinsic quality of their driving rather than its consequences, but argues that the law should depart from this in cases where death is caused and the driver's culpability is already high.[106] This is a frank recognition of the tension created by cases where there is the supreme harm (death) combined with some culpability but no foresight of the risk of death. There is a well-known risk in motoring that certain kinds of driving may cause accidents, and that accidents may cause death. The rules of the road are designed not only to produce the orderly and unhampered movement of traffic, but also to protect property, safety, and lives. One who deviates so manifestly from these rules as to drive recklessly

---

[103] Report of the Interdepartmental Committee on the Distribution of Criminal Business between the Crown Court and the Magistrates' Courts (1975, Cmnd. 6323), App. K.

[104] 14th Report (1980), paras. 140–8.   [105] Ibid., paras. 116–123.

[106] Report of the Road Traffic Law Review (1988), Ch. 6; for discussion, see J. R. Spencer, 'Road Traffic Law: A Review of the North Report' [1988] Crim. LR 707.

ought to realize—because the driving test requires a driver to realize—that there is a considerable risk of an accident. If an accident happens as a result of driving which deviates from the proper standard, then that may well be a case of negligence even if the driver had never thought of the risk in that particular case, because the driver is presumed to know the Highway Code. It is this negligence which is termed 'recklessness' by the decisions in *Caldwell* and *Lawrence*.

There is, however, another dimension to the debate, and this appears from the CLRC's view that, where reckless driving causes death, this should not affect the label of the offence but may be treated as an aggravating factor in sentencing in appropriate cases. This assumes that there is a tension between the causing of serious harm (death) and the relatively low fault ('recklessness', as here defined), and that this tension should be resolved in favour of the fault element when we are deciding on the labels of offences, thereby making no reference to the result, but should be resolved in favour of the serious harm when sentencing, increasing the sentence according to the gravity of the resulting harm. In short, we should call the offence reckless driving, but the occurrence of death, even though it may be regarded as bad luck, should aggravate the sentence. Is it defensible to have different principles for sentencing and for the labelling of offences?

Much depends on the social function of labelling criminal offences, and on the particular labels chosen. We are referring here to the offence of causing death by reckless driving, not to manslaughter. It is therefore, one may assume, a label of intermediate stigma (falling short of the stigma attached to the offence of manslaughter). The fault element is fairly substantial, since the *Lawrence* definition refers to an obvious and serious risk of at least substantial damage to property: there will be few cases where only such damage, and no risk to personal safety, is involved; moreover, as argued above, a major reason for having rules of the road which all drivers should know is to reduce the risk of injuries and deaths resulting. Retaining the more serious label which refers to the causing of death may therefore perform a useful educative function; it is hardly unfair to the driver, since this is the very risk against which the rules are intended to guard. As for sentencing, English courts have been unclear about the proper approach. In *Krawec* (1984),[107] a case of

---

[107] (1984) 6 Cr. App. R(S) 367.

careless driving where a death resulted, the Court of Appeal held that the proper basis for sentence is 'the quality of driving, the extent to which the appellant on the particular occasion fell below the standard of the reasonably competent driver', to which 'the unforeseen and unexpected results of the carelessness' are not relevant. However, there are other decisions which have taken account of unexpected and chance results as aggravating factors.[108] The problem, surely, is to find a satisfactory starting-point for the level of sentences. The degree of risk created by the bad driving should be regarded as the crucial factor; it is not so much a question of whether the sentence should be more severe when the risk eventuates, as whether the sentence should be more lenient when the risk does not materialize. If the aim of the rules of the road is to protect safety, and if the driver broke those rules in a way which may be labelled 'reckless', then the risk has been taken and the sentence should not be affected significantly by the materialization or non-materialization of the risk. But, as a risk to safety taken recklessly, the offence deserves a penalty which places it above many intentional offences against property. The argument, then, is that the causing of death by bad driving should not be regarded as a significant aggravating factor, but nor should the non-causing of death or injury be regarded as a significant mitigating factor. The level of sentence should be set primarily, as the Lord Chief Justice stated in *Krawec*, according to 'the degree of carelessness and culpability'.

It will therefore be seen that many of the issues involved here are similar to those raised by the law of involuntary manslaughter, save for the fact that driving offences constitute deviations from a code of conduct on which all persons are tested before they are granted driving-licences. This factor serves to distinguish driving cases from those of deaths resulting from a single punch, and also to bolster the argument that the penalties for the former should be higher than for the latter.

7.7. ENDANGERMENT IN OTHER SITUATIONS

Our discussion so far has stressed the relationship between endangerment on the roads and the detailed rules of the road, including the driving test. Some preventive rules, together with endanger-

---

[108] The conflicts were recognized in *McNamara* (1984), 6 Cr. App. R(S) 356.

ment offences, can be seen in a variety of other situations, but nowhere is there such a detailed and fairly widely known set of standards as that applicable to drivers on the roads. For example, there are regulations about the storage of explosives, and the dangers of handling explosives are well known. The main thrust of the Explosives Act 1883, however, is contained in the offences of causing an explosion likely to endanger life (section 2), and the possession of explosives with intent to endanger life (section 3). The latter offence is an inchoate offence of a familiar kind:[109] possession with intent, in circumstances where an innocent reason for possessing explosives is fairly hard to come by (unless the defendant is engaged in quarrying or another business in which explosives are used). The justification for the possession offence is preventive, and there is little difficulty in holding that a person caught in possession of explosives with intent to endanger life has sufficiently crossed the threshold of criminality to justify punishment. True, there may yet be the possibility of repentance as the time for using the explosives draws near, but the very step of taking explosives into one's possession with this intent is culpable. As for the endangerment offence itself, two features in section 2 of the 1883 Act stand out. One is that no actual endangerment is required: the explosion need only have been inherently likely to endanger life, and the offence is committed whether or not anyone's life was put in danger. In its style of labelling, therefore, this differs from the present driving law, with its separate offences of reckless driving and causing death by reckless driving: the equivalent would be a single offence of driving in a manner likely to endanger life. The second feature of the offence of causing an explosion likely to endanger life is that there appears to be no distinct fault requirement. So long as the prosecution proves that D caused the explosion, and that the explosion was likely to endanger life, that would suffice for conviction. The reason for this must be that one can hardly cause an explosion without realizing that one is about to do so, and that explosions usually create danger and must be known to do so, unless they are carefully controlled in an area away from members of the public. However, these arguments are not particularly strong, for, if the inference of fault is so great, why not include a requirement of proof of fault, at least at the level of subjective recklessness?

Further offences of endangerment may be found in the Firearms

---

[109] See below, Ch. 11.1 and 11.9.

Act 1968. Section 16 contains an offence of possessing a firearm with intent to endanger life, which corresponds to the offence under section 3 of the Explosives Act. Again, the circumstances of the possession are likely to raise an inference of intent, unless the possession was clearly connected with some authorised shooting activity. There are then three possession offences of a slightly different type. Section 18 penalizes the possession of a firearm with intent to commit a crime or to resist arrest: this is a more specific variation of section 16, catering for the defence that the firearm was being carried for use in a robbery but with no intention that it would actually be used to endanger anyone, only to frighten—that would be a section 18 offence. Section 19 penalises possession of a loaded firearm in a public place, presumably in circumstances where the section 16 offence cannot be proved, but on the argument that the mere possession is sufficiently dangerous because accidents can happen with loaded guns, and the consequences might be life-endangering. Section 20 penalizes possession of a firearm when trespassing: again, there might be a defence to a section 16 charge if D was merely intending to shoot animals or fowl, but the gun could be turned on a human being and therefore represents a source of danger. What these firearms offences appear to amount to is a criminalization of the carrying of firearms in all but the most innocent of contexts. If the firearm is discharged and property is damaged, then an offence of criminal damage may be charged. If it is discharged and a person is injured or killed, the appropriate offence against the person can be charged. What the Firearms Act provides is a series of inchoate or preventive offences which criminalize conduct even before it has reached the stage of an attempt to commit some substantive offence. The offences do not require any endangerment at all: that is taken to be inherent in the carrying of firearms, since their potentialities are grave and the risk of accidents as well as deliberate use is well known.

Offences relating to the operation of aircraft, ships, and railways have not been prominent in the practice of English criminal law. But the law does contain such offences, and it is more a matter of prosecutors making little use of them. It is true that over the years a few railway signalmen have been convicted of manslaughter for wrongful acts and omissions leading to fatal train crashes, but there is not the natural resort to the criminal law which is now a feature of road-traffic cases. In a sense, greater values are at stake in the operation of aircraft, ships, and railways, because many lives are involved, more than would normally be risked by the bad driving of a motor vehicle (although there is an important exception here in the operation of buses and coaches, which are more akin to planes, boats, and trains). But there is another significant difference between the individual driving a car or a lorry and all these other forms of transport, and that is the chain of responsibility. A company's management policies might be just as much to blame for a particular 'accident' as the actions of the driver, pilot, or captain: Sheen J made this point in his report on the Zeebrugge ferry disaster,[110] but English prosecution practice has tended not to invoke the criminal law against managers of transport systems. One reason for this may be the doctrine of corporate liability in English criminal law (discussed in Chapter 4.3, and found to be unsatisfactory); in particular, it may be difficult to establish the fault necessary for manslaughter, although easier to secure a conviction under legislation on railways or merchant shipping. There may also be a reluctance among prosecutors to look beyond the individual driver, pilot, or captain in each case. It is not just the operation of systems of transport which is a source of endangerment: the actions of individuals may be designed to take advantage of the possibility of causing several deaths at once. The longest determinate prison sentence ever upheld by English courts was the sentence of forty-five years' imprisonment in the case of *Hindawi* (1988),[111] a man who sent his pregnant girl-friend on a flight with a bag which contained a bomb timed to destroy the aircraft and its 350 passengers in mid-flight. The offence in this was 'an attempt to place on an aircraft a device likely to destroy or damage the aircraft, contrary to the Aviation Security Act 1982'—an inchoate offence, and one worded without any express reference to the endangerment of lives. The sentence, however, was intended to reflect the attempt to kill so many people.

Injuries and deaths at work are a significant and reducible source of danger to the citizen, and the Health and Safety at Work Act 1974 provides the framework for the regulation of safety in work-places with an offence of failing to ensure that, 'so far as is reasonably practicable', employees are not exposed to risks to their health or safety.[112] Other fragmentary legislation is to be found in recent years, e.g. the Safety of Sports Grounds Act 1975. However, in

---

[110] *MV Herald of Free Enterprise*, Report of the Court No. 8074, para. 14; see Ch. 4.3 above, and S. Field and N. Jorg, 'Corporate Manslaughter: Should We Go Dutch?' [1991] Crim. LR 156.   [111] (1988) 10 Cr. App. R(S) 104.
[112] See *Austin Rover Group Ltd. v. HM Inspector of Factories* [1990] AC 619.

addition to all these specific offences of endangerment, English law does contain one fairly wide-ranging offence, and that is the aggravated offence of criminal damage. Under section 1(2) of the Criminal Damage Act 1971 it is an offence—punishable with life imprisonment—to damage property 'intending by the destruction or damage to endanger the life of another or being reckless whether the life of another would be thereby endangered'. Criminal damage itself is an offence carrying up to ten years' imprisonment, but this is a more serious offence—more of an offence against the person. One might well ask how important the element of criminal damage is to the rationale of the aggravated offence. One answer could be that, where the damage is caused by fire, the consequent danger to life may be similar to that created by an explosion, and the inferences may be the same: who could cause such a fire in such a place without appreciating the danger to others?

However, the major question raised by section 1(2) of the Criminal Damage Act is why English law does not have a general offence of endangerment. Why should the fact that D was engaged on causing damage to property at the time (even damage to D's own property) make his conduct into an offence punishable with life imprisonment when, if D were engaged on some other activity, it would not be punishable as such and would only amount to manslaughter if a death happened to be caused? Section 211.2 of the Model Penal Code has been enacted into the laws of many American states, providing a general endangerment offence. The offence is committed where a person recklessly engages in conduct which places another person in danger of death or serious bodily injury.[113] It does not require any result, although it does require actual danger. Its great merit is that it is not confined to particular activities, and therefore has an across-the-board application to different sources of endangerment. On the other hand, such a general offence does not fulfil the educative function of singling out situations which carry a particular risk of danger. For that reason, it would be wise to retain a special offence for road-traffic cases, and there may be merit in retaining offences with particular labels in other spheres. What is more pertinent is whether the different styles of the offences discussed above have some justification. Should the fault standard require D's actual awareness, or merely an objective probability of danger? Should there be proof of actual danger to someone, or is potential danger enough?

[113] See below, Ch. 8.3(*j*) and K. J. M. Smith, 'Liability for Endangerment: English *Ad Hoc* Pragmatism and American Innovation', [1983] Crim. LR 127.

8

NON-FATAL VIOLATIONS
OF THE PERSON

8.1. VARIETIES OF PHYSICAL VIOLATION

In this chapter we shall be discussing two main forms of physical violation: the use of physical force, and sexual assaults. It is quite obvious that each type of violence varies considerably in its degree: physical force can be anything from a mere push to a brutal beating which leaves the victim close to death, and a sexual assault may be anything from a brief touching to a gross form of sexual violation. One problem which the criminal law has to confront, therefore, when dealing with physical violation, is how to grade the seriousness of the conduct. The variations are so wide that it would contravene both the principle of fair labelling (see Chapter 3.3 (*l*)) and the principle of maximum certainty (see Chapter 3.3 (*i*)) if there were just a single offence of non-fatal harm and a single offence of sexual assault: this would often leave little to be decided at the trial and would transfer the effective decision to the sentencing stage. Given that it would be unsatisfactory to have a single offence, then the question is how best to divide up the forms and degrees of physical violation and of sexual assault.

We shall look first at physical violation. Although many cases of sexual assault also involve significant physical violation, this is not always so, and the essence of many sexual assaults lies in their destruction of the freedom of choice in the most intimate area of personality, and in psychological damage. By considering physical violations first, this will enable us to identify more accurately the distinctive element in sexual assaults. The general term 'sexual assault' is used here to include non-consensual sexual offences: there are various forms of sexual activity which are criminal even if they are indulged in consensually by adults of sound mind, and there was a brief discussion of these in Chapter 2.1 and 2.4 (b).

8.2. REPORTED PHYSICAL VIOLATIONS

Recent decades have seen significant increases in the numbers of offences of violence reported to, and recorded by, the police. Between 1974 and 1984 the rise was 72 per cent, slightly above that for all recorded offences (69 per cent). The increases were lowest in the most serious forms of violent offences, and highest in the less serious offences of violence and in robbery.[1] Three-quarters of these offences each year are 'cleared up', and it transpires that most of them are committed by young males aged between 14 and 29. It seems that the use of a weapon is important in determining the legal classification of offences (not surprisingly, since offences involving weapons may tend to have more serious consequences): some three-quarters of the serious woundings involved a weapon, whereas the proportion was only one-fifth for the less serious offences.[2] Patterns of victimization vary: females are more likely to fall victim to violence in their homes; whilst males are more likely to fall victim to violence in a 'road, street or park', or in a place of recreation.[3] This trend may in fact be more marked, since it is acknowledged that victims may be considerably reluctant to report, and police to record, offences of violence committed in the home. Recent studies are beginning to uncover the true extent of so-called 'domestic' violence,[4] and many police forces have adopted more consistent policies of recording such incidents and dealing with them as true offences of violence.[5]

Two particular points may be made about offences of physical violation. First, there is evidence of a strong correlation between drinking and violence, in the sense that large numbers of violent offences are committed after consuming alcohol. It may be added, of course, that most of those who drink alcohol do not commit offences of violence thereafter.[6] But the first point remains, and means that the special rules relating to fault and intoxication, discussed in Chapter 6.3, come into play. A second general point is

---

[1] R. Walmsley, *Personal Violence*, Home Office Research Study No. 89 (1986), 3.
[2] Ibid. 8.   [3] Ibid. 62.
[4] e.g. S. S. M. Edwards, *Policing Domestic Violence* (1989).
[5] L. J. F. Smith, *Domestic Violence*, Home Office Research Study No. 107 (1989), Ch. 7. In August 1990 the Home Office issued a circular emphasizing this policy (Circular No. 59).
[6] Walmsley, *Personal Violence*, 16; cf. the perceptive study by Mary Tuck, *Drinking and Disorder: A Study of Non-Metropolitan Violence*, Home Office Research Study No. 108 (1989).

that many offences of violence have consequences for the victim which extend well beyond any injury caused. There are psychological effects of fear and depression, which may significantly impair the victim's enjoyment of life long after the physical wounds have healed. Such effects are well documented in the case of female victims of 'domestic' violence.[7]

The values which underlie the offences of physical violation are not far to seek. They are the values of physical autonomy and freedom from molestation, the liberty to decide for oneself the level of pain to subject one's body to (e.g. in sport). The value of privacy is central here: the body is part of one's private identity, and, apart from any physical hurt inflicted by violence, a violent assault constitutes a challenge to one's personal identity, peace, and well-being.

8.3. OFFENCES OF NON-FATAL PHYSICAL VIOLATION

We have seen something of the various situations in which non-fatal physical harm might occur. How does the law classify its offences? How should it respond to these various invasions of physical integrity, a quality which is highly valued by most citizens? One approach would be to create separate offences to cover many of the situations in which violence occurs, and to single out those situations in which there is some element of aggravation, such as attacks on law-enforcement officers. This was the nineteenth-century English approach, and many such offences still survive in the Offences against the Person Act 1861 (relating, for example, to injuries caused by gunpowder, throwing corrosive fluid, failing to provide food for apprentices, setting spring guns). A second approach would be to attempt to rank the offences by reference to the degree of harm caused and the degree of fault in the person causing it. The 1861 Act also contains some offences of this kind, but, as we shall see below, its ranking is impaired by obscure terms, uncertainties in the fault requirements, and some overlapping. Thorough reform of the law is long overdue.

(a) Attempted Murder

If we were to construct a 'ladder' of non-fatal offences, starting with the most serious and moving down to the least serious, the offence

---

[7] Smith, *Domestic Violence*, 18–20.

of attempted murder should be placed at the top. There is an immediate paradox here though: attempted murder may not involve the infliction of any harm at all, since a person who shoots at another and misses may still be held guilty of attempted murder. What distinguishes this offence is proof of an intention to kill, not the occurrence of any particular harm. The fault element for attempted murder is therefore high—higher than for murder, under English law, since murder may be committed by someone who merely intended to cause really serious injury and not death.[8] An intention to kill must be proved in order to convict someone of attempted murder.[9] Beyond that, all that is necessary is proof that D did something which was 'more than merely preparatory' towards the murder.[10] Although a conviction is perfectly possible where no harm results—and such a case might still be regarded as a most serious non-fatal offence, since D tried to cause death, and the subjective principles[11] confirm the high guilt—there are also cases where D's attempt to kill results in serious injury to the victim. In such cases a prosecution might be brought for attempted murder—and will succeed if the intention to kill can be proved. However, the court might not be satisfied of that 'beyond reasonable doubt', and might find that D only intended to cause grievous bodily harm. In that event, the conviction will be for the offence of causing grievous bodily harm, but both offences carry the same maximum punishment—life imprisonment.

(b) Wounding or Grievous Bodily Harm (GBH) with Intent

Section 18 of the Offences against the Person Act 1861 creates a serious offence which may be committed in a number of different ways. There are two alternative forms of conduct, and either of two forms of intent will suffice. The conduct may be either causing a wound or causing grievous bodily harm. A wound has been defined as an injury which breaks both the outer and inner skin—a bruise or a burst blood-vessel in an eye would not amount to a wound.[12] Grievous bodily harm has never been defined with any precision, and the authoritative description is 'really serious harm'.[13] Turning

---

[8] See the discussion above, Ch. 7.3(c), where this is viewed as one argument against the 'gbh' rule for murder.

[9] Recently confirmed in *Walker and Hayles* [1990] Crim. LR 44.

[10] This is the conduct requirement of all attempted crimes: see below, Ch. 11.3(b).

[11] See above, Ch. 5.2(a).

[12] *C. v. Eisenhower* [1984] QB 331.   [13] *DPP v. Smith* [1961] AC 290.

to the fault requirements, the one most commonly relied on in prosecutions is 'with intent to cause grievous bodily harm'. The meaning of 'intention' here is the same as outlined earlier.[14] It was observed above that most serious woundings involve the use of a weapon,[15] and that may make it easier to establish intention. Where the prosecution fails to establish intention, the offence will be reduced to the lower category, to be considered in section 8.3 (c) below, so long as recklessness is proved. But there is an alternative fault element: 'with intent to prevent the lawful apprehension or detainer of any person'. Whilst the policy of this requirement—classifying attacks on persons engaged in law enforcement as especially serious—is perfectly understandable, one result of the wording of section 18 of the 1861 Act is that D can be convicted of this offence (with a maximum penalty of life imprisonment) if he simply pushes a police-officer in order to prevent an arrest, and the officer loses balance, falls awkwardly, and suffers serious injury. There is no requirement that such serious results should have been foreseen or foreseeable, so long as D was trying to prevent an arrest. This is a stark example of constructive criminal liability.[16]

(c) Reckless Wounding or GBH

Section 20 of the Offences against the Person Act 1861 creates the offence of unlawfully and maliciously wounding or inflicting grievous bodily harm. The conduct element in this offence is similar to that for the more serious offence under section 18, and the meanings of 'wound' and 'grievous bodily harm' are no different. Considerable attention has been focused on the distinction between *causing* grievous bodily harm (section 18) and *inflicting* grievous bodily harm (section 20): for many years it was believed that the more restrictive word 'inflict' meant that section 20 required proof of a sufficiently direct action by D to constitute an assault, but the House of Lords has now decided that there can be an 'infliction' of GBH without proof of an assault.[17] The decision is controversial in its reasoning,[18] but it may be explained as an attempt by the judiciary to improve the workability of an ageing legal structure.

---

[14] See above, Ch. 5.3(b).   [15] See above, n. 2 and accompanying text.
[16] On which, see Ch. 5.2(b) above.   [17] *Wilson; Jenkins* [1984] AC 242.
[18] The decision has important procedural as well as substantive implications: see J. C. Smith [1983] Crim. LR 37–9; Glanville Williams, 'Alternative Elements and Included Offences' [1984] CLJ 290.

The main difference between sections 18 and 20 lies in the fault element, and it is a considerable difference. Section 18 requires intention. Section 20 requires recklessness, in the common-law sense of the conscious taking of an unjustified risk.[19] The fault element in section 20 has been further broadened by the decision in *Mowatt* (1968):[20] there is no need to prove recklessness as to wounding or grievous bodily harm, so long as the court is satisfied that D was reckless as to some physical harm to some person, albeit of a minor character. This is another example of constructive liability, and it is particularly inappropriate here, in so far as the law is aiming to produce a 'ladder' of offences graded in terms of relative seriousness. However, even without the *Mowatt* extension, one might ask whether the distinction between intention (section 18) and recklessness (section 20) is so wide in crimes of violence, often impulsive reactions to events, as to warrant the difference in maximum penalties between life imprisonment and five years' imprisonment.

(d) Aggravated Assaults

Common assault is the lowest rung of the 'ladder' of non-fatal offences, with a maximum penalty of six months' imprisonment, and it is discussed in more detail below.[21] But certain aggravated assaults are singled out by the law for higher maximum penalties, and three of them may be mentioned here. One is assault with intent to rob, which, like robbery, carries a maximum of life imprisonment:[22] it is, in effect, an offence of attempted robbery. Another aggravated offence is assault with intent to resist arrest or to prevent a lawful arrest, contrary to section 38 of the 1861 Act and carrying a maximum penalty of two years' imprisonment. The third, which is usually regarded as representing the rung of the 'ladder' below reckless wounding or GBH (contrary to section 20) but above common assault, is assault occasioning actual bodily harm. The conduct element is causing 'actual bodily harm', which has been given the wide definition of 'any hurt or injury calculated to interfere with the health or comfort of the victim' so long as it is not merely 'transient or trifling'.[23] One consequence of the breadth of this

[19] See above, Ch. 5.3(c).
[20] [1968] 1 QB 421, criticized in *Parmenter*, (1990) 92 Cr. App. R 68.
[21] In section 8.3(e).
[22] Theft Act 1968, s. 8(2); note that robbery itself (discussed in the context of property offences in Ch. 9.3 below) may also be classified as an offence of violence.
[23] *Donovan* [1934] 2 KB 498.

definition is that it has been held to cover psychological harm—where D causes V to become hysterical or to suffer substantial fear or fright, for example.[24] Since research shows that this is a frequent and long-lasting result of many attacks,[25] it is important that it be given some recognition.

The fault required for the offence of assault occasioning actual bodily harm, contrary to section 47 of the 1861 Act, is now in doubt. Formerly, all that needed to be established was the fault required for common assault, i.e. intent or recklessness as to the application of some unlawful force to another. This was open to the criticism that it imposed constructive liability: a person who risked a minor assault might be held guilty of a more serious offence if 'actual bodily harm' happened to result. Moreover, the maximum penalty for the section 47 offence is five years' imprisonment, with no apparent justification for the strange approach of making the *penalty* equivalent to the higher offence on the 'ladder' (the section 20 offence), and the *fault requirement* equivalent to the lower offence on the 'ladder' (common assault, with a maximum of six months' imprisonment). However, the Court of Appeal has now attempted to rectify the anomaly by holding that the prosecution must prove intention or recklessness as to physical harm, not as to a mere assault.[26] The Court was critical of the antiquated and illogical structure of the 1861 Act, which causes practical problems and yet remains unreformed.

Section 51 of the Police Act 1964 contains the offence of assaulting a police-officer in the execution of his or her duty. Procedurally speaking, this is not an aggravated assault, since it carries the same maximum penalty as common assault (six months' imprisonment) and is also triable summarily only. However, in practice the courts tend to impose higher sentences for assaults on the police, and it is therefore worth noting that this offence is committed even though D was unaware that he was striking a police-officer. A decision by a single judge on assize in 1865[27] is still regarded as authority for this proposition, but there is surely little justification for this today. The

---

[24] *Miller* [1954] 2 QB 282.
[25] J. Shapland, J. Willmore and P. Duff, *Victims in the Criminal Justice System* (1985), Ch. 6; M. Maguire and C. Corbett, *The Effects of Crime and the Work of Victim Support Schemes* (1987), Ch. 7.
[26] *Parmenter* (1990) 92 Cr. App. R 68, preferring *Spratt* (1990) 91 Cr. App. R 362 to *Savage* (1990) 91 Cr. App. R 317, and also criticising *Mowatt* [1968] 1 QB 421.
[27] *Forbes and Webb* (1865) 10 Cox CC 362.

proper approach should be to convict D of the aggravated offence only where he knew that V was, or might be, a police-officer. Otherwise, a conviction for common assault is more appropriate.

(e) Common Assault

The lowest offence on the 'ladder' is what is known as common assault. Strictly speaking, the term 'assault' is used here in its generic sense, as including two separate types of offence, assault and battery. In simple terms, battery is the application of unlawful force to another person, whereas assault consists of causing another person to apprehend or expect the application of unlawful force. Most batteries involve an assault, and the tendency is to refer generically to 'assaults', but the exposition of the law is clearer if the two offences are kept separate.

The essence of a battery is the application of any unlawful force to another. Examples might include a push, a kiss, or throwing a projectile or water which lands on another person's body. Indeed, it seems that the merest touching of another may constitute a battery, and this prompts the question of whether the criminal law ought to extend to such trivial incidents. The traditional justification is that there is no other sensible dividing line, and that this at least declares the law's regard for the physical integrity of citizens. As Blackstone put it: 'the law cannot draw the line between different degrees of violence, and therefore totally prohibits the first and lowest stage of it; every man's person being sacred, and no other having a right to meddle with it, in any the slightest manner.'[28]

Many unwanted touchings are 'technical' batteries, and prosecutors are relied upon to avoid prosecutions of minor incidents. One might be able to construct a law which penalized only those batteries which cause, or are likely to cause, significant annoyance, but it is doubtful whether the insertion of a (necessarily vague) standard would alter the nature of the problem. Individuals have a right not to be touched if they do not wish to be touched, since the body is private. Someone who knowingly touches another without his consent violates this personal right as surely as if he had taken his property. This is most evident in cases of indecent assault, which may be committed by the least unwanted touching or stroking of one person's body by another.[29] These are culpable acts, often regarded as being more serious than thefts of property. If the law is

[28] Blackstone, *Commentaries*, iii. 120.
[29] Discussed below, section 8.6(c).

to recognise the significance of the individual's physical integrity, then it must provide for offences of this kind even if some of the conduct falling within the definition of the offence is properly kept out of the courts by prosecutorial discretion.[30]

There are a number of disputed points about the ambit of the offence of battery. There is no clear decision on whether battery can be committed by the indirect application of force by digging a hole into which people subsequently fall, for example, but there are judicial statements in favour of including indirect force.[31] One major problem is that if the offence is defined so as to include all touchings to which the victim does not consent, it seems difficult to exclude everyday physical contact with others. This could be resolved by assuming that all citizens impliedly consent to those touchings which are incidental to ordinary everyday life and travel; but the judicial preference seems to be to create an exception for 'all physical contact which is generally acceptable in the ordinary conduct of daily life'.[32] The cases decide that this exception extends to touching a person in order to attract attention, although there can be no exception when the person touched has made it clear that he or she does not wish to be touched again. The problem arose in *Collins v. Wilcock* (1984),[33] where a police–officer, not empowered to arrest D, touched D in order to attract her attention and then subsequently took hold of D's arm. D proceeded to scratch the police–officer's arm, having previously made it clear—in colourful language—that she did not wish to talk to the police–officer. The Divisional Court quashed D's conviction for assaulting a police-officer in the execution of her duty, on the ground that the officer herself had assaulted D by taking hold of D's arm. The key issue here was D's obvious refusal of consent to any touching; in other cases there might be a general issue of whether the touching goes 'beyond generally acceptable standards of conduct'.[34] A number of decisions have suggested what appears to be an alternative approach: to ask whether D's touching was 'hostile'. This seems to be an inferior method of identifying the question of the boundaries of permissible conduct, and it is arguable whether this requirement forms part of the criminal law.[35]

---

[30] See above, Ch. 2.6.
[31] See *Clarence* (1888) 22 QBD 23, per Stephen and Wills JJ.
[32] Per Goff LJ, in *Collins v. Wilcock* (1984) 79 Cr. App. R 229, at 234.
[33] Ibid.
[34] Ibid. 234; cf. *Donnelly v. Jackman* (1969) 54 Cr. App. R 229.
[35] A requirement of hostility was reasserted in the civil case of *Wilson v. Pringle*

The essence of the crime of assault, as distinct from battery, is that it involves an apprehension of the immediate application of unlawful force. It is therefore possible to have a battery without an assault (e.g. where D strikes V from behind), as well as an assault without a battery (e.g. where D threatens to strike V but is prevented from doing so), but most cases involve both. One disputed point is whether words alone can constitute an assault: the preponderance of authority is probably that mere words, unaccompanied by any threatening conduct, cannot amount to an assault,[36] but if the point of the offence is to penalize the creation of fear of imminent attack, it is difficult to see why utterances such as 'Get out the knives' or 'Let's hit them' should be regarded more indulgently than a raised hand. Another disputed issue concerns the ambit of immediacy. In one case the Divisional Court held that assault was committed where a woman was frightened by the sight of a man looking in through the window of her house,[37] although there seems to have been little suggestion that the man was threatening to apply force either immediately or at all. The decision might be explained as an attempt to remedy the absence of an offence which penalizes such *voyeurs*. It is a different matter if D intends to cause, and does cause V to *apprehend* the immediate application of force in a case where none is objectively likely (e.g. the gun which D points at V is a toy). That clearly fulfils the definition of assault, and rightly so.

What fault element is required for assault and battery? The law is now settled that either intention or recklessness as to the respective conduct elements is sufficient.[38] After a brief period of uncertainty, it is now clear that common-law recklessness, not *Caldwell* recklessness, is the relevant test.[39] There remains, however, a question of principle which has not been fully considered:[40] should the fault element in offences against the person be widened so as to criminalize some negligent causing of physical harm? If physical integrity is so highly valued, would it be inappropriate to make it clear that an

---

[1986] 2 All ER 440, although the criminal cases of *Collins v. Wilcock* (1984) 79 Cr. App. R 229, and *Faulkner v. Talbot* (1981) 74 Cr. App. R 1, are against it.

[36] The older authorities were reviewed by Glanville Williams, 'Assaults and Words' [1957] Crim. LR 216.

[37] *Smith v. Chief Superintendent of Woking Police Station* (1983) 76 Cr. App. R 234.

[38] *Venna* [1976] QB 421.

[39] *Spratt* (1990) 91 Cr. App. R 362, overruling *DPP v. K* (1990) 91 Cr. App. R 23.

[40] See the criticisms by A. Ashworth and K. Campbell, (1991) 107 LQR.

offence would be committed by any normal adult who failed to see an obvious risk of physical harm to another?[41]

(f) Questions of Consent

In order to explain why offences of violence are regarded so seriously, reference has been made to the values of privacy and physical integrity. However, if individual autonomy is to be regarded as one of the fundamental values, the question arises of whether individuals might consent to the infliction of physical harm on themselves. The owner of property can consent to someone destroying or damaging that property.[42] We shall see below that consent may constitute the difference between the sexual expression of shared love between two people and the serious offence of rape.[43] If a person wishes to give up his physical integrity in certain circumstances, or to risk it for the sake of sport or excitement, should the criminal law allow the consent to negative what would otherwise be a crime?

The Court of Appeal was asked to rule on this question in *Attorney-General's Reference (No. 1 of 1980).*[44] The reference concerned a fight in the street between two youths to settle an argument. The essence of the court's answer was that 'It is not in the public interest that people should try to cause or should cause each other actual bodily harm for no good reason.' In other words, the Court held that, if the fight merely involves assault or battery, consent can be effective as a defence. But if the results constitute actual bodily harm—which extends to 'any hurt or injury calculated to interfere with the health or comfort of the victim'[45]—consent cannot be a defence. This applies whether the fight takes place in public or in private. The Lord Chief Justice added that:

Nothing which we have said is intended to cast doubt on the accepted legality of properly conducted games and sports, lawful chastisement or correction, reasonable surgical interference, dangerous exhibitions, etc. These apparent exceptions can be justified as involving the exercise of a legal right, in the case of chastisement or correction, or as needed in the public interest, in the other cases.[46]

---

[41] See above, section 5.3(c).
[42] Criminal Damage Act 1971, except in circumstances where life is endangered: see above, Ch. 7.7.
[43] See below, section 8.5(c).
[44] [1981] QB 715.
[45] *Donovan* [1934] 2 KB 498.   [46] [1981] QB 715, at 719.

This passage is somewhat unsatisfactory in its lack of certainty and in the wide discretion it appears to leave to the courts. It is true that the *Attorney-General's Reference* did not confront these particular issues directly, and the Lord Chief Justice perhaps intended no more than a sweeping reference to other kindred situations. But the allusion to 'properly conducted' games or sports is vague, and the notion that such dangerous exhibitions as circus acts or trying to vault over twelve buses on a motorcycle are 'needed' in the public interest seems strained.

Beneath all these particular situations there are conflicting values which claim the law's attention. Fundamental respect for individuals as autonomous, rational beings suggests that their liberty to risk injury or to undergo assaults, however serious, ought also to be respected. It is an aspect of self-determination: the point is conceded in the fact that suicide is no longer an offence, and it should therefore follow that consent to injury should negative any offence. That argument is not watertight, however, because existing law does not allow euthanasia. What distinguishes suicide from euthanasia is that the former is the individual's own act, whereas the latter involves the direct act of another. Why should this make so great a difference? It seems that problems of proof loom large here: there is a fear that the unscrupulous would manipulate any law permitting 'mercy killings', and the argument is presumably that this would put at risk more unwilling parties than a law allowing euthanasia would benefit willing parties. There are those, however, who find it objectionable that one person should ever be permitted to take the life of another.[47]

If we bring the argument back to consent to non-fatal physical harm, we may recall that the Lord Chief Justice relied on the phrase 'not in the public interest' to justify the restrictions. This phrase must be regarded as the starting-point for analysis rather than as an explanation. One reason that he ruled out was the argument, derived from earlier cases,[48] that fights in public should be prohibited because they tend to create disorder. This may be true, but there are other offences to deal with that aspect, and, in any case, violence in private raises the same issues of physical integrity and self-determination. Another old argument is that 'manly sports' help to keep people fit to fight for the Crown if necessary, whereas fights which involve maiming rob the Crown of able-bodied men for

[47] A. Kenny, *Freewill and Responsibility* (1978), and above, Ch. 7.4(*h*).
[48] Notably *Coney* (1882) 8 QBD 534.

the armed forces.[49] Although this precise reasoning is of doubtful relevance today, it contains the seeds of an argument to the effect that the public interest lies in having a society with fit and healthy citizens. Several laws have been passed in modern times to restrict dangerous activities and to impose criminal sanctions on citizens who fail to protect themselves against injury—for example, the offences of failing to wear a safety helmet when riding a motor cycle, and failing to wear a safety harness when travelling in the front seat of a car. Such laws are partly paternalistic,[50] based on the argument that the State is in a better position to assess the risks of injury, and partly economic, in the sense that conformity with the law would save millions of pounds in medical expenses (as well as much grief for citizens). Thus one social argument which might be mobilised in favour of the rule in the *Attorney-General's Reference* case is that the savings of medical expenses resulting from conformity with the law are more important than the liberty of individual citizens to engage in fights. That is a matter for debate.

A further paternalistic argument is that a law restricting consent helps to protect individual citizens from themselves by counteracting some of the social pressures and shame which might otherwise occur. The criminal law took a strong line against duelling in the nineteenth century, despite the notions of honour which still regarded it as appropriate or correct for settling certain disputes.[51] Similar pressures might be felt by some people today—to fight, or to risk injury in certain situations, and so on. On the other hand, the extent to which judicial decisions can influence patterns of social behaviour must remain an open question.

Physical sports would probably be widely accepted as an exception to restrictive rules on consent, but two points must be borne in mind. First, there has been a growing number of prosecutions in recent years for injuries resulting from organized matches of Association and Rugby football.[52] It is accepted that not every 'foul' committed in breach of the rules amounts to a crime, and it seems to be assumed that players do, and may lawfully, consent to physical force over and above the minimum permitted by the rules. But this does not exclude the possibility of convictions for the use of physical

---

[49] Sir Michael Foster, *Crown Law* (1762), 260.
[50] See above, Ch. 2.1.
[51] On this and generally, see Glanville Williams, 'Consent and Public Policy' [1962] Crim. LR 74, 154, and his *Textbook of Criminal Law* (2nd edn., 1983), Ch. 21.
[52] e.g. *Billinghurst* [1978] Crim. LR 553 *Lloyd* [1989] Crim. LR 513.

force well beyond that which may reasonably be expected in a game: the borderline is vague, but presumably the courts will decide particular cases by reference to the degree of violence used, its relation to the play in the game, any evidence of intent, and so on. Second, there should be constant reappraisal of the suitability of certain forms of 'sport'. Advances in medical knowledge might lead to the conclusion that some are simply too dangerous: there has long been a debate about the status of boxing, with increasing knowledge of the risks of brain damage to boxers.[53] Here, as elsewhere, there are difficult questions to be answered: whether membership of a society should involve a positive duty to take care of one's body for the general social good, either to avoid becoming a burden on other members of the community or even to preserve oneself as a positive contributor to that community. The question of 'positive contribution' raises again the issue of the social worth of sport, recreation and dangerous exhibitions.

(g) Offences under the Public Order Act 1986

Despite its title, the Public Order Act creates some offences which apply whether the conduct takes place in a public or a private place.[54] Of particular relevance here are those offences which involve violence or the threat of violence. The Act provides a 'ladder' of offences, of which the most serious is riot (section 1). The essence of riot is the use of unlawful violence by two or more persons in a group of at least twelve persons who are using or threatening violence. The maximum penalty is ten years' imprisonment, compared with a maximum of five years for the lesser offence of violent disorder. The essence of violent disorder (section 2) is the use or threat of unlawful violence in a group of at least three persons who are using or threatening violence. Beneath violent disorder comes the crime of affray (section 3), now defined in terms of threatening or using unlawful violence towards another, and carrying a maximum of three years' imprisonment. Affray may be committed by one individual, and, like the other offences, it may be committed in a private place. The term 'violence' includes conduct intended to cause physical harm and conduct which might cause harm (such as throwing a missile towards someone); and, for the two most serious offences of riot and violent disorder, 'violence'

[53] See Glanville Williams, at [1962] Crim. LR 80.
[54] For general analysis, see A. T. H. Smith, *Offences against Public Order* (1987), and R. Card, *Public Order: The New Law* (1986).

bears an extended meaning which includes violent conduct towards property.[55]

Is it necessary to have an extra ladder of offences so closely linked with the general ladder of offences of violence? One reason might be the unsatisfactory state of the law under the Offences against the Person Act 1861: that Act fails to provide both a clear and defensible gradation of offences and any general offences of threatening violence against another.[56] The provisions of the Public Order Act are, however, usually justified on other grounds. One supposed justification is that these extra offences are needed to cope with 'group offending', which causes fear in ordinary citizens, and extra difficulties for the police and for prosecutors (in obtaining persuasive evidence). Offences committed by groups may well occasion greater fear than offences committed by individuals, and it may also be true that groups have a tendency to do things which individuals might not do: there is a group bravado, a group pressure, which may lead to excesses.[57] On the other hand, the criminal law already makes some provision for such cases. The law of conspiracy is aimed at group offending, but conviction depends on proof of some prior agreement.[58] The law of complicity enables the conviction of people who aid and abet others to commit offences, and spreads a fairly wide net in doing so.[59] However, the law of complicity is technical, and the 1986 Public Order Act is a response to the call for a simplified and more 'practical' scheme of offences for dealing with public disorder. Thus the Act goes a long way in smoothing the path of the prosecutor. It is indeed an element of all three offences that the conduct must be such as would cause a person of reasonable firmness, present at the scene, to fear for his personal safety; and yet it is provided, for each offence, that 'no person of reasonable firmness need actually be, or be likely to be, present at the scene'. This not only removes the need for the prosecutor to prove this element, but also removes part of the rationale for the offences. This is 'practical' in the sense that the prosecution need not rely on members of the public to come forward and give evidence, which there is often a reluctance to do. But one effect of this is to limit the opportunities for the defence to contest the issue.

[55] Public Order Act 1986, s. 8.
[56] It does contain the offence of threatening to kill (s. 16); and common assault may be committed by threatening unlawful force.
[57] Cf. E. Trivizas, 'Sentencing the "Football Hooligan"' (1981) 21 *BJ Criminology* 342.
[58] See below Ch. 11.5.   [59] See below, Ch. 10.3.

Another justification for having separate 'public order' offences is that group activities of this kind may, over and above the features discussed above, constitute a special threat to law enforcement and the political system. This argument comes close to a constitutional paradox—that people who are protesting against the fairness of the political system may find themselves convicted of serious offences because their mode of protest is a realistic one. There ought to be a right to protest in public, it might be argued, and where the bona fide exercise of this right happens to lead to some form of disorder, it is wrong to visit the perpetrators with severe sanctions. The counter-argument is that peaceful protest is one thing but violent protest crosses the boundaries of acceptability; the value of physical integrity is such that violence and threats of violence ought not to be downgraded simply because their origins lie in some political protest. One problem here is that the two most serious offences include violence against property, so that conviction may result from threats against a person's property. Another issue is whether a refurbished general code of offences against the person, including clearly graded offences and 'threats' offences, would not cater adequately for these occasions. This brings the argument back to the justifications for those provisions of the Public Order Act which smooth the path of the prosecutor with dispensations from proof.[60] And yet there remains the fact, noted at the outset, that the Act applies to violence and violent threats *in private*. Practical experience will determine whether this heralds an assimilation of prosecution policy within public disorder and private or 'domestic' violence. Would this strengthen the case for a set of offences skewed towards the prosecution?

(h) Causing Illness

The Offences against the Person Act 1861 contains a number of crimes concerned with the administration of noxious or toxic substances. Section 22 penalizes the use of any overpowering drug or substance 'with intent to enable the commission of an arrestable offence' (maximum sentence of life imprisonment). Section 23 penalizes the intentional or reckless administration of any poison or noxious thing which results in danger to the victim's life or grievous bodily harm (maximum sentence of ten years' imprisonment). Section 24 penalizes the administration of any poison or noxious

---

[60] See A. Ashworth, 'Defining Offences without Harm', in P. F. Smith (ed.), *Criminal Law: Essays in Honour of J. C. Smith* (1987).

thing, 'with intent to injure, aggrieve or annoy the victim' (maximum sentence of five years). This section has been applied so as to cover the administration of a drug which causes harm to the victim's metabolism by overstimulation, if D's motive for this is malevolent rather than benevolent.[61] The three offences seem to provide a 'ladder' but, once again, the distinctions between them vary considerably, with section 23 being more concerned about the result than about D's fault. It seems likely that a redefinition of the principal crimes of physical violation would cover most of these cases anyway, and the Criminal Law Revision Committee saw the need to supplement the general offences with only one special offence—administering to another, without his consent, any substance which D knows to be capable of interfering substantially with the other's bodily functions.[62]

(i) Neglect of Duty

Several of the offences discussed above may be committed by omission. One can cause grievous bodily harm by omission, and a person who does so intentionally in a case where a duty of care exists may be convicted under section 18 of the 1861 Act. An example would be starving a child for whom one has parental responsibility, with the result that the child suffers serious harm.[63] It is unclear whether battery can be committed by omission,[64] but it is certainly possible to convict of battery someone who accidentally causes the unlawful application of force to another and then intentionally desists from stopping that application of force. The example is the famous case in which a man unintentionally drove his car on to a police-officer's foot and then declined to remove it, for a minute or two, when asked.[65]

There are also cases in which the criminal law creates special offences attached to certain duties of care, of which the parent's duty towards a child is one example. Section 1 of the Children and Young Persons Act 1933 contains an elaborately worded offence which may be termed 'child neglect'. It consists, essentially, of wilfully assaulting, ill-treating, neglecting, abandoning, or exposing a child in a manner likely to cause unnecessary suffering or injury

---

[61] *Hill* (1986) 83 Cr. App. R 386.
[62] CLRC, 14th Report, *Offences against the Person* (1980 Cmnd. 7844), 84–7, and the draft Criminal Code, Law Com. No. 177, clause 73.
[63] *Gibbins and Proctor* (1918) 13 Cr. App. R 134; see above, Ch. 4.3.
[64] *Fagan v. Metropolitan Police Commissioner* [1969] 1 QB 439.
[65] Ibid.

to health. The maximum penalty for child neglect is now ten years' imprisonment, which should be sufficient to deal with cases involving considerable fault and actually or potentially serious consequences. The Mental Health Act 1983 contains a somewhat similar offence of ill-treating or wilfully neglecting a patient in a mental hospital, which has a maximum penalty of two years' imprisonment.[66]

(j) Weapons, Motor Vehicles, and Endangerment

Most of the offences considered above involve the occurrence of physical harm plus intention or recklessness. It is also justifiable, however, for the criminal law to penalise conduct which may lead to the causing of physical harm, particularly in situations where the conduct has little social utility or where the risk is well known. In fact, English criminal law has a wide range of such offences, of which those involving firearms, offensive weapons, motor vehicles, and other endangerment will be outlined here.

The Firearms Act 1968 sets out to control the possession of firearms and ammunition, and contains several offences. The basic offence in section 1 is that of possessing a firearm without a certificate, an offence which (despite elements of strict liability[67]) carries a maximum of three years' imprisonment. The Act also contains a number of aggravated offences of possessing a firearm with various intents, and these were set out in Chapter 7.7 above.[68] Lower down the scale comes the offence of possessing an offensive weapon without lawful authority or excuse, contrary to the Prevention of Crime Act 1953. This offence, with its maximum penalty of two years' imprisonment, encompasses two classes of weapon: first, an article made or adapted for use as a weapon; and second, any article intended for such use. Much attention has been focused on the concept of 'reasonable excuse', where the courts have attempted to impose a fairly stringent test on persons whose reason for carrying a weapon is said to be fear of attack.[69]

[66] S. 127, and the decision in *Newington* [1990] Crim. LR 593; cf. s. 27 of the Offences against the Person Act 1861, an obsolete offence of neglect in providing for apprentices.

[67] See *Howells* [1977] QB 614, discussed above Ch. 5.3(a).

[68] For further discussion, see P. J. Clarke and J. W. Ellis, *The Law Relating to Firearms* (1981). Sentences of imprisonment for offences of possessing an unlicensed shot-gun with a sawn-off barrel are frequent: see e.g. *Jeffries* (1987) 9 Cr. App. R(S) 497, *Horne*, (1987) 9 Cr. App. R(S) 539.

[69] See above, Ch. 4.7, and, more generally, A. Ashworth, 'Liability for Carrying Offensive Weapons' [1976] Crim. LR 725.

Where motor vehicles are concerned, the problems are different. Although they are no less lethal than firearms in their potential to cause injury or even death, their considerable social utility (indeed, the dependence of much social interaction on them) indicates the need for a different approach. That approach consists of a code of good practice (The Highway Code), a requirement that drivers pass a qualifying test, and a network of offences to penalize those who deviate from proper standards. Leaving aside manslaughter and causing death by reckless driving, offences discussed in the previous chapter,[70] the ladder of offences runs from reckless driving, through drunken driving and careless driving, down to various offences of failure to obey traffic signs and failure to maintain a vehicle in a roadworthy state. Reckless driving, contrary to section 2 of the Road Traffic Act 1972, is committed where D's driving creates an obvious and serious risk of causing physical injury to some other person or of doing substantial damage to property, and where D either saw the risk or failed to give any thought to the risk. This is the test of *Caldwell* and *Lawrence*.[71] The effect of restricting the offence to reckless driving, a restriction which was enacted in 1977 (previously it had included dangerous driving, a less demanding standard),[72] has been that relatively few convictions for this offence are obtained. The offence immediately below is careless driving contrary to section 3 of the Road Traffic Act 1972, which is committed by anyone who drives without due care and attention. This offence is punishable only with a fine, whereas reckless driving carries a maximum of two years' imprisonment. The gap between the two offences is therefore considerable. The other major offence is drunken driving, an offence bristling with technicalities[73] which carries a maximum prison sentence of six months' and a minimum period twelve months' disqualification from driving. This structure of serious road-traffic offences was recently examined by the North Committee, which came to the conclusion that the criminal law does not treat traffic offences with the gravity they deserve, given the potential consequences of any deviation from proper standards of driving. During the 1980s there was evidence of harsher

---

[70] See above, Ch. 7.5 and 7.6.
[71] *Lawrence* [1982] AC 510; the decision in *Caldwell* is discussed extensively above Ch. 5.3(c).
[72] See the report of the James Committee, *The Distribution of Criminal Business between the Crown Court and Magistrates' Courts* (1975, Cmnd. 6323), App. K.
[73] For a general discussion of them, see R. Cross, P. A. Jones, and R. Card, *Introduction to Criminal Law* (11th edn., 1988), 505–20.

punishments being handed out to reckless drivers,[74] and of a wider appreciation of the risks created and the misery inflicted by deviations from proper standards of driving.[75] The North Committee recommended a reformulation of the offence of reckless driving so as to encompass 'very bad driving' of a wider kind, retaining careless driving as the lower offence.[76] The essence of both offences would be the intrinsic quality of the driving and its deviation from the proper standard, not the consequences which happen to result or happen not to result in a particular case. However, the Committee did accept the relevance of resulting harm in one sphere, namely, in its proposal of a new offence of causing death by careless driving when over the alcohol limit. This might be justified as a means of signalling the connection between drunken driving and fatal accidents. It is open to the obvious objection that it focuses on an outcome which may be a matter of pure chance: if such driving happens not to result in death, the charge will merely be drunken driving. One reply to this is that most offences of bad driving have the potential to cause death or serious injury; and that the North Committee's proposals *under*value the element of endangerment where no harm occurs rather than *over*-value the resulting harm where it does occur.

The question of endangerment has already been raised in a more general fashion in Chapter 7.7. English criminal law contains a number of discrete offences of endangerment, created in particular circumstances to deal with particular problems. For example, in addition to the road-traffic offences, there are offences under sections 32 and 33 of the Offences against the Person Act 1861 of endangering railway passengers; there are the offences under section 1(2) of the Criminal Damage Act 1971 of endangering the lives of others by causing damage to property (usually by fire); the Health and Safety at Work Act 1974 penalizes employers for failure to ensure that employees are not exposed to risks to their health or safety; and there are offences, such as that under section 12 of the Consumer Protection Act 1987, of selling goods in contravention of safety regulations. These are all offences of endangerment, in the

[74] This was the intention of Lord Lane CJ, in delivering the guide-line judgment on sentencing in these cases in *Boswell* (1984) 79 Cr. App. R 277.
[75] See the discussion by J. R. Spencer, 'Motor Vehicles as Weapons of Offence' [1985] Crim. LR 29.
[76] Report of the Road Traffic Law Review (chairman: Dr P. North; 1988) discussed by J. R. Spencer, 'Road Traffic Law: A Review of the North Report' [1988] Crim. LR 707.

sense that no harm need have resulted from the dangerous behaviour. Their importance lies in the value of the interest in freedom from physical violation. However, they do not accord with traditional conceptions of crime—perhaps because many of the offences may be committed in 'normal', situations, such as driving a car or conducting a business—and this may tend to obscure their direct relation to the issue of physical safety. It was argued in Chapter 2.5 and 2.6 that social attitudes towards various sources of harm are too hidebound by convention and ought to be re-examined. Chapter 7.7 commended the approach of the American Model Penal Code in creating a general offence of endangerment.[77] A different approach would be to introduce *Caldwell* recklessness into the non-fatal offences of causing injury, with a view to labelling cases of endangerment in the same way as 'traditional' crimes.[78] This would only be effective if it were accompanied by changes in policing practice and prosecution policy.[79] The advantage would be that the law would move closer towards proportionality based on degree of harm and degree of risk, untrammelled by conventional views of what does and what does not count as 'crime'.

(k) The Structure of the Non-Fatal Offences

This survey has shown that, generally speaking, the existing range of offences seems to emphasize the result, the degree of foresight and the status of the victim as the critical issues in grading crimes of physical violation. The crimes in the 1861 Act form a somewhat shakily constructed ladder, with rather more overlapping of offences and elements of constructive liability than is necessary. Factors which undoubtedly influence judgments of seriousness, such as the existence of provocation, or the difference between premeditated and impulsive violence, are accorded no legal significance and are left to the sentencing stage.[80] The main exception to this concerns the status of the victim, with separate offences for assaults on police-officers and wilful neglect of children, for example.

How might the non-fatal offences be reformed so as to conform with the principle of fair labelling? The approach recommended by

[77] Model Penal Code, s. 211.2; see, generally, K. J. M. Smith, 'Liability for Endangerment: English *Ad Hoc* Pragmatism and American Innovation' [1983] Crim. LR 127.
[78] See above, Ch. 5.3(*c*).
[79] See above, Ch. 2.6.
[80] See T. Hadden, 'Offences of Violence: The Law and the Facts' [1968] Crim. LR 521.

the Criminal Law Revision Committee illustrates the difficulties.[81] The Committee proposed three major offences in the field between attempted murder and common assault: causing serious injury with intent to cause serious injury; causing serious injury recklessly; and causing injury either with intent or recklessly. Separate offences for cases involving police-officers and children would be retained, to mark out the extra heinousness of such crimes in general. The scheme depends chiefly on the seriousness of the harm caused and the degree of foresight, though in a much more structured fashion than the 1861 Act. There are three obvious difficulties. First, what is the meaning of 'injury'? The only element specifically defined is that it includes unconsciousness; otherwise, its definition remains vague. Second what is the distinction between injury and serious injury? Once again, it is left to the courts to draw the line according to their overall judgment of the facts. These are two respects in which the reformed law would not achieve maximum certainty, and those who argue that the terms would 'cause little problem of interpretation' are surely giving way to unwarranted optimism.[82] Third, why are there two separate offences of causing serious injury—with intent, or recklessly—when the two mental states are combined in a single offence for mere injury? The Committee's view was that there is 'a definite moral and psychological difference' between causing serious injury with intent and causing serious injury recklessly, and that this difference should be reflected in separate offences. However, since it is 'not an easy distinction for the police, magistrates and juries to have to make', no attempt should be made to draw such a legal distinction at the lower level of 'injury' offences.[83] In order to support this position, one has to accept: (i) that the intention–recklessness distinction is the most significant dividing line for serious injuries, more relevant than factors such as pre-meditation or provocation; (ii) that this is a workable distinction for the courts, especially in impulsive crimes, where the definition of intention may be fulfilled by a momentary realization of what is happening; (iii) that it is so significant that a difference in maximum penalties between life imprisonment and five years' imprisonment is appropriate; and (iv) that there is not a strong case for phrasing the

---

[81] CLRC, 14th Report (1980), pt. iv, incorporated in the draft Criminal Code (Law Com. No. 177), clauses 70–2 (using the term 'personal harm' instead of the CLRC's 'personal injury').

[82] CLRC, 14th Report (1980), para. 154; cf. p. 71, n. 1.

[83] Ibid., para. 152.

offences in terms of endangerment rather than of causing physical harm. The Committee's proposals are a distinct improvement on the anomalies of the 1861 Act, but they leave these four issues open to doubt.

8.4. REPORTED SEXUAL ASSAULTS

The kinds of sexual assault repörted to the police cover an enormous range of conduct. Among the most serious are those now defined as rape (sexual intercourse without consent), and about one-sixth of these cases involve the perpetration of further sexual indignities upon the victim. Reported rapes have increased considerably in the 1980s,[84] but it is difficult to tell to what extent this represents a real increase in the number of rapes or an increase in the reporting of them. The approach of the police to the investigation of rape cases has been subject to much criticism—and then to considerable improvement[85]—and it seems quite possible that these improvements, together with the advent of rape-crisis centres and victim-support facilities, have led more women to report rapes than did so formerly. Reporting a rape remains a strenuous and harrowing experience, however, and it is likely to continue as an under-reported offence. Another serious offence is buggery (intercourse per anum), but that constitutes a crime whether committed consensually or non-consensually, and it is the non-consensual form which ranks as a serious sexual assault. Many of the other forms of sexual assault on males or females do not take the form of sexual intercourse as defined in the offences of rape and buggery, and English law classifies these as indecent assaults. This offence, with a maximum penalty of ten years' imprisonment, covers a wide range of conduct, from a stolen kiss on the cheek to forced fellatio (oral sex). Then there is a group of offences which prohibit sexual activities with young people, whether they appear to consent or not: whilst there is little dispute about the need for some such offences, there is room for disagreement on the proper boundaries of the criminal law and on the role of prosecutorial discretion. The offence of incest prohibits certain sexual relations within the family, thus providing a distinct label for some forms of child sexual abuse by

---

[84] There were 1,225 rapes reported in 1980, and 2,855 rapes reported in 1988: *Criminal Statistics: England and Wales 1988* (1989 Cm 847), Table 2.9.

[85] L. J. F. Smith, *Concerns about Rape*, Home Office Research Study No. 106 (1989), Chs 2 and 4.

parents and grandparents, although it also covers brother–sister relationships.

Before we consider each of these offences in outline, let us examine the practical and theoretical foundations for them. The practical effects of sexual assault can be considerable. There are well-documented consequences of rape victimization: some authorities write of a 'rape trauma syndrome', signifying deep disruption of the victim's life-pattern and thought-processes not just in terms of the physical effects of rape (physical pain, inability to sleep, prolonged distress), but also in terms of the effects on well-being (new-found fears, mistrust of surroundings and other people, embarrassment, and so on).[86] Young's New Zealand report concludes that 'rape is an experience which shakes the foundations of the lives of the victims. For many its effect is a long-term one, impairing their capacity for personal relationships, altering their behaviour and values and generating fear.'[87] There is no reason to suppose that such effects are confined to the victims of rape as traditionally defined: although sexual assaults vary in their degree, there may be many other forms of sexual assault which are serious enough to create such profound physical and psychological after-effects.

What, then, are the interests typically threatened or destroyed by sexual assaults? They may be described generally in terms of sexual autonomy and sexual choice. The argument must begin from the proposition that our body is our own: it is our private zone, and respect for privacy and personal autonomy both support this. Since these values are high among those which the criminal law ought to respect, no further demonstration of this starting-point is necessary. Each citizen may be said to have the right not to have sexual choices imposed on him or her; whether the law should go further, and hold that each citizen has the right to pursue his or her sexual choices consensually with another (subject to public-decency laws and to the protection of the young), is a question to be considered separately. Is respect for sexual choice any more important than respect for another's property rights? The answer to this requires us to assess the relative centrality of sexual choice to life choices and living standards. It may be argued that sexuality has a certain uniqueness which is absent from much property: sexuality is an intrinsic part of one's personality, it is a mode of expressing that personality in relation to others, and it is therefore fundamental that one should

---

[86] See the discussion by Jennifer Temkin, *Rape and the Legal Process* (1977), 1–6.
[87] W. Young, *Rape Study: A Discussion of Law and Practice* (1983), 34.

be able to choose whether to express oneself in this way—and, if so, towards and with whom. The essence of such self-expression is that it should be voluntary. Thus, even where a sexual assault involves no significant physical force, it constitutes harm in the sense that it invades a deeply personal zone, gaining non-consensually that which should only be shared consensually. In case this formulation of 'taking without permission' sounds too close to an analogy with theft, it must be emphasized that the crucial element in sexual assault resides in the close interrelationship between the body and the personality. This close relationship, some would say identity, emphasizes that central values such as autonomy and privacy are bound up in all sexual cases. It is the threat to these values which brings the real, deep, and sometimes long-lasting effects of sexual assault. There can therefore be little doubt that, in general, sexual assaults constitute a substantially more serious form of harm than mere property offences—which is not to deny that some forms of theft or destruction of property can be more serious than some minor sexual assaults.

There is much to suggest that the attitudes of society towards sexual offences, particularly the attitudes of many men (who hold most of the leading posts in the making of policy and law), have tended to undervalue the seriousness of sexual assaults. Among the manifestations of these attitudes are the statements of some defendants in rape trials, which may show an indifference towards the wishes of women, or a belief that the wearing of attractive clothes or an invitation to coffee is a sure sign of willingness to engage in sex; and the attitudes of some police-officers in the early 1980s, influenced by any one of a number of assumptions about the prevalence of false complaints of rape, about the 'typical' rape as an attack by a stranger, about the presence of injuries or bruises in 'genuine' rapes, and so forth.[88] Recent years have seen a growing awareness that most of these assumptions about rape are myths. The police have improved both their procedures and their training, but it is not known whether social attitudes in general have changed greatly. Studies of rape in England and Wales suggest that two-thirds of rapes take place in the home of the victim or the offender, and that only one-third involve strangers; that two-fifths of victims suffer physical violence as well as rape, and one-sixth suffer additional

---

[88] See the Scottish research by G. Chambers and A. Millar, *Investigating Sexual Assault* (1983).

sexual indignities;[89] that recent years have seen an increase in the reporting of rapes between acquaintances, and that rapes are increasing a little in their intrinsic seriousness (i.e. in terms of the violence used, other sexual acts, etc), but that the most significant rise has been in the average length of sentences imposed on rapists by the courts.[90] Longer sentences may be applauded by some,[91] but it is doubtful whether they will make any significant contribution to the protection of women. A recent Home Office survey concludes that there is no simple solution to the prevention of rape, other than 'the willingness both to question and to change the pattern of social life'.[92] The argument is that serious sexual assaults, and the attitude of many men towards them, derive from a male-dominated approach to sexuality in which aggressive sexual behaviour by males is praised or condoned whilst women are associated with passivity. To alter this cluster of attitudes to one in which sexuality is seen as an expression of an equal, sharing relationship will require a widespread change in social attitudes through education and other media.

8.5. NON-CONSENSUAL SEXUAL INTERCOURSE

The structure of sexual offences in English criminal law places rape and buggery at the top of the 'ladder', each carrying a maximum of life imprisonment, with the offences of attempted rape (maximum penalty of life imprisonment) and indecent assault (maximum penalty of ten years) beneath them. The conduct which constitutes rape is unlawful sexual intercourse with a woman without her consent; the fault element required is that the man intends to have sexual intercourse,[93] and either knows that the woman is not consenting or 'could not care less' whether she is not consenting. A number of issues arise for discussion.

---

[89] Smith, *Concerns about Rape*, Ch. 3.

[90] C. Lloyd and R. Walmsley, *Changes in Rape Offences and Sentencing*, Home Office Research Study No. 105 (1989), 40.

[91] One purpose of the guideline judgment in *Billam* (1986) 82 Cr. App. R 347, was to increase the length of sentences for rape, in the belief that the crime was being undervalued in proportion to other offences; another approach would be to lower the sentences for some other crimes.

[92] Smith, *Concerns about Rape*, 36. For further argument, see F. Olsen, 'Statutory Rape: A Feminist Critique of Rights Analysis' (1984) 63 *Texas LR* 387, and S. Estrich, 'Rape' (1986) 95 *Yale LJ* 1087.

[93] Cf. S. White, 'Three Points on *Pigg*' [1989] Crim. LR 539.

(a) The Concept of 'Sexual Intercourse'

Rape is only committed where the man has sexual intercourse with the woman without her consent. Sexual intercourse is defined as the penetration of the penis into the vagina: ejaculation is not required, and the offence is committed as soon as penetration takes place, although it has been held that the offence continues throughout penetration (so that if the woman revokes her consent during intercourse and the man fails to withdraw, he commits rape).[94] Is English law right to define rape in this way, and thereby to exclude from this offence such conduct as forced oral sex (fellatio), cunnilingus, and buggery? It can be argued that these offences may be no less traumatic for the victim than 'conventional' rape,[95] and therefore that any attempt to classify sexual offences by reference to their seriousness should place these forms of sexual assault in the highest category. In its review of sexual offences the Criminal Law Revision Committee argued in favour of preserving the existing classification, on the basis that rape has a settled popular meaning and that the distinguishing feature of 'conventional' rape is the risk of pregnancy. However, the latter point fails to take account of the fact that rape is committed even if there is no ejaculation, and even if the woman is infertile, and it has been strongly argued that 'penetration involving the penis, vagina or anus is perceived differently and regarded more seriously than other forms of penetration'.[96] It may therefore be questioned whether English law takes the right approach in confining its most serious sexual offence, rape, so narrowly.

(b) Marital Rape

Rape is only held to have been committed in English law where the sexual intercourse is 'unlawful', and it is generally assumed that the function of that term is to remove non-consensual intercourse between a man and his wife from the ambit of rape. If the man uses force or inflicts emotional shock on his wife in order to obtain sex, he is liable to conviction for assault occasioning actual bodily harm or some other offence against the person.[97] But if he obtains his wife's submission to intercourse without resort to those means,

---

[94] *Kaitamaki v. R* [1985] AC 147.
[95] See the evidence of victims collected by the Law Reform Commission of Ireland, *Rape*, Law Reform Commission No. 24 (1988).
[96] Temkin, *Rape and the Legal Process*, 33.
[97] *Miller* [1954] 2 QB 282.

there is no offence. The origins of this marital-rape exemption seem to lie in the notion that the wife is the husband's property, or that the wife promises intercourse on demand,[98] but it has been defended in modern times on the basis that such cases raise essentially family matters, better suited to examination in a non-criminal court, and that in any case proof would be difficult.[99] However, it is questionable whether the doors of the family home should be closed to the criminal law when so many offences of wife-battering, child battering, and sexual abuse of wives and children seem to go on behind them. Are persons who inflict physical or sexual assault in the domestic context really less blameworthy than their counterparts on the street? Are victims within the family any less worthy of the protection of the criminal law? Should the criminal law really distinguish between unmarried and married couples when it comes to dealing with rape? It is perhaps in recognition of the awkward position of English law that exceptions have been made to the marital-rape exemption in recent years. Where the court is able to conclude that the wife's 'implied consent to marital intercourse' has been formally revoked, non-consensual intercourse by the husband amounts to rape. This may be the case where there has been a separation order, a decree nisi for divorce, a non-molestation order, or a separation agreement between the parties.[100] However, these particular instances do not meet the general proposition that if the husband and wife have drifted apart, and the woman has made it known that she no longer wants to have sex with her husband, it is wrong that the husband who has sex with her without her consent is exempt from conviction for rape. There may be many reasons why the husband and wife do not make any formal agreement about separation, but this should not entitle a husband to return and force himself upon his wife weeks, months, or even years since he last saw her. The inadequacy of this part of English law was signalled recently in *Kowalski* (1988),[101] where the Court of Appeal upheld an estranged husband's conviction for indecently assaulting his wife by forcing her to have oral sex with him. The defence argument was that this

[98] See Temkin, *Rape and the Legal Process*, 43–9.
[99] CLRC, 15th Report, *Sexual Offences* (1984, Cmnd. 9213), paras. 2.64–2.70 (the view of a narrow majority of the Committee).
[100] See the decisions in *Clarke* [1949] 2 All ER 448; *Miller* [1954] 2 QB 282; *O'Brien* [1974] 3 All ER 663; *Steele* (1977) 65 Cr. App. R 22; *Roberts* [1986] Crim. LR 188; and *Sharples* [1990] Crim. LR 198; and discussion by R. Brooks, 'Marital Consent in Rape' [1989] Crim. LR 877.
[101] (1988) 86 Cr. App. R 339.

was a preliminary to 'conventional' intercourse, and that if the husband was exempt from liability for rape, he should equally be exempt from liability for indecent assault. The Court held that marriage does not imply consent to fellatio. This decision goes a long way towards demonstrating the untenability of the marital-rape exemption in modern times.

The Law Commission has now proposed the abolition of the marital-rape exemption,[102] bringing English law into accord with the many other jurisdictions where it does constitute rape for a husband to have non-consensual sexual intercourse with his wife. Reported cases are small in number, and it may be true that in some (not all) of these cases the degree of trauma suffered by the wife is less than if the rape had been by another man; but abolition of the marital-rape exemption is surely important as a statement of the married woman's autonomy and freedom of choice in sexual matters. These fundamental values should not be jettisoned simply because marriage is a factor in the case, as indeed the Court of Appeal affirmed when holding that a husband may be convicted of kidnapping his wife.[103]

(c) Mistaken Belief in Consent

The fault element in rape is that the man knows that the woman is not consenting or 'could not care less' that she is not consenting. It would seem to follow from this that a man who *believes* that the woman is consenting, even though she is not, ought to be acquitted. Lord Hailsham, in the leading decision of *DPP v Morgan* (1976)[104] held that this follows as a matter of 'inexorable logic'. It is not, then, a question of deciding on the elements of a 'defence' of mistake, because, where the man is mistaken, this means that he quite simply lacks the fault element required for the offence. It is not a 'defence' so much as the negation of the elements of the crime. So where, as in *Morgan*, defendants claim that they believed the woman was consenting, because her husband (who was present) had told them that she enjoyed a struggle, their case is simply that they lacked the fault element required for the crime.

The decision in *Morgan* has been hailed as a turning-point in English criminal law, inasmuch as the House of Lords resoundingly

---

[102] Law Commission Working Paper No. 116, 'Rape within Marriage' (1990); cf. the first instance decisions culminating in *C* [1991] Crim. LR 60.
[103] *Reid* [1973] QB 299.   [104] [1976] AC 182, discussed above Ch. 5.3(*d*).

affirmed the subjective principle of guilt. Fairness requires that we judge a defendant on the facts *as he or she believes them to be*. Previous decisions had held that a mistake must be based on reasonable grounds if it is to excuse, a doctrine which is illogical for the reason given by Lord Hailsham. Where a crime requires knowledge or recklessness as to a certain circumstance, and the defendant holds a mistaken belief about that circumstance, logic demands that an acquittal should follow. Moreover, the supporters of *Morgan* add, this should not lead to unmeritorious acquittals, because juries will not allow bogus defences to succeed: in *Morgan* itself the House of Lords was satisfied that the basis for the defence was so weak that a correctly directed jury would have found the defendants guilty.

However, it is possible to concede that defendants should be judged on the facts as they believe them to be, and yet to argue in favour of an exception in rape cases. This would be a bold argument, since its thrust would be that *Morgan* is correct as a case on general principles but wrong as a rape decision. How might the argument run? One could argue that there are certain situations in which the risk of serious harm is so obvious that it would be right for the law to impose a duty to take care to ascertain the facts before proceeding. In other words, mistakes must be based on reasonable grounds where the offences are serious—which would cover not only rape but also cases involving a risk of death or serious injury, such as the use of force in self-defence. One drawback of this style of argument is that not only is the harm serious for the victim, but conviction for such an offence is serious for the defendant: a single class of offenders (rapists, serious wounders) would contain not only those with subjective fault but also those who merely failed to take proper care, all of whom would be convicted of a grave offence carrying a maximum of life imprisonment. Perhaps a more fruitful line of argument is to emphasize that not only is rape a serious matter for the victim, but the ascertainment of one vital fact—consent—is a relatively easy matter for the man. There is a clear contrast here between cases of the use of serious force in self-defence, where there may be a need to act instantaneously on a hastily formed view of the situation, and sexual intercourse with another, where consent or non-consent is the essence of the crime and can be ascertained by asking a plain question of the victim. Thus the argument is that the victim's right to autonomy and freedom of sexual choice does not need to yield to the principle that a defendant should be judged on the facts as he believes them to be; it would be so simple (because of the inevitable physical proximity of the man and woman) for the man to ascertain the facts here. Of course, this involves a departure from the general subjective principle of criminal liability, since it involves imposing a duty on the defendant to ask about the victim's consent before continuing with his conduct. But compared with the potential sacrifice of victims' rights, this duty is so undemanding that the arguments in its favour are powerful. Critics will say that it converts rape into an offence of negligence, in one respect at least. The answer is that it does, and that the justifications for doing so have been set out above—not so much because rape is a serious offence, but rather because ascertainment of the facts is so easy that there should be little substantive unfairness to defendants.[105]

If the criminal law is to impose further duties on citizens, it is important to take account of the legality principles, particularly the principle of maximum certainty (see Chapter 3.3 (i) and (g)). This brings the discussion back to whether changes in social attitudes are the most effective way of preventing sexual victimization. There is no shortage of examples of defendants in rape cases who assumed that a woman who said no really meant yes, or who inferred from other supposed clues (make-up, clothing, accepting a drink) that the victim had consented, despite her apparent protests. Changing the law on mistake in rape could help to change these social attitudes, even though for some time to come defendants might find themselves charged with rape because of such ingrained attitudes towards women.

(d) Reckless Rapes

One of the many reactions to the decision of the House of Lords in *Caldwell* (1982)[106] was that it went against *DPP v. Morgan* and cut down its ambit. In fact, although the two decisions are opposed in spirit, their practical spheres of operation can be separated. For one thing, *Caldwell* deals with cases where D has either recognized the risk or has failed to give any thought to it, whereas *Morgan* applies only where D has formed a distinct belief that the victim is consenting, a situation not explicitly covered by *Caldwell*. It may also be said that *Caldwell* is concerned with foresight of consequences, whereas *Morgan* is concerned with knowledge of circumstances. It is doubtful whether either of these distinctions would bear scrutiny

---

[105] See T. Pickard, 'Culpable Mistakes' (1980) 30 *U. Toronto LJ* 75 and C. Wells, 'Swatting the Subjectivist Bug' [1982] Crim. LR 209.
[106] [1982] AC 341, discussed above Ch. 5.3(c).

on the broader canvas of moral and social philosophy: the moral thrust of *Caldwell* is that people are often just as much to blame for *failing* to think as they are for thinking about their actions and its consequences, and this very argument was applied to rape in the paragraphs above.

In fact, the *Caldwell* definition of recklessness has not been followed in rape cases, even though that offence would seem to fulfil the criterion of being a modern statute in which the term 'reckless' is used. The Court of Appeal's decisions have wavered somewhat, but the test which they now favour is that D is reckless if he 'could not care less' whether the woman is not consenting.[107] This test is ambiguous as to whether or not D must have thought about whether the woman is consenting, but there are those who argue that one cannot be said 'not to care less' about something unless one has considered it. There are arguments here, as there are in relation to mistake, that the law should impose a duty on men to consider consent, and therefore should treat them as reckless if they have failed to give any thought to the matter. Plausible cases are likely to be extremely rare in practice.

(e) Fraud, Deception, and Consent

How should the law deal with cases where the woman's consent to sexual intercourse stemmed from a mistake on her part? English law has tended to confine narrowly the situations in which a mistake is held to negative the consent apparently given by the woman: only where the victim was made to believe that the man was her husband, or that the act to which she was being asked to consent was not sexual intercourse, is the mistake sufficiently fundamental to convert the apparently consensual sex into rape. The latter question has arisen where young girls have been invited to submit to acts in order to train their voice or to improve their breathing[108]—unbeknown to them, the act which they were permitting was sexual intercourse. Other types of fraud and mistake are held to be insufficient for the offence of rape, and bring the case within the lesser offence of procuring a woman by false pretences or false representations to have unlawful sexual intercourse (section 3, Sexual Offences Act 1956, carrying a maximum penalty of two years' imprisonment).

Does the existing dividing line reflect the relative seriousness of

---

[107] *Satnam S and Kewal S* (1984) 78 Cr. App. R 149, adopting the approach of Lawton LJ, in *Kimber* (1983) 77 Cr. App. R 225.

[108] *Flattery* (1877) 2 QBD 410; *Williams* [1923] 1 KB 340.

these mistake-related offences? Since the identity of one's sexual partner may be assumed to be of fundamental significance, it is surely unjustified to give effect to this only where the mistake concerns whether the man is the woman's husband?[109] But there are wider issues here, too, implicit in the promiscuous use of the words 'mistake', 'false representations', 'fraud', and so on. Analogies with the effect of mistake in the law of contract may appear obvious, but it is questionable whether they are appropriate. The issues are: when the defendant should be convicted of a crime; how the crime should be labelled; and how seriously it should be viewed. It could be argued, therefore, that the focus should not be the victim's mental state but the defendant's intentions. If D set out to trick V into having sex, realising that she probably would not consent otherwise, are not his intention and his method sufficient to condemn him for rape, as they would be for obtaining property by deception? Similarly, if D knowingly takes advantage of the fact that V is labouring under a mistaken belief in order to have sex with her, when (as he realises) she probably would not consent otherwise, should this not be sufficient? The answer to those questions may be said to depend on whether it is generally as serious to obtain sex by deception as it is by other means (threats, force, fear). In England the Criminal Law Revision Committee took the view that it is not,[110] and therefore supported the division between fundamental deceptions (as to identity or the nature of the act) and lesser deceptions, placing the latter within the less serious category of procuring sex by deception. According to this view, the woman who agrees to have sex with D only when he promises to marry her (never intending to keep this promise)—and because he has promised to marry her—is a victim not of rape but of the lesser offence of procuring sexual intercourse by false representations. The Committee proposed to raise the maximum penalty for this offence to five years, but limited its recommendation to cases where D actively deceives V and failed to make any provision for cases where D takes advantage of a known mistake.

(f) Threats, Fear and Consent

More frequent in practice, and more problematic, are the cases involving threats and fear. At one time it was the law that rape is

---

[109] CLRC, 15th Report (1984) para. 2.25, recommending abolition of the limitation now contained in the Sexual Offences Act 1956, s. 1(2).
[110] Ibid.; cf. Temkin, *Rape and the Legal Process*, 63–7 and 69–71.

committed only where the woman submits through force, fear, or fraud. This is no longer a requirement, because decisions in the nineteenth century made it clear that rape can be committed whenever the woman does not consent—is asleep, for example, or too drunk to consent.[111] However, there are both practical and legal problems in cases where the woman says that she consented through fear only: she did not resist, because she thought that it would be hopeless in the circumstances, she was terrified, or she feared serious violence. The practical problems are that there may be no evidence of violence on the woman's body, which usually means that the case will be a question of the victim's word against the defendant's; this may lead the police to be sceptical of the woman's complaint, or may incline the prosecutor to accept a plea of guilty to the lesser charge of indecent assault. The legal problems are similar to those in the cases of mistake and deception: are all threats serious enough to justify regarding the crime as a rape, or should some threats be accommodated within a lesser offence? English law has the lesser crime of procuring unlawful sexual intercourse by threats or intimidation, and appears to limit rape to those cases where there is a threat of violence.[112] However, there is a wider dimension to the question, which encompasses fear as well as threats, and this hinges on the distinction between submission and consent.

In the case of *Olugboja* (1981)[113] two girls were picked up by two men and taken to a remote house. The victim was already distressed after being raped by the other man when D announced his intention to have sex with her. She asked him why he could not leave her alone, in view of what the other man had already done to her, but he turned off the lights and told her to undress. She did not resist. The Court of Appeal rejected the defence argument that there must be actual violence or threats of violence for the offence to be classified as rape. It also rejected the Crown's argument that the issue of consent should be left to the jury—in the same way as the question of dishonesty is left to them in theft cases—but its actual decision comes fairly close to this position. Thus, the jury should be instructed that the term 'consent' covers a whole range of situations from actual desire to reluctant acquiescence, and that the dividing line between real consent and mere submission must be drawn by the jury by applying its knowledge of human nature to the facts of the case.

[111] *Camplin* (1845) 1 Car & Kir 746; *Mayers* (1872) 12 Cox cc 311.
[112] Sexual Offences Act 1956, s. 2.   [113] [1982] QB 320.

The law of rape may therefore extend to threats other than threats of violence, but its boundaries are most uncertain. Resort to such concepts as 'common sense' and 'knowledge of human nature', is little more than a veiled admission that no satisfactory criteria have been found. The narrowest position is to say that rape is committed only where D threatens violence or knows that V is in fear of violence, and that any other threat must fall within the lesser offence of procuring sex by threats.[114] A broad position would be to hold that any threat may negative consent, and this might include a threat to send a compromising photograph to someone, a threat to report a driver for exceeding the speed limit, and so on. Among intermediate positions, one possibility is to draw an analogy with the offence of blackmail, holding that any unwarranted demand for sex with menaces should amount to rape, the menaces being either sufficient to influence an ordinary person or sufficient to influence the mind of this victim.[115] But the difficulty with this discussion is that it lacks a firm point of reference because it cannot be taken for granted that there should be two levels of offence, rape and procuring sex by threats. If there is to be a single offence of serious sexual assault, there are arguments for including all cases of obtaining sex by fear or threats within that. If the present division is regarded as desirable, the next step is to ensure that the maximum penalty for the lesser offence is sufficient to deal with cases of serious threats which are not enough to negative consent in rape. Then one can address the question of whether rape should be confined to cases where submission arises from a threat or fear of violence, or whether it should be phrased more widely. At that stage, questions about the appropriateness of labels, sentencing powers, and the principle of legality (in terms of certainty requirements) come to the fore. These questions will be considered on a broader canvas in section 8.7 below.

8.6. OTHER NON-CONSENSUAL SEXUAL OFFENCES

So far the discussion has focused on the offence of rape in English law, which is confined to cases of 'sexual intercourse' where the penis penetrates the vagina. Other kinds of sexual assault are classified in English law as buggery, attempted buggery or rape, or

---

[114] The CLRC would restrict the offence of rape to threats of 'immediate' violence: 15th Report (1984), para.2.29.
[115] See Temkin, *Rape and the Legal Process*, 67–9.

indecent assault, and there are also offences against young people and the mentally disordered. These will be considered briefly before the general subject of sexual offences is re-examined.

(a) Buggery

One of the circumstances constituting this offence is where the penis penetrate the anus of a male or a female,[116] and the maximum penalty is life imprisonment. The law therefore allows the offence to be treated just as seriously as rape, and we have seen how some would argue that it should be included as a form of rape, or at least as a form of the most serious offence of sexual assault, in any reformed law. In ordinary parlance one might say that anyone who has been forcibly subjected to this offence has been raped; the psychological effects are likely to be deep, and even if there is no risk of pregnancy (as there is not from some rapes, since ejaculation is not part of the definition), there may be the risk of disease.

(b) Attempted Rape or Attempted Buggery

If a defendant fulfils the requirements for the offence of rape or buggery but failed to achieve penetration, liability for attempted rape or attempted buggery may be possible. These are serious offences, carrying the same maximum penalty as the full offences. A survey in the 1970s showed that almost one-third of rape charges resulted in conviction of attempted rape.[117] According to the law of attempts, the least that a defendant must be proved to have done is something 'more than merely preparatory' to sexual intercourse, with intent to have unlawful sexual intercourse without the woman's consent.[118] Whether the prosecution can prove attempted rape rather than the lesser offence of indecent assault will often depend on proof of the defendant's intention to go beyond the indecent acts already committed. A legal problem has arisen here in respect of defendants who 'could not care less' whether the woman was not consenting: we have seen that such men can be convicted of rape in cases where they achieve penetration, but there is a problem in convicting them of attempted rape where they fail to achieve penetration but clearly intended to do so. The problem is that

---

[116] Sexual Offences Act 1956, s. 12; this is also an offence when committed consensually: see e.g. *Cowley* (1988) 10 Cr. App. R(S) 465.

[117] R. Wright, 'A Note on the Attrition of Rape Cases' (1984) 24 BJ Criminology 399.

[118] Criminal Attempts Act 1981, s. 1(1); see below Ch. 11.2.

conviction for an attempted crime requires an intent to commit the full offence whereas the 'reckless' attempted rapist intends to have sexual intercourse but is merely reckless as to the woman's non-consent. The strong argument in favour of classifying such offences as attempted rape rather than merely indecent assault has now been recognized by the Law Commission's draft Criminal Code,[119] and the Court of Appeal has recently found its way to this conclusion by 'interpreting' the Criminal Attempts Act 1981.[120]

(c) Indecent Assault

In English law the offence of indecent assault is charged for all forms of sexual assault other than rape, buggery, and attempts to commit those crimes. Until 1985 the maximum penalty for indecent assault on a female was two years' imprisonment, compared with ten years for indecent assault on a male—a legacy of the horror with which homosexuality was viewed, and of the undervaluing of female sexual and physical autonomy—but the maximum penalty for both forms of indecent assault is now ten years.[121] This is a far more realistic maximum for cases involving forced oral sex and other indignities, but the real question is whether such serious forms of sexual assault should be classified differently. At present they 'share' the offence of indecent assault with many minor forms of misconduct, such as giving an unwanted kiss or fondling clothes being worn by someone else, for which the penalty is likely to be a long way down the scale. This suggests that there is a strong argument for having two grades of indecent assault in English law, or for moving some of the more serious forms of the crime (such as forced fellatio or cunnilingus) into a broadened crime of rape or 'serious sexual assault'.

Most of the technical legal controversy has concerned not the more serious varieties of indecent assault but the more ambiguous forms, where the element of indecency is used to separate the sexual offence from the non-sexual. In *Court* (1988)[122] the House of Lords upheld the conviction of a man who had spanked a young girl several times on the seat of her shorts. The House distinguished, in effect, three types of case. First, where the conduct would not be thought indecent by any right-minded observer, indecent assault

---

[119] Law Com. No. 177, ii, 244.   [120] *Khan* (1990) 91 Cr. App. R 29.
[121] Sexual Offences Act 1985, s. 3.
[122] (1988) 87 Cr. App. R 144; see G. R. Sullivan, 'The Need for a Crime of Sexual Assault' [1989] Crim. LR 331.

could not be committed. Second, where right-minded observers would agree that the conduct was indecent, that would be an indecent assault. In a third class of cases, where the right-minded observer would be unsure, the court would look at the defendant's motive and, only if that was indecent, would the offence be made out. One result of this is that much will turn on the court's initial characterization of the incident, using the 'right-minded person' test. That test is vague, but could it be improved upon in this context? Is it possible to predetermine the types of conduct regarded as indecent? Should the defendant's motive be so crucial in cases where the act is not obviously indecent, in the sense that 'right-minded persons' would not unhesitatingly classify it as such? (One might argue against the concept of 'right-minded persons', which moves away from a statistical concept such as 'most people' or 'the ordinary citizen' and seems to seek a moral plane which is 'right-minded', a question-begging approach in this context.) Does it matter if a person derives some kind of sexual satisfaction from an act which most people or 'right-minded persons' would not regard as indecent? There is no parallel here with punishment for attempts and other inchoate offences, because there is no proof that the defendant was aiming to do something harmful: the harmfulness of the action is supposedly constituted by the indecent motive, not by anything actually done, or about to be done, to the victim.

The two main issues in the crime of indecent assault are therefore: whether the crime ought to be divided into two grades so that the more serious forms of sexual assault can be labelled separately; and how to draw the line between indecent and non-indecent contact with another. There is no indecent assault where the other party consents to the conduct, and the fault element for the crime includes knowledge or recklessness as to whether the other party is consenting. Here, as with rape, it seems sufficient to show that D 'could not care less' whether the other party was not consenting.[123] However, a person under the age of 16 cannot give valid consent. Thus, if a woman were to have sexual intercourse with a boy under 16, this would be the offence of indecent assault by the woman even if the boy consented to, or instigated, the act.[124] This restriction on consent is designed for the protection of the young, to which we will now turn.

---

[123] *Kimber* (1983) 77 Cr. App. R 225.
[124] Sexual Offences Act 1956, ss. 14 and 15; *Faulkner v. Talbot* (1982) 74 Cr. App. R 1.

(d) Sexual Intercourse with Girls under 16

A male commits an offence if he has sexual intercourse with a girl under 16. Even if she consents in fact, this has no effect in law and the offence is still committed. If the girl is under 13, the maximum penalty is life imprisonment, since a girl of 12 or under cannot have sufficient knowledge of the consequences of sex, or sufficient maturity of judgment to take decisions on those consequences. Where the girl is aged 13 to 15, the maximum penalty is two years. There is a defence for a young man under 24 who has not previously been charged with a similar offence and who believes that the girl is 16 years old.[125] In practice, the vast majority of reported offences of unlawful sexual intercourse with a girl of 16 involve young men of a similar age or a few years older, and the general trend is to administer a formal caution to such persons rather than to prosecute them. Prosecution is thus reserved for the cases in which some unfair advantage has been taken of the girl, particularly where the girl is under 13 (when lack of proper understanding is assumed), where the man is considerably older than the girl, where the man held some position of trust in relation to the girl, and where there is some element of deception involved. The law does not specify any of these elements: everything is left to prosecutorial discretion. The Criminal Law Revision Committee took the view that, if the law did try to restrict the offence in this way, it would inevitably legalize some cases which should remain contrary to the law.[126] Thus the law continues to sacrifice the principle of maximum certainty (see Chapter 3.3 (i)) to the supposed dictates of practicality. The law is framed widely, in the expectation that it will be enforced selectively. In one particular sphere, however, other legal systems seem to disagree with the practicality argument: namely, cases of sexual intercourse with a girl under 16 committed by a person in a position of trust towards her. Many countries have an offence of 'abuse of authority' to differentiate these crimes, in accord with the principle of fair labelling (Chapter 3.3 (l)), but anxieties about the problem of listing the types of authority (should it include persons undertaking voluntary responsibility, such as choirmasters and youth-club leaders?) have led to the continuation of the pragmatic all-encompassing provisions in England and Wales.

---

[125] Sexual Offences Act 1956, s. 6(3).
[126] CLRC, 15th Report (1984), paras. 5.19–5.21.

There are sharp divisions about the fault element for the offence of unlawful sexual intercourse with a girl under 16. The limited 'defence' of mistake about the girl's age, available to young men under 24, was explained above, and the reason for creating such a limited 'defence' is that in general it has been held that the crime does not require any fault element as regards the girl's age. For many years the decision in *Prince* (1875), in effect that the man is strictly liable when the girl is under 16, has been paraded by academic lawyers as the acme of injustice.[127] The decision may certainly be said to be out of line with the recent trend, that a defendant should be judged on the facts as he believes them to be; and this led the Criminal Law Revision Committee to recommend that the rules should be harmonized and that the prosecution should prove that the man realized that the girl was under 16.[128] Once again, one must question whether consistency is the highest value here. Critics argue that the whole point of this offence is to provide protection for young girls, and that this will be undermined if it is open to men to seek an acquittal on the ground that the girl looked 16. Without directly embracing the 'protection' element in this argument, it can be suggested that there should he a duty on the man to ask the girl about her age before entering into sexual relations, even though the answers may be untruthful in some cases.

(e) Other Rules against Exploitation of the Vulnerable

Mention might be made of four other special rules relating to the involvement of vulnerable persons in sexual activity. The *Prince* rule of strict liability as to age, which applies equally to indecent assault, has already been noticed. Another judge-made rule is that in *Tyrrell* (1894), which provides that a person cannot be convicted as a party to an offence if the offence was created for the protection of such persons.[129] Thus, in cases where a young girl or young boy of 15 leads an adult into sexual activity, the youth cannot be convicted as a party to either unlawful sexual intercourse with a girl under 16 or indecent assault (as the case may be). The adult commits the offence; the law imposes on him or her the duty to resist whatever temptation is provided by the under-age person.

Among the specific offences designed to protect the vulnerable,

---

[127] (1875) LR 2 CCR 154, on which see R. Cross, 'Centenary Reflections on Prince's Case' (1975) 91 LQR 540.

[128] CLRC, 15th Report (1984), paras. 5.5–5.15.

[129] [1894] 1 QB 710.

there are various offences of sexual relations with mentally handi-capped persons.[130] There is a crime of gross indecency with or towards a child under 14, which may be committed even though there is no indecent assault on the child by the adult—by inviting the child to touch the genitalia of the adult, for example.[131] However, there seems little reason for limiting the offence to cases involving children under 14 when the general age of consent to sexual activity stands at 16. And it is an offence for a man to commit gross indecency with another man: this offence usually concerns mutual masturbation or oral sex between two males (there is no equivalent offence between females). The reason for discussing it here is that, under the Sexual Offences Act 1967, this offence is not committed where the act is done in private, between consenting males, both aged 21 or over. This means that it is regarded as criminal for a man of 21 to commit this offence with a consenting male under 21. The age of 21 seems exceptionally high, since a person has the right to vote at 18 and the age of consent for other sexual conduct is 16. Logic suggests that 16 should be the age of consent for this conduct, too, but the CLRC took the view that young men of 16 and 17 need protection from this kind of behaviour, whereas they do not from other kinds of sexual contact.[132] The anomaly is increased by the fact that, under the present law, two young men under 21 who consensually commit 'gross indecency' are both liable to conviction for the offence: the rule in *Tyrrell* is inapplicable here, but the maximum penalty is two years' imprisonment where the offender is under 21, compared with five years where he is over 21.[133]

8.7. INCEST

A parent or grandparent who has sexual contact with a child or grandchild may well be guilty of one of the offences already con-sidered—rape, if there is sexual intercourse without consent; in-decent assault, if there is sexual contact with a child under 16; and even gross indecency with or towards a child, if the child is under 14. These other offences do not cover all eventualities, and, moreover, it may be argued with some force that child sexual abuse at home

---

[130] e.g. Sexual Offences Act 1956, s. 7; Sexual Offences Act 1967, s. 1(3).
[131] Indecency with Children Act 1960, s. 1.
[132] CLRC, 15th Report (1984), para. 6.18.
[133] Ibid., paras. 6.13–6.15; see J. C. Hindley, 'The Age of Consent for Male Homosexuals' [1986] Crim. LR 595.

ought to be labelled separately. It is not merely a sexual offence, but one of the deepest breaches of trust which can take place in a family-based society. The home ought to be a safe haven, the place where people go to get away from fear and violence, and it is this fundamental feeling of safety which can be destroyed by child sexual abuse. Incest was introduced into English law as a distinct offence by the Punishment of Incest Act 1908.[134] Although the eugenic risk (that the child of an incestuous relationship between father–daughter or brother–sister will have congenital defects) was known at the time and was probably a factor, most of the arguments of the reformers were based on the protection of children from sexual exploitation. Those arguments have great force today, as increasing evidence of child sexual abuse within the family comes to light. Fathers may have considerable power within the home, using that power to lead a daughter into sexual activity from a relatively early age. All kinds of pressure may be exerted on the child to keep quiet about the behaviour, with sometimes disastrous effects on his or her emotional development. Indeed, the primacy of this anti-exploitation rationale over eugenic reasons makes it desirable to extend the offence to cover adopted children as well as blood-relationships.[135]

The offence of incest is committed by a man who has sexual intercourse with a person whom he knows to be his granddaughter, daughter, sister or mother, and by a woman aged 16 or over who permits her grandfather, father, brother, or son to have sexual intercourse with her.[136] The first thing to notice about this definition is that, like the offence of rape, it is restricted to 'sexual intercourse'. In the context of incest this is even less defensible—first, because eugenic reasons no longer provide the main grounds for criminalization; and second because the primary rationale of punishing the sexual exploitation of children within the family applies no less to other serious sexual behaviour, such as oral and anal sex. Surely the offence of incest should cover all cases of vaginal or anal penetration or penetration involving the penis. Another feature of the offence is that it applies irrespective of the ages of the parties (save

---

[134] See V. Bailey and S. Blackburn, 'The Punishment of Incest Act 1908: A Case Study in Law Creation' [1979] Crim. LR 708, and S. Wolfram, 'Eugenics and the Punishment of Incest Act 1908' [1983] Crim. LR 308.

[135] CLRC, 15th Report (1984), para. 8.28.

[136] Sexual Offences Act 1956, ss. 10 and 11; sentencing guidelines for the offences were laid down in *Attorney-General's Reference (No. 1 of 1989)* (1989) 11 Cr. App. R(S) 409.

that a woman cannot commit the offence of 'permitting' intercourse unless she is aged 16 or over). Thus the crime of incest covers sexual relations by mature adults, in situations where the rationale of punishing exploitation of the young should no longer apply. One question, therefore, is whether the age should be reduced to 16, which is the general age of consent for sexual activity. There might appear to be an argument in favour of consistency here, but it is surely eclipsed by the need to recognize that many children remain dependent on their parents until they are at least 18. Indeed, the CLRC recommended that the age should be no lower than 21.[137] Another issue is whether brother–sister incest should remain criminal where both parties are aged 18 or over: when sentencing, the courts treat this as a much less serious form of the offence than father–daughter incest, and a majority of the CLRC accepted that brother–sister incest should cease to be an offence when both parties are aged 21 or over.[138] The reasoning behind this proposal seems to be that the two parties are adult, and any exploitation deriving from the family tie seems no more likely than in other adult relationships. However, adulthood begins at 18 rather than 21, and once again we have an example of a desire to shield those aged under 21 which may actually lead to the penalization of some brothers and sisters of that age.

8.8. PARAMETERS OF THE LAW ON SEXUAL ASSAULT

It is evident from this survey of English law on sexual assault that the parameters are open to considerable argument. Rules of antiquity (such as the definition of rape, and the marital exemption), of modernity (such as the definition of incest), and of recent creation (such as the doctrine of mistake in rape) are being called into question. There can be little doubt that the administration of criminal justice has paid insufficient attention to problems of sexual abuse over the years, and recent improvements in police procedures and in services for victims are to be welcomed. The difficult issue is how far this movement should be taken: changes which make it easier to convict men of sexual assault on women, or parents of the sexual abuse of children, cannot be welcomed unless one has a clear conception of the rights of defendants as well as the rights of victims. It is one thing to maintain that victims of sexual assault have

[137] CLRC, 15th Report (1984), paras. 8.15–8.17.
[138] Ibid., para. 8.22.

in the past suffered oppressive questioning by the police and oppressive cross-examination in court. It is quite another thing to suggest that it is therefore proper to place higher burdens of proof on defendants, and to restrict the presentation of the defence. Each of these proposals deserves careful examination from both points of view.[139]

The starting-point must be the empirical evidence of the effects of sexual assaults. These are variable, of course, but in many cases there are severe psychological after-effects—trauma, fear, and mistrust—which deeply affect the victim's ability to lead a normal life for some time to come. It is not suggested that each offence should be ranked according to the seriousness of its after-effects on the particular victim— although there is an argument for assuming that young victims will be particularly damaged by unwanted sexual experiences, and therefore for regarding such offences as more serious. To transfer this judgment of seriousness into desirable legal responses is no easy matter, however, for two powerful reasons. First, children might refrain from reporting or at least giving evidence if they know that a substantial prison sentence for a member of their family is the probable outcome. Second, defendants might defend cases more vigorously, causing greater trauma to child witnesses, if substantial imprisonment is probable. It can therefore be argued that, serious as the offence usually is, a policy of non-custodial treatment might be preferable in view of the effects on child victims.[140]

So far as ranking the relative seriousness of sexual assaults is concerned, however, full account should be taken of the psychological effects of such offences. Above all, one must avoid any tendency to equate the degree of harm with the degree of physical injury in a particular case, since the psychological harm may be far more severe. This chapter has dealt chiefly with the non-consensual offences, and this is important, because it is the absence of consent which is the crucial factor in many cases of sexual assault. Such offences attack the principle of freedom of choice in sexual matters, and this, together with the punishment of those who exploit the young, the mentally handicapped, and those for whom they have responsibility, should form the bedrock of the scheme of offences.

---

[139] Temkin, *Rape and the Legal Process*, 119–49.

[140] See D. Glaser and J. R. Spencer, 'Sentencing, Children's Evidence and Children's Trauma' [1990] Crim. LR 371.

This is not the place to embark upon detailed discussion of possible schemes for grading sexual assaults, but questions have been raised about the exclusion from the English offence of rape of oral and anal intercourse and penetration of the vagina by other objects. There is evidence to suggest that victims of these other forms of serious sexual assault regard them as no less serious than rape (narrowly defined). There is a strong argument for extending the offence of rape to cover these other sexual indignities, or for restructuring the law so that there are degrees of sexual assault. The sentencing decision in *Billam* (1986)[141] marks out some of the more serious varieties of sexual assault, and this could be used as a basis for introducing a new scheme of three or four graded offences: there are precedents for this in other countries. One approach would be to have first-degree sexual assault defined so as to include penetration involving the penis, vagina, or anus, together with the threat or infliction of grievous bodily harm; then a second-degree offence of the same nature involving a threat or infliction of actual bodily harm; and then a third-degree offence covering all other sexual assaults involving penetration, and a fourth offence to cover indecent assaults not involving penetration.[142] The CLRC did give serious consideration to dividing indecent assault into two grades, so the idea of grading is not entirely alien to England. One argument sometimes raised against it is that it would lead to plea-bargaining, and thus to offenders escaping with lesser convictions and lesser sentences. The fact is that this is a prominent feature of the existing law, in which there are only two major offences (rape and indecent assault) and in which some 42 per cent of those charged with rape have a plea of guilty to indecent assault accepted by the court.[143] A more refined gradation of offences could not be worse in this respect, and might improve the fairness of the labels and sentences imposed on sexual offenders. One other consequence of a fresh gradation of sexual offences might be that they would cease to be gender-specific: there are some strange inconsistencies in the law at present, and it is not at all difficult to draft offences which might be committed by males or females against males or females.

One feature of the discussion in this chapter has been to challenge the use of the concepts of consistency and 'inexorable logic' as

[141] (1986) 82 Cr. App. R 347.
[142] See Temkin, *Rape and the Legal Process*, 95–109.
[143] Wright, 'A Note on the Attrition of Rape Cases', 400.

unanswerable standards of appraisal of the law. This is not to suggest that consistency is an unworthy value: the argument is rather that there is a need to decide upon the categories to which the argument of consistency is being applied, and above all to recognize that simple resort to the allegation of inconsistency might serve to conceal the conflict between a number of social interests or principles. One example is the doctrine of mistake in rape: it might appear to be 'inexorable logic' that if the offence of rape is only committed where D knew that the woman was not consenting or was reckless as to her non-consent, a mistaken belief that she was consenting would lead to an acquittal. The inexorable logic does not, however, establish that the result is morally or socially desirable. There is a powerful argument that as far as sexual behaviour is concerned, an area in which consent makes the difference between gross violation and shared pleasure, and in which physical proximity makes it relatively easy to ask about consent, the law should in effect impose a duty to enquire. This would be done by limiting exculpatory mistakes to those based on reasonable grounds. It would partly alter the definition of rape or serious sexual assault; it would introduce an element of negligence liability; and it would also make D liable for an omission. But all those changes could be justified out of respect for the principle of freedom of choice in sexual matters, particularly where the enquiry is so straightforward. A similar argument could be mounted in relation to mistakes about age in the offences against girls and boys under 16: the basic principle of fairness to defendants underpins the subjective requirement of fault, but there is also the social policy against exploitation of the young and vulnerable. This social policy might support a duty to enquire about age wherever there might be room for doubt, and the ease of compliance (because of the inevitable physical proximity of the parties) again favours the requirement. In practice, there might be situations of doubt; a man might claim that there was nothing to alert him to the girl's age (e.g. a 15-year-old girl, who looks much older, soliciting in a street with other prostitutes). Moreover, if the criminal law is to impose duties of these kinds, it should publicize them widely, so as to ensure compliance with the principle of legality. The point of this argument is not to maintain that there would be no practical problems, but to demonstrate that there are weighty issues of principle on both sides. Appeal to 'inexorable logic' or consistency cannot conclude the argument: it over-simplifies the issues.

One policy, already mentioned, which should continue to shape the law of sexual offences is the criminalization of those who exploit the young and vulnerable. This is achieved through special offences and through rules invalidating apparent consent given by those under 16, and it is supported by the *Tyrrell* rule against convicting a participant who falls within the class protected by the offence concerned. The relevant ages of consent in English law vary: 16 seems to be the general age, but the offence of gross indecency with or towards children only applies where the child is under 14, and the age of consent for homosexual offences is 21 and the recommendation is to lower it only to 18. Once again, consistency is a proper starting-point for critical appraisal, but it is important to examine any special circumstances attendant on particular offences. For example, is there any substance in the claim that young men of 16 and 17 are more vulnerable, socially and psychologically, than young women of a similar age? Certainly there appears to be some sense in restricting any changes in the law of incest so that it continues to be an offence for a parent or grandparent to have sexual relations with a child aged 16 or 17, because children of that age are often dependent and living at home, and so the conditions for exploitation are still present at that age. Once again, the policy of using the law against those who indulge in sexual exploitation of the vulnerable may conflict with the 'logic' of overall consistency in age-limits, and this conflict must be acknowledged and confronted.[144]

9

OFFENCES OF DISHONESTY

9.1. INTRODUCTION

The principal statute in this part of the criminal law is the Theft Act 1968, and the principal offence is referred to as theft or stealing. These terms seem to convey the idea of permanently taking another's property, but in fact the definitions in the Theft Act extend the notion of stealing to a wide variety of dishonest violations of another's property rights. There is no requirement that D should have permanently deprived V of the property, but it must be proved that D *intended* to do so. D's conduct does not have to amount to a potential destruction of V's ability to use the property or act as owner: on the contrary, the courts have held that the merest interference with any right of an owner may suffice, so long as it is accompanied by dishonesty and an intention permanently to deprive. There are also some offences of temporary deprivation of property or of services, which strike at those who obtain the use of others' property rather than the property itself.

Indeed, it is the great variety of offences of dishonesty, and the breadth of their definitions, which raises problems of proportionality and the proper limits of the criminal sanction. The proportionality issues revolve partly round the problem of deciding which concept of property rights should be employed (discussed in the next paragraph) and partly round the prevalence of 'white-collar crime'. For many years there has been criminological interest in the notion of 'white-collar crime',[1] particularly deprivations of property perpetrated in commercial settings, but this has not really been reflected by changes in the law or in enforcement practice. The police have traditionally concerned themselves more with stealing from shops and burglary than with embezzlement and the various forms of frauds upon and by companies. And, although the modernization of property offences achieved by the Theft Act 1968 did have the effect of freeing the law from such constricting notions as

[1] See e.g. E. H. Sutherland, *White Collar Crime* (1949), and Michael Levi, *Regulating Fraud: White Collar Crime and the Criminal Process* (1987).

thieves having to 'take and carry away' property in order to be convicted, the Act provides little indication of a determination to treat white-collar offences as equivalent to other forms of theft: only sections 17 and 19, on false accounting and on false statements by company directors, achieve this. It is true that the 1980s saw the creation of several new offences in the spheres of white–collar crime and 'city fraud', but these offences remain outside the Theft Acts and the proposed Criminal Code,[2] making it difficult to claim that they have been integrated into a new scheme of property offences which achieves a realistic proportionality among the degrees of offending. There remains more than a suggestion that the Theft Acts are 'real crime', whereas the Companies Acts, Financial Services Acts, and other legislation are 'regulatory' in nature, despite the indictable offences they contain, and despite some maximum penalties (e.g. seven years for misleading statements or practices contrary to section 47 of the Financial Services Act 1986, and for fraudulent inducement to make a deposit contrary to section 35 of the Banking Act 1987) which are only slightly less than the maxima for theft and deception (ten years' imprisonment).[3] This chapter's discussion of the 'traditional' property offences will attempt to keep the 'new' offences of dishonesty well in sight.

The idea of dishonesty, explored in the context of the crime of theft below (see Chapter 9.2 (e)), seems to be the notion which binds these offences together. But they are also often grouped together as 'property offences', since they involve some violation of the property rights of another. Personal property is one of the basic organizing features of many modern societies, and it may be defended as an institution on grounds of individual autonomy and rights.[4] Individuals should generally be free to decide how to spend their money; if they choose to purchase property with it, this should be respected in the same way as their own physical integrity. This liberal political philosophy does not exclude the compulsory payment of taxes, and the approach should therefore find room for the notion of state property—property in public ownership, which no individual citizen is free to take for his or her exclusive use. So, the foundation of these property or dishonesty offences is that it is

[2] See Law Com. No. 177, clauses 139–77, which cover only the offences under the Theft Act and forgery.
[3] If the Criminal Justice Bill 1991 is enacted as proposed, the maximum for theft will be reduced to 7 years.
[4] See e.g. R. Nozick, *Anarchy, State and Utopia* (1974).

wrong for any person to take more than his or her fair share—'fair' being interpreted in the light of legally ordained methods of property distribution (including, at present, such things as earned income, inherited wealth, public funds derived from taxation, state benefits paid to certain citizens, etc.).

Agreement with the proposition that the law should uphold and respect property rights leaves the question of proportionality: what priority should it give to them? There has long been an allegation that English criminal law is too concerned with property offences—at the expense of offences against the person and against the environment. Whether, or to what extent, this allegation is factually accurate cannot be tested fully here, but two points should be made. First, the allegation may concern enforcement as much as the written laws. The police investigate and prosecute relatively fewer crimes within business and commercial circles. This may, in turn, be because offences are dealt with informally in other ways, by dismissing an employee who has been caught committing an offence, for example.[5] Recent years have seen the creation of the Serious Fraud Office as part of a stated determination to pursue commercial frauds more vigorously,[6] but the early results have done little to answer the critics who denounce its creation as 'tokenism', aimed at concealing the persistent imbalance in the prosecution of 'crimes in the streets' and 'crimes in the suites'. Second, there is the question of whether the threshold of the criminal law is lower in property offences than elsewhere. Civil law has a far greater involvement in offences of dishonesty than in violent or sexual offences; the very questions of property ownership and property rights are the subject of a complicated mass of rules relating to contracts, trusts, intellectual property, restitution, and so forth. Many property losses could be tackled through the civil courts, by suing under one of these heads of civil law. It may be true that the amounts concerned are often too small to justify the time and expense of civil proceedings, but should that not make us pause to consider whether the criminal sanction is being properly deployed here, and whether adequate weight is being given to the policy of minimum criminalization discussed in Chapter 3.2(a)? If the criminal law is to be reserved for significant challenges to the legal order, should there not be vigilance about the extension of the criminal sanction into spheres in which

---

[5] See Levi, *Regulating Fraud*, and id., 'Suite Justice: Sentencing for Fraud' [1989] Crim. LR 420; see also L. H. Leigh, *The Control of Commercial Fraud* (1982).

[6] J. Wood, 'The Serious Fraud Office', [1989] Crim. LR 175.

civil remedies exist, or where some non–criminal procedure might be more proportionate? And is it not true that many dishonest dealings which amount to criminal offences are in practice the subject of nothing more than regulatory action or civil penalties, from commercial frauds to income tax frauds? These are questions to which we will return at the end of this chapter.

Attention should also be drawn at this introductory stage to the respective roles of the legislature and the courts in property crimes. Parliament has, through the Theft Acts of 1968 and 1978, provided some fairly broad offences. The appellate courts have, in dealing with appeals, developed the law in ways which often extend the ambit of already wide offences in order to criminalize persons whose conduct seems wrongful. Although the decisions have not been all one way, there is much evidence here of the relative impotence of the principle of restrictive construction.[7]

9.2. THE OFFENCE OF THEFT[8]

Theft is not the most serious of the English offences against property, but it must be discussed first, because it is an ingredient of some more serious offences, notably robbery and burglary. The offence of theft, contrary to section 1 of the Theft Act 1968, may be divided into five elements. The three conduct elements are that there must be: (i) an appropriation; of (ii) property; which (iii) belongs to another. The fault elements are that this must be done: (iv) with an intention of permanent deprivation; and (v) dishonestly. Discussion of each of these five elements in turn will demonstrate just how extensive the English law of theft is in some directions, and how restrictive in other directions.

(a) Appropriation

Before the Theft Act 1968, English law used to require proof that D had taken and carried away the property, a requirement far too stringent for some types of property (e.g. bank balances), and yet a requirement which at least ensured that certain overt physical acts had to be established before conviction. The Theft Act broadens the law's basis by requiring merely an appropriation. In most cases this will involve taking possession of someone else's property

---

[7] See the examples given above, Ch. 3.3(*k*).

[8] There are two monographs on the law of theft: J. C. Smith, *The Law of Theft* (6th edn., 1989), and Edward Griew, *The Theft Acts* (6th edn., 1990).

without consent. Section 3 of the Act defines an appropriation as 'any assumption by a person of the rights of an owner', and that causes no problems in the normal type of case. Section 3(2) makes special provision for a person who acquires property by purchasing it in good faith and then discovers that there was a defect in the seller's title (e.g. the goods were stolen): in these circumstances it is not an appropriation if D continues to exercise the rights of an owner.

Some idea of the breadth of the concept of 'appropriation' is given by the other provision in section 3(1), which extends it to cover a case where D has come by the property without stealing it and where D subsequently assumes 'a right to it by keeping or dealing with it as owner'. This includes cases where D finds property which he does not initially intend to keep (perhaps intending to report the finding), but later decides to do so. The wording of section 3(1) seems to allow a simple change of mind, unaccompanied by any overt act, to constitute appropriation. Put another way, the mere omission to return the goods or to report the finding constitutes (together with the change of mind) the keeping which amounts to an appropriation. This is a dramatic demonstration of how far the law has retreated from the requirement of 'taking and carrying away' which characterized the previous law. It also raises questions about the justification for this omissions liability, and whether citizens have fair warning of it.

Let us explore further the breadth of the definition of appropriation as 'any assumption of the rights of an owner'. Does this mean that one can appropriate property even if one obtains it with the consent of the owner? On the face of it, this might seem absurd: surely one cannot be said to steal property if the owner consents to part with it. But the House of Lords has pointed out that the definition of theft does not include the phrase 'without the consent of the owner', as did the previous offence; and in *Lawrence* (1972)[9] it held that a taking can amount to theft, even though the owner consents to it. The facts in that case were that V, an Italian who spoke little English, arrived in England and wished to hire a taxi to take him to an address in London. He offered D, the taxi–driver, enough money to cover the lawful fare, but D asked for more and, as V held his wallet open, D took more notes from it. The defence argued strenuously that this could not be theft because V consented

[9] [1972] AC 626.

to D taking the extra money, but the House of Lords held this irrelevant. The definition of theft does not *require* the taking to be without the owner's consent, and D had appropriated V's property dishonestly and with the intention of depriving V permanently of it. This decision has given rise to much controversy and to diverse interpretations.[10] One technical question is whether the money still belonged to V when D took it from V's wallet: if it was V's intention that ownership should pass to D, maybe element (ii) in the definition was missing. But perhaps the most regrettable fact is that D was prosecuted for theft at all, since the case seems to be an obvious one of obtaining by deception. An English appeal court cannot alter the charge or order a retrial on the different charge, and so the choice lay between quashing the conviction of a manifestly dishonest person and reaching a decision which might well destabilize the law of theft. The courts are understandably loath to take the former course.

The effect of *Lawrence*, then, was to broaden the law of theft to cover many occasions of consensual taking—so long as the required fault elements could be proved. In practice, if a taking was manifestly dishonest, it could probably be squeezed within the notion of appropriation. The difficulty in stating that this remains the law derives from another House of Lords decision, *Morris* (1984).[11] The essence of the two cases consolidated in the appeal was that D took goods from a supermarket shelf, replaced their existing price-labels with labels showing lower prices, and then took them to the checkout, intending to buy them at the lower price. As in *Lawrence*, the cases proceeded on theft charges rather than on obtaining or attempting to obtain by deception. The House of Lords upheld the convictions, but propounded a more restrictive idea of appropriation. It was held that the concept of appropriation involves 'an act by way of adverse interference with or usurpation of' the owner's rights, and that this will generally require D to have committed some unauthorized act. This was clearly fulfilled in *Morris*, since the attaching of price-labels by customers is unauthorized. The House of Lords also made it clear that an appropriation occurs when D assumes 'a right of the owner', and that it is not necessary to show that D assumed all the rights of the owner.

[10] In addition to the monographs by Smith (*The Law of Theft*) and by Griew (*The Theft Acts*), see Glanville Williams, 'Theft, Consent and Illegality' [1977] Crim. LR 127.

[11] [1984] AC 320.

It will readily be appreciated that there are cases in which the test in *Lawrence* and the test in *Morris* conflict and indicate different results. The former test holds that there can be an appropriation even if it is with the consent of the owner; the latter that there can be an appropriation only if it involves an act which is not authorized expressly or impliedly by the owner. To give one example: if D takes goods from the shelf of a supermarket and places them in the wire basket provided, this cannot be an appropriation according to *Morris* (no unauthorised act) but it can be according to *Lawrence* (appropriation despite consent of owner). English law on this point is uncertain, with some decisions following one precedent, some following the other, and one decision claiming that the two tests are not inconsistent.[12] Reconciliation of the decisions is possible with ingenuity—*Lawrence* might apply where D actually obtains rights of ownership by his conduct, and *Morris* in other cases—but the courts have not stated this.

What is more important in the present context is the extensive reach of the law of theft, whichever test the courts prefer. On the *Lawrence* test, a taking with consent can amount to theft if the two fault elements are present: this effectively reduces the conduct element almost to vanishing point, since D's act is neutral or even permitted. On the *Morris* test, D's act must be unauthorized, but even that does not narrow the offence substantially. In the case itself, D would have committed theft as soon as he attached the wrong label to the item—before he had even presented the goods at the check-out point, let alone tried to leave the shop with them. So long as the fault elements can be proved—and they may, of course, be proved by inference—the committing of any unauthorized act which cannot be dismissed as a joke may amount to the completed offence of theft.

In terms of the logic of the Theft Act, this means not only that many offences of obtaining or attempting to obtain property by deception are also offences of theft, but also that theft is committed in such cases at a much earlier point than even an attempt to obtain by deception. Any policy of minimum criminalization (see Chapter 3.2(a)) seems to have little effect, and the principle of maximum

---

[12] Among the decisions favouring the *Lawrence* approach is the civil case of *Dobson v. General Accident Fire & Life Assurance Corporation* [1989] QB, and among the decisions favouring the *Morris* approach are *Skipp* [1975] Crim. LR 114, and *Fritschy* [1985] Crim. LR 745. The Court of Appeal in *Philippou* (1989) 89 Cr. App. R 290, made a rather unconvincing attempt to reconcile the two decisions.

certainty in the law (see Chapter 3.3(i)) also seems to be sacrificed to notions of social defence against rogues. In terms of the structure of English criminal law, the offence of theft goes much further in criminalizing those who threaten the property rights of others than most of the equivalent offences against the person. The offence of theft has been reduced to the assumption of *any* right of a property owner, if the court is satisfied as to D's dishonesty and intention to deprive the other permanently. The actual circumstances of the assumption need not represent a permanent or even temporary threat to V's property rights: after all, the full offence is committed by label–swapping inside a supermarket. What offence against the person criminalizes someone who is so far from the infliction of actual harm with which the crime is concerned?

(b) Property

In order to be stolen, the object concerned must be 'property' within the meaning of section 4 of the Theft Act 1968. In the vast majority of cases this will cause no problem, but the relevant definition of property is such as to exclude some things of value. Since, as we have just seen, the offence merely requires an appropriation, and does not require any realistic threat to the permanence of another's property rights, one might expect the definition of property to cover a wide range of property interests.

There are, however, various limitations in section 4. In the first place, the general proposition is that land cannot be stolen. There are some exceptions to this, and of course it is quite possible to convict someone of theft of title–deeds or of obtaining them by deception, but the land itself, being of a certain permanence, remains. Various rules exist about the application of the law of theft to flowers, fruit, and berries.[13] Section 4(1) appears to be couched in very broad terms—'property includes money and all other property, real or personal, including things in action and other intangible property'—and it is certainly appropriate to include some forms of property with which the previous law could not cope. For example, one can steal from another person's bank account by transferring money out of it. The property which one appropriates here is not the account-holder's *money*, strictly speaking, but the account-holder's *right to sue the bank* for whatever money stands to credit in

---

[13] See ss. 4(2) and (3) of the Theft Act 1968.

that account.[14] The same analysis is possible where the account-holder has an overdraft arrangement with the bank, and someone else dishonestly draws money out.[15]

But there are limits. There is no property capable of being stolen in electricity or in a dead body or its parts. More importantly, there is no property in confidential information, such as business secrets and examination papers. Thus, if D purloins a confidential document of this kind, photocopies it and replaces it, he cannot be charged with theft: what has been taken does not constitute property.[16] Injunctions may be obtained in the civil courts to prevent interference with, or the abuse of, such secrets, but the criminal offence of theft does not extend so far. The problem has become more pertinent with the increasing use of computers as means of storing information: if D 'hacks into' V's computer system, retrieving from it some confidential information which is then noted down, has any 'property' been stolen? The answer is no, and this indicates the need for further legislation to deal specifically with this kind of stealing.[17] This is provided by the Computer Misuse Act 1990, which creates three offences of unlawfully entering another's computer system, with dishonest intent. It is right that this form of property violation should be the subject of special provisions: any artificial extension of the present structure of the law of theft to cover such cases, which lie far from the ordinary stealing of tangible property, would probably be less successful and might have unexpected side–effects. It is also right that the law should criminalize this kind of property violation, which might be much more serious financially than many of the takings which fulfil the basic definition of theft.

(c) 'Belonging to Another'

The old law of larceny was concerned mainly to penalise those who took possession of property from those in possession, whereas there are many other ways of depriving a legal owner of property. How far should the law go in criminalizing appropriations of property from persons other than the legal owner? Section 5 of the Theft Act 1968 succeeds in spreading the net wide: property is regarded as belonging 'to any person having possession or control of it, or

[14] See the discussion by E. Griew, 'Stealing and Obtaining Bank Credits' [1986] Crim. LR, 356.

[15] See Smith, *The Law of Theft*, para. 110.

[16] *Oxford v. Moss* (1978) 68 Cr. App. R 183, and generally R. G. Hammond, 'Theft of Information' (1984) 100 LQR, 252.

[17] See Martin Wasik, 'The Computer Misuse Act 1990' [1990] Crim. LR 767.

having in it any proprietary right or interest (not being an equitable interest arising only from an agreement to transfer or grant an interest)'. The first phrase, 'possession or control', may be wide enough to enable D to be charged with theft of, say, a radio–telephone from V, even if V is merely borrowing it for two weeks while the owner is on holiday, or if V has acquired it on a day's trial, etc. There is no need to establish the precise legal relationship between the possessor and the supposed owner of the goods; for Theft Act purposes, the goods are treated as belonging to the temporary possessor, too.

The second phrase of the definition shows that one part-owner of property can be convicted of theft from the other part-owner. For example, a partner who appropriates property in order to deprive the other partner of partnership property may be liable to theft so long as the other elements (notably dishonesty: there must be no claim of right) are present.[18] A controversial question is whether company controllers may be convicted of stealing the property of the company—meaning by 'company controllers' one or more persons who, between them, own the entire shareholding in a company. If D and E (being the sole shareholders) transfer money from the company's account to their own personal accounts, it might seem strained to say that the company's property 'belongs to another' when the sole shareholders are the very persons who are doing the appropriating. One possible answer to this, adopted in the two leading English decisions,[19] is that such cases may in principle amount to theft because the company is a separate legal entity from its controllers. However, a company can only act through human agency, and where the controller's act is within the powers delegated to him or her by the company, it will in effect be the act of the company. It would be rare for a prosecution to be brought where the shareholders, acting together, simply shifted funds from the company to their personal accounts: there may be no aggrieved victim and no dishonesty. Different principles apply where the purpose of the transaction is dishonestly to remove funds from the reach of the company's creditors. Where a company becomes insolvent and is unable to pay its creditors in full, the courts have developed a principle that the overriding duty of the directors is to

---

[18] *Bonner* (1970) 54 Cr. App. R 257.
[19] *Attorney-General's Reference (No. 2 of 1982)* [1984] QB 624, and *Philippou* (1989) 89 Cr. App. R 290.

preserve the assets for the benefit of the creditors.[20] In these circumstances a decision to remove assets for their own benefit would clearly be a personal act of the directors, and might well, if dishonesty were established, constitute theft.

In view of the gain and of the dishonesty, such cases are surely as proper a concern of the criminal law as shoplifting. Whether they should be classified as theft, or dealt with under the Companies Act offence of fraudulent trading,[21] bears on such matters as the stigma of conviction (theft may be more stigmatic than a 'breach' of the Companies Act) and the mode of enforcement. Thus there are arguments in favour of criminalization—and against the marginalization of such offences—by placing them within the Theft Act. Whether the troubled concept of appropriation and the existing definitions within section 5 are adequate to the purpose is doubtful, and legislative amendment seems desirable.

Section 5 of the Theft Act also elucidates, and perhaps extends, the definition of 'belonging to another' in two distinct ways. Section 5(3) expressly includes property received 'from or on account of another' where the person receiving it is 'under an obligation to the other to retain and deal with that property or its proceeds in a particular way'. This applies to the treasurer of a sports club or a holiday fund who misappropriates some of the funds; it does not extend to the travel agent or other trader who receives a deposit for a purchase and then fails to fulfil the contract.[22] The latter case is governed by the principle that it is not necessary to criminalize mere breach of contract: the civil law generally provides adequate remedies. The former, 'club treasurer' cases are distinguished by the fact that the subscribers retain a specific interest in the way in which particular money is dealt with. Section 5(3) provides only for those cases where D is responsible for a particular sum of money or its proceeds on another's behalf, in which case there will usually (but not always) be a trust created.[23] Section 5(4) extends the definition of 'belonging to another' to cases where D 'gets property by another's mistake and is under an obligation to make restoration (in whole or in part) . . . '. The obvious example of this is the mistaken overpayment: if money is credited to D's bank account in error, and

---

[20] See C. A. Riley, 'Directors' Duties and the Interests of Creditors' (1989) 10 *Company Lawyer* 87.
[21] Companies Act 1989, s. 41.
[22] *Hall* [1973] QB 126.
[23] The case would therefore be covered by s. 5(1) of the Theft Act 1968.

D resolves to keep it, this amounts to theft of the overpaid sum.[24] If the overpayment is by a bookmaker, there is no legal obligation involved and so section 5(4) cannot be invoked to support a theft conviction.[25]

(d) 'The Intention Permanently to Deprive'

It must be proved that D intended that the person from whom he appropriated the property should be deprived of it permanently. We have already seen that permanent deprivation itself is not necessary for theft: a temporary appropriation will suffice. But the ambit of the offence is restricted by the need for an *intention* permanently to deprive. Thus, the essential minimum of the offence becomes temporary appropriation with the intention of permanent deprivation.

The Theft Act does not define 'intention permanently to deprive'. Intention presumably bears the same meaning as elsewhere in the criminal law,[26] and therefore covers cases where D knows that a virtually certain result of the appropriation will be that the other is deprived of the property permanently. In practice, most cases will fall into place fairly easily, and there will usually be no theft where D takes property and then abandons it where it might be found. The description 'stolen car' is therefore inaccurate if it refers to a car taken from its owner and then abandoned some distance away, since cars are normally returned to their owners by the police, and this is well known. Section 12 of the Theft Act 1968 provides a special offence for taking a car without the owner's consent, which does not require proof of an intention permanently to deprive. A car *would* be stolen, however, if it were taken with a view to changing its identity marks and then reselling it.

Although the Theft Act does not define 'an intention permanently to deprive', it does provide, in section 6, an extension of the concept. It states, in a poorly drafted compromise provision,[27] that persons are to be treated as having an intention permanently to deprive in certain circumstances. The general principle is that where D's intention is 'to treat the thing as his own to dispose of regardless of the other's rights', this is equivalent to an intention

---

[24] *Attorney-General's Reference (No. 1 of 1983)* [1985] QB 182; it is arguable whether s. 5(4) is needed to achieve this result after the civil case of *Chase Manhattan Bank NA v. Israel–British Bank* [1981] Ch. 105.

[25] *Gilks* (1972) 56 Cr. App. R 734.   [26] See above, Ch. 5.3(*b*).

[27] See J. R. Spencer, 'The Metamorphosis of Section 6 of the Theft Act' [1977] Crim. LR 653.

permanently to deprive. One example of this is the ransom principle, where D takes V's property, telling V that he will return it only if V pays the asking price. D is clearly treating the property as 'his own to dispose of regardless of the other's rights'.[28] As a general principle, this is surely correct: there can be some takings where, as section 6 puts it, D does not mean 'the other permanently to lose the thing itself', and yet where the substance of D's intended taking and V's intended loss is little different from permanent deprivation.

Section 6 goes on to give two examples of this. One, set out in section 6(2), is where D parts with V's property under a condition as to its return which D may be unable to fulfil: the obvious example of this is pawning another's property, hoping to be able to redeem it at some time in the future. The other example, in section 6(1), is where D borrows or lends V's property: this may amount to D treating it as his own to dispose of 'if, but only if, the borrowing or lending is for a period and in circumstances equivalent to an outright taking or disposal'. Although this is an extension of the idea of intending permanent deprivation, it is hedged about with fairly tough conditions. Its scope was considered by the Court of Appeal in *Lloyd* (1985),[29] where a cinema employee removed films from the cinema for a few hours, thereby enabling others to copy the films with a view to selling 'pirate' copies. The employee always intended to return the films, and always did. Clearly, his conduct in allowing others to make copies did significantly reduce the value of the films, but it is not possible to say, as section 6(1) requires, that his borrowing constituted an outright taking. He did not render the films valueless, even though he did reduce their commercial value by enabling the production of copies. Fewer people might pay to watch the films at the cinema. Lord Lane CJ stated the effect of section 6(1) in these terms: 'A mere borrowing is never enough to constitute the necessary guilty mind unless the intention is to return the "thing" in such a changed state that it can truly be said that all its goodness or virtue has gone.'[30]

The application of this test may be illustrated by D, who takes V's railway season-ticket, which expires on 31 January, and maintains that it was always his intention to return it on 1 February. His intention clearly is to return the ticket, which may be physically unchanged but, since it will no longer be valid, it is fair to describe it as being in a 'changed state'. 'All its goodness' will have gone by

---

[28] *Coffey* [1987] Crim. LR 498; cf. *Chan Man-Sin v. R* [1988] 1 All ER 1.
[29] [1985] QB 829.   [30] Ibid. 836.

1 February and so D is liable to conviction. But if D maintains that it was always his intention to return the ticket on 30 January, it will still be valid for one more day and, on the *Lloyd* test, D would have to be acquitted (if the court believed the story). Thus, by using the word 'all', Lord Lane made it clear that few borrowings will amount to theft. Some might argue that the wording of section 6 is slightly more flexible—'in circumstances making it *equivalent* to an outright taking'—but the only way of introducing greater flexibility would be to hold that an intention substantially to reduce the value of the property would suffice, and such a broad reading would go against the principle of maximum certainty (see Chapter 3.3(*i*)). The real problem here is that there is no general offence of temporary deprivation, and judicial attempts to stretch an offence based on an intention permanently to deprive are likely to produce difficulties.

Any review of the law of theft ought to consider whether there is not a strong case for dispensing with the requirement of an intention permanently to deprive. At present there are only two such offences in the Theft Act—section 12, penalizing the taking of cars, bicycles, etc., without the owner's consent; and section 11, penalizing the removal of an article on display in places open to the public, such as museums and galleries. Among the arguments for penalizing temporary deprivation generally,[31] probably the strongest is that the chief value of many items lies in their use, and if someone obtains an item for a period and deprives the other of its use for the same period, there may be far more gain and loss involved than in many cases of theft in which there is an intention permanently to deprive. In many similar cases where deception is used, there will be an offence of obtaining services by deception;[32] but if the advantage is gained boldly, without deception, the criminal law is rarely broken. The usual counter–argument is that the criminal law would be extended to many trivial 'borrowings' without consent, and that the police and courts would be flooded by such cases. However, this does not appear to have occurred in those European and Commonwealth jurisdictions which have extended their law of theft in this way. The real question is whether a sufficiently strong case for extending the ambit of the criminal law has been made: police and prosecutorial discretion might serve to eliminate minor cases, but

---

[31] See Glanville Williams, 'Temporary Appropriation Should Be Theft' [1981] Crim. LR 129, considered by the Law Commission Working Paper No. 104, 'Conspiracy to Defraud' (1988).

[32] See below, Ch. 9.7(*a*).

does not the existence of major cases justify legislation? Could these major cases, such as unauthorized copying of materials and other commercial malpractices, be covered adequately by specific offences?[33] Would one advantage be the removal of any need for provisions for the artificial extension of the idea of 'an intention permanently to deprive'?

(e) The Element of Dishonesty

Perhaps the core concept in the Theft Acts of 1968 and 1978 is dishonesty. The breadth of the definition of appropriation means that the finding of dishonesty may often make the difference between conviction and acquittal. In most cases, the presence or absence of dishonesty turns not so much on D's view of the situation but on the characterization of D's conduct by the jury or magistrates—and that characterization may be grounded in social attitudes and moral judgments which proceed from a particular social perspective. Let us consider the details.

The 1968 Act does not provide a definition of dishonesty, but it does stipulate in section 2 that, in each of three instances, an appropriation may not be considered dishonest for the purposes of the crime of theft.[34] The first instance, in section 2(1)(a), is where D believes that he has the legal right to deprive V of it. An example of this is where D seizes money from V, believing that V owes him the money.[35] It will be noticed that this turns on D's actual belief, however unreasonable that might be (so long as the court is left in reasonable doubt on the matter), and that it will often involve a mistake of law. It therefore constitutes an exception to the general policy that citizens are presumed to know the law,[36] although the mistakes covered by section 2(1)(a) will invariably be mistakes of civil law. The second instance, in section 2(1)(b), is where D believes that V would have consented if V had known of the circumstances. The third, in section 2(1)(c), is where D believes that the owner of the property cannot be discovered by taking reasonable steps. This applies chiefly to people who find property and conclude that it would be too difficult to trace the owner.

The main feature of section 2, then, is that it removes three types

---

[33] On which, see Law Com. WP 104.
[34] Section 2 does not apply to the term 'dishonesty' as used in other offences under the Theft Act such as the deception offences and handling, nor to conspiracy to defraud.
[35] *Robinson* [1977] Crim. LR 173.   [36] See above, Ch. 6.7.

of case from the possible ambit of 'dishonesty', making it clear that it is the personal beliefs of defendants which are crucial here. The only other legislative clue to the meaning of 'dishonesty' is the declaration in section 2(2) that an appropriation may be dishonest even though D is willing to pay for the property. Apart from that, the definition of dishonesty is at large, and the courts have been left to develop an approach. They have insisted that the meaning of dishonesty is a matter for the jury or magistrates and not a matter of law, but the judges have gone on to lay down a proper approach to the question. It seems that there are three stages. First, the court must ascertain D's beliefs in relation to the appropriation—the reasons, motivations, explanations. Second, the jury or magistrates must decide whether a person acting with those beliefs would be regarded as dishonest according to the current standards of ordinary decent people. Third, if there is evidence that D thought that the conduct was not dishonest according to those general standards, D should be acquitted if the court is left in reasonable doubt on the matter.

The first and second stages in the test were laid down in *Feely* (1973),[37] where D had 'borrowed' money from his employer's safe despite a warning that employees must not do so. D's explanation was that he intended to repay the sum out of money which his employer owed him (which amply covered the deficiency). The Court of Appeal held that the key question for the court should have been whether a person who takes money in those circumstances and with that intention is dishonest according to the current standards of ordinary decent people. The third stage was added by *Ghosh* (1982),[38] where the Court of Appeal tried to reconcile two lines of earlier cases. The example given by the court was of a foreigner failing to pay when travelling on English public transport in the belief that it is free. However, as has been pointed out,[39] this is a poor example, which would render the third stage superfluous. D's own beliefs are already considered at the first stage, so that, in the example given, the court would then consider at the second stage whether a foreigner with that belief would be dishonest according to the current standards of ordinary decent people. The answer would surely be no. Moreover, even though the third stage does not provide a defence where D acts on strong moral or social beliefs which he knows are not shared by 'ordinary decent people', it may

---

[37] [1973] QB 530.   [38] [1982] QB 1053.
[39] See K. Campbell, 'The Test of Dishonesty in *R v. Ghosh*' [1984] CLJ 349.

provide a defence for the person who thinks that 'ordinary decent people' would not regard his conduct as dishonest. Whether people who are so out of tune with current standards should be acquitted is a difficult issue. But the overall complexity makes it hardly surprising that the Court of Appeal has declared that the third stage should not be mentioned to a jury unless the facts specifically raise it.[40]

This three-stage test of dishonesty evolved by the courts is complex and controversial. Moreover, its sphere of operation is enormous: around one-half of all indictable charges tried by the courts include a requirement of dishonesty. The few specific instances covered by section 2 are relevant only to a few theft charges. Where the charge is deception or any other offence covered by the Theft Act, it is the three-stage judicial test which governs completely. Yet that test is open to serious objections.[41] The root of the problem has been the assumption, first stated by the Criminal Law Revision Committee[42] and then espoused by the courts in the 1970s,[43] that dishonesty is easily recognized and that the concept should therefore be treated as an ordinary word. Neither part of this assumption is well founded. Dishonesty may be easily recognized in some situations, but it is far more difficult in situations with which a jury or magistrates are unfamiliar—such as alleged business fraud or financial misdealing. Moreover, much depends on who is responsible for characterizing conduct as dishonest. In a multi-cultural society with widely differing degrees of wealth, it may often happen that someone who is poor or is a member of a minority community may have his or her conduct characterized as honest or dishonest by people who are relatively wealthy and are members of the majority community. There may well be an additional element of hypocrisy in this, since it is well known that practices which are strictly dishonest abound in the business or private lives of people at all levels.[44] Many, or most, forms of employment have their 'perks', according to which some practices of employees taking or using company property have become so traditional as to be thought of

---

[40] *Roberts* (1985) 84 Cr. App. R 117, *Price* [1990] Crim. LR 200.
[41] E. Griew, 'Dishonesty: The Objections to *Feely* and *Ghosh*' [1985] Crim. LR 341.
[42] Criminal Law Revision Committee, 8th Report, *Theft and Related Offences* (1966, Cmnd 2977), para. 39.
[43] But strongly criticized in Australia: see e.g. *Salvo* [1980] VR 401.
[44] For details from the most specific to the most general, see e.g. S. Henry, *The Hidden Economy* (1978); G. Mars, *Cheats at Work* (1982); and F. Pearce, *Crimes of the Powerful: Marxism, Crime and Deviance* (1978).

almost as an entitlement, and employers are content to connive at this. This all tends to suggest that there are situations in which dishonesty cannot be regarded as an ordinary word with a clear, shared meaning.

There are further objections to using the 'current standards of ordinary decent people' as a test for establishing dishonesty. It embodies a derogation from the principle of maximum certainty in the criminal law.[45] It also increases the risk of different courts reaching different verdicts on essentially similar sets of facts, and leaves room for the infiltration of irrelevant factors. The *Feely* problem of 'borrowing' money without permission is not unusual, but differently constituted juries might take a different view of its dishonesty. The inherent uncertainty of the test might also work against the efficiency of the system, by encouraging defendants to contest charges in the hope of finding a tribunal which is either sympathetic in its view of current standards or confused by the complexity of the three-stage test.

It is far easier to criticize the test, however, than to propose a replacement which overcomes all the objections. One thing which is certain is that dishonesty has a wide variety of manifestations. Any notion that Parliament could simply add further situations to the three instances specified in section 2 of the 1968 Act, to the point where most cases of dishonesty are covered, is chimerical. There may be an argument for some expansion of section 2, but the most fruitful line of development is likely to be a general legislative definition, interpreted by the courts. One proposal for a general definition is that a person is dishonest when acting 'knowing that the appropriation will or may be detrimental to the interests of the owner in a significant practical way'.[46] This may have the advantage of ruling out doubtful and trivial cases, but it would fall well below the principle of maximum certainty until the courts had developed some specific criteria. It appears to depend on D's 'subjective' knowledge, but in reality the notion of significant and practical detriment would probably become a judgment for the court in all but the rare cases where D could advance a particular explanation for his own belief. In that sense, the proposed test would not cure any tendency of the concept of dishonesty to be a tool used on

---

[45] See above, Ch. 3.3(*i*) and (*j*).

[46] D. W. Elliott, 'Dishonesty in Theft: A Dispensable Concept' [1982] Crim. LR 395, adapting the words of McGarvie J, in the Australian case of *Bonollo* [1981] VR 633, at 656.

behalf of wealthy people to convict the poor and members of minority communities; but it is arguable that legal definitions and procedures themselves cannot achieve that, since it depends on policing decisions, prosecution policy, and wider social attitudes.

9.3. ROBBERY

Robbery can be one of the most serious offences in the criminal calendar, and average sentences are higher than for any other crime apart from rape and murder. The definition of the offence is within the Theft Act 1968, but it is largely an offence of violence and is triable only in the Crown Court. Some 4,500 persons are convicted of robbery each year, and many of these offences are planned attacks on persons in charge of money or other valuables at banks, building societies, or in security companies. The starting-point when sentencing someone convicted of robbery of a bank or security vehicle in which firearms were carried and no serious injury done has been held to be fifteen years' imprisonment.[47] Sentences are therefore high, but the detection rate is rather low, with fewer than 25 per cent of robberies 'cleared up' in recent years.

The legal elements of robbery contrary to section 8 of the Theft Act 1968 are theft accompanied by the use of force. It follows from this that if D has a defence to theft, there can be no conviction for robbery. Thus where D brandished a knife at V in order to get V to hand over money which D believed he was owed, it was held that this could be neither theft nor robbery if the jury found that D did believe that he had a legal right to the money (and so was not dishonest: section 2(i)(a)).[48] Conviction for another offence, such as possessing an offensive weapon or blackmail, might be possible on these facts. But if there is no theft, there can be no robbery.

The legal definition of robbery has given rise to little case-law. The only noteworthy development has been the courts' interpretation of the minimum amount of force needed to convert a theft into a robbery. Section 8 of the Act requires it to be proved that, immediately before or at the time of stealing, and in order to steal, D 'used force on a person or put or sought to put any person in fear of being then and there subjected to force'. As a matter of statutory interpretation there are several points here. The force or threat of

---

[47] *Turner* (1975) 61 Cr. App. R 67, at 89–92, above p. 336.
[48] *Robinson* [1977] Crim. LR 173; cf. *Attorney-General's Reference (No. 2 of 1989)*, (1989) 11 Cr. App. R(S) 481.

force must take place immediately before or at the time of the theft: this seems to exclude the use of force immediately after the offence, but the Court of Appeal has circumvented this limitation by holding that the appropriation element in theft continues while the thieves are tying up their victims so as to make good their escape.[49] The force must be used in order to steal, not merely on the same occasion as the stealing. Where there is a threat of force, the threat must be to subject a person (not necessarily the victim of the theft) to immediate violence—a threat to injure at some time in the future would be insufficient for robbery. The question which has engaged the attention of the courts is, at first sight, a perfectly simple one: what does the phrase 'uses force on a person' mean?

The result of *Dawson and James* (1976)[50] seems to be that bumping into someone so as to knock him off balance is sufficient force. The result of *Clouden* (1987)[51] seems to be that pulling V's handbag in a way which causes her hand to be pulled downwards amounts to using force on a person. None of the defendants in these cases could claim great social or moral merit in their activities, but should they be classified as robbers rather than mere thieves? Of course it is difficult to draw the line between sufficient and insufficient force, but if robbery is to continue to be regarded as a serious offence, triable only on indictment and punishable with life imprisonment, surely something more than a bump, a push, or a pull should be required. There is a case for requiring at least the threat or the actual causing of injury, together with theft, as constituents of robbery. This would leave lesser cases to be dealt with by means of the laws on theft and assault, reserving the label 'robbery' for non minor cases, and thereby promoting the principle of fair labelling (Chapter 3.3(*l*)).

9.4. BLACKMAIL

It was noted earlier that the criminal law does not penalize all threats of violence,[52] although it does criminalize threats made in order to obtain sexual intercourse.[53] We have just seen that robbery

---

[49] *Hale* (1978) 68 Cr. App. R 415, above p. 133.

[50] (1976) 64 Cr. App. R 150.

[51] [1987] Crim. LR 56; the decision also goes directly against the Criminal Law Revision Committee's view (8th Report (1966), para. 65), that 'we should not regard mere snatching of property, such as a handbag, from an unresisting owner as using force for the purpose of the definition, though it might be so if the owner resisted'.

[52] See above, Ch. 8.3(*e*).　　　　　　[53] See above, 8.5(*f*).

is committed if a person uses a threat of immediate violence in order to steal property. The essence of blackmail contrary to section 21 of the Theft Act 1968 is the making of a demand, reinforced by menaces, with a view to making a gain or inflicting a loss. Blackmail is therefore wider than the other offences committed by threats, since it is not confined to threats of violence. The word 'menaces' has been held to extend to threats of 'any action detrimental to or unpleasant to the person addressed',[54] and may involve a threat to disclose some compromising information. On the other hand, blackmail is narrower than some other 'threat' offences, in that the offence is only committed where D makes the demand 'with a view to gain for himself or another or with intent to cause loss to another'. The definitions of 'gain' and 'loss',[55] are supposed to establish blackmail as a property offence, although the notion of 'gain' has been extended to cover the obtaining of a pain-killing injection from a doctor.[56]

What, then, are the elements of blackmail as a property offence? First, there must be a demand: this is a question of substance not form, and, in an appropriate context, the politest words can amount to a demand. Second, the exact nature of the demand does not matter, but there must be the elements of gain or loss, discussed above. Third, the demand must be accompanied by menaces. Fourth, it must be established that the demand was 'unwarranted', within the special definition of section 21: 'a demand with menaces is unwarranted unless the person making it does so in the belief—(a) that he has reasonable grounds for making the demand; and (b) that the use of menaces is a proper means of reinforcing the demand'. It will be noticed that this definition incorporates a fault element which focuses on the presence of two beliefs in D's mind. The first element classifies a demand as unwarranted unless D thinks there are reasonable grounds for making the demand. This will usually mean that D believes that he has a right to whatever he is demanding, and this roughly parallels section 2(1)(a) of the Theft Act 1968, which holds that there is no dishonesty in theft if D believes that he has a legal right to the property taken. The second element classifies a demand as unwarranted unless D believes that the menaces are a 'proper' means of reinforcing the demand. This element plugs a gap which we noticed in the definition of robbery: someone who threatens

---

[54] *Thorne v. Motor Trade Association* [1937] AC 797.
[55] In s. 34(2)(a) of the Theft Act 1968.
[56] *Bevans* (1988) 87 Cr. App. R 64.

another in order to obtain what he believes to be his rightful property is not guilty of robbery—he is not being dishonest—but he may be guilty of blackmail if the second element is fulfilled.

The wording of this second element might seem to be 'doubly subjective' again—in that D's own moral standards seem to set the standard of liability. If D was brought up to think that it was proper to threaten those who do not pay their debts, he would be immune from conviction for blackmail. But it is not certain that this is the correct meaning of this element. The Committee which proposed the test intended the word 'proper' to refer to what was thought to be morally and socially acceptable.[57] This would move away from D's own standards towards a test similar to *Ghosh* (on dishonesty): did D believe that people in general would regard the use of menaces as proper? It seems that both elements should be left to the jury, but that does not settle the issue of whether it is D's own standards or general social standards which are the focus of the second element. One decision went so far as to lay down that if D knows that a threatened act is unlawful, it cannot be maintained that it was believed 'proper'.[58] That favours the view that it is general social standards which apply here, but one might then go on to ask how one discovers what they are. As with the *Ghosh* test of dishonesty, there is much ambiguity and potential for inconsistent verdicts. It would be clearer and simpler to place the matter entirely on D's own belief as to what was 'proper': the issue will rarely arise, and where the courts have doubts about D's understanding of what was proper, there is a case for avoiding criminal liability. Of course, this amounts to a deviation from the policy of presumed knowledge of the law[59]—by allowing one individual's standards to set the bounds of the criminal sanction—but it does so at a point where clear objective standards peter out. Any objective standard would inevitably be uncertain, thus derogating from the principle of maximum certainty.

9.5. BURGLARY

One of the aims of the Theft Act 1968 was to reduce the mass of earlier prolix offences to a reasonable minimum. The law thus abandoned a definition which distinguished between burglaries of

---

[57] CLRC, 8th Report (1966), para. 123.
[58] *Harvey, Vylett and Plummer* (1981) 72 Cr. App. R 139.
[59] See above, Ch. 6.7(*a*).

dwellings and other premises, although sentencers continued to reflect the widely felt difference in seriousness by imposing more severe sentences on those who break into dwellings. The psychological effects of residential burglary are well documented: Maguire and Bennett found that about a quarter of victims 'are, temporarily at least, badly shaken by the experience', and that a small minority of victims suffer longer-lasting effects.[60] The Criminal Justice Act 1991 will reduce the maximum penalty for non-residential burglary to ten years, whilst retaining the fourteen-year maximum for residential burglaries. But the legal definition will continue unchanged, with no reference to the psychological harm which constitutes the gravamen of residential burglary.

The offence of burglary contrary to section 9 of the Theft Act 1968 has a wide—perhaps unexpectedly wide—ambit. Its essence, however, may be summarised thus: it may be committed either by entering a building as a trespasser with intent to steal, or by stealing after entering a building as a trespasser. 'Entry' does not require entry of the whole body: it is sufficient if, say, an arm is put through a broken window to take goods from within.[61] What must be entered is a building or part of a building: this is drafted so as to cover the person who enters the building itself lawfully, but then trespasses by going into a forbidden part of the building. The requirement of trespass places a civil-law concept at the centre of the offence. There is no general offence of trespass in English law— it is regarded as merely a civil matter between the parties—but a stealing or intent to steal converts trespass into the serious offence of burglary. In broad terms, someone who trespasses in another person's building is one who enters it without permission. Usually the permission will take the form of a direct invitation, but there may be cases of implied permission which raise difficulties of interpretation.

Two Court of Appeal decisions have been responsible for developing the element of entry as a trespasser in different, and possibly inconsistent, ways. In *Collins* (1973)[62] it was held that it is not enough that D would be classified as a trespasser in civil law: the criminal offence of burglary requires that D knew, or was reckless as to whether he was a trespasser. This protects from conviction the person who enters at the invitation of the householder's daughter, without realizing that she is not authorized to give such permission.

[60] M. Maguire and T. Bennett, *Burglary in a Dwelling* (1982), 164.
[61] *Brown* [1985] Crim. LR 611.   [62] [1973] QB 100.

This decision kept the offence fairly narrow, by insisting on a fault element on this point, but the decision in *Smith and Jones* (1976)[63] broadened it by suggesting that the fault element is intrinsically sufficient. The defendants here had entered the house of Smith's father and stolen two television sets. The father maintained that his son would never be a trespasser in his house, but this did not prevent the Court of Appeal from upholding the convictions. The Court reasoned that Smith had entered 'in excess of the permission' given by his father, since the father's general permission surely did not extend to occasions when his son intended to commit a crime on the premises. The result of this decision seems to be that anyone who enters another person's building with intent to steal is a trespasser by virtue of that intention. This approach has what some would see as the great merit of removing questions of civil law from the centre of the offence and replacing them with a straightforward test more appropriate to criminal trials: did D enter the building with the intention of stealing? More turns on D's intent than on the technicalities of trespass.

Simplicity is a virtue in the criminal law, and yet *Smith and Jones* introduces difficulties. In the first place, it seems inconsistent with *Collins*, where D had a (conditional) intent to rape the woman who invited him in, but this was not held to invalidate her permission. More importantly, the boundaries of burglary are being pushed wider than is necessary or appropriate. Surely the proper label for what was done in *Smith and Jones* is theft, and the availability of the charges of theft and attempted theft makes it unnecessary to strain the boundaries of trespass by inserting unstated reservations into general permissions given by householders. There is no element of suspicion, fear or threat when the person who enters is someone who is generally permitted to do so. Of course, part of the problem here is that the present definition of burglary includes no reference to the factors which make it such a serious crime in some cases. Convictions for the offence might be rare if the prosecution had to prove that D intended to cause, or was reckless as to causing, fear, alarm, or distress—a burglar might try to avoid such effects by entering a house when the occupier is out and taking property without damaging or ransacking the premises—but even then the crime can cause considerable distress and fear (feelings that one's property has been sullied by another, for example, or that one's

---

[63] (1976) 63 Cr. App. R 47.

home is no longer a safe place).[64] The difficulty is that the real gravamen of many burglaries lies in an unintended, unforeseen, or even unwanted effect upon the victim. It is fair to fix the level of sentences by reference to that element, since the psychological effects ought to be widely recognized, but it is more problematic to make it a requirement in the definition of the offence.

Section 9 creates two forms of burglary. The first, contrary to section 9(1)(a), is a truly inchoate offence: entering a building as a trespasser with intent to steal, etc. The offence is complete as soon as D has entered with the requisite intent. What ordinary people might regard as an 'attempted burglary', since D has not yet stolen anything, is in fact the full offence. The second form is, having entered as a trespasser, stealing or attempting to steal etc. (section 9(1)(b)). Either form of the offence becomes the more serious crime of aggravated burglary (section 10, punishable with life imprisonment) if D is carrying 'any firearm or imitation firearm, any weapon of offence or any explosive'. In most of these instances there could be a conviction for an additional offence in respect of the weapon, but this provision incorporates the aggravating element into the label.

Burglary also has another unexpected element. Not only does it have the inchoate form of entering a building with intent, but it also covers four different intents. The discussion thus far has concentrated on the intent to steal, since that is what one would expect. But, in fact, burglary is also committed by entering a building as a trespasser with intent to rape, inflict grievous bodily harm or commit criminal damage. This means that section 9(1)(a) burglary functions as an inchoate sexual offence and an inchoate violent offence: the intending rapist who enters, say, a nurses' home has not yet committed attempted rape, but he may well have committed burglary or (if armed) aggravated burglary. This illustrates the considerable reach of section 9(1)(a) burglary, going beyond that of an attempt to commit the substantive crime (e.g. rape). If it can be justified, it is on the ground that entering a building as a trespasser is a non-innocent act which should be sufficient (when combined with evidence of a proscribed intent, often inferred from surrounding circumstances or from the absence of any other plausible explanation) to warrant criminal liability.

---

[64] See Maguire and Bennett, *Burglary in a Dwelling*, Ch. 5.

D has crossed the threshold between mere intent and an attempt to translate that intent into action.

We have seen that what makes most residential burglaries more serious than most thefts is the element of invasion, with all the possible psychological effects which make it a more personal offence It should therefore be mentioned that there are other offences which 'protect' the home: the Protection from Eviction Act 1977 (as amended) criminalizes the unlawful eviction or harassment of a residential occupier, and there are various offences in Part II of the Criminal Law Act 1977, which penalize the adverse occupation of residential premises. These offences are re-stated in the draft Criminal Code.[65]

9.6. HANDLING STOLEN GOODS

It has often been said that if there were fewer receivers of stolen goods, there would be fewer thieves.[66] This may well be true—there are professional 'fences' who act as outlets for stolen goods, and goods are sometimes stolen 'to order'[67]—and it is advanced as the justification for the fact that there is a higher maximum penalty for handling stolen goods (fourteen years) than there is for theft (seven years). In 1968 section 22 of the Theft Act considerably extended the liability of persons concerned in dealing with stolen goods, creating a broad offence which covers many minor acts of assistance which might more naturally fall within inchoate offences or complicity. The aim was 'to combat theft by making it more difficult and less profitable to dispose of stolen property'.[68]

The essence of the offence of 'handling' is dealing with stolen goods. The concept of stolen goods includes goods obtained by means of theft (including robbery and burglary), deception, or blackmail, and it often covers the proceeds of such goods. Goods may, however, lose their classification as stolen if returned to their owner or to police custody, even temporarily.[69] The fault elements required for handling are dishonesty, and that D must 'know or believe' that the property is stolen, terms which include 'wilful

---

[65] Law Com. No. 177, clauses 187–96.

[66] e.g. *Battams* (1979) 1 Cr. App. R(S) 15.

[67] See C. B. Klockars, *The Professional Fence* (1975), and Maguire and Bennett, *Burglary in a Dwelling*, 70–5.

[68] CLRC, 8th Report (1966), para. 127.

[69] For an example, see *Attorney-General's Reference (No. 1 of 1974)* [1974] QB 744.

blindness'[70] but not suspicion, even strong suspicion. The prohibited conduct may take one of four forms, but merely touching stolen property does not amount to the offence. 'Handling' is simply the compendious name for the four types of conduct. Type (i) is 'receiving' stolen property, which means taking control or possession of it. This is the most usual form of the offence, and applies to the 'fence' who takes the property from the thief for resale, and to the person who knowingly buys stolen goods from another. Type (ii) is 'arranging to receive' stolen goods, and here we meet the broadening of the offence. If D agrees to buy stolen goods from the thief, who is to deliver them later, D has 'arranged to receive' even before the thief has taken any action to bring the goods to him. Type (iii) is 'undertaking or assisting in their retention, removal, disposal or realisation by or for the benefit of another person'. This is an extremely wide provision designed to criminalize those who help a thief or a receiver. It is rendered even wider by type (iv), which penalises arrangements to do an act or omission within (iii). Thus, a person who does, assists in, or arranges to do or assist in any of the acts or omissions within type (iii) is criminally liable—on one condition. The condition is that it must be 'by or for the benefit of another person'. In the leading case of *Bloxham* (1983)[71] D bought a car, subsequently realizing that it was stolen. He then sold the car to someone else and was charged with type (iii) handling. The House of Lords quashed his conviction, on the ground that he sold the car for his own benefit, not for the benefit of another. He did not sell the car for the benefit of the original thief or handler, of whom he knew nothing; and it would be ridiculous to suggest that he sold it for the buyer's benefit. Moreover, D was originally a purchaser in good faith, and the policy of the Theft Act is not to criminalize such purchasers, even if they later discover the unwelcome truth about their purchases.[72]

The offence of handling is therefore drafted widely so as to cast a net around the main Theft Act offences. 'Since thieves may be helped not only by buying the property but also in other ways such as facilitating its disposal, it seems right that the offence should

---

[70] Discussed above, Ch. 5.3(*d*).

[71] [1983] 1 AC 109, responding to the promptings of J. R. Spencer, 'The Mishandling of Handling' [1981] Crim. LR 682.

[72] Ss. 3(1) and (2) of the Theft Act; and see the exchange on 'Handling, Theft and the Purchaser who Takes a Chance' between J. R. Spencer [1985] Crim. LR 92, Glanville Williams [1985] Crim. LR 432, and J. R. Spencer [1985] Crim. LR 440.

extend to these kinds of assistance.'[73] But in doing so the offence assumes the role normally played by the doctrine of complicity and the inchoate offences, although those doctrines themselves apply to the already widened offence. The definition of handling eschews maximum certainty in favour of flexibility for prosecutors. And any impact of the policy of minimum criminalization is obviously muted where there are offences of attempting to arrange the removal of stolen goods, or counselling the retention of such property.

9.7. DECEPTION OFFENCES

(a) The Range of Deception Offences

Stealing and swindling seem to be nothing more than two means of obtaining the same thing. And, as we saw earlier, English law has developed in such a way that the same event can fulfil the definitions both of theft and of obtaining property by deception.[74] But there seems to be a general feeling that the criminal law should continue to draw a distinction between the two types of offence: it is said that people expect the law to mark the difference.[75] But what is this difference? Theft is typically a non–consensual taking of property. Deception, on the other hand, is a means of securing another's consent to the taking of property: deceptions may be practised for a whole range of purposes (e.g. obtaining consent to sexual familiarities, or obtaining consent to a surgical operation). There seems to be no general assumption that, in relation to property, deception is more heinous than a simple taking; it is just a different method. The criminal law provides a broad range of deception offences related to property, only a few of which are in the Theft Acts. The basic offence is obtaining property by deception (section 15 of the 1968 Act), and it is supplemented by the offences of obtaining services by deception (section 1 of the 1978 Act), evasion of liability by deception (section 2 of the 1978 Act), and obtaining a pecuniary advantage by deception (section 16 of the 1968 Act). Beyond these offences lie several fraud offences, some of them in the Theft Act 1968 (section 17, false accounting; section 19, false statements by company directors; section 20(2), procuring the execution of a valuable security by deception); others in the Forgery and Counterfeiting Act 1981; others in such legislation as the Companies Acts; and all

---

[73] CLRC, 8th Report (1966), para. 127.
[74] *Lawrence* [1972] AC 626, discussed above, p. 326.
[75] CLRC, 8th Report (1966), para. 38.

of them surrounded by the ample girth of common-law conspiracy to defraud.[76] More will be said about the control of fraud below, but first we will explore the essence of these deceptions.

(b) The Meaning of 'Deception'

The classic definition here is that 'to deceive is . . . to induce a man to believe that a thing is true which is false'.[77] That involves proof of causation, which is discussed further below. For the moment, we must consider what representations may amount to a deception (or attempted deception, in cases where causation is not established). Section 15(4) of the Theft Act 1968 casts the net wide: deception 'means any deception (whether deliberate or reckless) by words or conduct as to fact or as to law, including a deception as to the present intentions of the person using the deception or any other person'. The breadth of this definition makes plain the legislature's purpose of avoiding doubt about whether misstatements of the law or deceptions as to intention should fall within the reach of the criminal law. Deceptions may, of course, be express or implied, and this is where the notion of deception as to conduct becomes important. Many everyday transactions are conducted on certain assumptions which it would be tedious to spell out or to check on every occasion. We assume that the woman wearing a police uniform is a policewoman, or that the woman wearing a nurse's uniform is a nurse. We also assume that when a person pays by cheque there will be the funds to meet the cheque. The representations implied by giving a cheque in payment have now been formalized in a number of decisions: it is implied (i) that the drawer has an account at the bank; and (ii) that the cheque will be met on presentment, which may mean in practice that there are sufficient funds in the account, or that sufficient funds will be paid in before the cheque is presented, or that there is an arrangement with the bank for a sufficient overdraft facility.[78]

The courts have adopted a particularly zealous approach to cases involving a cheque card or credit card. In *Metropolitan Police Commissioner v. Charles*[79] it was held that the use of a cheque card with a cheque implies not only that the bank will meet the cheques (provided they fall within the relevant conditions), but also that D

---

[76] Discussed at pp. 353–6 below.

[77] Per Buckley J, in *Re London and Globe Finance Corporation Ltd.* [1903] 1 Ch. 728, at 732.

[78] *Gilmartin* [1983] QB 953.   [79] [1977] AC 177.

has the authority to use the cheque card in this way or to this extent. Similarly, in *Lambie* (1982)[80] it was held that the use of a credit card implies not only that the credit-card company will ensure that the money is paid, but also that D has the authority to use the credit card in this way or to this extent. Thus, in both these decisions a person was convicted because he or she had knowingly exceeded the borrowing limit imposed by the bank or credit-card company. The key question here should be whether it is generally implied in such transactions that D has the authority (from the bank or credit-card company) to use the card for this transaction: in practice, it seems doubtful whether that implication is conveyed to most traders, since the whole point of the card is to ensure that, if the proper formalities are observed, the trader will be paid.

Can silence on a particular point amount to a deception? According to the House of Lords in *DPP v. Ray* (1974),[81] a person who enters a restaurant and orders a meal is impliedly representing that payment will be made. If the person then has a change of mind and decides not to pay, the very act of remaining there (eating the meal, drinking coffee, etc.) amounts to an implied misrepresentation and therefore a deception. A person who obtains property under such circumstances will be obtaining property by deception. (Where the change of mind occurs after the meal has been consumed, no further property is obtained by the deception; but there is a special offence under section 3 of the Theft Act 1978 of making off without payment.[82]) A further example would be where D, a builder, had done work for V and her family over the years and, on request, gave her a quotation for building work which was excessively high. In *Silverman* (1988)[83] the Court of Appeal held that this might amount to a deception by silence: V had grown to trust D by virtue of their previous dealings, and so when D quoted a price for the work to be done, V assumed (and D knew that she would assume) that it was a fair price. These do not seem to be objectionable extensions of the notion of deception: indeed, in view of the commercial significance of assumptions, it would be artificial to exclude deception by silence. Where D is under a duty to supply information to V as the basis for charging D money, and D refrains from supplying the information so that no charges are made, the omission can properly be held to amount to deception.[84]

---

[80] [1982] AC 449.
[82] Discussed in Griew, *The Theft Acts*.
[84] *Firth* [1990] Crim. LR 326.

[81] [1974] AC 370.
[83] (1988) 86 Cr. App. R 213.

(c) Causation and Deception

It is axiomatic in deception offences that the deception must cause the obtaining. In practical terms, this means that the deception must precede the obtaining, and that it must explain why V allowed D to obtain the property, services, or whatever. In most cases these propositions cause no difficulty: D says he is an investment agent when he is not, and V hands over a sum of money; D tricks V into believing that she is a student and therefore entitled to a student discount on a purchase or on entry to a concert. The problems occur when the requirement of causation is linked to the notions of deception by conduct and by silence. Let us take *Metropolitan Police Commissioner v. Charles*, for instance:[85] in evidence the casino manager said that, when he saw that D had a cheque card, he had no hesitation in cashing the cheques because he knew that his employers would be assured of payment by the bank. So, even if (as the House of Lords held) there was an implied representation by D that he was authorized to use the cheque card to this extent, no such representation made an impact on V's decision to cash the cheques. Yet, later in his evidence, V stated that he would not have cashed the cheques if he had known that D was acting beyond the bank's authority. Does this mean that, in *Metropolitan Police Commissioner v. Charles*, the deception caused the obtaining? The answer is: only if causation is established by holding that V would not have acted as he did, if he had known the facts of the situation. This may seem to be a difficult proposition to accept, since V clearly knew all the facts relevant to his decision to accept the cheques—he said so, regarding only the validity of the cheque card as relevant. So the causation test which the courts appear to be using here is not one of actual causation, asking the factual question of whether any mistaken belief implanted or encouraged by D operated on V's mind at the crucial time, but a test of hypothetical causation, asking whether V would have acted in the same way if he or she had known the true position.

Some have condemned this hypothetical test of causation as wrong and inappropriate.[86] It certainly diverges from the general test of an operating and significant cause. It also succeeds in widening the net of criminal liability so as to convict of a deception offence when alleged misrepresentation was never actively pre-

---

[85] [1977] AC 177, above, p. 350.
[86] J. C. Smith, commentary [1977] Crim. LR 617; A. T. H. Smith, 'The Idea of Criminal Deception' [1982] Crim. LR 721.

sented to the victim's mind. But does this mean that there can never be a deception by omission? All omissions cases present difficult causation problems,[87] and there are surely some in which a conviction for a deception offence might appear quite proper. For example, where D fails to reveal a key fact about a claim under an insurance contract, few would dispute the appropriateness of holding that D deceived V. In this context, a definition of deception which insists on the mistake being present in V's mind at the time D is allowed to obtain the property or services, seems unsuitably narrow. It is, in fact, a situation in which there is a clear duty on the claimant to disclose all material facts.[88]

The question then is whether this analysis of deception by omission can fairly be extended to many of the 'assumption' cases, where V acts on the basis of the usual assumptions and D hopes that V will do so. Opponents of the courts' broad approach in *Metropolitan Police Commissioner v. Charles* and *Lambie* say that this is inconsistent with the legislature's use of the concept of deception, as distinct from 'fraud' or 'false pretences': the Criminal Law Revision Committee proposed the term 'deception' because it has 'the advantage of directing attention to the effect that the offender deliberately produced on the mind of the person deceived',[89] whereas the two House of Lords decisions effectively negate this requirement. Once again, broad 'social defence' arguments in favour of convicting manifest rogues are mobilized as reasons for drawing the courts away from a constitutionally proper deference to legislative purpose.

9.8. FRAUD OFFENCES

In addition to the deception offences in the Theft Acts, there are a considerable number of offences of fraud scattered through the statute-book and at common law. Among the statutory offences are several under the Forgery and Counterfeiting Act 1981, the offence of carrying on a business with intent to defraud creditors or for any fraudulent prupose (Companies Act 1985, section 458), and various offences of false and misleading statements under the Financial Services Act 1986 and the Banking Act 1987. Among the common-

---

[87] See above, Ch. 4.4(*b*).

[88] See the discussion by the Law Commission No. 104, *Insurance Law: Non-Disclosure and Breach of Warranty* (1988).

[89] CLRC, 8th Report (1966), para. 87; see also pp. 50–1 on the question of deception by omission.

law offences are cheating the public revenue (which is based on fraud, and does not require deception[90]) and conspiracy to defraud, to which we shall now turn.

The elements of the common-law crime of conspiracy to defraud were restated in *Scott v. Metropolitan Police Commissioner* (1975)[91]. The offence may take one of two forms. If it is directed at a private person, what is proscribed is an agreement between two or more persons 'by dishonesty to deprive' that person of something to which he or she is or may be entitled, or to injure some proprietary right of that person, with intent to cause economic loss. If the offence is directed at a public official, what is proscribed is an agreement between two or more persons 'by dishonesty' to cause the official to act contrary to his or her public duty. There seem to be few prosecutions for conspiracy to defraud directed at public officials. The controversies mainly concern the first form of the offence.

It is, in the first place, a crime of conspiracy. Conspiracy is one of the three inchoate offences in English criminal law, discussed in Chapter 11 below, but conspiracy may also be charged when the acts agreed upon have actually been committed. The reason given is that a charge of conspiracy may be a more accurate representation of the nature of the law-breaking than a number of specific charges. But an additional reason, in relation to conspiracy to defraud, is that its definition is so wide that it criminalizes agreements to do things which, if done by an individual, would not amount to an offence. Although conspiracy to defraud raises several issues of principle,[92] this is the nub of the problem. The boundaries of the law are unclear, and prosecutors and courts have a large measure of discretion in applying the law, and latitude in describing the nature of the offence. To be more precise, conspiracy to defraud goes beyond the standard offences of theft, deception, etc. in several known (and some unpredictable) respects. An agreement temporarily to obtain someone's property may amount to a conspiracy to defraud, even though there is no general offence of temporary deprivation. There is no offence of deceiving a machine, but there may be a conspiracy to defraud a machine's owner. Conspiracy charges may also be brought where a secret profit has been made

---

[90] *Mavji* (1987) 84 Cr. App. R 34; *Redford* (1989) 89 Cr. App. R 1.
[91] [1975] AC 819.
[92] See above, Ch. 3, on the principles of maximum certainty (3.3(*i*)) and of non-retroactivity (3.3(*g*)).

with another person's property,[93] for some gambling swindles, for 'long firm' frauds, and, in the area of commercial counterfeiting, for making and selling goods which are copies of famous branded goods.

The Law Commission is now considering the reform of this branch of the law, and it has two main options.[94] One, which has been followed in previous reforms of conspiracy law,[95] is to draft a number of specific offences to cover the types of case now prosecuted as conspiracy to defraud. This approach gives priority to legality principles, especially the principle of maximum certainty, but it risks the appearance of gaps in the law if new forms of fraud, no less serious than those presently criminalized, begin to develop. This risk has been taken in other parts of the criminal law, and the risk is minimized if the legislature acts swiftly to remedy gaps. A second option is to attempt to create as many specific offences as appear necessary, but also to retain a general and residual offence of fraud.[95a] The Law Commission's tentative proposal was as follows: 'Any person who dishonestly causes another person to suffer [financial] prejudice, or a risk of prejudice, or who dishonestly makes a gain for himself or another, commits an offence.' This would be an offence of staggering breadth, applicable to conduct by an individual as well as to agreements by two or more people. It will be evident that the flexible and amorphous concept of dishonesty lies at its centre. Some of the dangers of oppressiveness arising from its breadth could be minimized by the articulation and enforcement of restrictions on prosecutors—for example, through guidelines which form part of the Code for Crown Prosecutors.[96] Prosecutors and others argue that an offence of this breadth is necessary if some particularly serious fradusters are to be caught. Such an offence goes strongly against the principle of maximum certainty, but an

[93] The Court of Appeal has held that if done by one person, this is not theft: *Attorney-General's Reference (No. 1 of 1985)* [1986] QB 491.

[94] Law Com. WP 104, discussed by A. T. H. Smith [1988] Crim. LR 508.

[95] Law Commission No. 76, *Conspiracy and Criminal Law Reform* (1976), discussed below, Ch. 11.5.

[95a] G. R. Sullivan, "Fraud and the Efficacy of the Criminal Law", [1985] Crim. LR 616.

[96] This is the present position: there are guide-lines for prosecutors on the proper and improper use of the charge of conspiracy to defraud, proposed by the Criminal Law Revision Committee, 18th Report, *Conspiracy to Defraud* (1986, Cmnd 9873), as a counterweight to the greater prosecutorial freedom granted under s. 12 of the Criminal Justice Act 1987.

interesting feature is that the invocation of that principle would shelter people who are often in powerful commercial positions or are otherwise able to call upon substantial financial resources. The law generally favours such people by imposing civil and administrative penalties rather than criminal prosecution. Would it be inequitable now to suggest that the weight of the principle of maximum certainty should not tell in their favour, since the balance is tipped towards them socially and legally in any case? In this area, 'the more specific and certain the law is, the easier it is [for those with resources] to manipulate, to slip between its provisions, to distinguish one case from another.'[97]

9.9. DISHONESTY, DISCRETION, AND 'DESERT'

There is no shortage of issues of principle raised by the approach of the legislature and the courts to offences of dishonesty. The most obvious of these is the virtual abandonment of the principle of maximum certainty in relation to the offence of conspiracy to defraud, and, more generally, in the reliance on 'dishonesty' as the key element in most offences. Apart from the three exceptions in section 2 of the 1968 Act, which apply only to offences of theft, the meaning of 'dishonesty' is left at large, with only the 'current standards of ordinary decent people' to steer the jury or magistrates towards a conclusion. This ample discretion—which is what it amounts to, since there is no touchstone of social honesty—opens the way to inconsistent decisions (which detract from the rule of law) and discriminatory decisions (which detract from equality before the law). No doubt, prosecutors and some judges regard flexibility as a great virtue in the law, but it runs counter to any principles which regard respect for individual autonomy as a central value.[98] Efforts must be made to redefine at least some of the property offences in a way which cuts down or structures this wide discretion. It is a great irony that one of the few official references to 'the principle of English law to give reasonable guidance as to what kinds of conduct are criminal' comes in the report which preceded and proposed the Theft Act.[99]

The definitions of some of the offences under the Theft Act are also notable for breadth of another kind, inasmuch as they spill over

---

[97] See Doreen McBarnet, 'The Limits of Criminal Law' (unpublished conference paper, 1987).
[98] See the fairness principles discussed above, Ch. 3.3.
[99] CLRC, 8th Report (1966), para. 99(i).

into areas normally occupied by inchoate offences or by the law of complicity. The inchoate mode of definition is used with regard to burglary contrary to section 9(1)(a), 'entering as a trespasser with intent to steal', but—more significantly—it is adopted for the crime of theft itself: the main conduct element is an 'appropriation', which may be fulfilled by any adverse interference with a right of an owner.[100] There is nothing here about *depriving* V of a property right, merely interfering with it. One consequence is to push back the crime of attempted theft even further, so that in *Morris*[101] theft was constituted by swapping labels on goods in the supermarket, and attempted theft would presumably be committed by such acts as trying to peel off the labels prior to swapping them. This might be regarded as pressing criminal liability too far. For a similar reason, mention might also be made of the offence of handling, for which the legislature has cast the net so wide (assisting in, or arranging to assist in, the retention, removal, disposal, or realization of stolen goods) as to cover conduct which would normally be charged as aiding and abetting, etc.[102] Again, one consequence of this is that the law of complicity applies so as to extend the boundaries of the wide offence of handling still further. Just as attempted theft might be termed a doubly inchoate offence, so aiding and abetting an offence of handling stolen goods might be called a doubly secondary offence.

The historical explanation for the broad drafting of offences in the Theft Act was that the earlier law of larceny consisted of many technically worded offences covering fairly similar forms of conduct, an approach which had attracted technical interpretations and which resulted in a complex law often quite removed from its original purposes. The drive to eschew technicality was laudable. It could have gone further—by amalgamating theft and deception into a single offence for example—but it was thought desirable to retain conventional distinctions.[103] However, among the results of the new 'broad band' offence-structure have been (i) some difficulty in predicting the precise boundaries of the criminal law, which gives more power to prosecutors; (ii) greater discretion in the administration of the law by juries and magistrates; and (iii) wider discretion in sentencing, an intended result of the pattern of fewer offences with relatively high maximum penalties.[104] Yet the picture is blurred

---

[100] See above, pp. 326–329. [101] [1984] AC 320.
[102] See above, section 9. [103] CLRC, 8th Report (1966), para. 38.
[104] See A. Ashworth, *Sentencing and Penal Policy* (1983), 81–91, and above, Ch. 3.3(*l*) and (*m*).

by the fact that the Theft Act 1978 reverts to a more particularistic style of drafting.

The property offences both within and outside the Theft Acts do not form a readily comprehensible scheme, based on relative seriousness and proportionality. It was noticed earlier that the fairly serious offence of burglary is defined without any reference to the element of psychological harm to the victim, which is such a key factor in determining its relative seriousness. The piecemeal nature of the law's development is betrayed by several anomalies: it is an offence to obtain services by deception, but not to help oneself to them brazenly; temporary deprivations are criminal in some circumstances and not in others, irrespective of the loss inflicted on the victim; various commercial swindles are offences if done by two or more people (conspiracy to defraud), but not if done by an individual; and so forth.

The flexibility of the 'broad band' approach to definitions in the Theft Act 1968, together with the anomalous contours of criminalization, has meant that the outer boundaries of the law (and particularly the lower boundaries) are uncertain and shifting. This problem is compounded by the variable approaches to statute interpretation taken by the appellate courts. The concept of 'appropriation' is central to the offence of theft, yet the definition in section 3 of the Act has been interpreted in divergent ways by courts all the way up to the House of Lords.[105] What is common to the conflicting House of Lords decisions in *Lawrence* and *Morris* is simply the result that two persons of whose dishonesty the courts were convinced were ultimately convicted of theft. The patterns of reasoning have little in common, bear little relation to the recommendations of the Criminal Law Revision Committee, and do not follow any regular canons of statute interpretation. The courts were engaged in the unbridled pursuit of a notion of social defence, encouraged in part by the breadth of the statutory definitions and in part by their relative freedom in intepretation.

What is particularly objectionable about the many cases of stretching dishonesty offences is that they have stretched the law downwards, so that relatively minor acts render persons liable to conviction for offences with fairly serious labels. It is important to note here that English law has no provision equivalent to the *de minimis*

---

[105] See *Lawrence* [1972] AC 626, *Morris* [1984] AC 320, and the extraordinary decision of the Court of Appeal in *Phillipou* (1989) 89 Cr. App. R 290, which denies any conflict between the two earlier House of Lords decisions; see above, p. 328.

section of the Model Penal Code, allowing a defence where the conduct was not serious enough to warrant conviction.[106] There is a provision in the Code for Crown Prosecutors in England which states that it is not in the public interest to bring a prosecution where only a nominal penalty would be likely;[107] but that consigns the matter to discretion once more, leaving the boundaries of the criminal law in a distinctly uncertain state. The point is strengthened by the presence of civil remedies for many acts of dishonesty concerning property. The courts have recalled that in the two House of Lords decisions, *Metropolitan Police Commissioner v. Charles* and *Lambie*[108], the court strove to bring the defendants' behaviour within the criminal law rather than leaving the banks to pursue civil remedies against customers with whom they had regular and considered contractual arrangements. In *Clarke*[109] the Court of Appeal made strong criticisms of the banks for their poor precautions against the fraudulent use of credit cards. Unusually, in *Navvabi*[110] the Court of Appeal stopped short of convicting of theft a person who opened bank accounts in false names, and then passed cheques in excess of the balance in the accounts. There are some cases where the courts have taken a strong stance against the importation of civil-law concepts into the criminal law,[111] and others where they have willingly embraced civil-law reasoning in order to reach a desired conclusion.[112] Behind these inconsistencies of approach lies the fundamental question of principle—for the legislature rather than for the courts—about the proper division between criminal prosecution and civil suits.

The legislative and judicial development of dishonesty offences charted in this chapter shows little attachment to a policy of minimum criminalization, and ready resort to the criminal sanction as 'social defence' against relatively minor forms of dishonesty.[113] Otherwise, efforts would have been made to remove many of the lesser appropriations and handlings from the criminal law. The problem appears to be that it is hard to find a workable distinction between these

---

[106] Model Penal Code, s. 212.
[107] Code for Crown Prosecutors, para. 8(i).
[108] *Metropolitan Police Commissioner v. Charles* [1977] AC 177, and *Lambie* [1982] AC 449, discussed above, pp. 350–353.
[109] (1982) 75 Cr. App. R 119.   [110] [1987] Crim. LR 57.
[111] e.g. *Morris* [1984] AC 320, and *Attorney-General's Reference (No. 1 of 1985)* [1986] QB 491.
[112] e.g. *Metropolitan Police Commissioner v. Charles* [1977] AC 177.
[113] Cf. Ch. 3.2(b) with Chapter 3.2(a).

minor forms of dishonesty and dishonest appropriations of property which are quite serious. One approach is to regard the value of the appropriated goods or services as the crucial element, and to place all cases below a certain sum into a separate category—cancellation of the offence if the taker repays what was taken within seven days, for example, like the French bad-cheque law;[114] or a fixed penalty offence;[115] or a new category of civil infractions.[116] Of course, there are possible objections against each of these alternatives, not least the claim that offences of dishonesty have a significance in one's judgment of people which transcends the sum involved. But this is where we meet serious problems of proportionality and of social hypocrisy. Many forms of conduct amounting to dishonesty offences are routinely dealt with in some non-criminal manner—large companies required to repay money on government contracts, for example, executives dismissed from employment, tax fraudsters required to pay double the underpaid tax rather than being prosecuted, and so forth. Indeed, a recent Law Commission Working Paper argued that there is no need to criminalize those who deliberately use another person's profit-earning property in order to make secret profits, since it is generally adequate to leave the owner to sue the malefactor; yet restaurant bilkers who make off without paying a few pounds are routinely subjected to the criminal sanction.[117] Moreover, as argued above, there are few social standards of dishonesty which do not vary according to the background and circumstances of the group of citizens who are making the judgment. The argument is clearly one of social fairness: the present legal definitions and enforcement practices are failing to ensure equality before the law, by subjecting many minor offenders to conviction whilst adopting a different approach to some major offenders.

There are, then, at least five conflicting principles in dishonesty offences. The principle of significant harm argues in favour of a reconstruction of these offences so as to exclude some minor forms of dishonesty and to include some major ones. The principle of proportionality militates in favour of a more clearly structured

---

[114] For an outline, see C. Anyangwe, 'Dealing with the Problem of Bad Cheques in France' [1978] Crim. LR 31.

[115] For a radical proposal, see A. Ashworth, 'Prosecution, Police and the Public: A Guide to Good Gatekeeping' (1984) 23 *Howard JCJ* 65.

[116] See the discussion by Barbara Huber, 'The Dilemma of Decriminalisation: Dealing with Shoplifting in West Germany' [1980] Crim. LR 621.

[117] Pointed out by A. T. H. Smith, 'Conspiracy to Defraud' [1988] Crim. LR 508, at 513, commenting on the Law Com. WP 104.

restatement of dishonesty offences so as to integrate crimes from the Companies Acts and elsewhere into the general framework. The principle of maximum certainty urges that such a restatement should be less reliant on such discretionary terms as 'dishonestly'. On the other hand, the principle of keeping the criminal law to a minimum would support the exploration of non-criminal means of dealing with some forms of dishonesty: this has been the pattern for many years, but it has generally meant that companies and well-connected persons have succeeded in avoiding the criminal sanction, when others of lowlier status have been convicted. This goes against the principle of equality before the law, since it discriminates on grounds of wealth and social position. Some would argue that we should still not forsake non-criminal means of dealing with commercial fraud, since these can be more effective,[118] but that we should redouble our efforts to narrow down the ambit of the criminal sanction for minor forms of dishonesty.

[118] Cf. J. Braithwaite and B. Fisse, 'The Allocation of Responsibility for Corporate Crime' (1988) 11 *Sydney LR* 468, with Levi, *Regulating Fraud*.

10
COMPLICITY

10.1. INTRODUCTION

The question of complicity arises when two or more people play some part in the commission of an offence. It has already been noted, in discussing the various public-order offences,[1] and will be emphasized later, when discussing conspiracy,[2] that the criminal law regards offences involving more than one person as particularly serious—partly because they suggest planning and determination to offend and make it difficult for an individual to withdraw, and partly because group offences against an individual tend to be more frightening. There are, of course, different degrees of involvement in a criminal enterprise, and one of the main issues in the law of complicity is the proper scope of criminal liability: how much involvement should be necessary, as a minimum?

Let us take a hypothetical example of a burglary, in which A and B plan to raid a country house: they approach C, who has worked at the house, for information which will help them to gain entry; they arrange for D to drive them to the house in a large van and to transport the stolen goods after the burglary; and they agree with E that he should come and position himself near the main gates of the house in order to warn them if anyone approaches. If A, B, C, D, and E all do as planned, what approach should the law take to their criminal liability?

It is apparent that A and B are the only ones to have fulfilled the definition of the crime of burglary, by entering the house as trespassers and stealing property from it.[3] They are guilty as co-principals. It should then be asked whether there is sufficient justification for bringing C, D, and E within the ambit of the criminal law at all. Would the law not be more effective if it concentrated on the major offenders? The main difficulty in answering this question is that, in some crimes, the conduct of the accomplices, urging and threatening, is no less serious than that of the principals.

---

[1] See above, Ch. 8.3(g).   [2] See below, Ch. 11.4.
[3] Theft Act 1968, s. 9; see above, Ch. 9.5.

As a general reason for bringing accomplices within the ambit of criminal liability, one might say that culpably assisting one or more persons in a criminal enterprise deserves the criminal sanction; the culpability implies a decision to support the commission of the principal's crime, and the assistance is a practical manifestation of that support. A consequentialist reason for convicting those who help and support a criminal enterprise can also be found: penalizing helpers and other participants should act as a deterrent, thereby making offences less likely to occur.

What contribution to a crime must be made before the law regards a person as an accomplice? The neutral word 'assistance' was used in the previous paragraph, but must it be proved that the conduct of persons such as C, D, and E actually *caused* A and B's offence, in the sense that it would not have happened as it did but for their help? One practical answer to this question is that A and B might well have found others willing to help. The theoretical answer would begin by pointing out that A and B are responsible, autonomous individuals—one cannot, in general, trace causal responsibility through the voluntary act of another person[4]—so it will not usually be possible to hold that the accomplices *caused* the principals to act. The law of complicity does not require causation, then, but it does require certain conduct by the accomplice, perhaps more as evidence of the accomplice's commitment to furthering the criminal enterprise, in a similar way to the conduct requirement in attempts and other inchoate offences,[5] than as evidence that the crime would not have happened but for the accomplice's assistance. But there are cases of procuring, as we shall see in section 11.4 below, where the accomplice plays a major part, virtually 'controlling' the principal. Thus, even in a minimalist system of criminal law which aimed to reserve the criminal sanction for the 'big fish' and to ignore the 'minnows', penalizing the principals and not the accomplices would miss the target in a number of cases.

10.2. DISTINGUISHING PRINCIPALS FROM ACCESSORIES

The simplest way of drawing this distinction is to say that a principal is a person whose acts fall within the legal definition of the crime, whereas an accomplice (sometimes called an 'accessory' or 'secondary party') is anyone who aids, abets, counsels, or procures a

---

[4] See above, Ch. 4.6(*a*) and (*c*).   [5] See below, Ch. 11.3(*b*) and 11.6.

principal. It does not follow from this that where two or more persons are involved in an offence, one must be the principal and the others accomplices. Two or more persons can be co-principals, so long as each of them satisfies the definition of the substantive offence, by each inflicting wounds upon the victim with the required fault, for example. Indeed, English law goes further, holding that two or more persons can be co-principals if each of them satisfies some part of the conduct element of the offence, if all their acts together fulfil all the conduct elements, and if each of them has the required mental element. This is an unusual example of the attribution of one person's acts to another, which is thought to be justified by the concept of 'joint enterprise,' or 'common purpose' which binds together the several acts of persons who are acting in pursuance of an agreement.

Some criminal offences are so defined that they can only be committed by two or more co-principals. The public-order offences of riot and violent disorder are clear examples of this.[6] There can also be accomplices to such offences, but the broad definitions of the offences themselves make this unusual. A related rule, which operates only in the United States, is that all members of a conspiracy are deemed to be co-principals in the offence if it is committed. The rule eliminates from such cases the distinction between principals and accessories, and has led to the conviction, as principal in an offence, of someone who was in prison at the time for committing another offence. The result is that the conviction misrepresents the nature of the person's participation in the crime: a conspirator is labelled as a perpetrator, which is hardly fair or necessary.[7]

If we return to the more normal situations, in which there is one principal and one accomplice or (as in the earlier example) two principals and three accomplices, what are the practical implications of holding a person to be an accomplice rather than a principal? The answer, in English law, is that they are rarely significant. The leading statute is the Accessories and Abettors Act 1861, which provides that anyone who 'shall aid, abet, counsel or procure the commission of any indictable offence . . . shall be liable to be tried, indicted and punished as a principal offender'. This means that in practice, the prosecution can succeed against a defendant without

---

[6] See above, Ch. 8.3(g).

[7] It conflicts with the principle of fair labelling (discussed in Ch. 3.3(l)) and the principles of 'desert' (Ch. 5.2(b)). The leading American decision is *Pinkerton v. United States* (1946) 328 US 640.

specifying in advance whether the allegation is that D is a principal or an accomplice, or what form the alleged complicity took. This is undoubtedly a great convenience for the prosecution, particularly in cases where they can prove that each of two defendants was at least an accomplice but cannot prove which one was the principal.[8] It is surely right that some means be found of minimizing the extent to which defendants can escape criminal liability by blaming one another; if accomplices had to be subjected to separate charges from principals, for example, some unmeritorious acquittals might result. What the 1861 Act does not ensure, however, is that individual defendants receive fair warning of the case against them, although the House of Lords has encouraged prosecutors to frame indictments in as much detail as possible.[9] One must ask whether the present system succeeds in maximizing respect for the right to receive fair warning of charge(s), whilst minimizing the opportunities for avoiding criminal liability by resort to procedural rules which conceal the normal elements of criminal guilt.[10]

The 1861 English law is sometimes compared unfavourably with such systems as the German, which restricts the maximum penalty for an accomplice to three-quarters that of the principal.[11] The comparison is not a straightforward one, however. It is true that accomplices are normally less blameworthy than principals and therefore deserve less severe sentences. It is also true that a law which convicts someone of murder, sentencing them mandatorily to life imprisonment for giving relatively minor assistance to a murderer, is unjust (though the injustice stems as much from the mandatory penalty for murder as from the law of complicity). But systems like the German seem not to provide for those, admittedly rare, cases in which the accomplice is no less culpable, even more culpable, than the principal—as where a powerful figure orders a weak-willed person to commit a certain crime. One way of providing for all degrees of complicity would be to retain the legal power to impose any relevant sentence on the principal; to respect the accomplice's right not to be punished more severely than is proportionate to the

---

[8] See the cases discussed by E. Griew, 'It Must Have Been One of Them' [1989] Crim. LR 129.

[9] *Maxwell v. DPP for Northern Ireland* [1978] 1 WLR 1350.

[10] That, in itself, is a complex issue. If the avoidance of liability by 'technical' means is not regarded as a defendant's entitlement, it remains to be decided whether the point should be covered by a rule of evidence (such as reversal of the burden of proof), or by criminal procedure, or by substantive law.

[11] See G. Fletcher, *Rethinking Criminal Law* (1978) 634 ff.

gravity of his contribution by declaring a general rule that accomplices should receive no more than half the sentence of the principal —or even less, if the accomplice's contribution is minor; and to permit courts to exceed this normal level in cases where the accomplice's role was unusually influential. Some such approach would sacrifice the notion that the legal labels ought to reflect the different degrees of involvement in favour of a more flexible, yet regulated, response through sentencing.

10.3. THE CONDUCT ELEMENT IN COMPLICITY

We have seen that the 1861 Act refers to those who 'aid, abet, counsel or procure' a crime. As a matter of history, it seems that this Act was intended only to declare the procedure whereby accomplices could be convicted and sentenced as principals, and not to provide a definition of complicity. Earlier statutes had used a wide range of terms—contriving, helping, maintaining, directing—and it seems likely that the wording of the 1861 Act was intended merely as a general reference to the existing common law on accomplices. However, the words have taken on an authority of their own. There have been many decisions on the meaning of each term, and in 1976 the Court of Appeal declared that each of the four verbs should be given its ordinary meaning.[12] This 'ordinary language' approach to the interpretation of statutes now seems to be receding,[13] and since the 1976 decision paid no heed to the historical development of the law, its authority is open to doubt.

One factor which used to have considerable importance was presence during the commission of the crime. So long as the other conditions for liability were fulfilled, presence turned the accomplice into an aider or abettor, absence into a counsellor or procurer.[14] However, it appears that the distinction no longer has any practical consequences in English law.[15] Whether an accomplice is described as an aider, abettor, counsellor, or procurer seems to depend on the description most appropriate in ordinary language, and presence has no special significance.

[12] *Attorney-General's Reference (No. 1 of 1975)* [1975] QB 773.

[13] *Maginnis* [1987] AC 303, discussed by D. W. Elliott, '*Brutus v. Cozens*: Decline and Fall' [1989] Crim. LR 323.

[14] See e.g. Lord Goddard CJ in *Ferguson v. Weaving* [1951] 1 KB 814, and generally J. C. Smith, 'Aid, Abet, Counsel or Procure', in P. R. Glazebrook (ed.) *Reshaping the Criminal Law* (1978).

[15] *Howe* [1987] AC 417, overruling *Richards* [1974] QB 776.

(a) Aiding and Abetting

It has been traditional to consider the modes of complicity in terms of the two time-honoured pairings: 'aid or abet', and 'counsel or procure'. In fact, the concept of abetment seems to play no independent role now. Abetting involves some encouragement of the principal to commit the offence, and this usually accompanies, or is implicit in, an act of aiding. Aid may be given by supplying an instrument to the principal, keeping a look-out, doing preparatory acts, and many other forms of assistance. The disappearance of the old requirement of presence may be illustrated by two cases. In *Bainbridge* (1959)[16] a man who provided equipment for use in a burglary was treated as a counsellor and procurer, because the burglary was to take place some days hence, whereas it would now be more natural to refer to him as an aider since he gave assistance by supplying the equipment. In *Attorney General v. Able* (1984)[17] the discussion of D's criminal liability for supplying a booklet explaining various ways of committing suicide was conducted on the basis that this would be aiding and abetting, whereas in former times this would have been regarded as counselling, since the author of the book was not present at the suicides.

Once it has been shown that the accomplice's conduct helped or might have helped the principal in some way, it does not have to be established that the accomplice caused the principal's offence. But that leaves us with the problem of deciding on the lower boundaries of 'aiding and abetting'. Causation requirements often function so as to fix the threshold of legal liability. Since causation is not a requirement here, how can the boundaries be drawn? It has been argued that there is still a form of causation requirement here: the courts must be satisfied that the accomplice's help *might* have made a difference to whether the principal's offence was actually committed, in the sense that one could not be sure that it would have been committed but for the accomplice's assistance.[18] Even according to this view, which is not supported by the explicit reasoning of the courts, the causal connection is rather tenuous and would fall within the *de minimis* range normally excluded from legal causation (see Chapter 4.6(a) above). Surely the search for a causal connection should be abandoned. There would then be two options. One would be for the law to formulate an objective test, such as 'did the act or

[16] [1960] 1 QB 129.   [17] [1984] 1 QB 795.
[18] S. Kadish, *Blame and Punishment* (1987), 162.

omission make some actual or potential contribution to the principal's offence?'. This would leave the law well short of the principle of maximum certainty, and would not exclude the criminalization of minimal acts of assistance. The other option would be to focus on the accomplice's conduct as an outward manifestation of his or her willingness to be associated with the crime and to support its perpetrator. According to this view, the fault element in complicity is the main justification for imposing liability on accomplices, and it would also define the outer boundary of accessorial liability. This second option would tend to assimilate accomplice liability within the criteria for attempts liability, discussed in Chapter 11.3(*b*) below.

This raises the question of intended contributions by would-be accomplices. If we return to the hypothetical example given earlier, let us suppose that D had agreed with A and B that he would bring the van to a certain place, would carry them to the house, and would then bring them back with the proceeds of their crime. So, D drives the van to the meeting-place, ready to play his part, but A and B, having decided that they do not wish to rely on D, have obtained a van for themselves and have carried out the burglary without D's assistance. D's culpability remains the same as if A and B had relied upon his help. Yet there is no shadow of a causal link between D's acts and the offence committed by A and B. One suggestion is that D should be liable to conviction for attempting to aid and abet the burglary by A and B, but English law draws the line here: there is no offence of attempted complicity, because it is too remote from the occurrence of the harm.[19] If, on the other hand, English law were to criminalize accomplices separately, by having an offence of doing acts with intent to assist or instigate a crime, people in D's position would be liable to conviction. Existing English law places limits on accomplice liability, largely through its basic doctrine that the liability of the accomplice derives from the liability of the principal, of which more will be said as the chapter proceeds.

Two further situations illustrate these difficulties over the link between an accomplice's aiding and the principal's offence. In *Wilcox v. Jeffery* (1951) a jazz enthusiast attended a concert, applauding the decision of an American jazz musician to give an illegal performance. No point was taken in court about whether the

---

[19] Criminal Attempts Act 1981, s. 1(4), and J. C. Smith, 'Secondary Participation and Inchoate Offences', in C. Tapper (ed.), *Crime, Proof and Punishment* (1981).

musician was actually encouraged by the defendant's acts.[20] Indeed, in cases where several people applaud or encourage some kind of unlawful spectacle, it would be difficult to maintain that the performer(s) drew actual encouragement from the acts of any one of the spectators. One might say that a form of causal connection is assumed, but once again this is patently weak. Another type of situation occurs where the principal is unaware of the help given by the secondary party. In the famous American case of *State v. Tally* (1894),[21] Judge Tally, knowing that his brothers-in-law had set out to kill the deceased, and knowing that someone else had sent a telegram to warn the victim, sent a telegram to the telegraph operator telling him not to deliver the warning telegram. The telegraph operator complied, and the brothers-in-law committed the offence. The judge was convicted of aiding and abetting murder, even though the brothers-in-law were unaware of the judge's assistance when they killed the victim. It could be said that there was a causal connection in this case, but surely it should have been enough that the judge's act was more than minimal and he intended to aid.

(b) Accomplice Liability and Social Duties

We saw in Chapter 4.4 how accomplice liability has been used in English law to establish criminal liability for certain omissions, and the relevant authorities must now be considered in their adopted legal habitat. The cases raise issues of constitutional and social importance, but the key question in accessorial liability is simple to state: can a person be convicted as an accomplice merely for standing by and doing nothing while an offence is being committed?

Let us first consider whether presence at the scene during the principal's offence is sufficient for accomplice liability. The issue has deep implications, since an affirmative answer would amount to recognizing a citizen's duty to take reasonable steps to prevent or frustrate any offence which is witnessed. The citizen's choice would lie between taking some preventive action or being deemed to be an accomplice. The courts have responded by drawing some fine lines. Non-accidental presence, such as attending a fight or an unlawful theatrical performance, is not conclusive evidence of aiding and abetting.[22] It seems that the prosecution must establish both that D intended to encourage and that this encouragement had some effect on the principal.[23] The factual questions are for the jury or

---

[20] [1951] 1 All ER 464.
[22] *Coney* (1882) 8 QBD 534.
[21] *State v. Tally* (1894) 15 So. 722.
[23] *Clarkson* [1971] 1 WLR 1402.

magistrates. The inference of an intention to encourage might readily be drawn if D has gone to the place where the performance is taking place, especially if payment were made.[24] The position of spectators who simply come upon an illegal fight or event and stay to watch it is different: simply sitting or standing nearby is unlikely to be sufficient for liability, but any cheering or applause would probably tip the balance in favour of conviction. The problems are particularly acute in cases of public disorder. To impose duties on bystanders, even the duty to move away, might be regarded as an incursion on a citizen's right to freedom of movement. On the other hand, to remain at the scene might strengthen the resolve of aggressors, increase the fear of victims, and make it difficult for the police to separate the involved from the uninvolved, but it is questionable whether these considerations are sufficient to justify the imposition of criminal liability.

However, there are arguments in favour of the law going further and imposing a duty to take steps to prevent crime. The public-disorder example is complicated by the impotence of individuals to do anything to stop the affray, and, indeed, the imprudence of their trying to do so. But is it not arguable that there should be at least a duty to alert the police? If so, should failure to do so constitute a distinct offence (as in French law[25]) or complicity in the public disorder? Another example, which does not involve public disorder, occurs where a woman is living with a man who, she discovers, is dealing in drugs. If the police raid the dwelling and find drugs on the premises, should the law treat her as an accomplice even if there is no evidence of active assistance or encouragement towards the drug-dealing? In the case of *Bland* (1988)[26] the Court of Appeal quashed the woman's conviction as an accomplice. Cases such as this demonstrate a vivid conflict between individuals' rights of privacy in their personal relationships and the social interest in suppressing serious crime. Would it be right for the law to co-opt husbands against wives, parents against children, house-sharing friends against friends in order to increase public protection?

Probably the only way to answer this question is to balance the relative centrality of the right against the seriousness of the offence involved—not a simple exercise, but an inevitable one if the true

---

[24] *Wilcox v. Jeffery* [1951] I All ER 464.
[25] See A. Ashworth and E. Steiner, 'Criminal Omissions and Public Duties' (1990) 10 *LS* 153.
[26] [1988] Crim. LR 41.

nature of the problem is to be confronted. The same applies to the situation in *Clarkson* (1971):[27] two soldiers happened to enter a room where other soldiers were raping a woman. It was not found that they did anything other than watch, but they certainly did nothing to discourage continuance of the offence. The Court of Appeal quashed their convictions, because the judge had not made it clear that there should be proof of both an intent to encourage and actual encouragement. Nothing was said about a duty to alert the authorities immediately in the hope of preventing the crime's continuance. What if three persons came upon one man raping a woman? If it was within their power to put a stop to the offence and to apprehend the offender, should they have a duty to do so—or at least a duty to inform the police? The particular situation will vary from case to case, but the real issue is whether there is to be a principle that citizens ought to take reasonable steps to inform the police when they witness an offence. Variations in the facts of cases can be accommodated within the concept of 'reasonable steps',[28] and no court should require a person to place his or her own safety in jeopardy. Even if this is accepted, there would remain the question of whether it is fairer to convict the defaulting citizen of a new offence of failing to inform the police rather than making the citizen into an accomplice to the principal crime. The former is surely more appropriate in terms of fair labelling.

Can a person be said to aid an offence by an omission? There would surely be no awkwardness in describing the cleaner of a bank who, in pursuance of an agreed plan, purposely omits to lock the doors when leaving as 'aiding' a burglary of the bank. In such a case, there is a clear duty and a failure to perform it, and the causation problems are similar to those of omissions generally.[29] Another example would be the driving instructor who is supervising a learner-driver and who realizes that the learner is about to undertake a manoeuvre which is dangerous to other road-users: if, as in *Rubie v. Faulkner* (1940),[30] the instructor fails to intervene, either by telling the learner not to do it or by physically acting to prevent it, then this

[27] [1971] 1 WLR 1402.

[28] Cf. article 63(1) of the French Penal Code, discussed by A. Ashworth and E. Steiner, 'Criminal Omissions and Public Duties: The French Experience'.

[29] See above, Ch. 4.6(c) and 4.4(b).

[30] [1940] 1 KB 571, discussed by M. Wasik, 'A Learner's Careless Driving' [1982] Crim. LR 411, and D. J. Lanham, 'Drivers, Control and Accomplices' [1982] Crim. LR 419.

failure in the duty of supervision is rightly held to be sufficient to support liability for aiding and abetting the learner-driver's offence.

From these cases of duty we turn to cases of legal power. The owner of a car who is a passenger when the car is being driven by another has the legal power to direct this other person not to drive in certain ways;[31] the licensee of a public house has the legal power to require customers to leave at closing-time;[32] the owners of a house have the legal power to direct the behaviour of their children and of visitors to their premises. In the first two cases the courts have held the car owner and the licensee liable as accomplices to the crime of the offender who drives carelessly or remains drinking after hours. What is unusual about these cases is that they rest on a legal power to intervene and not, like *Rubie v. Faulkner* above, on the existence of a legal duty to prevent offences. The cases seem to transgress the principle that there should be no liability for an omission unless a clear duty exists. What the courts have done, in effect, is to assimilate these cases of power to cases of duty, thereby creating a new class of public duty. Even though English law does not impose liability for failing to take reasonable steps to prevent an offence which occurs in the street, these cases hold that a property owner will be liable for failing to take reasonable steps to prevent an offence which occurs on or with the property and in the owner's presence. The law has, in effect, co-opted property owners as law enforcement agents in respect of their own property.

Does it amount to aiding if a shopkeeper sells goods to an offender for use in crime, or if a borrower returns goods to their owner for use in crime? These could be said to be acts of assistance, in the sense that the physical conduct of selling or returning goods helps an offender: should they, if accompanied by the required mental element, amount to aiding the principal? The problem is that both acts are 'normal': the shopkeeper is simply selling goods in the normal course of business, and the borrower is merely fulfilling a duty to restore the goods to their owner. If the law were to regard either of these acts as 'aiding', it would be requiring the defendants to do something abnormal in the circumstances, and—in effect—punishing them for the omission to do the abnormal thing.

Three approaches to this problem may be considered. The first was described by Devlin J in *National Coal Board v. Gamble* (1959):

[31] *Du Cros v. Lambourne* [1907] 1 KB 40.
[32] *Tuck v. Robson* [1970] 1 WLR 741.

'If one man deliberately sells to another a gun to be used for murdering a third, he may be indifferent whether the third man lives or dies and interested only in the cash profit to be made out of the sale, but he can still be an aider or abettor.'[33] This view criminalizes the shopkeeper as an accomplice in every case where the customer's intention to commit that kind of offence is known. It might be justified by arguing that a small sacrifice may be required of shop-keepers in order to benefit the potential victims of crime. Surely, where an offence against the person is a possibility, it is right to place the potential victim's right not to be subjected to assault or injury above the shopkeeper's liberty to sell to all-comers. After all, the shopkeeper is not being required to intervene or even to notify the police of the customer's intentions. The requirement is not to sell goods when the customer is known to be bent on crime.

Despite the decision in *Gillick v. West Norfolk and Wisbech Health Authority* (1986),[34] the statement in *NCB v. Gamble* that selling goods in the ordinary course of business can satisfy the conduct element of 'aiding' remains good law. But English law as a whole now seems to be moving towards the second approach, long upheld in many American jurisdictions, namely, that a shopkeeper should only be liable as an accomplice where it was his or her purpose to further the customer's offence.[35] This stresses the notions of free trade and individual autonomy, treating the shopkeeper as a mere trader rather than as a fellow citizen's keeper. A third approach would not involve the law of complicity, but would treat the shopkeeper's liability as a matter of general criminal law—either by creating a special offence of selling goods which are likely to be used in the commission of crime (of which there are some examples now, such as the sale of flick-knives), or through a general offence of facilitating crime.

The situation of someone who has borrowed goods and who is asked by the owner to return them so that they may be used for a crime is slightly different. In *NCB v. Gamble* it was held by Devlin J that returning goods in these circumstances is a 'negative act' rather than a 'positive act': 'A man who hands over to another his own property on demand, although he may physically be per-forming a positive act, in law is only refraining from detinue.'[36]

---

[33] *NCB v. Gamble* [1959] 1 QB 11.
[34] *Gillick v. West Norfolk and Wisbech Area Health Authority* [1986] AC 112, criticized at pp. 152 and 378.   [35] Model Penal Code, s. 2.06(3).
[36] [1959] 1 QB 11, at 20, discussing *Lomas* (1913) 9 Cr. App. R 220.

Thus the return of the goods is not an act of aiding, because, according to this sophistry, it is not a positive act. In one sense the case is weaker than that of the shopkeeper, since the borrower has a duty to return goods to their owner, whereas a shopkeeper has no duty to sell; but in another sense it is just as strong, since a court would be reluctant to find liability in tort, and would be more likely to recognize a defence if it was known that a crime was contemplated. Devlin J's analysis, despite the fragility of the positive–negative distinction, commends itself as a pragmatic solution, but it is inadequate when it comes to dealing with a case where the borrower is returning a gun which is then to be used for killing someone. The potential victim's rights must count for more than the borrower's duty to return goods to their owner. Rather than concealing these conflicts behind an apparently logical rule, a preferable course would be to allow a defence of 'balance of evils' to any apparently criminal complicity.[37]

(c) Counselling and Procuring

The characteristic contribution of the counsellor or procurer is to incite, instigate, or advise on the commission of the substantive offence by the principal. One way of expressing this is to describe the role as 'influencing' the perpetrator. Some European legal systems provide a higher maximum penalty for an accomplice who incites or instigates than for a mere helper, and a general justification for this can readily be found. No offence might have taken place at all but for the instigation, and this is surely more reprehensible than assisting someone who has already decided to commit a crime. In practice, however, there are many shades of culpability between helpers and instigators, a point which strikes the English lawyer more forcefully, because of the uncertain limits of the terms 'counselling' and 'procuring'. The ordinary meaning of 'counselling' may fall well short of inciting or instigating an offence, and covers such conduct as advising on an offence and giving information required for an offence. The ordinary meaning of 'procuring' is said to be 'to produce by endeavour',[38] which goes beyond mere instigation.

The forms of counselling and procuring recognized by English law probably stretch from the giving of advice or information, through encouraging or trying to persuade another person to commit the crime, to such conduct as threatening or commanding that the

---

[37] See above, Ch. 4.8.
[38] *Attorney-General's Reference (No. 1 of 1975)* [1975] QB 773.

offence be committed. Generally speaking, the accomplice's culpability increases as one proceeds towards the extreme of a command
backed by threats. In that extreme situation the principal may have
the defence of duress,[39] and may be regarded as an innocent agent
of the threatener, who then becomes the principal.[40] There are also
cases in which the principal does not realize that someone is trying
to bring about an offence: for example, if D surreptitiously laces P's
non-alcoholic drink with some form of alcohol and P subsequently
drives a car, unaware of the consumption of alcohol, P would be
liable to conviction for drunken driving and D could be convicted of
procuring the offence, so long as it was shown that D knew P was
intending to drive. Such conduct fulfils the ordinary definition of
procuring: 'you procure a thing by setting out to see that it happens
and taking appropriate steps to produce that happening'.[41] P's case
may also look like one of innocent agency, but it may not be,
primarily because that doctrine only applies where it is D's purpose
to bring about the offence.

The ordinary meaning of procuring, 'to produce by endeavour', is
not restricted to cases where the principal is unaware of the accomplice's design. One can take the appropriate steps to bring about a
crime by persuading another to do the required acts—for example,
by hiring 'hit men',[42] or perhaps by shaming someone into committing an offence by taunts of cowardice. It can be said that there is a
causal relationship in such cases between the accomplice's procuring
and the principal's offence: the accomplice provides a reason for the
principal's act, and it is proper to say that the principal acts *in
consequence of* the accomplice's conduct.[43] These cases of procuring, then, represent the high-water mark of causal connection
among the various types of accessorial conduct, headed by the case
of procuring an unwitting principal (where D laces P's drink), in
which there is no meeting of minds between principal and accomplice. Such a strong causal connection is not found in counselling,
which may merely involve the supply of information, advice, or
encouragement. This has led Professor J. C. Smith to conclude that:
'Procuring requires causation but not consensus; encouraging requires

[39] See above, Ch. 6.4.
[40] See *Bourne* (1952) 36 Cr. App. R 125, discussed below, Ch. 10.6.
[41] See *Attorney-General's Reference (No. 1 of 1975)* [1975] QB 773.
[42] As on the facts of *Richards* [1974] QB 776, and of *Calhaem* [1985] QB 808.
[43] H. L. A. Hart and A. M. Honoré, *Causation in the Law* (2nd edn. 1985), 51—9,
and Ch. 4.6(c) above.

consensus but not causation; assisting requires actual help but neither consensus nor causation.'[44]

The uncertain and, indeed, vanishing quality of causation in the law of complicity is not the only difficulty with the conduct element required. The law has been largely developed by the courts, and they have tended to pursue a conception of social defence combined with flexibility in the boundaries of the criminal law, without explicit consideration of the claims of the policy of minimum criminalization (see Chapter 3.2(*a*)) or the policy of maximum certainty (see Chapter 3.3.(*i*)). The need for principled reform is manifest.

10.4. THE MENTAL ELEMENT IN COMPLICITY

The fault required before a person can be convicted as an accomplice differs from that required for all other forms of criminal liability. This is because it concerns not merely the defendant's awareness of the nature and effect of his own acts, but also his awareness of the intentions of the principal. It is a form of two-dimensional fault, which brings with it various complexities: the would-be accomplice's knowledge of the principal's intentions may be more or less detailed, and in any event the principal might not do exactly as planned.

Two basic fault requirements may be outlined. First, the accomplice must be aware that his or her acts will amount to some assistance in the principal's crime or will encourage that crime: mere recklessness on this issue would seem insufficient.[45] Second, the accomplice must know the 'essential matters which constitute the offence', i.e. all the relevant circumstances.[46] These requirements apply whether the principal's crime is one of recklessness, negligence, or strict liability. Why is a higher degree of fault required for the accomplice than for the principal? The answer, as for inchoate offences (see below, Chapter 11.3(*a*)), is that as the form of criminal liability moves further away from the actual infliction of harm, so the grounds of liability should become narrower. Otherwise, the law would spread its net wide indeed, and all kinds of people who did acts which, unbeknown to them, helped others to

---

[44] Smith, 'Aid, Abet, Counsel or Procure', 134; perhaps the words 'actual or potential help' might be preferable.

[45] See G. Williams, 'Complicity, Purpose and the Draft Code, II' [1990] Crim. LR 98.

[46] *Johnson v. Youden* [1950] 1 KB 544.

commit crimes of strict liability or negligence would find themselves liable to conviction. In fact, the practical problem arises mainly in cases of aiding, as there is rarely any doubt that a person intends the principal to commit the offence when that person encourages, instigates, or procures the offence. But the problems of the concept of 'aiding' are considerable—its definition is so wide, embracing any act of assistance to a principal offender; there is no requirement of causation; and there are particular problems in cases of omissions and ordinary business transactions—and therefore the mental element performs a necessary limiting function.

Just how narrow this mental element is depends on the resolution of a conflict of authority between two cases. The first is *National Coal Board v. Gamble* (1959),[47] where a weighbridge operator issued a ticket to a lorry-driver certifying the lorry's weight and thus allowing him to take his lorry out of the colliery and on to a public road. The Divisional Court held that the weighbridge operator was liable for aiding and abetting the driver's offence so long as he knew that the lorry was overweight and that it was about to be driven on a public road,[48] with Devlin J explaining that 'mens rea is a matter of intent only and does not depend on desire or motive'. Thus, it was irrelevant that the weighbridge operator was 'only doing his job' and had no personal interest in what the lorry-driver might do thereafter. His *knowledge* of what the lorry-driver *was about to do* was sufficient. This approach would also lead to the conviction of a shopkeeper who knows that his customer plans to use a certain item for a crime and who nevertheless sells the item, and it is dissatisfaction with this outcome which led the framers of the American Model Penal Code to impose the more stringent requirement that the accomplice should have acted with the purpose of promoting or facilitating the offence.[49] The effect of that narrower doctrine is to ensure that citizens are not treated as their fellow citizens' keepers, a sturdy individualist approach. The wider doctrine of *NCB v. Gamble*, which imposes accomplice liability wherever a person knows that the recipient intends to commit a certain crime with the property delivered, has the effect of placing a seller, a weighbridge operator, etc. under a duty not to make the sale or issue the ticket in these circumstances. Not only is this consistent with the general

---

[47] [1959] 1 QB 11.
[48] See also *Attorney-General v. Able* [1984] 1 QB 795.
[49] Model Penal Code, s. 2.06(3).

assimilation of foresight of practical certainty within intention,[50] but it also supports a more social and less individualistic notion of responsibility.

English courts have not always felt comfortable with the proposition that knowledge of the principal's intention (without purpose) should suffice for accomplice liability, and in the unusual circumstances of *Gillick v. West Norfolk and Wisbech Health Authority* (1986)[51] the House of Lords held that a doctor who supplies contraceptives to a girl under 16, knowing that this will assist her boyfriend to commit the offence of unlawful sexual intercourse with a girl under 16, is not an accomplice to the boyfriend's offence. The reason for this decision seems to be that the doctor's purpose would not be to assist the offence but to protect the girl. This runs directly counter to *NCB v. Gamble*, where it was held that mere knowledge of assistance is enough and that purpose is not required. *Gillick* may not be treated as conclusive on the issue of accomplice liability, since it could have been better explained as an example of a defence of medical necessity.[52] A much clearer decision is that in *Clarke* (1985),[53] where the Court of Appeal held that a person who knowingly assists others in a burglary, with the intent of ensuring that the police capture both the burglars and the stolen property, does satisfy the mental element of complicity (in that he knows that the principals will commit the offence) but may have a defence based on his purpose of assisting law enforcement. That decision keeps the question of the accomplice's knowledge separate from the question of whether there is any defence.

Much more could be written about the conflict between the cases of *Gamble* and *Gillick*. There are legal precedents in favour of each view,[54] and a further possibility is that the broader *Gamble* requirement of knowledge should be applied in cases of aiding and abetting, whereas the narrower *Gillick* concept of purpose is more appropriate

---

[50] As in *Moloney* [1985] AC 905, *Hancock and Shankland* [1986] AC 455, and the draft Criminal Code, clause 18(b), discussed above, Ch. 5.3(*b*).

[51] [1986] AC 112.

[52] The court did not mention such a doctrine, but see the discussion of this possibility above, Ch. 4.8(*b*).

[53] (1985) 80 Cr. App. R 344.

[54] For recent debate, see I. H. Dennis, 'The Mental Element for Accessories', in P. F. Smith (ed.), *Criminal Law: Essays in Honour of J. C. Smith* (1987), G. R. Sullivan, 'Intent, Purpose and Complicity', [1988] Crim. LR 641, with reply by Dennis [1988] Crim. LR 649; see also R. J. Buxton, 'Some Simple Thoughts on Intention' [1988] Crim. LR 484.

in cases of counselling and procuring.[55] What is regrettable is that the issue of principle has been obscured by confusions of terminology (e.g. different meanings of intention) and by refusals to give explicit recognition to a defence of medical necessity. The real issue concerns the proper scope of the criminal law in this sphere, and there remains the associated question of whether the difficulty in finding a reasonably certain definition of the conduct element in complicity renders it desirable to maintain a narrow fault requirement.

The conflict over whether mere knowledge or purpose is necessary for accomplice liability is not the only uncertain factor in the mental element. Problems arise from the fact that at least two people are involved, the accomplice and the principal, and so it is often a question of one person's knowledge of another person's intentions. Some issues can be resolved by basic principles. If the aider knows the nature of the offence which the principal intends to commit but does not know when it is to occur, that should be immaterial: time is rarely specified as an element in the definition of an offence. The same applies to the location of the offence: so long as the aider knows that the principal plans to burgle a bank, ignorance as to the particular bank is immaterial to accomplice liability.[56] The real difficulties begin when the aider or counsellor does not know precisely what offence the principal intends to commit, and has only a general idea. Should this be sufficient?

Let us suppose that D lends P some mechanical cutting equipment, knowing full well that P intends to use it in connection with a forthcoming crime but having no precise idea of the crime intended: D does not ask, and P does not tell. In fact, D uses the equipment in a burglary. On facts similar to these, the decision in *Bainbridge* (1960)[57] held that neither mere suspicion nor broad knowledge of some criminal intention is sufficient: the minimum condition for accomplice liability is knowledge that the principal intends to commit a crime of the *type* actually committed. Should this decision be regretted as widening the mental element—knowledge of the particular crime committed ought to be required, because the theory is that the accomplice's liability derives from the principal's offence—or should it be accepted as a pragmatic solution which avoids the acquittals of those who assist willingly without knowing the precise form of offence envisaged? This might depend on the breadth of the term 'type', and some light is thrown on this by the

---

[55] G. Williams, 'Complicity, Purpose and the Draft Code, I' [1990] Crim. LR 4.
[56] *Bainbridge* [1960] 1 QB 219.   [57] Ibid.

decision of the House of Lords in *Maxwell v. DPP for Northern Ireland* (1978).[58] Maxwell was persuaded to drive a car for a group of terrorists, knowing broadly what offences they *might* commit, but not knowing which one or ones they *would* commit. It was held that he was liable as an accomplice to the offence of planting explosives so long as he contemplated that offence as one of the possible offences and intentionally lent his assistance. As Lord Scarman put it: 'An accessory who leaves it to his principal to choose is liable, provided always the choice is made from the range of offences from which the accessory contemplates the choice will be made.'

It is not difficult to see why the courts reached the decisions in *Bainbridge* and in *Maxwell*. They probably believed that a narrow view of the mental element in complicity might open the door to acquittal for some persons believed to be sufficiently culpable, and in *Maxwell* there was the additional factor of the defendant's knowing involvement in terrorism which may have led the court to avoid a narrow view. Both courts appear to have decided to propound a test which stops short of proclaiming that a general criminal intent is sufficient (i.e. knowledge that the principal was going to commit some crime), and yet which goes wider than a requirement of full knowledge. The effect of the *Maxwell* test is to introduce reckless knowledge as sufficient: the accomplice knows that one or more of a group of offences is virtually certain to be committed, which means that in relation to the one(s) actually committed, there was knowledge only of a *risk* that it would be committed—and that amounts to recklessness. Since our discussion began with the principle that accomplice liability should be restricted to cases of full knowledge, and since the effect of *Gillick* may be to restrict it further to cases of purpose, the ruling in *Maxwell* does appear to be a significant departure. Yet there is surely no merit in acquitting a person who willingly gives assistance, knowing that one of a group of crimes will be committed but not knowing exactly which one. Such a person has surely crossed the threshold of blameworthiness, both in conduct and in the accompanying fault. The difficulty arises not so much from the *Maxwell* ruling itself as from English law's insistence that the liability of the accomplice should be derived from, and tied to, the precise offence committed by the principal. In situations like *Maxwell*, the main justification for convicting the

[58] [1978] 3 All ER 1140.

defendant is the willing assistance to persons known to be involved in serious crime. The logical way of dealing with this is to create a separate crime of facilitation, to be committed by anyone who assists a person who is known to be involved in a crime, and to be sentenced according to the level of seriousness of the crime contemplated by the facilitator.[59] In the absence of such an offence, the courts have created another *ad hoc* adaptation of the prevailing complicity doctrine, by extending the referential field of the accomplice's 'knowledge' to deal with the problems raised by *Bainbridge* and *Maxwell*.

10.5. COMMON PURPOSE AND LIABILITY FOR THE UNEXPECTED

Most complicity caces involve some kind of agreement between principal and accomplice. This is not necessarily the case where the accomplice's contribution is a form of 'aiding': as we saw earlier, 'aiding' can be effected without any consensus between the two parties—and, indeed, without the principal knowing about the accomplice's contribution.[60] However, most of the cases do involve some kind of common purpose, sometimes termed 'joint enterprise' or 'common design' by the courts. The questions we must now confront are: What view does the law take if the plan goes wrong and unexpected consequences ensue? What is the accomplice's liability if the principal deliberately deviates from the plan? What principles should govern these questions?

(a) Same Offence: Different Result

In one group of cases the law takes the same approach for joint enterprises as it does for offences by individuals. Thus, where the intended result occurs by an unexpected mode (e.g. death caused by drowning rather than by beating), this does not affect the accomplice's liability;[61] where the principal makes a mistake of identity and commits the offence against the wrong victim, this is also irrelevant;[62] and where the intended offence falls upon the wrong victim because the principal's attempt to harm one person succeeds

---

[59] A precedent for this would be s. 4 of the Criminal Law Act 1967; see further R. J. Buxton, 'Complicity in the Criminal Code' (1969) 85 LQR 252.

[60] See above, Ch. 10.3(*a*), and the case of *State v. Tally* (1894) 15 So. 722.

[61] For the unforeseen mode, see Ch. 5.4(*b*) above.

[62] For mistaken victim, see Ch. 5.4(*c*) above.

only in harming another, this too is irrelevant.[63] In so far as the policies of transferred liability and the other rules are sound for individuals, they should apply to principals and accomplices. The same should presumably be said of constructive liability: thus, if D helps P in an assault on V, as a result of which V unexpectedly dies, a law which renders P liable for manslaughter should also apply so as to render D an accomplice to manslaughter. These propositions all apply the logic of English law's 'derivative' theory of complicity, whereby the accomplice's liability derives from that of the principal. Most of the questions could be approached in other ways—for example, making the accomplice's liability turn on what he or she intended the principal to do, rather than attaching liability to what actually happened.[64]

The common factor in the above group of cases is that the result was unexpected by both principal and accomplice. The problem of the accomplice's liability is different in cases where the principal deviates intentionally from the agreed course of conduct. Causal principles would suggest that this change of mind constitutes a voluntary intervening act which should sever all connection between the accomplice's contribution and the principal's actual offence. This was the approach taken in the sixteenth-century case of *Saunders and Archer* (1573), where D had advised P to kill his wife by means of a poisoned apple; P placed the apple before his wife, but the wife passed the apple to their child, who ate it and died.[65] D was held not to have been an accomplice in the child's murder, on the basis that the events amounted to a deliberate change of plan by P. Although P did not actually give the apple to the child, he sat by and allowed the child to eat the apple when it was his parental duty to intervene, and this was enough to negative D's complicity in the actual result.

Behind this decision lies a conflict of principles. It seems to establish that an accomplice is relieved of liability if the principal deliberately deviates from the 'common design' by selecting a different victim, and causal reasoning may support that. But this seems inconsistent with English law's general disregard of the identity of the victim and of the method used to effect result-oriented crimes. Would the *Saunders and Archer* approach be used in cases of deliberate change of mode? If D had counselled P to kill his wife with a poisoned apple, and P had decided to use a knife or a

---

[63] For transferred fault, see Ch. 5.4(*d*) above.
[64] Discussed further below, pp. 393–394.   [65] (1573) 2 Plowd. 473.

gun instead, should D equally be acquitted of complicity in the killing? Perhaps accessorial liability should be determined on the basis that it is for the parties to stipulate which features of their common design are critical, rather than for the law to declare that neither the identity of the victim nor the method employed is legally relevant. For example, in the South African case of *S v. Robinson* (1968)[66] X and two others agreed with V that V should be killed by X so that V could escape prosecution for fraud and the others could obtain insurances monies. V withdrew his consent to the arrangement (not surprisingly), but X killed him nevertheless. The offence was as planned, the victim was as planned, but the element of consent was crucial to the common purpose, and that was absent: should the two others be convicted as accomplices to X's offence? In this case, as in the others, the accomplices have made a contribution which would in normal circumstances attract criminal liability, but because the principal has taken an unexpected decision, and because the common law maintains that the liability of the accomplice derives from that of the principal, a problem of legal logic arises. English law has struggled to resolve the problem by holding that a deliberate change of victim releases the accomplice from liability; it has also used the test of whether the principal's conduct was 'beyond the scope of his authority';[67] but it has not directly confronted the question of whether these *ad hoc* adaptations of the derivative theory of liability are satisfactory both in theory and in practice. One alternative would be to introduce a general offence of facilitation or instigation of crime.[68] This would make it unnecessary for there to be any connection between the accomplice's contribution and the actual result brought about by the principal. It thus disposes of the causal argument which appears to support *Saunders and Archer*, and places the emphasis squarely on what the accomplice believed was going to occur.

(b) Different, More Serious Offence

The cases discussed so far have chiefly concerned deviations by the principal which have none the less resulted in the commission of an

[66] 1968 (1) SA 666.
[67] *Calhaem* [1985] QB 808; see the discussion by K. J. M. Smith, 'Complicity and Causation' [1986] Crim. LR 663. The draft Criminal Code leaves the issue for judicial solution: Law Com. No. 177, clause 27(1) and para. 9.31.
[68] See the proposals of Buxton, 'Complicity in the Criminal Code', and J. R. Spencer, 'Helping Others to Commit Crimes', in Smith (ed.), *Essays in Honour of J. C. Smith*.

offence in the same legal category as that contemplated by the parties. What if the principal deliberately deviates so as to commit a more serious offence? English law on this point has developed in a curious way. A hundred years ago Stephen stated the test as whether the crime committed by the principal could be regarded as a 'probable consequence' of the common design—an objective test of foreseeability, to be applied to the point at which the assistance was given or the agreement reached.[69] To allow the accomplice's liability to turn on an objective test of foreseeability was open to criticism on the familiar unfairness grounds,[70] and the tendency in the last thirty years has been to phrase the test subjectively. However, the courts have been unable to decide on the proper formulation of the test, and there is a conflict of authorities. The broader view, supported by the stronger authorities,[71] is whether the would-be accomplice foresaw the higher offence as a 'real risk' or as a 'possible result'. This subjective test may be wider than the old objective one: indeed, it bases the accomplice's liability on recklessness, and is therefore similar in spirit to the *Maxwell* decision.[72] The justification for placing the same label on both accomplice and principal here is presumably that the accomplice's foresight of the possibility of a more serious offence, coupled with his failure to withdraw or to try to prevent the occurrence of that offence,[73] amounts to sufficient inculpation.

Another line of decisions supports the narrower view that the accomplice is only liable if he or she had the same degree of *mens rea* as is required for the principal.[74] As a general proposition, this does not represent the common law of complicity.[75] But the origins of this approach are not difficult to find. If D and E go out to burgle a house, and D hands E a knife on the understanding that it will only be used to frighten the victim, the broader test (above) would turn D into an accomplice to murder, liable to the mandatory penalty of life imprisonment, if E uses the knife and kills somone. E would be liable for murder only if the required intention is present, but D is

---

[69] Sir James Fitzjames Stephen, *A Digest of the Criminal Law*, art. 20.
[70] See above, Ch. 5.2(*a*) and 5.3(*a*).
[71] *Chan Wing-Siu v. R* [1985] AC 168 (Privy Council), *Ward* (1986) 85 Cr. App. R 71 *Slack* (1989) 89 Cr. App. R 252, and *Hyde* [1991] Crim. LR 133.
[72] See above, n. 57 and accompanying text.
[73] See below, Ch. 10.7.
[74] *Barr et al.* (1989) 88 Cr. App. R 362; *Wakeley et al.* [1990] Crim. LR 119; see M. Giles, 'Complicity: The Problems of Joint Enterprise' [1990] Crim. LR 383.
[75] Williams, 'Complicity, Purpose and the Draft Code, II.'

liable to conviction of the same offence, with the same mandatory penalty, on the basis of recklessness alone. The narrower test avoids this result by requiring some tacit agreement between the parties about the conduct which took place. This is, however, very much an *ad hoc* solution, driven by the inflexibility of the English law of murder rather than by policies relevant to complicity. Some will applaud it as a pragmatic device, but it would surely be preferable to consider the creation of a separate offence for those who help or facilitate the commission of crimes. This would keep the assessment of the accomplice's culpability independent from that of the principal, departing from the 'derivative' theory which underpins much of the common law of complicity.

(c) Different, Less Serious Offence

The English courts have recently stretched the law of complicity in the opposite direction: the House of Lords decision in *Howe* (1987)[76] holds that where D aids or counsels the principal to commit a certain offence, and the principal deviates by committing a less serious offence, D may be convicted as an accomplice to the intended (more serious) offence. The previous decision in *Richards*[77] laid down a different rule. In that case a woman paid two men to beat up her husband so as to put him in hospital for a few days. Her hope was that this experience would lead her husband to turn to her for comfort, thus repairing their relationship. The hired men inflicted less serious injuries than she had asked them to, and it was held that she could not be convicted as an accomplice to the higher offence unless she was present at the scene (an ancient rule). The effect of *Howe* is to sweep away such restrictions. Yet this new rule involves a patent departure from the derivative theory of accomplice liability: the (intended) higher offence was never committed, and so the accomplice's liability cannot derive from any such offence. The theory underlying the *Howe* ruling is that the culpability of the accomplice should be viewed as a separate issue from that of the principal, and based upon what the accomplice intended to happen or believed would happen. This result could have been achieved in *Richards* by charging the wife with the inchoate offence of incitement (see Chapter 11.6 below). Where the prosecution uses the law of complicity, the decision in *Howe* suggests that liability is determined

---

[76] [1987] AC 417.
[77] [1974] QB 776, discussed by Kadish, *Blame and Punishment*, 184–6.

according to which of two principles—the derivative and the subjective—has the further reach in a given case.

10.6. DERIVATIVE LIABILITY AND THE MISSING LINK

We now come to another set of cases in which the English courts
have departed from, or at least modified, the derivative theory of
accessorial liability. If the would-be principal is not guilty of the
substantive offence, because of the absence of a mental element or
the presence of a defence, does this mean that the accomplice must
also be acquitted? A straightforward application of the derivative
theory would lead to non-liability: one cannot be said to have aided
and abetted an offence if the offence did not take place, for there is
nothing from which the accomplice's liability can derive. Yet the
would-be accomplice has done all that he or she intended to do in
order to further the principal's crime, and, considered in isolation,
the accomplice is surely no less culpable than if the principal had
been found guilty. It is therefore not surprising that English courts
have responded by stretching the doctrine of complicity. In *Bourne*
(1952)[78] D threatened and forced his wife to commit bestiality with
a dog, and his conviction for aiding and abetting bestiality was
upheld despite the fact that his wife would have had a defence of
duress if charged as the principal. In *Cogan and Leak* (1976)[79]
Cogan had intercourse with Leak's wife, believing, on the basis of
what Leak had told him, that Mrs Leak was consenting. Leak knew
that his wife was not consenting. Cogan's conviction for rape was
quashed because his defence of mistaken belief in the woman's
consent had not been put to the jury, but Leak's conviction for
aiding and abetting rape was upheld. The judgments in these cases
contain little elaboration of the theoretical basis for conviction, but
they could be defended as a mere extension of the derivative theory.
The extension would be that a person may be convicted as an
accomplice to the commission of an *actus reus* or 'wrongful act',
where the reason for acquitting the would-be principal is the
absence of a mental element or the presence of a defence. This
approach does have theoretical and practical limitations, however.
One requirement of accomplice liability is that the accomplice must
know the essential elements of the offence (including the principal's
mental element); but in these cases the accomplice usually knows

---

[78] (1952) 36 Cr. App. R 125.   [79] [1976] 1 QB 217.

that the would-be principal lacks an element necessary for conviction. Bourne knew that his wife was acting because of his threats; Leak knew that Cogan was acting because of his lies. The suggested extension of the derivative theory would also do nothing to overturn the decision in *Thornton v. Mitchell* (1940).[80] A bus-conductor was directing the driver in reversing a bus when an accident was caused. The driver was acquitted of careless driving, because he was relying on the conductor's guidance, and it was held that the conductor must therefore be acquitted of aiding and abetting. Since the *actus reus* of careless driving was not committed, the suggested extension of the derivative theory would yield the same result. Only a suitably worded offence of facilitation would produce a conviction.

Convictions seem justified for Bourne and Leak, because they both chose to bring about a result which the law prohibits: their behaviour and culpability are as high on the scale of seriousness as many principals. The inchoate offence of incitement might appear to offer a solution, but it may not succeed where the inciter knows that the 'incited' lacks an element of the full offence.[81] One solution would be to change the law and to deem such persons principals, which the draft English Code proposes;[82] or the law could render the person liable as a principal for causing the prohibited conduct or result—for example, by imposing liability for causing an innocent or non-responsible person to engage in prohibited conduct where the person who causes this has the mental element required for the offence.[83]

Another possible approach is through the doctrine of innocent agency. A clear example would be where an adult urges or orders a child under the age of criminal responsibility to commit crimes, such as stealing from a shop. The young child is deemed 'innocent' in law, and so it is said that the adult commits the crime through the innocent agency of the child. No such notion is possible where two adults are involved, since it is presumed that adults are autonomous beings acting voluntarily, save in exceptional circumstances. One exceptional circumstance would be where the adult is mentally disordered; another would be where the adult is acting under duress. Thus, if, as in *Bourne*,[84] a man threatens and forces his wife to commit bestiality with a dog, her defence of duress may be said to establish that her conduct was insufficiently voluntary to be regarded

---

[80] [1940] 1 All ER 339.
[82] Law Com. No. 177, clause 26(1).
[83] Model Penal Code, s. 2.06(2)(a).

[81] See below, Ch. 11.6.

[84] (1952) 36 Cr. App. R 125.

as the cause of the event. In causal terms she 'drops out of the picture' as a mere innocent agent, leaving the person who uttered the threats as the principal responsible for the offence.[85] How much further can the doctrine of innocent agency be taken? If D gives a bottle to the nurse attending V, telling her that it contains a prescribed medicine when in fact it contains poison, D should surely be liable as the principal when the nurse administers the contents of the bottle to V, who dies. The nurse would be regarded as an innocent agent because, although she did not lack criminal capacity in the sense of being mentally disordered or overborne by threats, she was acting under a mistake which would relieve her of criminal liability for her acts.[86] If this is accepted, it would seem to follow that where (as in *Cogan and Leak*) D persuades P to have sexual intercourse with D's wife by inducing P to believe that she consents to this, P's mistake would mean that he drops out of the picture as an innocent agent and that D should be liable as a principal for rape.[87]

Various objections might be raised against this conclusion. The major counter-argument is that the doctrine of innocent agency should not be used where it is linguistically inappropriate. It is appropriate to describe D as killing (or, at least, causing the death of) V in the case involving the nurse, but it is manifestly inappropriate to describe a person as driving with excess alcohol in his blood, if what he has done is to lace the drink of someone who is about to drive a car,[88] or to describe D as having raped a woman if D tricked a man into having sexual intercourse with that woman,[89] or to describe D as having committed bigamy if she induced someone else to believe (erroneously) that the other person's marriage had been legally terminated and to remarry on the strength this belief.[90] The conflict here is plain. The law has to be expressed in words, and some verbal formulas are hedged about with linguistic conventions which do not correspond to moral or social distinctions in responsibility. It seems right that the person who gives poison to the nurse to administer unwittingly should be convicted as the principal in murder, because that person was the cause of the death. That element of causation remains prominent in the other examples of

---

[85] See above, Ch. 4.6(*b*).
[86] *Michael* (1840) 9 C & P 356, above p. 104.
[87] See generally the discussion by Kadish, *Blame and Punishment*, Essay 8.
[88] *Attorney-General's Reference (No. 1 of 1975)* [1975] QB 773.
[89] *Cogan and Leak* [1976] 1 QB 217.
[90] *Kemp and Else* [1964] 2 QB 341.

the 'lacer' of drinks, the encourager of non-consensual intercourse, and the orchestrator of bigamy, and the moral/social argument for criminal liability seems no less strong; but the conventions of language erect a barrier. Some offences are phrased in terms which imply personal agency (rape is said to be one) or which apply only to the holder of a certain office or licence. There is no reason why the law should be constrained by this linguistic barrier. The courts could simply ignore it and stretch the language.[91] Or Parliament could introduce a special provision which would make it possible to convict as a principal the person who uttered the threats, implanted the mistaken belief, or poured the alcohol clandestinely, on the basis that that person *caused* the wrongful act.[92] Or it could introduce a special provision which would render that person liable as an accomplice, even though no person could be convicted as a principal.[93] The difference between the last two alternatives would seem to turn on the the appropriateness of labelling the person as a principal or an accomplice: since he or she really is the motivator and the cause of the event, it would not seem wrong to label them as such. This could lead to a woman who tricked a man into having sexual intercourse with another woman being convicted as a principal in rape. This is said to be absurd. Any absurdity is, however, linguistic rather than moral or social. This is where the counter-argument started.

10.7 WITHDRAWAL FROM PARTICIPATION

Complicity often involves the accomplice in words or deeds prior to the principal's crime. If the accomplice has a change of heart before the principal commits the offence, can the accomplice's liability be removed? If an individual decides to commit an offence on his own, then obviously that individual can change his mind at will. However, once some steps have been taken towards the commission of the offence, the possibility of preventing liability by abandoning one's intentions depends in English law on how far one has gone towards the substantive offence. If the acts done so far amount to a criminal attempt, then the law states that there can be no legally effective abandonment—it becomes merely a matter in mitigation of sent-

---

[91] See A. Ashworth, 'Interpreting Criminal Legislation: A Crisis of Legality?' (1991) 107 LQR.

[92] See Model Penal Code, s. 2.06(2)(a).

[93] Confirming *Cogan and Leak* [1976] 1 QB 217, (above, note 78), and following the German law described by Fletcher, *Rethinking Criminal Law*, 664–7.

ence. Only if the acts done fall short of an attempt, can the person abandon the criminal plan with impunity. This is an over-strict doctrine which neither reflects culpability nor serves the goal of crime prevention.[94] If we now turn to complicity cases, where there is a principal and an accomplice, abandonment or withdrawal by the accomplice raises slightly different issues. Since the contribution of the accomplice may have had some influence over the principal, either by way of encouragement or assistance, one might expect the law to require not merely a change of mind communicated to the principal, but some endeavour to 'undo' the effects of what has been done. The older decisions tend to speak in terms of the principal acting with the authority of the accomplice, and withdrawal as a countermanding of that authority.[95] Modern decisions have emphasized the significance of the stage at which the principal's actions rest. Thus, where D's contribution consists of giving information to the principal about property to be burgled, and then, a week or so before the planned burglary D tells the principal that he does not wish to take part and does not want the burglary to take place, this may be an effective withdrawal.[96] In *Becerra and Cooper* (1975),[97] however, the situation was rather different. B had given C a knife to use if anyone disturbed them during the burglary they were carrying out. When B heard someone coming, he told C of this, said 'Come on, let's go', jumped out of a window, and ran off. C did not follow: he stabbed the inquisitive neighbour fatally with the knife. B was convicted as an accomplice to murder, and this was upheld in the Court of Appeal; when events have proceeded so far, an effective withdrawal was held to require far more than a few words such as 'let's go'. The Court did not decide exactly what was required, but it seems clear that if C had already been using or preparing to use the knife against the inquisitive neighbour, B might have had to go so far as to try to restrain C physically. The trial judge framed the general proposition that the withdrawing accomplice must 'take all reasonable steps to prevent the commission of the crime which he had agreed the others should commit,' and the Court of Appeal did not dissent from this. Thus the principle underlying withdrawal in complicity is that the accomplice must not only make a clear statement of withdrawal and communicate this to the principal, but must also (if the crime is imminent) take some steps to prevent its

---

[94] See further Ch. 11.3(*a*) below.
[95] e.g. *Saunders and Archer* (1573) 2 Plowd. 473, at 476.
[96] *Whitefield* (1984) 79 Cr. App. R 36.   [97] (1975) 62 Cr. App. R 212.

commission. The closer the principal's offence to commission, the more active the intervention required of the accomplice for effective withdrawal. In a sense, the argument seems to parallel the *Miller* principle—that one has a duty to prevent harm resulting from a train of events which one has started[98]—but the parallel is imperfect, since on the one hand complicity involves the actions of two autonomous individuals, and the accomplice is not causally 'responsible' for the principal's conduct, and on the other hand the accomplice is knowingly involved in initiating the train of events, whereas Miller did so unknowingly. But the parallel still has some rough equivalence. One cannot go further, and suggest that English law is supporting a limited duty to prevent crime here,[99] since the accomplice who gives information to the principal and then communicates a withdrawal in good time is not, it seems, required to counteract the effect of that information by informing the police of the planned crime.[100] This seems difficult to justify, given the influence which the accomplice's help or advice may have had on the principal, and it would surely be right to require more as a condition of legally effective withdrawal.

It is apparent that the English law of complicity is replete with uncertainties and conflicts. It has usually been assumed that there are two fundamental principles underlying the English doctrine— that the liability of the accomplice derives from that of the principal, and that intention or knowledge by the accomplice of the principal's offence is required for liability. Neither proposition can now be advanced without qualification. The derivative theory has given way in several situations to liability based on causal or subjective principles, and the fault requirements have in some spheres been relaxed so as to include recklessness and in other spheres narrowed to 'purpose' alone. What reasons have led the courts to develop the law in these ways? What principles ought to determine the boundaries of accomplice liability?

The early part of this chapter was concerned with the ambit of complicity liability: what forms of conduct should suffice? The variation in the level of accomplices' contributions is great. Someone who procures another to commit an offence by threats or by implanting a false belief may have substantial causal influence. This

---

[98] [1983] 2 AC 161.   [99] See above, Ch. 4.4(c) and Ch. 10.3(b).
[100] See the draft Criminal Code, Law Com. No. 177, clause 27(8); cf. *Hudson and Taylor* [1971] 2 QB 202, and Ch. 6.4(c).

suggests, by the way, that a rule restricting the penalty for the accomplice to half or three-quarters of the maximum for the principal would be too crude. In contrast, acts of aiding may be minor and hardly significant. It would be impractical to attempt a legislative listing of all the types of conduct which might amount to complicity. And to require that the accomplice contributed significantly or substantially to the principal's offence would introduce a further avenue for legal argument, without honouring the principle of maximum certainty. Yet the expedient of leaving prosecutorial discretion to determine (in practice) the lower threshold of criminal complicity may also be unsatisfactory: certainly, a prosecutors' code could urge them not to bring proceedings unless the contribution was significant, but this would still leave scope for pressure to be placed on fringe participants in offences to choose between facing prosecution and testifying in offences against the others. A flexible definition of complicity strengthens the prosecutor's hand considerably, and gives little weight to the principle of minimum criminalization (see Chapter 3.2(*a*)).

It is rather strange how the law of complicity has become the focal point for a number of arguments about the duties of citizens. The generally restrictive approach of English law towards liability for omissions has already been discussed,[101] but complicity is one sphere in which the courts have abandoned their general reluctance. In a sense, this may be compatible with the notion that the accomplice may be termed 'responsible' for the conduct of the principal, a notion implicit in the terminology of 'authority' which is sometimes used, and also in the requirements for withdrawal from complicity. But the idea of legal responsibility as an accomplice for the acts of those whose conduct one has the power to control—rendering the publican, the car owner, and the house owner liable for the conduct of their guests—is a bold step towards omissions liability under the camouflage of the law of complicity.[102] The debate about the liability of the gun-seller as an accomplice to murder turns on somewhat similar considerations of a citizen's duties towards law enforcement, but it has become wrapped up in an analysis of the distinction between intention and purpose. As suggested in Chapter 4.4(*c*) above, a more open and more principled solution would be to

---

[101] See above, Ch. 4.4(*b*) and (*c*).
[102] See A. Ashworth, 'The Scope of Criminal Liability for Omissions' (1989) 105 LQR at 445–7; Law Com. No. 177, clause 27(3).

create some discrete offences to cover those situations in which it is felt that citizens ought to take positive action.

Another respect in which English law on complicity is confused is the relationship between the accomplice's conduct and that of the principal. On the one hand the law gives itself extraordinary width by its procedural rule which draws no distinction between principal and accomplice in point of charge, conviction, and maximum sentence. Yet on the other hand it has still not relinquished the idea that the accomplice's liability derives from that of the principal, despite the inadequacies of that theory in dealing with cases where there is a missing link[103] or where the principal deviates from the agreed or understood course of action,[104] for example. In these two types of case the courts have stretched or abandoned the derivative theory—but why? The reason for wishing to secure convictions here is surely that the accomplice is no less culpable than would have been the case if the principal had done as intended. In terms of culpability and danger the accomplice stands on the same level: should we not then regard the accomplice's liability as established independently, rather than making it depend on the liability of the principal? The courts have responded by ensuring liability in these cases by one means or another, although there is the further constraint of linguistic awkwardness which may hinder the pursuit of sound policies here. The draft Code follows this approach, grafting specific exceptions on to a legal framework which still follows the derivative theory. The alternative approach is to place more reliance on the inchoate offences of incitement, attempt, and conspiracy, and also to introduce a new general offence of facilitating or instigating a criminal offence. The essence of the new offence would lie in acts or omissions done with intent to facilitate or to instigate a certain crime or in the knowledge that this would be the effect of the acts or omissions. The penalty should be related to the penalty for the crime envisaged.

Much has already been written about this kind of development,[105] and it is not proposed to discuss it at length here. But there remains one important ambiguity which awaits principled resolution. Should the law confine complicity liability to cases where it is the accomplice's purpose that the principal should commit the crime, or continue liability where the accomplice knows that the principal is

---

[103] See above, Ch. 10.6.   [104] See above, Ch. 10.5.
[105] See above, n. 67.

going to commit the crime, or support liability where the accomplice knows that the principal is going to commit one of a number of crimes, but does not know which one?[106] The English decisions do not give a coherent answer. Cases like *Gillick*[107] and *Maxwell*[108] might be explained better by reference to the respective positions of family doctors and Northern Ireland terrorists than by reference to any coherent theory of the mental element in complicity. Much depends on the view one takes of responsibilities for law enforcement. If one adopts a 'social responsibility' approach rather than an 'individualist' approach, this suggests that it should be sufficient for criminal liability if a person acts or omits to act (where there is a duty) in the belief that this will instigate or facilitate an offence or, for completeness, a prohibited harm. Intention or purpose should not be required, and the doctor in *Gillick* would be exonerated by a defence of clinical judgment rather than by a distortion of the law of complicity.

[106] See above, Ch. 10.6(*b*).   [107] [1986] AC 112, see above, p. 378.
[108] [1978] 3 All ER 1140, see above, p. 380.

11

INCHOATE OFFENCES

11.1 THE CONCEPT OF AN INCHOATE OFFENCE

The word 'inchoate', not much used in ordinary discourse, means 'just begun', 'undeveloped'. The common law has given birth to three general offences which are usually termed 'inchoate' or 'preliminary' crimes—attempt, conspiracy, and incitement. A principal feature of these crimes is that they are committed even though the substantive offence is not successfully consummated. An attempt fails, a conspiracy comes to nothing, words of incitement are ignored—in all these instances, there may be liability for the inchoate crime. Moreover, as we shall see later in the chapter, there are many substantive offences which are defined in such a way as not to require the actual causing of harm: offences which penalize a person who does a certain act 'with intent to do X' are in reality defined in an inchoate mode, having many of the characteristics of inchoate offences. Crimes of possession are also essentially inchoate: it is not the mere possession, so much as what the possessor might do with the article or substance, which is the reason for criminalization. However, the chapter begins with a discussion of the three traditional inchoate offences of attempt, conspiracy, and incitement, which will show that their ambit and their significance are rather wider than the term 'inchoate' suggests.

11.2. THE JUSTIFICATIONS FOR PENALIZING ATTEMPTS AT CRIMES

(a) Introduction

Let us begin with three examples: (i) X goes to the house of his rival, V, with a can of petrol, some paper, and a box of matches; he soaks the paper in petrol and pushes it through the letter-box, but he is arrested before he can do anything more; (ii) Y drives a car straight at V, but V jumps out of the way at the last moment and is uninjured; (iii) Z is offered money to carry a package of cannabis into Britain; she accepts, brings the package in, but on her arrest it is found that the package contains dried lettuce leaves. These are all cases in which there might be a conviction for attempt.[1] The first feature to be noticed is that no harm actually occurred in any of them—no damage was done, no injury caused, no drugs smuggled. Normally, criminal liability requires both culpability and harm: X, Y, and Z might appear culpable, but they have caused no harm. Why, then, should the criminal law become involved? The answer is that harm does indeed have a central place in criminal liability, but that the concern is not merely with the occurrence of harm but also with its prevention. According to this view, the first decision for legislators is exactly which harms should properly be objects of the criminal law (see Chapter 2). Once this has been decided, and taking the aims of the criminal law into account,[2] the law should seek to prevent the occurrence of those harms as well as punishing their perpetrators. The consequentialist justification for a law of attempts is therefore that it allows law-enforcement officers and the courts to step in *before* any harm has been done, so long as the danger of the harm being caused is clear. There is also a separate justification, stemming from the 'desert' theory of criminal liability, namely that a person who tries to cause a prohibited harm and fails is, in terms of moral culpability, not materially different from the person who tries and succeeds: the difference in outcome is determined by chance rather than by choice, and the criminal law should not so subordinate itself to the vagaries of fortune that it pays no attention to the failure, and concerns itself only with the actual harm-doer.

(b) Two Kinds of Attempt

The rationale for criminalizing attempts can best be appreciated by drawing a distinction between two kinds of attempt. First, there are incomplete attempts, which are cases in which the defendant has set out to commit a substantive offence but has not yet done all the acts necessary to bring it about. Our first example, of X putting petrol-soaked paper through the door of V's house, is such a case: he has still to strike a match and light the paper. Contrast this with the second kind of attempt, which will be called a complete attempt. Here the defendant has done all that he intended, but the desired result has not followed—Y has driven the car at V, intending to

---

[1] This depends on the accused's intentions and beliefs at the time: see section 11.3(*a*) below.
[2] As discussed in Ch. 1.3 above.

injure V, but he failed; and Z has smuggled the package into the country, believing it to be cannabis when in fact it is a harmless and worthless substance.

It is easier to justify the criminalization of complete attempts than incomplete attempts, and the two sets of justifications have somewhat different emphases. The justification for punishing complete attempts is that the defendant has done all the acts intended, with the beliefs required for the offence, and is therefore no less blameworthy than a person who is successful in committing the substantive offence. The complete 'attempter' is thwarted by some unexpected turn of events which, to him, is a matter of pure chance—the intended victim jumped out of the way, or the substance was not what it appeared to be. These are applications of what were called the 'intent' principle and the 'belief' principle earlier.[3] These principles heighten the subjective element in criminal liability, holding that people's criminal liability should be assessed on what they were trying to do, intended to do, and believed they were doing rather than on the actual consequences of their conduct. Rejection of this approach would lead to criminal liability always being judged according to the actual outcome, which would allow luck to play too great a part in the criminal law. Of course luck and chance play a considerable role in human affairs, but that is no reason why a human system for judging the behaviour of others should be a slave to the vagaries of chance. The 'intent principle' and the 'belief principle' would also be accepted by the consequentialist as justifications for criminalizing complete attempts: the defendant was trying to break the law, and therefore constitutes a source of social danger no less (or little less) than that presented by 'successful' harm-doers.

What about incomplete attempts? The 'intent principle' and the 'belief principle' do have some application here, inasmuch as the defendant has given some evidence of a determination to commit the substantive offence—though the evidence is likely to be less conclusive than in cases of complete attempts. Indeed, it may fairly be said that the incomplete attempter still has time to repent before doing all the acts necessary to bring about the substantive offence: that possibility weakens to some extent the case for criminal liability here. On the other hand, there is one distinct factor present in incomplete attempts, and that is the social

---

[3] Discussed above, Ch. 5.2(*a*).

importance of authorizing official intervention before harm is done. Since the prevention of harm has a central place in the justifications for criminal law, there is a strong case for stopping attempts before they result in the causing of harm. Detailed arguments about the point at which the law should intervene are discussed in section 11.3(*b*) below. Once this point has been agreed, then the agents of law enforcement may intervene to stop attempts before they go further. The culpability of the incomplete attempter may be less than that of the complete attempter because there remains the possibility that there would have been voluntary repentance at some late stage: after all, it may take greater nerve to do the final act which triggers the actual harm than to do the preliminary acts. But so long as it is accepted that the incomplete attempter has evinced a settled intention to continue, and to commit the substantive offence by doing some further acts, there is sufficient ground for criminalization.

These arguments in favour of criminalizing incomplete and complete attempts rely heavily on the assertion that there is no relevant moral difference between attempters and those who succeed in committing the full offence. To argue that the moral difference is not relevant, one may concede that the incomplete attempter is *somewhat* less culpable, given the possibility of voluntary renunciation of criminal purpose before the final act, but this difference is insufficient to take incomplete attempts below the threshold of culpability required for criminal liability. But is it true to say that there is no relevant *moral* difference? Does this not assume that morality is concerned only with the subjective culpability of individuals, which is the point to be proved? Certainly, it can be argued that the moral position of the complete attempter (who causes no harm) differs from that of the person who commits the full offence (and causes harm): but the difference lies, surely, in the latter's liability to pay compensation for the harm done, and does not suggest that the one should be criminally liable and the other not.[4] The criminal law does, in any event, mark the difference in outcome by convicting one of an attempted crime and the other of the full crime. Thus, once again, the argument is that the difference in terms of culpability between the complete attempter and the substantive offender is insufficient to exempt the former from all criminal liability. Rather the reverse: the similarity between them is

[4] Further discussion of this point may be found in H. L. A. Hart, *Punishment and Responsibility*, 130–1, and A. Ashworth, in J. Eekelaar and J. Bell (eds.), *Oxford Essays in Jurisprudence: Third Series* (1987), 16–20.

so great as to constitute a positive argument in favour of criminalizing the complete attempter.

None of this is to suggest that all attempts are no less culpable than completed crimes. On the contrary, it may be argued that incomplete attempts should be punished less severely than the full offence—because of the possibility of voluntary abandonment of the attempt, because it takes greater nerve to consummate an offence, and because it may be prudent to leave some incentive (i.e. reduced punishment) to the incomplete attempter to give up rather than to carry out the full offence. For complete attempts the case for reduced punishment is less strong, although there may be an argument for some reduction of punishment in order to give the complete attempter an incentive not to try again—otherwise D might reason that there is nothing to lose by this. It will be noticed that these arguments for reduced punishments are utilitarian in nature. Following the principle of 'desert', there is little reason for reducing the punishment of the complete attempter, but some reason for recognizing the possibility that the incomplete attempter might yet desist.

11.3 THE ELEMENTS OF CRIMINAL ATTEMPT

The relevant English law is now to be found in the Criminal Attempts Act 1981, which followed a Law Commission report on the subject.[5] It will be discussed by considering three separate aspects of the offence in turn—the fault element, the conduct element and the problem of impossibility.

(a) The Fault Element

It has been said that, where a person is charged with an attempt, 'the intent becomes the principal ingredient of the crime'.[6] The law on this point rarely causes much difficulty: it must be shown that the defendant intended to cause the proscribed harm, and had the necessary knowledge of facts and circumstances. There have been appeals in cases where D has been charged with attempting to cause

---

[5] Law Commission No. 102, *Attempt, and Impossibility in Relation to Attempt, Conspiracy and Incitement* (1980). For an analysis of the provisions of the 1981 Act, see I. Dennis, 'The Criminal Attempts Act 1981' [1982] Crim. LR 5. A more general discussion of the English law of attempts may be found in A. Ashworth, 'Criminal Attempts and the Role of Resulting Harm under the Code, and in the Common Law' (1988) 19 Rutgers LJ 725.

[6] Per Lord Goddard CJ, in *Whybrow* (1951) 35 Cr. App. R 141, at 147.

grievous bodily harm by driving a car at another person, and the defence has been that D did not intend to injure the other. These appeals have led the courts to establish that purpose is not required for the crime of attempt: what is needed, according to James LJ in *Mohan* (1976),[7] is proof of 'a decision to bring about . . . [the offence], no matter whether the accused desired that consequence of his act or not'.

Can there be liability for attempt where D intends to do the prohibited act but is only reckless as to the circumstances? This problem might arise on a charge of attempting to obtain property by deception, where D tries to induce V to part with property on the strength of a representation which D thinks may be false (but does not know to be false).[8] The problem is usually debated in the context of attempted rape, where D tries to have sexual intercourse with a woman, not knowing and not caring whether she consents. The Criminal Attempts Act does not give an unambiguous answer: it uses the phrase 'with intent to commit' the substantive offence, which is silent on the question of whether intent combined with reckless knowledge will suffice. One interpretation, based on the Law Commission report,[9] is that the phrase 'with intent to commit' implies that D has full knowledge of the required circumstances. Reckless knowledge is not enough, and so there could be no conviction of attempted rape on the above facts. The counter-argument is that the Act fails to deal with the degree of knowledge needed for conviction: it refers only to the requirement of intent as to conduct or consequence, and that is present in the example given. Moreover, the offence of rape itself is satisfied by recklessness as to the woman's consent. If two men set out to have sexual intercourse with two women, not caring whether they consent or not, it would be absurd if the one who achieved penetration was convicted of rape, whilst the other, who failed to achieve penetration despite trying, was not even liable for attempted rape. It may be true that the latter commits indecent assault, for which the maximum is ten years' imprisonment, but would not attempted rape be a more appropriate label for something so close to the full offence? These strong arguments for convicting the attempted reckless rapist have

---

[7] [1976] 1 QB 1, applied to the 1981 Act in *Pearman* (1985) 80 Cr. App. R 259.
[8] This offence was discussed in Ch. 9.7 above.
[9] Law Com. No. 102 (1980), para. 2.15; there was subsequent academic debate between Glanville Williams, 'The Problem of Reckless Attempts' [1983] Crim. LR 365, and R. J. Buxton, 'Circumstances, Consequences and Attempted Rape' [1984] Crim. LR 25.

now found favour with both the Law Commission and the Court of Appeal.[10]

One wider question of principle is how far criminal liability should be taken. Those wedded to a linguistic approach seem to say that the word 'attempt' connotes trying, trying connotes purposeful behaviour, and therefore there can be no such thing as a reckless or negligent attempt. The opposite view focuses on the element of luck in whether behaviour results in the commission of a substantive offence or not. A milkman is found to have bottles of contaminated milk in his crates: if he had sold them, not knowing that they were contaminated, he would be guilty of a strict liability offence. But there is no strict liability in attempts. A person plans an explosion near to a procession; the procession is cancelled at the last minute, but the explosion occurs. Had the procession taken place, there would have been a risk of injuries. There is no offence of recklessly attempting to cause bodily harm. The question resolves itself into a choice of which is to govern, the historical principles of the law of attempt or the policy of each particular substantive offence? English law has resolved the question pragmatically, by creating a few specific offences of endangerment to deal with reckless behaviour on the roads and in other situations where there is a risk, but no actual occurrence, of serious consequences (see Chapter 7.6 and 7.7). A general doctrine of reckless attempts would be a simpler solution, but it might extend the reach of the criminal law considerably. Since we are concerned here with preliminary offences which go beyond the definitions of substantive crimes, might it be more judicious to proceed piecemeal (as English law does), thereby ensuring that the outer boundaries of the criminal law are carefully regulated?

(b) The Conduct Element

Since the effect of the law of attempts is to extend the criminal sanction further back than the definition of substantive offences, the question of the minimum conduct necessary to constitute an attempt has great importance. The issue concerns incomplete attempts: when has a person gone far enough to justify criminal liability? Two schools of thought may be outlined here. First, there are the subjectivists, who argue that the essence of an attempt is trying to commit a crime, and that all the law should require is proof of the

[10] Law Com. No. 177, 244; and now *Khan et al.* (1990) 91 Cr. App. R 29. See generally S. White, 'Three Points on *Pigg*' [1989] Crim. LR 539.

intention plus any act designed to implement that intention. The reasoning is that any person who has gone so far as to translate a criminal intention into action has crossed the threshold of criminal liability, and deserves punishment (though, for the reasons given above—the possibility of abandonment, for example—the punishment would be less than for a complete attempt). On the other hand there are objectivists of at least two strains. One strain bases itself on the argument that one cannot be sure that the deterrent effect of the criminal law has failed until D has done all the acts necessary, since one could regard the law as successful if D did stop before the last act out of fear of detection and punishment. The other strain of objectivists are those who see great dangers of oppressive official action—to the detriment of individual liberties—if the ambit of the law of attempts is not restricted tightly. If any overt act were to suffice as the conduct element in attempts, wrongful arrests might be more numerous; conviction would turn largely on evidence of D's intention, so the police might be tempted to exert pressure in order to obtain a confession; and miscarriages of justice might increase. To safeguard the liberty of citizens and to assure people that justice is being fairly administered, the law should require proof of an unambiguous act close to the commission of the crime before conviction of an attempt. Otherwise, we would be risking a world of thought crimes and thought police.

The choices for the conduct element in attempts might therefore be ranged along a continuum. The least requirement would be 'any overt act', but that would be objectionable as risking oppressive police practices and as leaving little opportunity for an attempter to withdraw voluntarily. The most demanding requirement would be the 'last act' or 'final stage', but that goes too far in the other direction, leaving little time for the police to intervene to prevent the occurrence of harm and allowing the defence to gain an acquittal by raising a doubt as to whether D had actually done the very last act. The Model Penal Code requires D to have taken a 'substantial step' towards the commission of the full offence.[11] This might appear to breach the principle of maximum certainty,[12] but the Model Penal Code seeks to avoid this by listing a number of authoritative examples of a 'substantial step'. Thus, the approach recognizes the inevitable flexibility in questions of degree such as

[11] Model Penal Code, s. 5.01, discussed by Ashworth, 'Criminal Attempts and the Role of Resulting Harm', 751–3.
[12] Discussed above, Ch. 3.3(*i*).

this but seeks to give some firm guidance. The Criminal Attempts Act 1981 requires D to have done 'an act which is more than merely preparatory to the commission of the offence'. Opinions differ on whether this is closer to the subjectivist end of the spectrum than the 'substantial step' test, but it is certainly more vague (since there are no authoritative examples), and the Act leaves the application of the test entirely to the jury, once the judge has found that there is sufficient evidence of an attempt.[13] English judges have used various tests to explain the Act's requirements to juries. One popular test was the so-called Rubicon test, which holds that a person is not guilty of an attempt until he has 'crossed the Rubicon and burnt his boats'.[14] This is almost as demanding as the 'last act' test, since it requires D to have reached a stage from which there is no turning back. It has now, rightly, been rejected as an explanation of the current law. The proper test is whether D was *still* engaged in merely preparatory acts, in which case he is not guilty of attempt, or whether his conduct was more than merely preparatory. Thus, in *Gullefer* (1987)[15] a man who placed a bet on a race jumped on to the greyhound track in an endeavour to have the race declared void so that he could recover his stake-money. He was held not to have gone past the stage of mere preparation for the crime of theft, and so he had not committed an attempted theft. If his plan was to work, it remained for the race stewards to declare the race void and for him to demand his money back. Jumping on to the track was 'mere preparation'.

It is not really possible to say, after one decade of the Criminal Attempts Act, whether it strikes an acceptable balance between individual liberties and the social interest in preventing harm. However, the test does abandon the principle of maximum certainty (see Chapter 3.3(i)) in favour of a more flexible law giving greater discretion to the courts. Maximum certainty would be well satisfied by the 'last act' test, but it has been argued that this is too narrow a basis for the law. It is right to seek an earlier point of criminalization, and at least the Model Penal Code's formulation endeavours to increase certainty by the articulation of examples.

[13] Criminal Attempts Act 1981, ss. 1(1) and 4(3).
[14] *DPP v. Stonehouse* [1978] AC 55.
[15] [1987] Crim. LR 195, affirmed in *Jones* (1990) 91 Cr. App. R 351.

(c) The Problem of Impossibility

Just as the conduct element in attempts relates chiefly to incomplete attempts, so the problem of impossibility usually arises in connection with complete attempts. Once again, there are subjectivist and objectivist perspectives to be considered.

What might be termed the subjectivist approach to impossible attempts is a straightforward application of the belief principle: a person should be judged on the facts or circumstances as he or she believed them to be at the time. We have seen how the belief principle operates as a ground of exculpation where D is labouring under a mistake of fact (see Chapter 5.3(c)). Here it operates as a ground of inculpation. In other words, where D *believes* that he is committing an offence, it is justifiable to convict of an attempt to commit that offence. D's state of mind is just as blameworthy as it would be if the facts *were* as they are believed to be. Thus, we are justified in convicting the person who smuggles dried lettuce leaves in the belief that they are cannabis, and the person who puts sugar in someone's drink in the belief that it is cyanide, and the person who handles goods in the belief that they are stolen. In all these cases there is no relevant moral difference between their culpability and the culpability of others where the substances *really* are cannabis, cyanide, and stolen goods.

The objectivist stance on attempts points to the absence of actual danger in these cases, and argues that there is a risk of oppression if the law criminalizes people in objectively innocent situations.[16] Part of the concern here is that convictions might be based on confessions which are the result of fear, confusion, or even police fabrication.[17] Without the need to establish any objectively incriminating facts, the police might construct a case simply on the basis of remarks attributed to the accused person. Anyone carrying a bag might be liable to be arrested and to have attributed to him or her the remark: 'I thought it contained drugs'. These arguments based on the threat to individual rights are too important to be dismissed peremptorily, but they raise the question of whether stronger controls on police powers, requirements of tape recording, and so on, can be expected

---

[16] Three expressions of the objectivist view are J. F. Stephen, *History of the Criminal Law* (1883), ii. 225; J. Temkin, 'Impossible Attempts: Another View' (1976) 39 MLR 55; and Lords Bridge and Roskill in *Anderton v. Ryan* [1985] AC 560.
[17] This is one of the concerns expressed in the lengthy discussion of attempts by G. Fletcher, *Rethinking Criminal Law* (1978), 137 ff.

to obviate the danger. Recent research findings on this are rather pessimistic: it seems that new controls on the police tend to be manipulated in practice so that the intended goals may not be achieved.[18] It may therefore be unsafe to expect the laws of criminal procedure to prevent any dangers to individual rights. This leaves untouched the subjectivists' point that there really is no difference in terms of moral culpability or dangerousness between persons who actually do make an impossible attempt and many ordinary attempters. Objectivists focus on the absence of danger in the actual situation, and subjectivists on the 'desert' or potential dangerousness of the person involved. But if a subjectivist law leads to police malpractice which cannot otherwise be prevented, it ought to be narrowed.

There would be little argument between objectivists and subjectivists over the case of D, who fired a shot at V and missed because his aim was not good enough. That is a classic criminal attempt. But what is the difference between that and a case in which E puts sugar in X's drink in the belief that it is cyanide? Objectivists say that there is no social danger in the latter case, because sugar is innocuous; yet it is equally true that there is no danger in the first case, because shooting and missing is innocuous. Some might say that D might try again and the shot might not miss; yet it is equally possible that E might try again and might choose an ingredient which actually is poisonous. It seems, then, that objectivists accept the intent principle—that people should be judged on the consequences they intend to happen—but not the belief principle—that people should be judged on the facts as they believe them to be. There is no principled explanation of why they accept one and not the other, apart from the argument about police powers and individual liberty, which ought (if possible) to be tackled directly, and not through a distortion of the law of attempts.

The recent history of English law contains evidence of both approaches. The House of Lords in *Haughton v. Smith*[19] preferred an objectivist stance, but the Law Commission accepted the arguments above and recommended a subjectivist approach, in which impossibility would be no defence to liability. Debate continued during the passage of the new law, and one result of further changes

---

[18] See e.g. I. McKenzie, R. Morgan, and R. Reiner, 'Helping the Police with their Inquiries' [1990] Crim. LR 22, and A. Sanders and L. Bridges, 'Legal Advice and Police Malpractice' [1990] Crim. LR 494.

[19] [1975] AC 476.

of mind by the government was two strangely worded provisions in section 1(2) and (3) of the Criminal Attempts Act 1981. The Act purported to follow the Law Commission and to criminalize impossible attempts, but the House of Lords interpreted the provisions so as not to achieve this result, and it was only in *Shivpuri* (1986)[20] that it was settled that, in the English law of attempts, D is judged on the facts as he or she believed them to be. Thus, if a person buys a video recorder believing that it is stolen when it is not, that constitutes an attempt to handle stolen goods.

The application of the belief principle here is limited to facts. If D is mistaken about the law, believing that certain conduct is an offence when it is not; there is no liability for an attempt. Thus, where D believed that he was smuggling currency into the country but there is no offence of importing currency, there could be no conviction.[21] This is easily explained: there is no crime to be attempted, only an imaginary crime. But it can also be seen as a corollary of the policy that ignorance of the law is no excuse:[22] a mistake about the criminal law neither exculpates nor inculpates. By contrast, a mistake as to the facts may exculpate (subject to other policies relevant to mistakes)[23] or inculpate (as an impossible attempt), since the general principle is that D is judged on the facts as he or she believed them to be.[24]

11.4 THE JUSTIFICATIONS FOR AN OFFENCE OF CONSPIRACY

The essence of conspiracy is an agreement between two or more persons to commit a criminal offence. Thus defined, conspiracy takes its place as one of the three inchoate offences at common law, penalizing the conspirators before any substantive offence has been committed. The justification for this is largely preventive, as in the law of attempts, since it enables the police and the courts to intervene before any harm has actually been inflicted. Whereas in attempts the doing of a 'more than merely preparatory' act is required as evidence of the firmness of the intent, in conspiracy it is the fact of agreement with others which is regarded as sufficiently firm evidence that the parties are committed to carrying out the

---

[20] [1987] AC 1, overruling the House's own decision of the previous year in *Anderton v. Ryan* [1985] AC 560. A considerable influence in bringing about this judicial volte-face was the article by Glanville Williams, 'The Lords and Impossible Attempts', [1986] CLJ 33.

[21] *Taaffe* [1984] AC 539.

[22] Discussed above, Ch. 6.7.

[23] See above, Ch. 5.3(*d*).

[24] See above, Ch. 5.2(*a*).

crime. Another part of the justification for an offence of conspiracy is that persons who conspire and then try unsuccessfully to implement the conspiracy are not likely to be significantly less blameworthy or less dangerous than persons who conspire and succeed in bringing about the substantive offence, and so it is right that the former should be liable to conviction.

However, this fairly traditional analysis of conspiracy as an inchoate offence neglects the other social functions which conspiracy law has been called upon to perform. In the nineteenth century it was accepted that a charge of criminal conspiracy would lie for an agreement to do any unlawful act, even though that act was not criminal but only a civil wrong, such as a tort or breach of contract. This gave the criminal law a long reach, particularly with regard to the activities of the early trade unions, and the courts upheld conspiracy convictions for what were, in effect, agreements to strike until the law was changed by the Conspiracy and Protection of Property Act 1875 and the Trade Disputes Act 1906.[25] In social terms, the criminal law lent its authority to those who wished to suppress organized strikes. In legal terms, the reasoning seemed to be that acts which were insufficiently antisocial to justify criminal liability when done by one person could become sufficiently antisocial to justify criminal liability when done by two or more people acting in agreement. Such a combination of malefactors might increase the probability of harm resulting, might in some cases increase public alarm, and might in other cases facilitate the perpetration and concealment of the wrong.[26] These prosecutions were often brought in cases where the agreement had been carried out and the unlawful acts done, since there was no substantive criminal offence to be prosecuted (in that the conspiracy was to do an unlawful but non-criminal act). Thus the legal definition turned on an 'agreement', but the social reality centred upon the actual commission of the tort or breach of contract, from which a prior agreement was inferred. In these contexts, conspiracy functioned more as an additional criminal offence than as an inchoate crime.

The Acts of 1875 and 1906 curtailed, but did not remove, this use of the offence of conspiracy against conduct thought to be antisocial,

---

[25] For a general account of the social history of conspiracy, see R. Spicer, *Conspiracy: Law, Class and Society* (1981); see also G. Robertson, *Whose Conspiracy?* (1974).

[26] For further discussion, see R. Johnson, 'The Unnecessary Crime of Conspiracy' (1973) 61 Cal. LR 1137, and I. Dennis, 'The Rationale of Criminal Conspiracy' (1977) 93 LQR 39.

and the idea of conspiracy as an extra substantive offence experienced a revival in the 1960s and early 1970s. The signal for this was probably the House of Lords decision in *Shaw v. DPP*,[27] the case which created the offence of conspiracy to corrupt public morals. The high-water mark was the decision in *Kamara v. DPP*,[28] where students who occupied the High Commission of Sierra Leone in London were convicted of conspiracy to trespass, even though trespass is itself a tort and not a crime. However, a judicial retrenchment was evident in *DPP v. Withers*,[29] where the House of Lords quashed convictions of conspiracy to effect a public mischief and declared that no such general offence was known to the law. The gist of the decision was that criminal conspiracy should be extended no further than had already been established.

The decision in *Withers* may be seen as a belated gesture towards the principles of non-retroactivity and maximum certainty, after a whole host of earlier decisions had ignored the principles in favour of a broad policy of social defence.[30] In a way, it presaged the Law Commission's report on conspiracy in 1976, which recommended that the offence of conspiracy should be coextensive with the substantive law.[31] Conspiracies should only be criminal if the conduct agreed upon would constitute a crime. The principles of non-retroactivity and maximum certainty were accepted, even to the point of asserting that if some new form of wickedness were to arise which did not fall within existing offences, the proper approach would be to await a response from the legislature rather than for the judges to exploit the elasticity of the law of conspiracy.[32] Parliament adopted the substance of the Law Commission's report, and enacted the Criminal Law Act 1977. Part I of the Act creates the new offence of statutory conspiracy, limited to agreements to commit one or more criminal offences; Part II provides a handful of new offences of trespass on residential premises. An agreement to commit one of these distinct trespass offences would be a statutory conspiracy, and the common-law offence of conspiracy to trespass, upheld in *Kamara*,[33] was abolished.

The 1977 Act did not, however, accomplish a clean sweep of common-law conspiracy. The Law Commission had been unable to

---

[27] [1962] AC 220.   [28] [1973] 2 All ER 1242.   [29] [1975] AC 842.
[30] Cf. *DPP v. Bhagwan* [1972] AC 60, where the House of Lords held that there is no general crime of conspiracy to defeat the purpose of an Act of Parliament.
[31] Law Commission No. 76, *Conspiracy and Criminal Law Reform* (1976).
[32] Ibid., paras. 1.8–1.9.   [33] [1973] 2 All ER 1242.

complete its examination of conspiracy to defraud and any new offences which might be needed to replace it (see Chapter 9.8 above); and another committee was engaged in a review of the laws on obscenity, which led the government to exclude from the 1977 Act conspiracies to corrupt public morals and to outrage public decency.[34] Thus the controversial decision in *Shaw*[35] remains authoritative on conspiracy to corrupt public morals, as does the decision in *Scott v. Metropolitan Police Commissioner*[36] on conspiracy to defraud, whose precepts owe more to the 'thin ice' principle (Chapter 3.3(*b*)) and the policy of social defence (Chapter 3.3(*j*)) than to any notion of maximum certainty in criminal law (Chapter 3.3(*i*)).

Leaving aside the common-law conspiracies to defraud, to corrupt public morals, and to outrage public decency, is it true to say that statutory conspiracy functions primarily as an inchoate offence? Few conspiracies can be prosecuted at the stage of agreement, because meetings of conspirators usually take place in private and it is rare for sufficient evidence to become available until some acts in furtherance of the agreement have been done and observed. So the rationale of early prevention, even before an attempt has been committed, is often far from the social facts. However, another function of inchoate offences is to criminalize those who try and fail, as well as those who are caught before they have the chance to succeed or fail. Conspiracy does fulfil this function, being used against those who join together to commit a crime in circumstances where it is impossible to do so.[37] Yet there remains a way in which even statutory conspiracy also functions as an extra criminal offence. The rules of evidence in conspiracy cases are somewhat wider than in other trials: for example, the statements of one co-conspirator are admissible in evidence against another if they relate to an act done in furtherance of the conspiracy, by way of exception to the general rule that the admissions of one co-defendant cannot be adduced in evidence against the other.[38] Moreover, all that has to be proved for conspiracy is the agreement, and this may be inferred from behaviour. Prosecutors who wish to take advantage of these rules may prefer to charge conspiracy instead of the substantive

[34] The Williams Committee, which reported on *Obscenity and Film Censorship* (1979, Cmnd. 7772), but whose recommendations were not adopted in legislation.
[35] [1962] AC 220.   [36] [1975] AC 819.
[37] The 1977 Act contained no provision on impossibility, but s. 5 of the Criminal Attempts Act 1981 makes it clear that impossibility is no more a defence to conspiracy than it is to attempt.
[38] Sir Rupert Cross, *Evidence* (6th edn., 1985), 526–7.

crime in a case where the substantive offence has been committed: it is bad practice for them to charge both conspiracy and the substantive crime,[39] but it is no answer to a conspiracy charge alone that the substantive offence was in fact committed. In the terminology of English criminal procedure, a conspiracy does not 'merge' with the substantive offence.

The crime of conspiracy therefore remains more than an inchoate offence. Whilst it can be used against agreements to commit crimes which have not yet been consummated, and against agreements which are carried out and yet fail to produce the intended crime, it can also be charged where the elements of the substantive offence have been completed. The justification for this is that the offence of conspiracy gives a more rounded impression of the nature of the criminal enterprise, in terms of planning and concerted action and the different roles of the various participants. The deliberate involvement of two or more people alters the character of the offence. Thus one individual who declares an intent to steal certain property has committed no offence; two or more individuals who agree to do the same thing may be convicted of conspiracy to steal. How strong are the justifications?[40] One argument is that it may be more difficult to reverse a conspiracy than for an individual to change his or her mind: conspiracies are therefore more likely to result in harm-doing. It is easy to raise the counter-argument of one resolute individual compared with two weak and dithering conspirators. Another argument is that the involvement of several people in an offence creates greater fear in victims and greater public alarm. It is easy to raise the counter-argument of one terrifying individual compared with two incompetent and hesitant bunglers. However, these succeed only in showing that it is problematic to use a numerical division (between one and two persons) to distinguish between serious and less serious criminal activities. They cast little doubt on the qualitative difference between most criminal gangs and the activities of most lone offenders. In many cases group crimes are more terrifying, and sentencers may well be justified in treating this as an aggravating factor.[41] In many cases group behaviour may acquire a momentum of its own, with individuals being

[39] See the case of the Shrewsbury pickets, *Jones et al.* (1974) 59 Cr. App. R 120, and the Practice Direction [1977] 2 All ER 540.

[40] See Johnson, 'The Unnecessary Crime of Conspiracy', and Dennis, 'The Rationale of Criminal Conspiracy'.

[41] Sir Rupert Cross, *The English Sentencing System* (3rd edn, 1981), 156–7.

afraid to withdraw and participants spurring each other on.[42] Whether considerations such as these justify the creation of special public-order offences aimed at group behaviour, with separate rules of proof favouring prosecutors, was questioned earlier.[43]

Even if it is conceded that group offences are often qualitatively more serious than offences by individuals, does it follow that the law needs the offence of conspiracy? What if the doctrine of merger was extended, so that conspiracy ceased to be chargeable if the substantive offence had been committed? Any special characteristic of group criminality would not be lost, because there remains the doctrine of complicity. The law of principals and accomplices may lack the evidentiary advantages to the prosecution which conspiracy has, but it does favour the prosecution procedurally by not requiring it to charge defendants separately as accomplices or principals.[44] And there is the same discretion at the sentencing stage to reflect the element of aggravation in planned group offending. A similar question about the dispensability of the offence of conspiracy may be asked in relation to its inchoate function. Many conspiracies will already have been carried far enough to fulfil the test for a criminal attempt, at least under the broad 'more than merely preparatory' test of English law. Much of the ground might therefore be covered by the law of attempts and by prosecutions for complicity in attempts. This leaves only the few cases where clear evidence is obtained of an agreement to commit a crime, without any action having yet been taken to implement the agreement. This brings the discussion back to the original, narrow justification for the crime of conspiracy—does an agreement, without more, go far enough to warrant criminalization?

This question raises issues of principle and policy. On the one hand, there is the principle of maximum certainty: the requirement of an agreement is considerably more certain than the requirement of a 'more than merely preparatory act' for attempts. But agreements usually involve words, and issues of freedom of speech and of association may arise here, in the sense that the existence of this offence might encourage the police to use intrusive tactics (such as bugging premises). Freedom to plan crimes is not being advocated, but freedom to develop controversial ideas may also be inhibited.

---

[42] See the discussion of duress and fault in Ch. 6.4(c) above.
[43] See above, Ch. 8.3(g).
[44] See further, Ch. 10.2 above, and *DPP for Northern Ireland v. Maxwell* [1978] 3 All ER 1140.

Furthermore, there are the dangers of conviction based on inference and mere association, which leave opportunities for prosecutions to be brought without much hard evidence. The offence of conspiracy may be defended as a vital tool against organized crime, but the difficulty is that it bears oppressively on individuals who are prosecuted. At present, the same law could be used against both Mafia leaders and a couple of bungling burglars who happened to meet in a pub.

11.5 THE ELEMENTS OF CRIMINAL CONSPIRACY

(a) An Agreement between Two or More Persons

Agreement is the basic element in conspiracy. The idea of an agreement seems to involve a meeting of minds, and there is no need for a physical meeting of the persons involved so long as they reach a mutual understanding of what is to be done.[45] Whether the understanding amounts to an agreement may be a matter of degree: if the parties are still at the stage of negotiation, without having decided what to do, no criminal conspiracy has yet come into being. But what if the parties have reached agreement in principle, leaving matters of detail to be resolved afterwards? What if arrangements have been made, but may be unscrambled later? The judicial tendency is to regard these as conspiratorial agreements, and this is consistent with the rule that there is no defence of withdrawal for a person who has become a party to a conspiracy.[46] Moreover, since all human arrangements are vulnerable to changes in circumstances, the possibility that a planned robbery might be cancelled if there are police in the vicinity at the time does not negate the existence of a conspiracy. Further problems over 'conditional' agreements are discussed in section 11.5(b) below.

Certain agreements are excluded from the law of conspiracy. First, by section 2(2)(a) of the Criminal Law Act 1977, agreements between husband and wife only (without a third person) cannot amount to criminal conspiracies. This rule places the value of marital confidence above the public interest in having conspirators brought to justice, a priority which has been partly abandoned in other areas of the law (e.g. by compelling one spouse to give evidence against the other in certain proceedings).[47] If a husband

---

[45] G. Orchard, ' "Agreement" in Criminal Conspiracy', [1974] Crim. LR 297.
[46] e.g. *Mulcahy* (1868) LR 3 HL 306; *Thomson* (1965) 50 Cr. App. R 1.
[47] Police and Criminal Evidence Act 1984, s. 80.

and wife go so far as to commit an attempt or a substantive offence, they can be convicted jointly of that. Second, by section 2(2)(b), agreements in which the only other person is under the age of criminal responsibility cannot result in D's conviction for conspiracy—an application of the rule of criminal capacity. Third, by section 2(2)(c) of the Act, agreements in which the only other person is an intended victim cannot result in D's conviction for conspiracy. This parallels the rule that a person who falls within the class protected by the offence (e.g. persons under a given age) cannot be convicted as a party to that crime.[48] Fourth, section 4(1) provides that a prosecution for conspiracy to commit one or more summary offences requires the consent of the Director of Public Prosecutions. Although this appears to restrict the practical use of conspiracy charges, it should be noted that the crime of attempt does not apply to summary offences at all. Once again, the 'double life' of conspiracy as an inchoate and a quasi-substantive offence is evident. One argument is that the deliberate planning of numerous offences, even if summary only, may justify prosecution as a conspiracy. Presumably, also, the number of persons involved in an agreement to commit summary offences might persuade the Crown Prosecution Service that it is in the public interest to prosecute for a single conspiracy rather than bringing various separate small charges.

Agreement is the basic element in criminal conspiracy, but the evidence offered to a court may often be inferences from behaviour rather than direct testimony or recording of a meeting of conspirators. Thus the typical process is to infer a prior agreement from behaviour which appears to be concerted.

(b) The Criminal Conduct Agreed Upon

We move now to the subject-matter of the agreement. The Criminal Law Act 1977 provides, in section 1(1), that a conspiracy is criminal if it is agreed that 'a course of conduct will be pursued which, if the agreement is carried out in accordance with their intentions . . . will necessarily amount to or involve the commission of any offence or offences by one or more parties to the agreement'. The essence, therefore, is that two or more persons should agree on the commission of a crime. It is well established that they need not know that the agreed course of conduct does amount to a crime—ignorance of

[48] *Tyrrell* [1894] 1 QB 710, discussed in Ch. 10 above.

the criminal law does not excuse here[49]—and the 1977 Act provides for some other eventualities.

In interpreting the section, one's eyes are drawn to the word 'necessarily': can it ever be said that, if an agreement is carried out in accordance with the parties' intentions, it will *necessarily* involve the commission of an offence? This unduly concrete term seems to run counter to the proposition that all agreements are conditional in some way or another, and thus to ignore the possibility of an unexpected failure (the bomb which fails to detonate, the shot which misses, etc.). Does it therefore leave all fallible agreements outside the law of conspiracy? Is it enough for the defence to raise a reasonable doubt that the plan might have miscarried for some reason? Such an argument would put the principles of statutory interpretation to a stern test: should the court apply the plain meaning of 'necessarily' or the principle of strict construction—and acquit—or should it apply the purposive approach and the policy of social defence—and convict? One challenge to the wording was heard in *Jackson* (1985).[50] Four men arranged for one of their number to be shot in the leg; the aim was to provide mitigation in the event of his being convicted at his trial for burglary. He was shot in the leg before the end of the trial. On a charge of conspiracy to pervert the course of justice, it was argued that there was no certainty that he would be convicted and therefore the agreement would not necessarily lead to a perversion of the course of justice. The Court of Appeal rejected the argument, drawing a distinction between the inevitability of the substantive offence being committed (which section 1(1) does not require) and the inevitability that it would be committed if the agreement was carried out in accordance with their intentions. In this case the key issue of whether the jury convicted V was entirely outside the defendants' control, and so it is difficult to regard it as part of their 'intentions'. The decision must be seen as an affirmation of social defence, since the court did not trouble to consult the Law Commission report as a step towards the purposive approach. It is noticeable that the draft Criminal Code abandons the word 'necessarily', leaving the question to the general rules about conditional intention.[51]

Section 1(1) of the 1977 Act was amended by section 5 of the Criminal Attempts Act 1981 to make it clear that impossibility is no more a defence to conspiracy than to a charge of attempt. It is

---

[49] *Churchill v. Walton* [1967] 2 AC 224.
[50] [1985] Crim. LR 442.   [51] Law Com. No. 177, s. 48.

sufficient to establish that the agreement *would* have involved the commission of an offence but for the existence of facts which rendered it impossible. The justifications for this follow those outlined in section 11.3(*c*) above.

(c) The Fault Requirements

The basic fault requirements for conspiracy are that each defendant should have knowledge of any facts or circumstances specified in the substantive offence, and that each defendant should intend the conspiracy to be carried out and the substantive offence committed. Section 1(2) makes it clear that these requirements of full intention and knowledge apply no matter what offence is agreed upon. Thus, for conspiracies to commit offences of strict liability, negligence, or recklessness, full knowledge and intent are required. Why is the fault element for conspiracy kept so narrow? If the substantive offence is satisfied, say, by recklessness as to some elements, why should the crime of conspiracy not likewise be satisfied? The answer seems to be the general principle encountered elsewhere: that inchoate crimes are an extension of the criminal sanction, and the more remote an offence becomes from the actual infliction of harm, the higher the degree of fault necessary to justify criminalization. Whilst an individual may be convicted of selling unsound meat despite ignorance that it is unsound and despite the taking of normal precautions, it is thought wrong to convict suppliers and wholesalers of conspiracy to sell unsound meat if they are unaware of its unsoundness. In fact, the general principle cannot be applied completely to conspiracy, because of its 'double life' as an inchoate and a quasi-substantive offence. Thus, once again the doctrinal position is confused, although on this occasion the confusion works in favour of defendants rather than against them, by requiring full knowledge and intention even where conspiracy is used as a quasi-substantive offence.

Should this principled restriction of the fault requirement in conspiracy apply to offences of intention which may include an element of recklessness? If X and Y agree to go to a woman's room and to have intercourse with her, thinking that she may well consent but not caring whether she will or not, are they guilty of conspiracy to rape? The wording of section 1(2) of the 1977 Act says no, and the general principle says no. Yet it was argued earlier[52] that there

---

[52] See section 11.3(*a*), and *Khan* (1990) 91 Cr. App. R 29.

should be a conviction for attempted rape where there is recklessness as to consent, and that argument might apply no less strongly to conspiracy. One might say, pragmatically, that there is no need to extend conspiracy in this way because one can wait until an attempt has been committed and then prosecute for that. But the argument in favour of thus extending conspiracy is surely powerful.

In applying the 1977 Act, the concern of the courts has not been with these arguments but with other questions about the meaning of section 1(1). In *Anderson* (1986),[53] the House of Lords chose to reinterpret the words of the section in order to uphold a conviction. They held, first, that a person may be convicted of conspiracy even without intending the agreement to be carried out; and, secondly, that a person is guilty of conspiracy if, and only if, it is established that he or she intended to play some part in the agreed course of conduct. The second point appears to run counter to one of the rationales of conspiracy, which is to bring those who plan offences but do not take part in them (the 'godfathers') within the ambit of the criminal sanction. It has now been reinterpreted by the Court of Appeal[54] so as to mean the opposite of what the House of Lords said: a passive conspirator, who concurs in the activities of the person(s) carrying out the crime without becoming involved himself, is guilty of criminal conspiracy. However, if the law contained a general offence of facilitating crime,[55] this might be a more appropriate label for minor participants in conspiracies.

11.6. INCITEMENT

The third of the trio of inchoate offences in English criminal law is incitement. The essence of this is that someone who instigates or encourages another person to commit an offence should be liable to conviction for those acts of incitement, both because he is culpable for trying to cause a crime and because such liability is a step towards crime prevention. The offence of incitement is committed irrespective of whether the person(s) incited respond by committing the offence concerned. Indeed, when they do go on to commit the offence, the inciter becomes a party to that crime, and is liable to conviction for counselling the offence.[56]

---

[53] [1986] AC 27.
[54] *Siracusa* (1989) 90 Cr. App. R 340.
[55] See the discussion below, n. 61 and accompanying text, and above, Ch. 10.8.
[56] See above, Ch. 10.3(c).

The conduct required for incitement is some form of encouragement or persuasion to commit an offence, although there is authority which would regard threats or other forms of pressure as incitement.[57] The terms of the incitement must be communicated to person incited or to someone who may fairly be considered as the object of the incitement: if there is no such communication, then the offence may be an attempt to incite.[58] Where D's incitement to an offence is impossible of commission, perhaps because of a mistake of fact or circumstance, it appears that the offence of incitement may not be committed. In making this ruling in *Fitzmaurice* (1983),[59] the Court of Appeal took the view that it was keeping the common-law offence of incitement in line with the common-law rules for attempt and conspiracy. However, as we have seen, the offences of attempt and incitement have now been put into statutory form, and impossibility is no defence to either of them. The result is that incitement is out of line with the other inchoate offences, so far as impossibility is concerned. The arguments of principle and policy seem no different for incitement, and it is therefore desirable that incitement should be put into a statutory form compatible with attempt and conspiracy as soon as possible.[60]

The fault element in incitement is that D should intend the substantive offence to be committed and should know the facts and circumstances specified by that offence. This is unlikely to cause a problem in most cases, since someone who either encourages or exerts pressure on another person to commit an offence will usually, by definition, intend that offence to be committed.

The offence of incitement is not widely used by prosecutors in England. It could serve to close some of the gaps left by the law of complicity and conspiracy, but what is really needed here is a new form of inchoate offence. The problem is that if D helps E to commit a crime by lending equipment or providing information, D is liable as an accomplice if E goes ahead and commits the crime, but he is not straightforwardly liable for any offence if E has a change of mind. As in the cases of impossible attempts, discussed in section 11.3(c) above, D is just as culpable in both situations, and it is a

---

[57] *Race Relations Board v. Applin* [1973] QB 815.
[58] See below, 11.8.   [59] [1983] QB 1083.
[60] In their 1980 report the Law Commission took the view that it was not necessary to state in legislation that impossibility is no defence to incitement (Law Com. No. 102, para. 4.4), but the decision in *Fitzmaurice* showed otherwise, and the draft Criminal Code includes a general provision on impossibility in attempt, conspiracy, and incitement: Law Com. No. 177, cl. 50.

matter of chance whether E commits the principal offence or not. Courts have striven to fill this gap by bending the law of incitement, and offences of possession may be invoked, but the preferable approach is to recognize the deficiency in the law and to fill it with an offence of facilitating a crime.[61]

11.7 VOLUNTARY RENUNCIATION OF CRIMINAL PURPOSE

Since a major function of attempt, conspiracy and incitement is as inchoate offences, the question arises of the legal effect of a change of mind before the substantive offence is committed. What if D abandons the attempt, or withdraws from the conspiracy, or countermands the incitement? English law has generally taken the view that this cannot alter the legal significance of what has already occurred: there is no defence of voluntary renunciation of criminal purpose, and it is a matter for mitigation of sentence only.[62] On the other hand, many other European systems allow such a defence,[63] and the American Model Penal Code also makes provision for it.[64] What are the main arguments on either side?

The main argument against allowing such a defence is that it contradicts the temporal logic of the law. The definition of attempt, conspiracy, or incitement is fulfilled once D, with the appropriate culpability, does the 'more than merely preparatory' act, or reaches the agreement, or utters the words of incitement. Anything that happens subsequently cannot undo the offence: it has already been committed. The situation is no different from that of the thief who decides to return the stolen property: theft has been committed and the offence cannot be undone, even though voluntary repentance may well justify substantial mitigation of sentence. A subsidiary argument is that it would in any event be difficult for a court to satisfy itself of the voluntariness of the renunciation of criminal purpose, and that such occasions might well involve a mixture of motives of D's part. This makes the matter much more suitable for the sentencing stage than the trial itself.

---

[61] The proposal may be found in R. J. Buxton, 'Complicity in the Criminal Code' (1969) 85 LQR 252, and has recently been advanced powerfully by J. R. Spencer, 'The Need for an Offence of Facilitation', in P. F. Smith (ed.), *Criminal Law: Essays in Honour of J. C. Smith* (1987).
[62] *Lankford* [1959] Crim. LR 209, and Law Com. No. 102 (1980), para. 2.133; cf. M. Wasik, 'Abandoning Criminal Intent' [1980] Crim. LR 785.
[63] Fletcher, *Rethinking Criminal Law*, 184–97.
[64] Model Penal Code, s. 5.01(4).

Against this, and in favour of a defence of voluntary renunciation, may be ranged various moral and prudential arguments. The principal argument is that it is the intent or criminal purpose which is the essence of inchoate offences; that the criminal liability is premised on the firmness and continuance of that purpose until the commission of the substantive crime; and that voluntary renunciation shows that the original criminal purpose was not sufficiently firm. This coincides with the view that it often takes more 'nerve' to go through with a crime than to plan or encourage it. Thus, where D voluntarily abandons an attempt, withdraws from a conspiracy, or countermands an incitement, this should be sufficient to negative criminal liability. According to this view, D can be said to 'undo' the offence by a change of mind, because the criminal purpose is a continuing one—not a once-and-for-all mental state—and its effect can be neutralized by subsequent decision or action on D's part. There is a difference from the thief who voluntarily decides to return the property to its owner, for theft is a substantive offence and is not criminalized simply because it is one stage on the way to another crime. A further argument is that if D renounces before harm is caused, this shows that the criminal sanction has had a deterrent effect. To punish D none the less would be needless, and the case should be regarded as a success for the law rather than a failure. Both these arguments depart from the principle of contemporaneity (see Chapter 5.2(d)) in favour of a broader time-frame for criminal liability.[65] We have already observed the abandonment of contemporaneity in cases of prior fault (see Chapter 5.2(e)): this deviation would be on the ground of subsequent non-fault.

The argument for allowing a defence of voluntary renunciation becomes stronger as the conduct element in the inchoate offences is taken further back from the occurrence of the harm. In attempts, for example, the fact that there may be ample time for a change of mind between the commission of a 'more than merely preparatory' act and the completion of the substantive offence surely strengthens the case for a defence. There are prudential arguments as well—first, that a defence may act as an incentive to inchoate offenders to give up before they cause harm; second, that the renunciation shows that there was no real social danger from this person—but they are not particularly convincing. Whether inchoate offenders ever do contemplate the legal effect of renunciation, and whether

[65] See M. Kelman, 'Interpretive Construction in the Substantive Criminal Law' (1981) 33 *Stanford LR* 591, at 611–14 and 628–30.

they would be influenced by a complete defence rather than by a substantial sentencing discount, is difficult to say.

Those systems which have a defence of voluntary renunciation do not appear to find it problematic.[66] It is rarely raised, and the issue usually turns on the voluntariness of the change of mind, which is likely to be explored more fully at trial than at the sentencing stage. At a theoretical level, there is a strong argument for reduced culpability, but this does not conclude the case for a complete defence. The allocation of excuses as between the liability and the sentencing stages turns on questions of degree (see Chapter 6.9), and one might well take the view that voluntary renunciation is not sufficiently fundamental to warrant a complete defence to criminal liability.

11.8. THE RELATIONSHIP BETWEEN SUBSTANTIVE AND INCHOATE CRIMES

We have seen that the general function of inchoate crimes is to penalize preparation, planning, or encouragement towards the commission of a substantive offence. It has also been noted that the crime of conspiracy is sometimes invoked where the substantive offence has occurred, and that 'complete' attempts are cases in which D has done everything intended for the commission of a crime: in both those instances, the inchoate offences come very close to substantive crimes. The same phenomenon also appears the other way round: modern legal systems often define what are essentially inchoate offences in the terms of substantive crimes.

A clear example of this is the offence of doing an act with intent to impede the apprehension of an offender.[67] This is not worded as a crime of attempt, but in essence it is a crime of attempt since it requires the doing of an act with the required intent—no result need be proved, no result need have happened. The standard analysis of a substantive crime is 'harm plus culpability', whereas the standard analysis of an attempt is 'culpability without actual harm'. Clearly, the offence of doing an act with intent to impede the apprehension of an offender resembles the latter rather than the former. We can therefore say that the offence is defined in the inchoate mode. There are many other examples of this type of offence—notably

---

[66] See the discussion by Fletcher, *Rethinking Criminal Law*, 184–97.
[67] Criminal Law Act 1967, s. 4.

burglary,[68] perjury,[69] and perpetrating a bomb hoax.[70] The prosecution's task is made easier in these offences; they do not have to establish that D caused a certain result if they can persuade the court that he did an act with intent to produce that result. Moreover, since these are substantive offences, inchoate liability can be incurred as well, through the three inchoate offences.[71] Thus there can be an attempted burglary or an attempted bomb hoax, which criminalizes D's conduct at an even earlier point than the actual causing of any harm. There is little evidence that these extensions of the criminal law are carefully monitored, or that the implications of applying the inchoate offences to crimes defined in the inchoate mode have ever been systematically considered. It is, for example, possible to convict a person of attempting to incite an offence. The reach of criminal liability is simply pushed further and further.

Another prominent example of offences defined in the inchoate mode is possession—possessing offensive weapons, possessing drugs, possessing instruments for use in forgery, and possessing articles for burglary or deception. A major difference here is that most of these articles are non-innocent, in the sense that their possession calls for an explanation at least. That certainly cannot be said of offences defined so as to penalize 'any act done with intent', although it can perhaps be said of an offence of burglary, which penalizes the entering of a building as a trespasser with intent to steal. Much depends on the way in which a legal system uses and defines its offences of possession, but there is at least one major objection to them, namely, that they presume a criminal intent from the very fact of possession. Some possession offences leave no opportunity for the defence to argue that possession was for a non-criminal reason;[72] others, like the offensive weapons law, impose on the defendant the burden of proving a 'lawful excuse' or 'reasonable excuse' for the possession.[73] Now it is true, and worth bringing into the calculation, that possession offences often have the merit of certainty: there is nothing vague about the warning they spell out to citizens.[74] Yet it must be questioned whether this is enough to

---

[68] Theft Act 1968, s. 9(1)(a); see above, Ch. 9.5.
[69] Perjury Act 1911, s. 1.   [70] Criminal Law Act 1977, s. 51.
[71] For discussion of such liability, see I. P. Robbins, 'Doubly Inchoate Offences'.
[72] Cf. s. 5(4)(b) of the Misuse of Drugs Act 1971, providing a defence for those who take possession of drugs for the purpose of handing them to the police or other authorities.
[73] Prevention of Crime Act 1953, s. 1; see above, Ch. 8.3(j).
[74] On the principle of maximum certainty, see above, Ch. 3.3(i).

outweigh the remoteness from harm and the absence of a need for the prosecution to prove criminal intent which characterize most crimes of possession. One might have thought that, as with the fault element for attempt and conspiracy, the more remote offences should be confined to cases of proven intention that the substantive crime be committed. Some offences of possession have no such requirement at all.

11.9. THE PLACE OF INCHOATE LIABILITY

There appear to be sound reasons for including inchoate offences within the criminal law, both on the consequentialist ground of the prevention of harm and on the 'desert' ground that the threshold of culpability has been crossed. Indeed, our argument has gone further in suggesting that some inchoate offences are no different, in terms of culpability, from substantive offences. This is so with completed attempts, where D has done everything intended but some unexpected—or at least, undesired—circumstance has prevented the occurrence of the harm and the same may apply to some impossible conspiracies. The belief principle and the intent principle (see Chapter 5.2(a)) are fulfilled no less in these cases than in substantive crimes. This does not mean that harm is an unimportant component of criminal liability. On the contrary, the determination of which harms should attract criminal liability remains a major, step in determining the ambit of the law (see Chapters 2 and 3.3(a)). What it does mean is that criminal liability need not be dependent on the occurrence of the harm if it can be related to its prospective occurrence. As we have seen in this chapter, this relationship is a difficult one at times. The conduct element in attempts has been drawn so vaguely in English law that it sacrifices values of legality (see Chapter 11.3(a) and Chapter 3.3(i)), and there are also uncertainties over the conduct element in conspiracy (section 11.5(b)) and in incitement (section 11.6) which ought to be eliminated.

It is certainly arguable that the reach of the inchoate offences should increase with the seriousness of the harm—meaning, for example, that the law should stretch further against crimes of violence than against mere property offences. Surveys of English law suggest that there is no such scheme,[75] and that inchoate offences (and, more particularly, substantive offences in the incho-

---

[75] See Ashworth, 'Criminal Attempts and the Role of Resulting Harm', 764–6.

ate mode) have simply been increased on an *ad hoc* basis. There is, however, some evidence of a general proposition that the inchoate offences should be subjected to more restrictive principles than other crimes: thus intention and knowledge alone are generally required for the inchoate offences, and recklessness is insufficient,[76] and the crime of attempt does not apply to summary offences (nor does conspiracy, unless the Crown Prosecution Service decides otherwise). The need for an overall consideration of this sphere of criminal liability applies equally to the law of complicity, which overlaps at some points with the inchoate offences. As argued in Chapter 10, there is a case for removing the derivative theory from the English law of complicity and replacing it with liability based on the culpability of the individual concerned. This might be achieved through general offences of facilitating crime and of instigating crime, offences which (if suitably drafted) could encompass much of the behaviour now falling within the inchoate offences and other substantive offences defined in the inchoate mode. In considering such changes, due account should be taken of such doctrines as the policy of minimum criminalization (see Chapter 3.2(a)), the principle of maximum certainty (see Chapter 3.3(i)), and the various policy arguments drawn together under the banner of social defence (see Chapter 3.2(b) and 3.3(j)).

---

[76] Cf. the treatment of recklessness as to circumstances, in sections 11.3(a) (attempt) and 11.5(c) (conspiracy).

INDEX